Dear Diary

A Girl's Book of Devotions

Other books in the Young Women of Faith Library

The Lily Series

> *Here's Lily*
> *Lily Robbins, M.D. (Medical Dabbler)*

Non-fiction

> *The Beauty Book*
> *The Body Book*

Young Women of Faith

Dear Diary

A Girl's Book of Devotions

Susie Shellenberger

Zonderkidz™

The Children's Group of ZondervanPublishingHouse

00 01 02 03 04 05 06 / ❖ DC/ 10 9 8 7 6 5 4 3 2 1

To Phyllis and Amber Gingerich,
who both love God's Holy Word.
Thanks for being Jesus to me.

Hey, Girlfriend!

I'm so excited that you're holding this book in your hands! Know why? Because if you actually read it and do the stuff inside, it will help you get to know God really well. Can you imagine knowing the Creator of this whole universe on a first-name basis? It's possible! This book will help you understand the most important book ever written—the Bible. If you're looking for adventure and surprises and strength and answers, you're ready to begin the journey of becoming God's girl! C'mon, let's go!

Susie Shellenberger

Dear Diary ...

Something's been bugging me since yesterday. We were in Sunday school, and the lesson was about being a Christian. Mrs. Johnson asked us to think about when we became a Christian. I don't get it. I've always gone to church! But Gabrielle said when she was seven, she asked her mom to pray with her, and that's when she invited Jesus into her heart.

Alicia said she became a Christian two weeks ago when Pastor Samuelson asked people to come forward who wanted to give their lives to Christ. And when Janie asked me when I became a Christian, all I could think of was, "I don't know."

I'm totally confused!

Good news! You don't *have* to be confused. You can know beyond all doubt if you're a Christian. But before we chat about that, take a few minutes to take this quick quiz, okay?

1. You're a Christian if
   a. you go to church and invite your friends.

  b. you know right from wrong.

  c. you've asked Jesus into your heart and are following him.

 2. You're *not* a Christian if

  a. you don't read the Bible every day.

  b. you've never confessed your sins and asked
Christ to come into your life.

  c. you get angry.

 3. Christians

  a. will go to heaven when they die.

  b. can never know for sure if they'll go to heaven.

  c. need to give a certain amount of money to the
church over a period of years to make sure
they'll go to heaven.

 4. If you're a good person,

  a. you're a Christian.

  b. God will love you more.

  c. you'll probably still mess up.

Let's compare answers. The correct answer for the first question is C. Going to church doesn't make anyone a Christian. And lots of people know right from wrong (even Satan knows that!). A true Christian is someone who has confessed her sins, asked Jesus into her heart and is following him.

If you chose B for the second question, you're right! Forgetting to read your Bible yesterday or getting angry because someone stole your lunch isn't a sign of not being a Christian. Christians are still human, and we're packed full of emotions. We'll still get angry (although God wants to help us with that), and we'll still be forgetful.

What about the third question? I hope you chose the first answer. Isn't it exciting that you can know *for sure* that you'll spend eternity in heaven with Christ?

The correct answer for the last question is C. Being a good person doesn't make you a Christian. And even good people will still fail. Becoming a Christian is done on faith. Let's open your Bible and check out what God has to say . . .

and we'll keep chatting about being a Christian for the next few pages, okay? After all, becoming God's girl is all about following him . . . and that means understanding this whole thing called Christianity.

Read Psalm 139:13–14. Who created you?

List some words that pop into your mind that describe how God feels about you as you read this Scripture. Here are a few ideas to get you started:

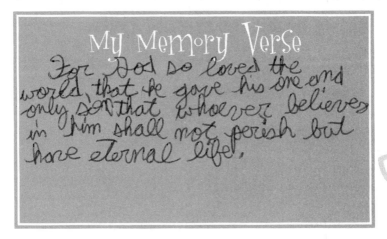

valuable

God thinks I'm wonderful!

God's in love with me

I'm wonderfully made

special

Read John 3:16 to find out how much God loves you. Write the verse here in the space provided and memorize it.

My Memory Verse

For God so loved the world, that he gave his one and only son, that whoever believes in him shall not perish but have eternal life.

Dear Diary ...

This is blowing my mind! I thought being a Christian was just being a good person. I'm beginning to realize that there's more to it than that.

I'm a good person, and I go to church with my family. And I thought since my parents are Christians, I was automatically one, too. I still don't have it all figured out yet, but I'm super excited about becoming God's girl! I think I'm finally on the right track.

❀❀❀

Ready for some mind-boggling truth? Here it is:

There's nothing you can do to make God love you any more than he does right now.

Let's personalize it, okay? Repeat after me: "There's nothing I can do to make God love me any more than he does right now." Let's say it again: "There's nothing I can do to make God love me any more than he does right now."

Cool, huh! Ready for *another* mind-boggler? Here it is:

There's nothing you can ever do to make God love you any less.

Ready to make it personal? Okay, here we go! "There's nothing I can ever do to make God love me any less." Let's say it again: "There's nothing I can ever do to make God love me any less."

Many people think God is hiding and that he's a big secret. But that's totally bizarre! God wants—more than anything in the world—for you to know him. Look up John 17:3. What does it say about knowing God?

According to the above verse, how can we have eternal life? *If we know Jesus, and know the only true god.*

❀❀❀

Now for the BIG question: How do we get to know God? Hmmm. Think of all the things you do (and did and are still doing) to get to know your friends. Make a quick list right here. *Talk to them*
- *ask questions about them / family*
- *play with them*
- *make conversation*

❀❀❀

We can do some of those same things to get to know God. Circle the things you think will help you know God.

talking with him   *drinking Coca-Cola*

making cookies

reading the letter he wrote to you (the Bible)

asking him questions

begging Mom for a new dress

listening to him

skipping school

doing homework

spending time with him

memorizing Scripture

playing Monopoly

sleeping

eating a candy bar

watching MTV

telling him what you're thinking

disobeying Mom

going to church

this book

Dear Diary ...

I never thought getting to know God would be so much fun! I mean, it's kind of like getting to know a brand-new best friend. Only, I'm beginning to realize that he's way more than just another best friend—he's totally in love with me!

I don't have time to write any more, K? Gotta go!

Later.

❀❀❀

Yes, God wants to be your best friend. But guess what! He also wants to be your Savior, your Guide, your Truth, your reason to live, your power source, your answers, your Lord, your Master, your King. He wants to be your *all*.

This frightens some people. They're afraid to give God total control of their lives. But when we truly realize that God is in love with us, and when we begin to fall in love with *him*, it's not scary at all. It's exciting!

People who are scared of God don't really understand who he is. Maybe they think he's a mean ruler who can't wait to punish them when they mess up. How can we know what God is like?

By reading the Bible! The Bible tells us over and over and over again that God is full of love and compassion. We don't need to be afraid of a loving, compassionate God.

Check out 1 John 4:18. What does perfect love to do fear?

Now read 1 John 4:16 and fill in these blanks.

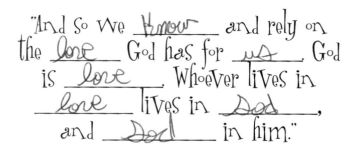

"And so we ___know___ and rely on the ___love___ God has for ___us___. God is ___love___. Whoever lives in ___love___ lives in ___God___, and ___God___ in him."

Is being a Christian just about understanding who God is?

(Circle one)   YES NO

Is being a Christian just about knowing Scripture?

YES NO

Do Christians need to live in fear of God?

YES NO

I hope you answered "no" to the above three questions. Being a Christian is all about having a personal *relationship* with God. Make a list of four people with whom you have a personal relationship.

1. mom
2. dad
3. brother
4. sister

Why do you think so many people do not have a personal relationship with God?

Dear Diary ...

I'm so jazzed I don't have to be afraid of God. It's a humongous comfort to realize that he loves me so much! Tee hee. He loves me!

❀❀❀

God loves me!

Jesus Christ is crazy about me.

I'm the apple of God's eye.

I love it that he loves me so much!

I am a star of God's creation.

He loves me.

God loves me more than I'll ever fully comprehend.

I love to think about his love.   Hee hee!

I am so special!

Jesus loves me so much that he died for me!

No one will ever love me as much as God does.

Jesus loves ME!!!!

Yes, God is totally in love with us. But there's also another side of him that he wants us to know about: God is perfect.

And because God is perfect, he can't tolerate sin. (That means he can't put up with it—can't allow it into heaven, his kingdom.)

Yikes!

Here's the catchy part.

Question: Who was born with sin?

Answer: You. Me. All of us.

Question: If we're born with sin, that means we're sinful, right?

Answer: Right.

Question: If God can't tolerate sin, wouldn't our sin separate us from God?

Answer: You got it.

Question: But I was so pumped about God loving me! Now you're telling me God can't even tolerate me? That I can't go to heaven and hang out with him forever?

Answer: True . . . *unless* . . .

Question: Unless what?

Answer: Unless you pay for your sins.

Question: What's the price?

Answer: It's found in the first part of Romans 6:23: "For the wages of sin is death."

Question: So I gotta *die* to pay for my sins?

Answer: Yes. Unless . . .

Question: Unless what???

Answer: Unless someone would do it for you.

Question: *Die* for me? That's ridiculous. No one would ever love me enough to die for me. Would they?

Answer: Yes. Someone does. His name is Jesus.

Question: I thought Jesus died for the *world*. You're saying he died for *me*?

Answer: He sure did! God loves you so much that he gave his only Son to die a horrible death to pay for your sins—so you wouldn't have to! In fact, check out the last part of Romans 6:23.

Question: "But the gift of God is eternal life in Christ Jesus our Lord." Wow! What did I do to deserve such a gift?

Answer: You *don't* deserve it! But God loves you so much, he wants you to spend forever with him. The only way he can allow you into heaven is if your sin has been paid for. That's what Jesus' death is all about. He paid for *your* sins.

Question: Wow. I feel like I should do something. But what?

Answer: You can thank him and accept this wonderful *gift* of eternal life.

Question: Yeah! Can I do that right now?

Answer: Sure. Let's pray, okay?

Dear Jesus,

Thank you sooooo very much for dying for my sins. I certainly don't deserve that! I'll never deserve that! But I sure am grateful for it. I accept this incredible gift of eternal life.

Amen.

Dear Diary ...

I always thought I knew a lot about God, because I'm a pretty good kid, and I go to church. But there's a ton of stuff I don't know, and I'm excited about learning it! Like . . . if Jesus didn't die for my sins, I would've had to die for them. And his death wasn't quick or painless. He was crucified! He was tortured for me!

That blows my mind!

❀❀❀

We can't even imagine how much physical and emotional pain Jesus experienced on the cross. And yes, though he died for the entire world, he also died just for *you*. Think of it this way: If you were the only person in the whole world, Jesus still would have died on the cross . . . just for you.

But becoming a Christian is more than simply believing in Jesus and being grateful for his death. A lot of people believe in Jesus who aren't truly Christians. Even Satan believes in Jesus! He knows all too well how very real Jesus is . . . but Satan isn't a Christian.

Although the gift of Christianity—or eternal life—is something we can't earn and will never deserve, there *is* something we have to do to get it. We have to accept it and receive it. I could offer you a million dollars, but until you actually *received* it, it wouldn't really be yours. Just knowing about the money doesn't make it yours. And simply believing it's yours doesn't make it yours. Action is required. You have to accept it.

When you accept Christ's gift of eternal life, there are some important ingredients in the acceptance process that people sometimes overlook: confession, repentance. Think of it as a recipe. Each ingredient is important.

Question: Yeah, but just a few pages ago, I prayed. I mean, I accepted God's gift of eternal life. So what's going on?

Answer: Right. You did. But you want the full recipe, don't you? There are still a couple of ingredients we need to put into your acceptance prayer.

Question: So I'm not finished praying?

Answer: That's right.

Question: Well, I wanna get this right. I wanna make sure I really understand it. So can we keep praying?

Answer: You bet! But since you want to make sure you understand the whole picture, let's take a peek at a few Scriptures first. Check out Acts 3:19. Go ahead. Read it right now.

Question: Okay. "Repent, then, and turn to God, so that your sins may be wiped out, that times of refreshing may come from the Lord." Wow. According to that, I totally left out the repent part, didn't I?

Answer: Yes. And you left out something else, too.

Question: What's that?

Answer: The "turning" part.

Question: Whaddya mean?

Answer: God doesn't want lip service. Anyone can *say* she's sorry for her sins. But God looks at your heart. If you're really sorry, you'll *turn away* from sinful things.

Question: So . . . God's looking for action, right?

Answer: Right.

Question: Can we keep praying? I wanna get this right!

Answer: Let's do it right now.

Dear Jesus,

Not only do I accept your incredible gift of eternal life that I don't deserve ... but I want you to know how truly sorry I am for the sin in my life. Oh, Father! I don't deserve to be forgiven, but I'm so glad you want to forgive me. I don't want to live a sinful lifestyle any more. I want to live as you want me to live. Will you forgive me for my sins? I confess to you right now that I am a sinner. And I repent of my selfishness and my horrible attitudes. I repent of lying and disobeying my parents and you. I repent of all the wrong in my life.

Will you come into my life and flood me with your forgiveness and power and grace? I want you to have total control. Yes, I want you to be my best Friend, but I also want you to be my Master, my Guide, my Savior, my King, my all in all.

Jesus, you make me into all you want me to be. I give my life to you right now, and I turn from my sin. I'll follow you and obey you, Father. Make me more like you every day as I read the Bible and talk with you.

I love you so much, Jesus!

Amen.

Dear Diary ...

Guess what?

I KNOW now! I mean, I really KNOW! I really, really, really truly KNOW that I'm a Christian now. I asked Jesus to come into my life. He's living inside of me, now.

And I confessed my sins—I repented—and guess what? He forgave me! He really, truly did!

Ya-Hoo!

I hope I feel this great forever!!!!

I gotta call Amy.

❀❀❀

When you asked Jesus to come into your heart, you may have felt like screaming in joy. Or you may have felt a deep, quiet reverence. Or like you'd been hit by an exciting electrical current. You may have even cried because you were so grateful. Or ... you may have felt nothing.

Nothing?

Question: What if I felt *nothing?* Does that mean I'm really not a Christian?

Answer: Absolutely not. We accept Jesus Christ
             into our lives, and we accept his forgive-
             ness for our sins by *faith*.

Question: What's that mean?

Answer: It means that you *trusted* God to do all
             that he promised in the Bible he *would* do.
             He said he'd forgive your sins if you asked
             him. He said you could have eternal life if
             you'd accept it as a gift.

Question: So why wouldn't everyone who becomes a
             Christian *feel* it?

Answer: Let's answer a question with a question:
             Do you always *feel* the sun?

Question: No. But what's that got to do with faith?

Answer: Just because you don't *feel* the sun, you
             don't doubt its existence. So why would
             you doubt all that God has done—and *is*
             doing in your life—simply because you
             can't *feel* it?

Question: Because . . . well, feelings are important.
             Aren't they?

Answer: Sure! They're important. But they're not
             as important as *faith*.

Question: Okay, so what's the most important ingre-
             dient in my relationship with Jesus?

Answer: Faith. Faith is the very *foundation* of your
             life with Christ.

Question: I think I'm really starting to understand
             this Christianity stuff. It's all about having
             a *relationship* with Christ! And that rela-
             tionship isn't based on feeling—it's
             grounded on faith.

Answer: Yes! You're absolutely right!

Question: It's all coming together. I wanna pray
             some more.

Answer: There's nothing God enjoys more than
             hearing your prayers.

Dear Jesus,

I think I'm getting it. I don't always feel like brushing my teeth, but I know it's the right thing to do. I won't always feel like doing the right thing, but I'm going to do it anyway—with your help. And I probably won't always feel like a Christian, but I'm going to keep trusting you.

Jesus, help me to grow stronger in my faith. I want to trust you more and more and more. If I ever start to doubt, remind me to turn those doubts over to you.

I love you so much, Father. I'm excited about following you.

Amen.

Dear Diary ...

I'm growing in Christ! I really am! I'm becoming a stronger Christian. I'm so glad that God understands my doubts and that he wants to hear about them. I think it's way cool that I don't hafta keep all that stuff all crammed inside me. I love it that I can talk to him about anything!

Catch ya later.

❀❀❀

Let's recap, okay?

1. I'm a Christian because
   a. I believe in God.
   b. I repented and confessed my sins to Jesus and accepted his forgiveness by faith.
   c. I'm a good person.

2. I know God forgave my sins because
   a. I deserve to be forgiven.
   b. of John 1:12.
   c. of 1 Kings 21:1

3. If I don't feel God, I will
   a. assume I'm really not a Christian.
   b. continue to trust him in faith.
   c. give more in offering at church so I can feel him more.

If you selected B for all of your answers, you really *are* on the right track! Are you aware that God has made some exciting promises to you? Let's look at a few.

What does he promise in Hebrews 13:5?

According to John 14:20, where is God?

❀❀❀

What does Colossians 2:13–14 prove he has done for you?

❀❀❀

What is promised in 1 John 5:13?

❀❀❀

Would you like to make a promise to God? Rewrite Colossians 2:6–7 in the form of a commitment from you to God.

❀❀❀

Dear Diary ...

Erika thinks she's soooo cool. Today she walked into school wearing a brand-new pair of sandals and bragging about how much her dad paid for them. Then she looks at my shoes and starts laughing. "Where'd you get those clunkers?" she smirked. "Outta the trash?"

And I know I shouldn't have ... but I'd just had it with her! I mean, I'm sooooo tired of the way she treats me. So I said something really mean about her to Ashley, and guess what? Erika heard me.

Gross. I feel all yucky inside. I want to be nice to her, but there's just something about her that really makes me mad!

❀ ❀ ❀

Do you know what it's like to feel yukky inside? At one time or another, all of us say or do something we wish we could take back. But the weird thing about *words* is that once they're spoken, we *can't* get them back. When they're released, they're gone forever.

Words are powerful! Think about it: You can help those around you have a better day simply by the words you use. For instance, "Hi, Jessica! Those jeans look great on you," will probably help your friend feel good about herself. But choosing to say something mean—like Erika did—can really put a stink in someone's day.

So what kind of words are *you* using? Are you the giver of beautiful words? Encouraging words? Fun words? Or are the words you're delivering cruel, sarcastic, or mean?

All the words we use obviously come out of our mouth. That means the tongue is pretty important, huh? We wouldn't get very far in a conversation without being able to use our tongue. Because God knows how powerful words can be, he had some important stuff to say about the tongue.

He said that if we can't control our tongue (and the words we use), we're like a forest fire that's killing everything in sight. (Check out James 3:1–12.)

Are your words that deadly?

You have a decision to make. Are you going to have a bitter tongue that hurts people with poisonous, unkind words? Or will you use your tongue to deliver happy, thoughtful, and kind words that will give others a better day?

Do you know someone like Erika? Describe her.

She probably says unkind things because . . .

Something nice I can say to her tomorrow is . . .

❀❀❀

What unkind words did I use today and with whom?

❀❀❀

What encouraging words did I use today and with whom?

❀❀❀

God wants me to use my tongue to deliver positive words because . . .

❀❀❀

Read James 3:5–8. Rewrite verse 6 (put it in your own words), and insert your name somewhere inside this Scripture.

Dear Diary ...

Last night I saw these pictures of children on TV. They were real skinny with big stomachs sticking way out. The narrator said they were starving. I cried when I went to bed. I wish there was something I could do. But I'm just one girl. How can I ever make a difference?

❀❀❀

ONE can make a *big* difference. Have you ever heard the saying "one bad apple can spoil the whole bunch"? It's true. It you put a piece of rotten fruit in the midst of other fruit, it will spoil everything around it.

ONE can make a negative difference, or it can make a positive difference. Jesus dreams big dreams for you. He wants to use *you* to make a positive difference!

Did you know there was a man who served as President of the United States for only one day? His name was David Atchison, and he served in the Senate. Let's flash back to 1849, so you can get the full story, okay?

When it came time to swear in the new president, Zachary Taylor (no, not the blond-haired guy who plays Brad on reruns of *Home Improvement*), inauguration day happened to fall on a Sunday. Mr. Taylor didn't want to be sworn in on a Sunday. He decided to wait until Monday.

So that meant when President James K. Polk finished his term, there was a day between presidents. That's where David Atchison came in. He served as president for one day—just until Monday when President Taylor was sworn in.

Jot down some things that you'd do if *you* could be president for one day.

Guess what David Atchison did? He slept! Kind of makes you wonder what he *could* have done if he'd stayed awake, doesn't it? He was so tired of last-minute business from Congress that he decided to crash.

Don't be like David Atchison. Don't waste the valuable opportunities God is giving you every day to make a difference. Don't sleep through something important. No, you don't have the power of the presidency behind you. But you *do* have God's power—and that lasts forever! Are you using it to make a difference?

What is one thing you could have done today to make a positive difference for someone?

You can't keep children from starving, but you *can* contact a child-development organization about information on sponsoring a child. For about $24 a month (and with your family's help), you really *could* make a difference. Will you call for information?

—Compassion International (1–800–336–7676)
—Mission of Mercy (719–595–0099)
—World Vision (818–357–7979)

Get with your mom and jot down how these people—just one at a time—made a difference.

• Phoebe (Check out Romans 16:1.)

❀❀❀

• Onesimus (Take a peek at Philemon 1:1–2; 17–19.)

❀❀❀

Write out a prayer asking God to help you make a difference.

❀❀❀

Dear Diary ...

Hey. It's me again. I'm so totally bored. There's nothing to do. I'm tired of watching re-runs, and I don't wanna read a book.

I already ate a bowl of cereal and rode my bike around the block. My life reeks. There's never anything cool to do. Just the same ol' same ol'.

Sigh.

I wish you were a real person, Diary.

❀❀❀

It's no fun to be bored, is it? So grab some chips and lemonade and meet me back here. We'll do some fun, totally non-boring stuff right here in your very own diary.

Do you like stickers? Pretend you're making some really cool bumper stickers. List below the names of friends you're creating stickers for, and next to their name, write what your sticker will say.

Example: Courtney (You're a funtastic friend!)

-
-
-
-

Now grab the Yellow Pages and look for print shops. Make a few phone calls and ask if they have any scraps of paper with adhesive backing that you could have. Now grab your colored markers, glitter, and paints, and get busy making your sticker dreams a reality!

Place a few of your favorite stickers here, and write where you got them.

❀❀❀

Ever heard of "random acts of kindness"? It means doing nice things for others. Scribble down some acts of kindness *you* can do. (I'll get you started.)

1. Give a doggie treat to the neighbor's dog.
2. Rake leaves for someone down the street.
3.
4.
5. Write a nice note for your mail carrier.
6.
7.
8. Clean the house without being asked.
9.
10.

Let your imagination go wild! Dream up as many creative, wacky things you can think of to chase away the boredom blues. Use these as brain-ticklers to get rolling:

Invent a brand-new board game.

Create a rap, song, or poem based on John 3:16.

Write your own book.

Make up a new color.

My Memory Verse: 1 Corinthians 13. Yes, the whole chapter. It's the love chapter, and it's really, really, really important. It can change your life! After you've memorized the first five verses, write them from memory here in your diary.

My Memory Verse

Thank God for good ideas. Ask him to spark your imagination with creativity. Tell him you want to use your free time to be productive and useful. Now tell your mom you love her, and try not to go wacko the next time you get bored.

Dear Diary ...

I've known about this book report for almost a whole month. Now it's Friday, and it's due on Monday, and I haven't even started reading the book!

I feel gross about waiting so long to get started. I know. I know. I know. I could have read the book instead of going to Hillary's slumber party. I could have skipped riding my bike all those days after school and jumping on the trampoline with Alicia. But I didn't. Now I'm gonna have a rotten weekend because I've got to read the whole book plus write the report!

Ugh! This will be the most awful weekend of my life!

❀❀❀

Do you know what it means to procrastinate? It means to put something off and keep putting it off and *keep* putting it off . . . until it's finally the last minute.

Every year around Christmas, churches all over the world perform an exciting musical called *Messiah*. Maybe you've heard it—or maybe you're familiar with the famous "Hallelujah" chorus from *Messiah.* Perhaps your church has even sung it.

A man named George Handel composed *Messiah,* and while he was writing it, he worked almost non-stop for 24 hours! He didn't leave his house, and his servants brought his food to him on trays—but he only took a few small bites now and then. He didn't want to stop long enough to take the time to eat an entire meal.

I guess you could say he was pretty focused on what he was doing, huh? He stuck with it until the *Messiah* was completed.

Guess what? God wants *you* to be focused, too. And it's tough to be focused when you get into the sad habit of procrastinating.

Have you ever procrastinated? Think of three things you waited until the last minute to do, and list them here.

1.
2.
3.

How would the above three things turned out differently if you hadn't procrastinated?

What if God decided to "put off" or procrastinate forgiving our sins? Could that affect where we spend eternity? Explain how in the space provided.

Let's pray, okay?

Dear Jesus,
I don't want to be a procrastinator. I want to be focused. I want you to be able to use me to do big things. Help me to realize how important it is not to put stuff off for later that I should really be working on right now.
I love you, Jesus.
Amen.

Dear Diary ...

I don't get it. Amy's my best friend. Well ... I thought she was my best friend. Yesterday, we got a new girl in class—Megan. And Amy's been sticking to her like glue. What's the deal?

Amy and I used to always have lunch together, but today Megan was with us. I don't want her hanging out with us. I just want Amy and me to be friends ... without Megan cutting in.

❀❀❀

What do *you* think? Is Amy really backing away? Or is she simply reaching out to include a new girl? It's hard to be the new kid, isn't it? It's tough to walk into a class or club or group and not know anyone. It feels like everyone's watching you and forming opinions about you before you even get to meet them.

There's absolutely nothing wrong with having best friends. In fact, it's totally natural for you to hang out with the friends you feel most comfortable with and who share common interests. It becomes *wrong* when you begin to exclude others—you know, leave them out.

Amy is trying to do what Jesus did: He reached out to those who needed a friend. Are *you* reaching out and including others ... or are you excluding people from getting to know you and your friends?

Think of someone who doesn't have many friends. Write her name here in the space provided.

Now jot down what you can do to reach out to that person.

❀❀❀

What are some specific things you can do to try to include her?

(I'll get you started, then you complete the list, okay?)

1. I could invite her to Sunday school and church.
2. I could ask her to come home with me next Friday.
3. I could just call her on the phone to talk.
4.
5.
6.
7.
8.

Will you do it? If so, write a promise below.

❀❀❀

Dear Diary ...

Ryan wrote Sarah a note and said he liked her. I think she likes him, too.

Nobody's ever written me a note like that. I think Adam is kinda cute. How come no boys pay extra attention to me like they do to Sarah? Is something wrong with me?

I think maybe I want a boyfriend.

❀❀❀

Here it is—some of the best advice you'll ever read: Instead of worrying about getting a boyfriend . . . concentrate instead of simply being friends with *everyone*—guys AND girls!

Why is that such good advice? Because it screams volumes to boys. See, when guys notice that a girl is friends with everyone—nice to people, laughs easily, feels good about herself, is easy to talk to—they are automatically attracted to her. In fact, *everyone's* attracted to her. And if you're that person, you become sort of like a magnet. Everyone wants to be around you!

Sometimes when girls get impatient about wanting a boyfriend, they make the huge mistake of "chasing" a guy—writing him notes, calling him on the phone, always hanging around him. And you know what happens? Most of the time, the guy gets scared or frustrated and wants nothing to do with her.

Since God created you, he knows you better than anyone. Let's ask him right now to help you become the magnetic friend who people want to be around, okay? Will you write that out right here?

❁❁❁

And let's pray about it together, okay?

Dear Jesus,

I really want to be the kind of friend who's nice and caring and loving to everyone. Please help me not to get carried away wondering if a guy likes me or going out of my way to get his attention. I don't want to be the kind of girl who's always chasing a guy. I just want you to be in charge of all my friendships—and that means guys as well as girls.

Thank you, Jesus, for being my best Friend!

I love you!

Dear Diary ...

I'm so mad! I've got detention after school tomorrow! I can't believe it. This has never happened to me before.

It wasn't even my fault!

Shauna was talking to me . . . so, of course, I had to talk back to her. Well, Mr. Withers heard us and gave us both detention. It was really Shauna's fault. I wouldn't have even been talking if she hadn't talked to me.

Ugh!

❀❀❀

Have you noticed that when we get in trouble, we often try to blame someone else? Maybe we're trying to make ourselves feel better, but it doesn't really help, does it?

God has a lot to say about responsibility in the Bible. He wants his children (you and me) to take responsibility for our actions.

In Matthew 27, you can read the story of Jesus being tried before Pilate. Even though the crowd screamed, "Crucify him!" Pilate couldn't find any legal reason for Jesus to die.

He finally got tired of all the pressure, though, and he gave in. Check out the details: "When Pilate saw that he was getting nowhere, but that instead an uproar was starting, he took water and washed his hands in front of the crowd. 'I am innocent of this man's blood,' he said. 'It is your responsibility!'" (Matthew 27:24).

Again, God desires for us to take responsibility for our actions. When you're wrong, admit it. When something is even one percent your fault, go ahead and accept responsibility for it.

Why? Because you'll be much stronger and more admired in the long run. Think about it: The person who's always blaming someone else is a person who can't be trusted. Prove to God—and to those around you—that you're a young lady who can be trusted!

Take time to refresh yourself with the story of Adam and Eve in the Garden of Eden. There was one specific tree they were forbidden to eat from. Check it out in Genesis 3. Go ahead. Read the whole chapter right now. (It'll only take you about four minutes.)

____ I read the whole thing—Genesis 3.

Pop back up to Genesis 3:12. Whom did Adam blame when God found out he had eaten the forbidden fruit?

Why is it sometimes hard to take responsibility for our actions?

Are there a few things you tend to blame others for? List them here.

(homework, talking in class, chores ...)

Would you like to begin the process of becoming a young lady who can be trusted? If so, tell God right now. Go ahead. Write it out.

❀❀❀

Dear Diary ...

I blew the spelling test today. I had completely forgotten all about it—until Mrs. Parsons announced it was time to remove our books and take out a clean sheet of paper.

Ugh! I hate that announcement!

Erika said she'd let me copy off of her ... and part of me really wanted to, because she makes fantastic grades. But deep down inside I knew it wouldn't be right to take answers that didn't belong to me. I mean ... isn't that just like stealing?

I blew the test, but I have a clean conscience.

I just wish Mrs. Parsons graded on honesty instead of correct spelling!

❀❀❀

Lots of us have been tempted to cheat, but cheating really *is* stealing. Taking someone else's answers—even with their permission—is wrong. ALWAYS.

The reason you blew the test is because you forgot about it. How can you make sure that doesn't happen again? (Choose one.)

A. You should call your teacher at home every night and ask if there's anything you need to be studying.
B. You could make an assignment book and keep a record of when tests will be and when homework is due.
C. You should just repeat everything over and over in your head that you need to remember. You probably won't forget again.

Write down Exodus 20:15.

My Memory Verse

Let's list some material things that people are tempted to steal.

1. candy
2. jewelry
3. perfume
4.
5.
6.

Now let's list some *non-material* things that people are tempted to steal.

1. test answers
2.
3.
4. homework
5.
6. credit for doing something that you didn't do.

This is how God sees cheating: Cheating = Stealing = Sin. If you've ever cheated, please confess it to your heavenly Father right now.

Dear Jesus,

I'm totally sorry that I cheated. I realize now that in doing so, I sinned. Will you please forgive me? I don't want to be a cheater. I want to become a young lady who can be trusted. I want to live honorably.

I pledge to you that I won't cheat again. I know that you can give me the strength to keep this promise. And thank you, Father, for forgiving me for cheating.

I love you, Jesus!

Amen.

Dear Diary ...

I don't really enjoy being around Tasha anymore. Every time we're together she goes on and on about all the bad stuff that's happening in her life. And you know what? It's not that bad!

She's mad because her mom won't let her get a new pair of jeans. She's upset because she woke up late and had a bad hair day. She's angry because she didn't get elected class treasurer. She's ticked off at Adam because he laughed at her. (I think he was just teasing her!) It seems like something is always wrong. I'm tired of hearing it. And I think other kids are starting to back away from her, too.

Sure hope I never get that way. I'd hate to become a complainer without even realizing it!

❀❀❀

Corrie ten Boom had every right to be negative, angry, and bitter. She could have blamed the soldiers who sent her and her sister Betsy to a concentration camp during the reign of Hitler. She had nightmares of the horrible things she had witnessed during her days of imprisonment, yet she strove to keep her positive faith.

After her release—and many years down the road—she came face to face with one of the guards who had raped a woman in her camp. Can you imagine the battle Corrie must have fought within? She had every right to be angry, but silently, she asked God to fill her with love for this man.

After hearing her address a crowd of several hundred, he approached the stage and extended his hand. Only because she had surrendered her rights to God was she able to look into his eyes, smile, and take his hand in hers.

When bad things happen to you, how do you most often react?

    A. Like Tasha
    B. Like Corrie ten Boom
    C. It varies

We can allow the hard things in life to draw us closer to God or farther from God. Which do you choose?

Take a peek at Hebrews 12:15. What can happen if we allow bitterness to consume our lives?

Check out what the apostle Paul says in Philippians 1:12–14. How did he turn bitterness into opportunity?

Write a note to God, telling him that you want hard times to make you *better* instead of *bitter.*

Now choose a tangible object—one that you can feel and touch. Every time you see or touch this object, let it serve as a specific reminder of your new commitment.

(For example, you might choose a doorknob. Every time you open or close a door, say to yourself, "Better, not bitter." Or if you've chosen a mirror, say "Better, not bitter" every time you catch your reflection.)

Jot down what your tangible object will be.

Dear Diary ...

Jeremy's a high school kid at my church. Last Sunday, our pastor asked if anyone would like to share what God was doing in his life, and Jeremy stood. He said, "Everyone in my family is a Christian, and we've always gone to church. I've known for years that I should let God have total control of my life, but I decided I'd rather just go through the motions instead.

"So I kept coming to church and pretending that I was a Christian, but deep inside I knew I was a phony. Two weeks ago, though, God really got my attention. I was in a car wreck and had to stay in the hospital for two days. During that time, I gave him total control of my life. It feels so good to be real!"

Wow! I can't get his testimony off my mind. I want to always be real. Pretending takes too much work!

❀❀❀

Did you know it *costs* money to *make* money? Here's the breakdown of the manufacturing costs of American coins:

penny—$.63
nickel—$2.06
dime—$1.06
quarter—$2.79

For years, people have made counterfeit money. Many have been able to make the *outsides* of the coins look good, but when this counterfeit money is weighed and closely inspected, it becomes evident that the *insides* of the coins aren't filled with the ingredients of real money.

Sadly, many people try to live counterfeit Christian lives. They seem to think that if they can go through the right motions on the *outside,* it doesn't really matter what's on the *inside.*

Jesus has a strong word for this kind of "Christian": hypocrite.

In fact, let's see what the Bible has to say about hypocrites.

Flip over to Matthew 6:2. What kind of reward does Jesus say the hypocrites will get?

❀❀❀

Now turn to Mark 7:6–7. What are the hypocrites mentioned in these verses doing?

❀❀❀

What about *you?* Could there be some areas in your life in which you've become hypocritical? Let's talk to God about it, okay?

Go ahead. Right now. Doesn't matter if you're in school, in your bedroom, or in the school locker room. God doesn't care about the surroundings. He's concerned with your heart.

Ask him to bring to your mind any areas in your life that aren't right with him. As he does, ask for his forgiveness. Thank him for making you aware of the sin in your life. Accept his forgiveness, and commit these areas of your life to him.

Memorize these verses and write them in the box below: "Therefore, rid yourselves of all malice and all deceit, hypocrisy, envy, and slander of every kind. Like newborn babies, crave pure spiritual milk, so that by it you may grow up in your salvation, now that you have tasted that the Lord is good" (1 Peter 2:1–3).

My Memory Verse

Dear Diary ...

I want to tell others about God, but I never know what to say. I get all tongue-tied and scared. Ugh! Why does it have to be so hard?

❀❀❀

Surprise! Sharing God *doesn't* have to be hard! Repeat after me: "My life screams a lot louder than my words!"

Again: "My life screams a lot louder than my words!"

One more time: "MY LIFE SCREAMS A LOT LOUDER THAN MY WORDS!"

It really does. Actions carry a lot of weight—often-times even more than your words do! Let's prove it. Mark the action that would mean more to you:

1. Your family just moved to a new city. You don't know anyone, and naturally you're feeling awkward as the new kid at school.
   _____ Jodi has a locker next to yours and says, "It would be great to have you come to our youth group tomorrow night!"
   _____ Kacey sits across from you in science and says, "Can my family pick you up for Bible study tomorrow night?"
2. Your mom is in the hospital.
   _____ Jodi says, "I'll pray for you."
   _____ Kacey and her mom bring a yummy casserole and chocolate cake to your house at dinner time.

3. You tried out for the volleyball team but didn't make it.

_____ Jodi says, "Don't get discouraged. You did a good job. I heard the coach is looking for a team manager. Are you interested? You'd be great!"

_____ Kacey takes you to the bulletin board where all the other tryouts, clubs, and organizations are listed. "Look! Cheerleading tryouts are next week. Come on. I'll go with you to sign up. Afterward, I'll walk you to pottery club. If you're interested, I'll join with you, okay?"

Both Jodi and Kacey genuinely care, but Kacey's efforts are always backed with *action*. Words are important, but actions are remembered a lot longer!

Read the first seven chapters of Acts—a chapter for each day of the week. Each day, look for specific things the early Christians did to show Christ's love to those around them. Strive to do some of the same things they did.

For example, they shared with someone in need. In the space provided, list two or three names of people who can use some of the clothes you've outgrown.

❀❀❀

The early Christians grew in number daily. Jot down names of some kids you can invite to church.

The early Christians didn't hoard their possessions. List some things you can share with someone who's not as fortunate as you.

❀❀❀

What are three more things you can *do* (action!) to show Christ's love to those around you? (I'll get you started—you finish!)

1.   Rake leaves for your neighbor.
2.
3.   Surprise your mom by cleaning the house.
4.
5.
6.   Offer to baby-sit your brother or sister . . . for free!

Dear Diary ...

Today at lunch, Meredith mentioned that her family is throwing a birthday party for her older sister, Beth. I didn't think that was any big deal, but then Meredith said something that totally shocked me.

She goes, "I'm praying that God will help me find just the right birthday gift for Beth."

And I go, "What do you mean . . . you're asking God to help you. I don't get it."

And she goes, "Yeah. I'm trying to pray about everything—the big stuff and the smaller stuff. So I'm asking God to help me with things I used to think he wasn't interested in. I'm learning that he cares about helping me with everything I'm concerned about. Cool, huh!"

Whoa.

I never thought about that. I mean . . . does God really care about stuff other than earthquakes and famines and people who have cancer? Why would he be concerned with a birthday gift?

❀❀❀

Did you know that your eye muscles move an average of 100,000 times each day? That's what it takes just to keep you focused on whatever you look at!

Your inner ear contains as many circuits as the telephone system of an average city! Ever wonder about your heart? It beats 40,000,000 times a year. And get this: Your brain has 10,000,000,000 circuits and a memory of 1,000,000,000,000,000,000,000,000 bits, each one being five to ten times more complex than any computer ever built!

If God cared enough to take the time to create such a wonderful, complex, special thing as your body—and to give you life—don't you think he also cares about everything that happens in your life?

Jot down what Luke 12:7 and Matthew 10:30 say about your hair.

According to Ephesians 6:18, what should we pray about?

Since we're told to pray about *everything,* don't you think it's time you started doing it? The exciting thing about prayer is that God really, really, really wants to help you with the BIG stuff *and* the little stuff. He cares just as much about your English test as he does a starving child in Africa. Isn't it cool that you really *can* pray about *everything?!*

In the space provided, tell God your favorite foods.

Now tell him about the things you don't enjoy doing (chores, homework, etc.).

Now jot him a thank-you note for caring about every single thing that concerns you.

❀❀❀

Dear Diary ...

Pastor Samuelson asked Amber and Kelli to decorate the youth center for the party we're throwing for the senior citizens next week. I feel totally left out. Yeah, I know ... Amber and Kelli really are great at decorating. In fact, they did an incredible job with the '50s roller-skating party we hosted last year. But I still feel left out.

It's not that I wanna decorate. I hate decorating. I'm just not good at it. I'd rather be doing skits at a party instead of decorating it. You couldn't pay Amber and Kelli to get in front of a crowd and do something silly. I guess I'm good at stuff they're not, and maybe they're good at things I'm not.

But it still feels weird sometimes.

Goodnight.

❈❈❈

Zacchaeus was a wee little man, yes a wee little man was he ..."
   Remember that song? Uh, yeah. Didn't NSync record it on their last CD? No, wait. That's not right.

If you've heard that song at all, it's probably stuck so far back in your memory banks it may be hard to place. But I'm guessing you may have sung it yourself, along with a bunch of other little tune-tapping tots a few years back in vacation Bible school. More than just a fun memory-jogger, that mondo melody holds some major truth.

Zack was short. So short, he would not have been able to see Jesus through the crowd unless he could elevate himself somehow. Since helicopters hadn't been invented yet, he did the next best thing: He scaled a sycamore tree.

Now, the really cool thing about all this is the fact that he didn't allow his limitations to stop him! See, Zack knew his limitations, accepted them, and then did something about them! He could have said, "I'm just too short to see the Messiah, so I guess I'll have to wait and catch it on the late-night news."

Guess what? All of us have limitations—stuff we're not so good at; stuff that holds us back. We can either give up, or we can do something about it!

Let's flash back to your diary for a sec, okay? Instead of feeling left out because Amber and Kelli were asked to decorate, how can you change your feelings?

- You could call Amber and say, "I'm not the best decorator, but I'd love to learn. Do you guys need any help?"
- Talk with the pastor and say, "Decorating really isn't my thing, but I'd love to help with the entertainment. What can I do?"

By accepting your limitations and focusing on your strengths, God will be able to use you in exciting ways!

Okay. Now back to Zack. It's kind of funny—when the day began, he was the shortest guy in the community. By sunset, however, few could measure up.

In the space provided, paraphrase this verse (rewrite it in your own words): "'For I know the plans I have for you,' declares the Lord, 'plans to prosper you and not to harm you, plans to give you hope and a future'" (Jeremiah 29:11).

My Memory Verse

Can you think of some other people who aren't allowing their limitations to stop them? I'll get you started, and you fill in the blanks provided, okay?

1. Joni Eareckson Tada: She's paralyzed and confined to a wheelchair. She could have easily given up. Instead, she taught herself to write and draw with her mouth. She's an accomplished artist, speaker, and singer.

2.

3. Actor Christopher Reeves: He, too, is confined to a wheelchair. Before his tragic accident of falling off a horse, he acted as Superman in several movies. He hasn't given up. He has gone on to speak and even direct and produce other movies.

4.

Dear Jesus,

Instead of getting down about the things I can't do, help me to focus on the things I can do. I may be shorter, taller, skinnier, or larger than anyone in my class, but I realize you have given me special gifts to use for your glory.

I love you, Father!

Amen.

Hey, Diary ...

Today at school, Mrs. Parsons called me down for talking. And I wasn't the only one talking! Brittany and Chelsea were talking, too, but they didn't get called down.

Okay, enough. I just had to write it out and complain. I'm glad I can write anything I want to here in my diary!

When I got home from school, I had two messages on our answering machine. One was from Angela. She had called to invite me to her birthday party next week. And the other one was from my grandma who called to ask me what color I wanted the afghan that she's making me.

Ooops! Gotta go! Mom's calling me to supper. Later.

❋❋❋

Wow! We sure do juggle a lot of "calls," don't we? Getting called down, phone calls, call-waiting, long-distance calls, caller-I.D., name-calling, prank calls, collect calls, being called to supper. But the most important call you'll ever receive is . . . *God's* call.

Let's take a peek at Zack again. Remember where he is? He's at the top of a sycamore tree so he can see Jesus. It was probably a little weird for an adult to be in a tree. When Jesus came by, he could have easily said, "Look at you—all decked out in your business suit and crouched in a tree. Do you realize how stupid that looks?"

But, of course, Jesus didn't say that. He simply walked to the tree, looked up, and called to Zack. (Check out Luke 19:5.)

The incredible thing about Jesus calling Zack is not the fact that it was Zack he called, but the fact that he's calling everyone! (You included.) Pretty cool, huh?

Good news: It's okay if you're short. Doesn't matter if you're a little heavy, of if you're super skinny. You don't have to make straight A's or sing well or have a great complexion or be a good athlete.

More good news: You don't have to audition. No tryouts. You don't have to measure up or qualify. No sign-up sheet at the back of this book. All you have to do is answer the call!

God is calling you to

1. Follow him.
2. Make a difference in the lives around you.

God had all kinds of incredibly spectacular wonders in store for Zack, but he wasn't about to force his dreams on the guy. Zack had to accept. And guess what? You're in the same boat. God has fantabalastic stuff in store for you . . . but it's up to you to answer the call.

The highest call you'll ever receive is the call of God on your life. He's calling you. Have you accepted the call?

Let's flip over to the Old Testament. Look up Joel 2:32 and copy the Scripture right here. (You can stop at the word "saved").

My Memory Verse

According to the verse you just wrote out, what kind of call does God want you to make?

❀❀❀

Psalm 1 talks about someone who has accepted God's call and one who hasn't. Read that short chapter and list the differences between the two people.

Hey, Di!

Just because Latisha was complaining about her name, we got a homework assignment! That's right—Mrs. Parsons told us to do some research on our name. You know ... stuff like ask our parents why they named us what they did, try to find out what our name means—that kind of stuff.

I guess it won't really be that tough, but I never really thought about my name before. Latisha hates her name. She says she wishes she could change it. I like my name. And I especially like to hear it—if it's good, I mean. Like when Mrs. Parsons calls my name and says I did the best job on the science project. Or when Mom calls my name and says she loves me. It feels good, you know?

Zacchaeus probably wasn't called by his name very often. Because he was a tax-collector, he was hated and despised. People called him all kinds of names—cheater, jerk, swindler, crook. And because he was so short, he probably got some name-calling because of that, too: Midget, Shorty, Little Guy, Short-Stuff, Baby.

Imagine how good it must have felt when Jesus—the Creator of the universe, the head of the parade—stopped beside the tree Zack was in and call him by *name*. "Zacchaeus."

Our name is important. It's part of our identity. It helps explain who we are and who we belong to. As a *Christian*, we take part of *Christ's* name.

The God of all creation knows your name! Circle all the words that describe how that makes you feel.

How does Isaiah 43:1 prove that God is personally interested in *you*?

❀❀❀

According to Luke 10:20, if you're a Christian, where is your name written?

❀❀❀

Revelation 21:27 is talking about heaven. Read this verse and jot down who will *not* enter and who *will* enter.

❀❀❀

Dear Jesus,

Thanks so much for knowing my name! That makes me feel pretty special. And thanks that I can have the assurance that my name is written in your book of life—in your kingdom.

Father, help me to take your name seriously. Because I'm a Christian—because I carry part of your name—I want to live a holy life. I love you, Jesus. Help me to live a life that reflects your name to those around me.

Amen.

Hey, Diary!

The homework thing on names really wasn't that bad. In fact, a lot of kids found some interesting stuff about names. David reported on some famous people who changed their names. It was really cool.

Johnny Appleseed's real name was John Chapman. Sitting Bull's real name was Tatanka Iyotake (I like Sitting Bull much better!). Kareem Abdul-Jabbar's original name was Ferdinand Lewis Alcindor, Jr. (ha!). Hulk Hogan's original name was Terry Bodello. And Tom Cruise started out with Thomas Cruise Mapother IV.

Pretty funny, huh?

All in all . . . I'm pretty happy with what I've got.

❀❀❀

Believe it, it's true: A man with the name of Tonsilitis Jackson has brothers and sisters named Meningitis, Appendicitis, and Peritonitis.

Believe it, it's true: The following people have names that kind of, sort of, well, maybe not really, go with their professions. Mrs. Screech is a voice teacher in Victoria, British Columbia. There's an undertaker in Houston with the name of Mr. Groaner Digger. Mr. I. C. Shivers is an iceman.

Ever heard of a lawyer named Mr. Ronald Supena? He really exits! Dr. Slaughter is a surgeon. There's actually a pediatrician named Dr. Needles, and guess what profession Dr. Bonebreak belongs to? He's a chiropractor.

The study of names can be fascinating. But the Bible tells us there is one name above all names—and that's the name of our Lord and Savior, Jesus Christ.

Did you know that Jesus has a few other names?

Jot down the name of the Lord found in each of these Scriptures.

Proverbs 18:10 _____
Isaiah 42:8 _____
Isaiah 57:15 _____
Hosea 12:5 _____
Exodus 3:14 _____

Dear Jesus,
Help me to constantly know you better and better. I already feel I know you a little better by learning more about your name. Help me never get tired of learning more about you.
Amen.

Dear Diary ...

I never knew God had so many names! I'm really getting into this whole name thing! I mean it's totally fun finding out about famous people's names, what names are popular, and learning more about God's names.

❀❀❀

Betcha didn't know *these* famous people started out with different names!

Dr. Suess was named Theodore Suess Geisel. Cher's original name was Cherilyn Sarkisian, and guess what name Jodie Foster was born with? Alicia Christian Foster.

Chevy Chase began as Cornelius Crane Chase, Whoopi Goldberg used to be Caryn Johnson, and John Wayne was Marion Michael Morrison.

After discovering what some of these folks' original names were, it's easy to understand why they changed them to something else, isn't it!

Did you know that even Jesus gave himself different names? In various situations, he gave himself different names to help the people understand who he is and the role he wants to play in our lives. Find the name (or role) he gives himself in the following verses.

John 6:27 _____

John 6:35 _____

John 8:12 _____

John 10:7 _____

John 10:11 _____

John 14:6 _____

John 15:1 _____

Let's take a closer look at a few of these names. What does Jesus' name and role found in John 10:7 tell you about how to get into heaven?

❀❀❀

In John 15:1, Jesus calls himself the vine. What are we?

❀❀❀

What does his name and role say about his love for us in John 10:11?

❀❀❀

When you say the name of Jesus, realize that you are calling on the most powerful name in the entire world. There never was and never will be any name more powerful than that of your Savior. Express this in a prayer to him, and write it out in the space provided.

❀❀❀

Hey, Di!

This morning Aaron got sent to the principal's office for using some bad language in the hallway. Megan and I were talking about it at lunch. She says she hears kids say so much bad stuff so often that she's used to it.

In fact, she couldn't believe Aaron got sent to the office. "Lots of kids talk like that," she said. "It's no big deal."

Hmmm.

I always thought it was big deal. Now I'm confused.

❀❀❀

Have you ever heard the saying, "You'll know a tree by its fruit"? Well, it's not just a saying, it's actually in the Bible. Matthew 7:16 says, "By their fruit you will recognize them." And that same statement is repeated a few lines later in Matthew 7:20: "Thus, by their fruit you will recognize them."

When something is repeated, it's usually important. Jesus must have felt this thought was important enough to repeat. But what does it mean? He explains that we don't pick grapes from a thorn bush. That makes sense. If you wanted to pick roses for your mom, you wouldn't head for a patch of dandelions.

Jesus is saying that our "fruit" is what shows up on the outside. If you see roses growing, you know they're growing from a rose bush. If you see apples on a tree, you know it's an apple tree.

When people use bad language and misuse God's name, it's coming from inside. And just like a rose bush produces roses, an evil heart will produce evil talk, evil actions, and an evil lifestyle.

But wait a minute! you may be thinking. *Are bad words really evil?* Good question. What *is* evil? It's anything that goes against the nature of Jesus Christ. When you allow yourself to use bad language, you're not only breaking God's heart, you're also showing others that Christ doesn't rule the inside of your heart.

Let's see what the Bible has to say about all this. Read Colossians 3:8 and fill in the blanks.

"But now you must _____
yourselves of all such things as these:
_____, rage, _____,
slander, and _____
from your _____."

Copy Exodus 20:7 here in the space provided.

My Memory Verse

What does it mean to "misuse the name of the Lord"?

❀❀❀

Circle the words that describe how you'd feel if someone misused your name.

excited

angry

made fun of

hurt

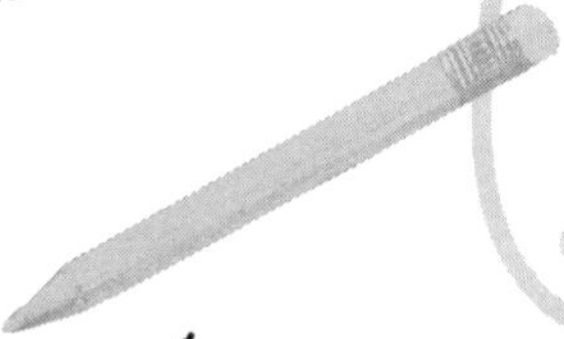

wouldn't care

sad

happy

relieved

powerful

unimportant

helpless

unappreciated

special

unloved

popular

cool

Read Philippians 4:8 and complete the list of all the things God wants you to focus your mind on.

Whatever is _____, Whatever is_____, Whatever is _____, Whatever is _____, Whatever is _____, Whatever is _____—if anything is _____ or _____—think about such things.

Dear Jesus,
I don't want to use language that makes you sad. I want the words that come out of my mouth to be helpful and kind. Please help me to think before I speak. I want a pure heart, and I want it to be reflected in the way I live my life.
I love you, Father.
Amen.

Dear Diary ...

I feel awful! I know I shouldn't have done it, but I did. I lied. I had just finished supper and was ready to watch my favorite TV show, when Mom asked me if I'd finished my homework.

Well, I really hadn't, but I knew I could do it on the bus tomorrow before I got to school. I told her everything was done, and I watched the show. I didn't even enjoy it. I felt too guilty.

I know the Bible says that lying is a sin. So does this mean I'm not a Christian anymore?

❀❀❀

The Bible tells us in 1 John 2:1 that we don't have to sin. In other words, once we become a Christian and allow Christ to rule our lives, we're no longer *slaves* to sin. But 1 John 2:1 also tells us that we *might* sin. In other words, the apostle John knew that with God's power within us, we can choose to claim that power and decide with God's help not to sin. But John also knew that we wouldn't always make the right choice. So he reminded us that if we *do* sin, there is hope. That hope is Jesus.

Remember, God is holy. Therefore, he will not tolerate sin in his kingdom. So when we sin, we need to ask Jesus to forgive us. He then is able to present us before God as pure and forgiven.

When you sin, you don't have to throw in the towel and start all over. Simply ask Jesus to forgive you, accept his forgiveness, and keep walking with him. God is always willing to forgive a heart that's truly sorry.

According to Mark 2:7, who alone can forgive sins?

How long will God remember your sins? (Check out Isaiah 43:25 for the answer!)

How far does God remove our sins from us when we seek his forgiveness? (You'll find the answer in Psalm 103:12.)

Through whom is the forgiveness of sins proclaimed to us? (Sneak a peek at Acts 13:26!)

Is there anything in your life for which you need to seek forgiveness? You can do that right now. Go ahead. Write out your prayer to Jesus in the space provided.

Hey, Di!

Kylee's mom is taking us to the mall this afternoon. Can't wait. We're gonna try on jeans and shoes. But you know what my fave thing to do at the mall is?

Hitting the perfume counter! Kylee and I'll spray each other with all the newest cologne, and we'll beg the clerk to give us some free samples. I love to smell good. Makes me feel special!

See ya tomorrow.

❀❀❀

We have all kinds of stuff to make us smell good, don't we? We have odor-eaters to put inside our shoes. We buy deodorant so we won't smell sweaty. We use bath gel and body powders so others can enjoy our sweet scent. And we spend money on cologne to use ourselves or to give away as a gift. Most of us think it's cool to smell good.

Did you know that people in the Bible also liked to smell good? They didn't have all the choices we have, but they mixed spices and herbs to create a variety of pleasing scents. Often when a visitor had traveled a long way to someone's home, the host would remove the guest's shoes, wash his feet, and sprinkle a tiny bit of perfume on his friend's feet. It was quite an honor to have someone rub perfume on his tired, dirty feet.

Has anyone told you recently that you smell? Well, you do! The apostle Paul says that Christians have a specific aroma. Check it out in 2 Corinthians 2:14. What is our fragrance?

❀❀❀

Now read 2 Corinthians 2:15. What aroma are we to God?

❀❀❀

According to 2 Corinthians 2:16, to non-Christians we smell like _____. But to Christians, we have the fragrance of _____.

Think about it: What are you smelling like? If you'll make time to read your Bible every day and talk with God, you're growing spiritually. Imagine the wonderful aroma Jesus gives through growing Christians!

My Memory Verse

He anointed us, set his seal of ownership on us, and put his Spirit in our hearts as a deposit, guaranteeing what is to come (2 Corinthians 1:21).

The best is yet to come! As you grow stronger in Christ, his beautiful fragrance through you will also strengthen.

Dear Diary ...

Kimberly is really getting on my nerves! She's so negative! She's mad because Ryan didn't sit with her at lunch. She's ticked off because it rained before school. She's steamed because her mom didn't have time to pack her lunch and Kimberly had to do it herself.

I go, "Kimberly, your life would seem a lot better if you'd find something positive to think about instead of always looking at the bad stuff."

And she's all, "There isn't anything good in my life. My life reeks. Everything is wrong!"

Oh, gimme a break.

Her friends are starting to ignore her because she's so negative. I hope I never become like Kimberly! Gag!

✿✿✿

You could say that Grace Vanderbilt went down in history as being the party hostess champion. She spent a whopping $300,000 a year for 50 years entertaining guests!

And the biggest bash in history was hosted in October of 1971 by the shah of Iran. He spent close to one hundred million dollars for the extravagant event.

Hey, these folks knew how to throw a party! And they were probably great parties because of the people who came. Think about it: What makes a party fun? Yeah, games, food, and prizes certainly help. But the main ingredient is the guests. If you have negative, sour guests that complain the entire evening, chances are the party will bomb. If your guests are excited and happy to be together, the party will probably be a success even if you run out of food!

As Christians, we're preparing for an incredible party. God—the Creator of rhyme and music and color and dance and laughter—knows how to throw a party! He invented them, remember?

I guess it's halfway understandable when non-Christians are so negative. They don't know Jesus as their personal Savior. But Christians really don't have a reason to be negative. We're going to heaven! Eventually, we'll be celebrating at the biggest party of all throughout eternity!

Attitude check: What's yours like? Jot down how you react when things don't go your way.

How do you think Jesus *wants* you to react when things go wrong?

Read Ephesians 5:1 and jot down who we should be imitating.

❀❀❀

According to Philippians 4:4, what does God want us to do in good times and in bad times?

❀❀❀

Instead of complaining, being negative, and wanting more, what did the apostle Paul learn in Philippians 4:11–12?

❀❀❀

Stop right here and think of six really good things you can thank Christ for.

1.
2.
3.
4.
5.
6.

Ask God to help you be positive and to always see the good things that are happening around you, instead of focusing on the negative.

Dear Di ...

I've got $42.67 saved from baby-sitting. It's taken me quite a while to get that much, but now that I have it, I'm wanting to buy a new pair of boots.

Mom says I don't need new boots. She's suggesting I keep saving it. I don't wanna save anymore. I wanna buy something!

Okay, I'll admit I already have two pairs of boots, but I really want this brand-new pair I saw at the mall. They'd look great with my cargos.

Sigh.

❀❀❀

In just one day, Americans ...

- produce more than 800,000 pairs of jeans.
- brush their teeth with more than 500,000 pounds of toothpaste.
- purchase more than 50,000 pairs of running shoes.

We can tell what's important in people's lives by looking at what they spend their money on, how they use their time, and who they hang out with.

It's been said that if you want to know what people's priorities are, go through their garbage. Police can actually learn quite a bit about people by simply digging through their trash. They find canceled checks or bills and immediately know what people spend their money on. They see fast-food bags and can develop a sense of people's schedules: Are they fast-paced, or do they have time to cook and sit down to a full meal? By noticing ticket stubs and other indications of entertainment, police can guess whether the people are social or like to stay at home.

What's important in *your* life? When we study the life of Jesus, it's easy to see what was important to him. He was on a single-minded mission: His goal was to spread the gospel and lead as many people as he could into a personal relationship with his Father.

Jesus knew his time on earth was limited. He knew his public ministry would last only three years. Therefore, he moved, spoke, healed, and lived with a sense of urgency. He calls us to do the same.

Instead of being sidetracked by things that don't have eternal value, strive to focus your energy, your time, and your life on influencing others for God.

What if you only had two more years to live? What would become more important to you?

How would you try to grow closer to your family?

Who would you apologize to?

❀❀❀

Who would you share Jesus with?

❀❀❀

According to Colossians 4:17, what are we to complete?

❀❀❀

Make a list of "urgents"—things you feel God wants you to do.

❀❀❀

Ask him to keep you focused on what he's calling you to do instead of getting sidetracked with new boots or other temporary things.

Dear Diary ...

Mrs. Parsons assigned us to write a paper on what we want to be and do someday. I used to be interested in nursing, but now I think I'd kinda like to be an astronaut. I don't know, though. Maybe God has something else in mind for me.

Wonder how I'll know?

❀❀❀

Let's imagine that Regis Philbin from TV's "Who Wants To Be a Millionaire?" shows up at your front door. "We had a million dollars left over from our game show," he says, "and the network told me I could give it to anyone I wanted. So I've decided to give it you!"

Whoa! Would you be screaming at this point? Or just jumping up and down unable to say anything?

"But there's a catch," he continues. "I've hidden the money in your yard. You'll have to find it."

Just as you're about to ask where to start, he says, "I won't spell it out for you, but I'll point you in the right direction. Don't worry—I'll make sure you find it. I really want you to have the money!"

He points you toward the swing set. As you head in that direction, you notice the sandbox and can't help but think, *That would be a perfect place to bury something! I'll start digging.* You throw yourself into the big pile of sand and start digging furiously. As

Regis shields himself from flying sand, he gently turns you around to face the swing set.

Suddenly you notice a big oak tree in the middle of the yard. *Of course!* you think. *People always hide stuff under trees. I'll look there.* Regis interrupts your digging and pulls you to your feet. He again points you toward the swing set.

You finally get the hint and start digging under the swing. After just ten minutes of digging, you pull out a beautiful treasure chest filled with your fortune.

Regis Philbin probably won't ever visit your house. But God's plan for your life is just like an incredible treasure. And he's going to make sure you find it!

God's plan for your life is *his* responsibility. It's up to him to make sure you know what he wants you to do. Trust him.

What kind of plans does God have for you? (Find out in Jeremiah 29:11 and list them here.)

If you're confused about God's plan for your life, what should you ask God for? (James 1:5)

According to James 1:6, how should you ask God?

What should you trust God with, according to Proverbs 3:5?

And what does God *not* want you to lean on?

❀❀❀

My Memory Verse

Trust in the Lord with all your heart and lean not on your own understanding; in all your ways acknowledge him, and he will make your paths straight (Proverbs 3:5–6).

Hey, Diary!

I've decided to trust God with his plans for my life. I'm not sure what he wants me to do yet, but I'm willing to do anything. I'll be a teacher, a missionary, a singer—I'll do anything he wants. I just want to serve him and be all he calls me to be.

❀❀❀

When we think about what we're going to do with our lives someday, it's easy to ask ourselves, "What can I do to make a lot of money? How can I become important? What can I do to be remembered?"

Those questions are never found in the Bible. In fact, Jesus gives us some very interesting advice! He says if we want to be great, we have to be the least. To be first, we need to be last. Want to be in charge? Then start by serving.

Hmmm. Maybe our prayer should be, "Lord, where can I serve you? How can you use my life to help others?"

God has blessed you with special gifts and abilities. As you grow, he wants to help you develop those skills so you can bring glory to him. So it's important to know what you're good at, but he doesn't want you to become obsessed with what you do well.

Look at Romans 12:6–8. Make a list of the gifts mentioned here as you read the Scripture.

Now make a list of all your skills. Don't hold back! Are you good with people? Put it down. Do you have a knack for throwing parties and making others feel welcome? Maybe you're good with numbers, or maybe you're a good athlete. Do you like to write? Maybe words and sentences come easily to you. Perhaps you have a vivid imagination. Good handwriting? List as many good things as you can.

Spend some time praying about each entry. Ask God to help you use these things according to his will. Tell him that your heart's desire is to be all that he wants you to be.

Hey, Diary ...

In Sunday school we made a list of some of the most important things in our lives. Michael listed his guitar, Hannah mentioned her golden retriever, several students listed their parents and family, and Danielle said God was the most important thing in her life.

You know what, Diary? That's what I want. I want God to be more important to me than anything. But it sure is easy to get attached to stuff like my stereo, our big-screen TV, my new bed, and my fave fleece vest.

❀❀❀

Suppose you were given the following items. Rank each item from 1 to 10 according to the value (1 is the most valuable; 10 is the least valuable) you would place on each one.

___a basketball signed by Michael Jordan
___four tickets for front-row seats to your fave concert group
___a cure for AIDS
___a $10,000 computer system, complete with *all* extras
___an original painting by van Gogh

___an all-expenses-paid snow-skiing trip in the Colorado Rockies

___a guarantee to achieve worldwide fame

___the ability to feed hungry people around the world

___incredible body shape and beauty

Unfortunately, we often place value on things in our lives that aren't eternal. It's natural to want to be liked, to be recognized for things we do, and to have the best that life has to offer. But when it's all said and done, the only thing that will *really* matter is our relationship with Jesus Christ. *That's* something that holds eternal value.

Read Matthew 6:19–21 and fill in the blanks.

"Do not store up for yourselves

_____ on _____,
Where moth and rust _____, and
Where _____ break in
and _____. But store up for
yourselves _____ in
_____, Where moth
and _____ do _____ destroy,
and Where thieves do _____ break in
and _____. For Where your
_____ is, there your
_____ Will be also."

List four things you're often tempted to put too much value on.

1.
2.
3.
4.

List some things that have eternal value. (I'll get you started, you fill in the rest, okay?)

1. faith
2.
3. prayer
4.
5. putting God first

Make a list of things you can do to place more value on your faith.

1.
2. talk more about God
3.
4.
5. give some of my belongings to people who need them
6. spend more time reading the Bible

Dear Diary ...

Amy's so funny! She invited me over to spend the night and said we'd order pizza. Well, by the time I got there, it had already been delivered.

"I thought we were gonna decide together what kind of pizza we want," I said.

Then she grinned really big and opened the lid. "I didn't have to wait," she said. "I know your favorite pizza is double cheese, so that's what I got."

We died laughing. And then she opened the fridge. "Mom got a six-pack of Squirt at the grocery store this morning," she said, "because I told her that was your favorite drink."

Wow! What a great friend!

✿✿✿

You've probably memorized the most important things about your best friends. For example, you know the sounds of their voices. When your friends call you, they probably don't have to tell you who they are.

Since you have your friends' voices memorized, you probably know exactly who's calling as soon as you hear the very first word they say. You don't even have to hear a complete sentence to know who it is. I'll bet you even know their favorite TV shows, what they like on their pizza, and which ice-cream they enjoy most.

You know these things because you've spent enough quality time together that you've actually *memorized* them without really trying.

It works the same way with God. The more time you spend with him, the better you know his voice. The more you *listen* to his voice, the more natural it is to *obey* his voice. Before you know it, you're memorizing the character of God. And the exciting part? His character begins to show up in your life!

Since your friendship with God is the most important friendship you'll ever have—one that will last forever—spend some quality time this week getting to know him better.

Deepen your relationship with God by talking to him and listening to him. Start by asking him the questions below.

- Jesus, how can I show your love to my family?

- Father, what are some things in my life that you're pleased with?

• What are some areas I need to work on?

• How can I grow closer to you?

Now list some questions of your own to ask God. (And don't forget to listen for the answers!)

•
•
•
•

My Memory Verse

For my thoughts are not your thoughts, neither are your ways my ways," declares the Lord. As the heavens are higher than the earth, so are my ways higher than your ways and my thoughts than your thoughts (Isaiah 55:8–9).

Dear Diary ...

Three weeks ago, I asked Keisha to go to camping with my family. She sounded interested. Well . . . last week, Jennifer—my best friend from last year—moved back. I couldn't believe it! We were so happy to see each other.

I was so excited, I asked her go camping with my family—then I remembered I had already invited Keisha. Since our tent isn't big enough for me to bring two friends, I just hoped Keisha would forget about it.

Jennifer and I had a total blast! We swam, hiked, roasted hot dogs, and picked wild flowers. But when I saw Keisha on Monday, she wouldn't even talk to me.

I know I should apologize, but . . . it's hard!

Choose one:

1. It's easier for me to
    a. notice my own faults.
    b. notice other people's mistakes.

2. It's easier for me to
   a. ask for forgiveness.
   b. hold a grudge.
3. It's easier for me to
   a. make excuses for my mistakes.
   b. forgive others.

Amber *said* she'd save you a seat at lunch, but you see her sitting with three new students. Do you get angry? Hold a grudge? Assume she's trying to reach out?

Lexi *said* she'd call. It's been four days. When you finally run into her at school, she says her brother was injured. Do you respond with concern, or do you think, *So what? You're not his doctor!*

Being willing to say we're sorry for an attitude, a misunderstanding, unkind words, or a mean reaction is simply part of growing up. In fact, real maturity is found in people who can easily admit their mistakes. When people apologize and accept the blame for something that's their fault, they're actually exhibiting a strong character trait—humility.

The best leaders, the most consistent friends, the most exciting people to be around are those who can admit they blew it. People want to follow that kind of disciple.

Think about this: Peter and Judas both denied Jesus. The difference? Peter had the humility to say "I'm sorry."

This might be tough, but ask God to help you think of people you need to apologize to. As he does, jot their names in the space provided and list what you need to apologize about.

Now write out a prayer asking God for the strength—and the right words—to make things right with these people *this week.*

Read Luke 6:37 and write down what happens to us when we forgive others.

Now look at Mark 11:25. Before we can experience true forgiveness from God, what must we do for others?

My Favorite Diary ...

Sometimes I think you're the only one who really understands. When Mom and Dad said we were going to Grandma's for dinner (she just lives two miles from our house), I got kinda mad because I knew I'd be missing my fave TV show.

That's when Dad asked me if that show had become too important to me. And Mom goes, "When a TV show keeps you from being with other people, it may be time to give it up."

Sigh.

I'm confused. I love my TV show. But I don't want it to be more important than it should.

❀❀❀

Wagga Wagga is an actual city in Australia. Like any good citizens, the people of Wagga Wagga are proud of their city. But let's imagine they became so proud that they made a bunch of Wagga Wagga T-shirts in seven different colors, and everyone wore a different one on each day of the week.

Next they manufactured Wagga Wagga toothpaste and toothbrushes. Everyone who lived in the city used them daily.

They even invented a special Wagga Wagga holiday. But let's say their new holiday fell on the same day that the Australian government called a special meeting of representatives from every city. And let's just say that Wagga Wagga citizens refused to participate because it got in the way of their own holiday.

We could easily say that what they had created kept them from serving a higher government. They failed to see the bigger picture because they couldn't get past their own devotion to their city.

It works the same way in our relationship with Christ. An idol is anything we allow to come between ourselves and Jesus Christ. An idol is usually something we place a great deal of value on—like a friendship, a favorite TV show, music, sports—*anything* that becomes as important or *more* important than God.

What does 1 Corinthians 14 say about idolatry?

❀❀❀

Fill in the blanks after you read Isaiah 44:9.

"All who make _____ are _____, and the things they _____ are

_____."

Read Psalm 139:23–24 and write it out in your own words.

My Memory Verse

Now make the above your prayer this week, okay?

Dear Diary ...

Zoe had a bunch of us over for a slumber party last night. It was so fun! We stayed up till 4 a.m., then finally started dozing off. I'm still pretty tired, but I had a total blast.

We watched videos, had a scavenger hunt, and played a bunch of crazy games. We munched on everything from caramel corn to oatmeal cookies to chips, and we even made pizza.

Okay ... so here's the only part I didn't like. I'm crazy about pizza. Who isn't, right? Well, we made a cheese pizza and a pepperoni pizza ... but, I know this is hard to believe, Zoe's mom forgot to buy tomato sauce. What's a pizza without tomato sauce? Is it really even a pizza?

Not only that, but we didn't have any mozzarella to sprinkle on top, either! Well, we did the best we could. And we still had a total blast. And we still ate the pizzas. But they didn't really have a lot of flavor. (I think Zoe was kind of embarrassed!)

❀❀❀

Can you imagine making sugar cookies without the sugar? Or oatmeal cookies without oatmeal? Or let's say you made a batch of brownies and forgot the chocolate! Your baked items probably wouldn't go too far, wouldn't they?

If you had made them for a fund-raising event at your school, it's doubtful anyone would purchase them. And if you intended to give away your goodies as a gift, the receiver probably wouldn't even eat them!

When baking or cooking, it's important to follow the recipe, isn't it? If we leave out just one ingredient, it can affect the outcome of the whole thing.

Guess what? Christianity has some pretty important ingredients, too. In fact, Jesus said that Christians are the salt of the earth. As you know, salt is a very important ingredient that gives our food flavor. Without it, most of what we eat would taste really bland. Can you imagine eating popcorn without any salt?

When Christians fall short of being the flavor God intends for them to be, the world around them seems tasteless. What are *you* doing to bring flavor to the lives of your non-Christian friends?

List five of your favorite things to salt:

1.
2.
3.
4.
5.

If you *had* to go without salt on one of these items, which one would it be? (Circle one)

Hamburger
French fries
chips
popcorn

Check out Matthew 5:13. What happens when salt loses its saltiness?

Jesus said that Christians are the flavor of the world. List some ways you can bring "flavor" to those around you. (I'll get you started; you do the rest.)

1. I can keep a positive attitude when everyone else is negative or complaining.
2.
3.
4. I can write a kind note and mail it someone who's had a rough day.
5.

Try going one entire week without putting any salt on your food. Then write about your experience in the space provided.

❀❀❀

Dear Diary ...

I can't believe what MacKenzie did! I'm so mad at her I could bust open into a trillion-zillion-gabrillion pieces!

Yesterday, she asked me if I thought Shawn was cute. "I guess so," I said. That's all I said.

Then this morning she blabbed to everyone in our ZIP code that I'm in love with Shawn. How could she do that? I didn't even say I liked him.

I passed Shawn in the hall, and he wouldn't even look at me.

Ugh!

❁❁❁

Being angry actually takes a lot of energy, and if you're angry *long* enough, you'll eventually become depressed (a deep, growing sadness). Depression is simply anger turned inward.

Yuk. Why would someone want to spend so much energy on something so negative?

The Bible tells us not to let the sun go down while anger is still in our hearts. In other words, don't go to bed when you're "ticked-off." Make every effort to set-tle your anger. That may mean talking it out, seeking counsel, asking forgiveness, praying, or putting your thoughts on paper.

No matter how you choose to deal with your anger, let God be your guide. He understands your emotions even better than you do. He invented them, remember?

Instead of wasting energy by harboring a grudge against someone who has hurt you, think of some things you could accomplish by putting that same energy into action.

1. I could write a song.
2.
3. I could make a new friend by becoming pen pals with someone in another country.
4.
5. I could write a children's story and try to get it published.
6.

Read 1 Corinthians 13:5. If we love someone, what kind of records should we keep when they anger us?

Check out James 1:20. What kind of life does God desire for us to live?

❀❀❀

What will keep us from living that kind of life?

❀❀❀

Now flip over to Ephesians 4:26–27 and complete these verses:

"In your _____ do not _____: Do not let the _____ go down while you are still _____, and do not give the _____ a _____."

Is there anyone with whom you're angry? Ask God to bring him or her to your mind. Next, ask God to give you the strength to forgive and forget.

Hey, Di ...

Sigh. Another ordinary day. Nothing major happened. Nothing to even write about. Seems like my life is in slow motion.

Sigh.

❀❀❀

There are a lot of ordinary days, aren't there? But guess what? It's how we spend our ordinary days that determine our great ones. Hey, it's easy to be happy and excited on the terrific days! When you've just aced that pop quiz in math, you just found out you were elected class secretary, Michael said you looked nice, and your school pictures turned out great, it doesn't take much effort to feel good about yourself.

Anyone can feel great on *those* kind of days! But how are you handling your ordinary days? Instead of seeing them as boring, not-much-happening, blah days, try to imagine that every day of your life is a fantastic one! In fact, there are actually some pretty special days on the calendar that you're probably not even aware of. For instance, do you know about *these* special days?

October 15	National Grouch Day (Just because, stay in an extra-nice mood all day long.)
November 1	Real Jewelry Month begins (Buy some candy necklaces, and give them to your friends.)

November 3   Sandwich Day (Invent a new sandwich.)

December 14   South Pole Discovery Day: 1911 (Act like a penguin.)

January 4   Trivia Day (Learn something new.)

February 11   Secret Pal Day (Slip someone a secret note of appreciation.)

Hey, why not make up a few special days of your own? After all, walking and living with Jesus Christ really *does* make every day an incredible one!

Let's make up some of our own special days right now! Grab a calendar and assign dates to these actions.

Date   _____   Eat an apple.

_____   Learn how to play a new game.

_____   Start a collection.

_____   Baby-sit for free.

_____   Give something away.

Now assign actions to the following dates.

September 10 _____

April 24   _____

July 16   _____

February 1   _____

August 28   _____

Read 1 Thessalonians 5:16–18. When should we be joyful?

❀❀❀

How often should we pray?

❀❀❀

What is God's will for us in all circumstances?

Dearest Di ...

Even though I didn't feel like it, I made chocolate chip cookies last night from scratch. And this morning I wrapped them up in a really cool basket and took them to Mrs. Foster next door. She's pretty old, and she doesn't get out much. You know what? I'm really glad I did it! The look on her face when I handed her the basket of cookies was worth a jillion dollars. I think I'll try to do that more often. It really wasn't that hard.

Later.

❀❀❀

You may think there's nothing more fun than being surprised with an unexpected gift. But you can actually have just as much fun—maybe even *more*—by being the surpriser who gives the gift!

When was the last time you did something unexpected for someone? Do you know that every time you're kind and giving to someone, you're actually representing Jesus? His entire life was unselfish. He gave and gave and gave. And he wants us to do the same.

Check out 1 Thessalonians 5:11. What two things are we supposed to be doing for others?

List a few people you have encouraged this week, and jot down what you did that encouraged them.

❀❀❀

Flip over to 1 Thessalonians 3:12. What does God want to do with our love?

❀❀❀

My Memory Verse

And do not forget to do good and to share with others, for with such sacrifices God is pleased (1 Thessalonians 3:16).

Hey, Di ...

This morning in church, Pastor Samuelson introduced the Westoff family. The Reverend and Mrs. Westoff are missionaries in East Africa, and they have a teen daughter and a little boy. The teen girl—Samantha—visited our Sunday school class and talked about what it was like to live overseas and be a missionary kid.

She said there are a lot of differences—like they don't have as much cereal to choose from as we do. She said it's really cool that we have an entire aisle in the grocery store just filled with cereal.

And she said there are no ATM machines in her village. No traffic lights, no ice-cream stores, and no mall nearby.

"Life as an M.K.," Samantha said, "is full of surprises and adjustments."

❀❀❀

Here are a few *more* surprises:

- Back in 1919, a giant 90-foot tank of molasses exploded and 13,500 tons of the sticky stuff spewed into a community. This wave of molasses measured 50 feet high and moved at 35 miles an hour. It swallowed eight buildings, engulfed more than 100 people, and killed 22 folks. The aftereffect? The town smelled like pancake syrup for years!

- The yummy chocolate Baby Ruth candy bar wasn't really named after baseball legend Babe Ruth. Surprise! It was actually named after Ruth Cleveland—"Baby Ruth"—President Cleveland's oldest daughter.
- A Miami Customs Service Agent searched the luggage of twenty-year-old Manuel Frade as he arrived in America from Venezuela. The agent opened Manuel's suitcase and touched a pair of jeans that wiggled suspiciously. Imagine the agent's surprise when she found 14 boa constrictors inside! By the time she finished searching Manuel's luggage, she had also accumulated hundreds of tarantulas, their eggs, and 300 poison-arrow frogs. What a surprise!

Imagine the surprise Noah had when it finally rained! And imagine Mary and Martha's surprise when Jesus brought their brother Lazarus back from the dead. And Job certainly had quite a series of surprises when most of his family died and he became seriously ill.

Life is full of surprises—both good and bad. It doesn't matter how many surprises we encounter or even if they're happy or disastrous. For Christians, the issue at stake is how we respond to life's surprises.

Rank yourself from 1 to 5 (1 being poor and 5 being great) on how you respond to the following surprises:

____ Your English teacher announces a surprise spelling test.

____ Your mom has cooked your favorite dinner.

____ The track meet you were looking forward to competing in is suddenly canceled because of rain.

____ Your parents tell you to clean the kitchen and vacuum the house before your best friend comes over.

___ Your Sunday school teacher announces that next week you'll be asked to give in a special offering to surprise a missionary family.

What does 1 John 3:13 tell you not to be surprised about?

❀❀❀

Check out 1 Peter 4:12–14 to complete these verses:

"Dear _____, do not be
_____ at the painful trial
you are _____, as though
something _____ were
happening to you. But _____ that
you _____ in the
sufferings of _____, so that you
may be _____ when his
glory is _____. If you
are _____ because of the
_____ of _____,
you are _____, for the Spirit
of _____ and of God rests
on _____."

The apostle Peter had some strong things to say about surprises. Grab your Bible and check out 1 Peter 5:8–11. Grab a few index cards or some blank paper and copy these verses. Put these pages or cards someplace where you'll see them often (inside your locker at school, above your light switch, on your mirror). And every time you see these verses, read them again and ask God to help you handle life's surprises in the way he wants you to.

Dear Diary ...

I feel really bad for Olivia. Someone stole her mountain bike. She'd only had it for two weeks, and it was a really expensive one. When I told her I'd pray for her, she looked at me totally weird.

"God doesn't care about my bike," she said. "Besides, my dad has already put an ad in the paper and talked with the police. There's nothing more we can do."

I couldn't believe it! She's not even willing to pray about it. I sure wish Olivia knew Jesus as her personal Savior—then she'd know that he cares about everything in our lives.

I'm still gonna pray for her. After all, not long ago, I was just learning about how God wants us to pray about everything that concerns us.

❀❀❀

It's totally true! God cares about everything *you* care about. The Bible tells us he even knows the exact number of hairs on your head. Hey, he understands when you're having a bad hair day!

It's fun to trade our school photos with friends, isn't it? We like to carry them in our purse, in our wallet, and even display them in our lockers. But if your friends all wore masks on picture day, you wouldn't be carrying an accurate photo of them, would you? You wouldn't be able to see their face because of the mask.

Some people have a tough time believing God truly cares about every detail of their lives, because they're carrying around the wrong picture of God. Here are a few snapshots some of your friends may have of God:

The traffic cop. Maybe your friends see God as someone who's hiding around the corner, waiting to issue a ticket when a mistake is made.

The Santa Claus. Do you have friends who think God is simply Someone who gives us stuff? And that we only get it when we're good?

The weak God. Lots of people see all the suffering in the world and don't think God is strong enough to stop it.

The silent God. Maybe your friends think God just sits on his throne in heaven, but he never really talks with us or makes his presence known.

None of these snapshots of God are shown in the Bible. That means all the above snapshots are false. So what kind of snapshot of God *does* the Bible show? Well, let's check it out. Start by turning to Psalm 34:18. Where is God when your heart is broken?

What does he do for those whose spirits are crushed?

Flip over to Psalm 104:13–15. List the specific ways God cares for the earth he created.

What does he do for the cattle?

What does he do for man?

Read Psalm 145:18 to answer this next question. When you call on God,

a. He listens to you sometimes, but not always.
b. He'll answer your prayer if you've said the right words.
c. He is always near.

I hope you selected the last answer to the above question. God is totally wrapped up in your life. He's crazy about you!

Dear Father,

Thanks so much for caring about all the big stuff—and all the little stuff in my life. Help me to show my friends how active you want to be in their lives, too.

Thanks for always hearing my prayers, Father. I love you so much!

Amen.

Hey, Diary ...

I know. I know. I know. I shouldn't have said the things to Riley that I did. It's just that ... well, sometimes he's really a pest. Don't get me wrong—I love my little brother—but gimme a break!

Keisha and I were working on our science project after school, and he kept coming into the kitchen and bugging us. "You want some lemonade, Keisha?"

So I told him to scram.

"You want me to turn off the TV, Keisha?"

I told him to beat it!

"Whatcha guys doin'?"

I chased him into the living room.

"Hey, how come I can't hang out with you?"

That was it! I'd had it! I called him a bratty, snot-nosed kid, and I shoved him so hard he fell down.

Now I feel bad. Kind of. I mean ... yeah, he was a total pest! But I shouldn't have hurt him that bad—or said the stuff I did. I found him in his room later, and he was crying.

*O*uch! When we hurt someone's feelings, it not only hurts *them*, it hurts *us* as well. It's easy to tell God that we're sorry. But it's a little tougher to tell someone else we're sorry.

Some people think, *It's no big deal. I can always apologize to the person I hurt, and I can always ask God to forgive me.*

Guess what? That's not true repentance. That's not genuinely being sorry—that's just temporarily feeling bad.

When we apologize to someone, and when we ask God to forgive us for hurting someone, we shouldn't plan on involving ourselves in that hurt ever again. In other words, to scream at your brother, shove him, and hurt his feelings and ask God for forgiveness should be with a pure heart, and you should truly want to change.

But to think, *I'll apologize to my bro, and I'll ask God to forgive me. Then tomorrow if Riley bugs me again, I'll just do the same thing over. God will always forgive me.*

God knows our hearts. He sees all the way inside us. When you apologize to someone, do it with a silent pledge not to hurt that person again.

According to Hebrews 4:13, what can we hide from God?

Read Hebrews 4:12. Make a list of all the words that describe how powerful God's Word is.

Take a peek at Acts 26:20. How can we prove we have a genuine and repentant heart?

Ask God to bring anyone to your mind that you need to seek forgiveness from. First ask God to forgive you; then seek forgiveness from the person you've hurt.

My Memory Verse

Godly sorrow brings repentance that leads to salvation and leaves no regret, but worldly sorrow brings death (2 Corinthians 7:10).

Dear Diary ...

Ugh! I barely got through the front door this afternoon, and Mom reminded me that I'd forgotten to take out the trash this morning. Then she told me to do the dishes while she started dinner.

I just got home! I'm still tired from school! Why do I always have to work around the house?

❈❈❈

Let's imagine for a few seconds, okay? Let's pretend frogs can talk. It's been raining all night, and when you leave for school in the morning, a frog approaches you.

"Man, all this rain is totally getting me down! I'm so tired of it. It's just not fair!"

What would your response be?

a. "I hate it, too. Let's run away together. We'll go somewhere very hot where it never rains."
b. "That's just part of life. We *need* rain. Besides, it helps all the plants grow stronger."
c. "If you just ignore the rain and pretend it isn't there, it'll eventually go away."

Sometimes chores just don't seem fair, do they? (Oh, yeah. You can stop pretending now.) But helping around the house is simply part of life. In fact, just as plants benefit from the rain, you also benefit from chores.

No way!

Yep. It's true. When you do your part around the house, you're actually demonstrating that you're part of a team. Your family is a unit, and each member of the unit needs to work together to keep your home running smoothly.

Have you ever thought about how your parents feel? I mean, *really* thought about it? Maybe they're worried about paying bills, your relatives, pressure at work, or making enough money to help you with college someday. And sometimes parents get so tired, they just don't *feel* good. Hey, that's where you can really shine!

List some questions you can ask your parents that will show your concern for them. (I'll get you started.)

1. "How was your day?"
2.
3. "Anything I can help you with?"
4.
5. "Do you know how much I love you?"
6.

What are some things you can compliment your mom on?

1. "You look nice today."
2.
3. "Thanks for dinner."
4.
5. "I'm proud of you."
6.

Read 1 Corinthians 13:4–7. Jot down all the characteristics found here about love.

❀❀❀

Are you showing your parents how much you love them? Start right now!

Hi, Diary ...

I really wish I was taller. And skinnier. And cuter. My nose is too big, and my ears are weird-looking. All the other girls in my class are already starting to develop ... and I'm still flat as a pancake.

I hate my body!

Get a load of this!

- It's against the law to annoy squirrels in Topeka, Kansas.
- In Natoma, Kansas, it's against the law to practice knife-throwing at men wearing striped suits.
- It's against the law in New York City to open or close an umbrella in the presence of a horse.
- In Greene, New York, you can't eat peanuts and walk backward on the sidewalks while a concert is in progress.

Even though we laugh at some of these old laws that were never taken out of the books, we sometimes create our own laws that are just as silly. Laws or expectations that require girls to wear a certain size clothing and have silky-smooth complexions are not only silly, they're also unrealistic.

Although we often hear messages that tell us we have to look perfect to be beautiful, nothing could be farther from the truth. God told the prophet Samuel that God is *way* more interested in what goes on inside the *hearts* of people than in our outward appearances.

Though no one is perfect, we *can* find things we like about our physical appearance. Take time to do that right now. Go ahead. List four things you like about the way you look.

1.
2.
3.
4.

Read Proverbs 31:30 and complete this verse.

"Charm is _____, and _____ is _____; but a _____ who fears the _____ is to be _____."

What does *fleeting* mean?

a. Made out of fleece.
b. Here today and gone tomorrow.
c. Popular.

If you chose B, you made the right choice. The Bible tells us that beauty is fleeting—in other words, it's only temporary. What are some other things that are temporary? (I'll get you started, you finish, okay?)

1. Clothing
2.
3.
4. Slang words
5.
6. Fads (Furby, Beanie Babies, computerized key chain pets)
7.

Read 1 Peter 3:3–4. What is of greater worth in God's sight?

a. Expensive jewelry
b. The latest hair style
c. A gentle and quiet spirit

Is there anyone you've been ignoring because she doesn't measure up to the world's crazy laws of beauty? Ask God to bring someone to your mind—right now—who needs your friendship. (Write her name in the space provided.)

I dare you to approach her backward: Get to know her from the inside out . . . instead of the outside in. Will you do that? If so, list some ways you can get to know this person from the inside.

Dear Diary ...

Our pastor is preaching on how we need to be like children to follow Jesus. I'm sick of being a kid! In fact, I'm loving growing up and getting more responsibilities.

Sigh.

This is so confusing!

❀❀❀

It was Friday, and Maggie, the director for "Jerusalem's Jovial Day-care Center," was short on staff. Sharon was out with the flu, and Craig had taken the camel to the vet. This left Maggie in charge of seventy-three enthusiastic children, full of energy and bored with Legos. So she took them all to the park.

Mikey and his friends headed for the jungle gym. Mallory, Jennifer, and Sylvia pulled out their dolls and set up house. Matt and his teeny-tiny tot friends waddled over to the big crowd of adults sitting right under the huge old oak.

Jesus was speaking. They hung on his every word. The disciples noticed the teeny-tiny tots inching closer to the attentive crowd. Not wanting to break the concentration of the listeners, they tried to shoo them away.

Just as Jesus was about to launch into some good stuff on eternal rewards, Scott smashed Brett with a green water balloon! Brett fell, knocking Matt and his teeny-tiny tot friends right into the feet of Jesus.

The disciples quickly picked the boys up and pushed them toward the edge of the crowd, admonishing them to play elsewhere.

But Jesus stood. Then he reached out his long arms and scooped up Scott (dirty from playing in the sand) and Brett (with a sliver of green balloon dangling from his left ear) and even teeny-tiny Matt (who needed a diaper change) and set all three boys in his lap.

Jesus wanted to know who launched the balloon. "I did," confessed Scott.

"It's okay, Scott," Brett said. "I know you didn't mean to hurt me."

Matt just sort of gurgled, content to be with the Master.

Then Jesus surprised the entire crowd by announcing that unless they became *just like these children* they would never enter the kingdom of God.

The crowd sat in wonder. And three boys who exhibited *confession, forgiveness, and a desire to be with the Savior* were never the same.

When Jesus tells us to be like children and follow him, what does he mean?

a. We should start sucking our thumbs again and crawling on the ground.
b. We should throw temper tantrums.
c. We should maintain some attractive child-like qualities.

Did you select C as your answer? Jesus doesn't want you to start eating baby food again, but he *does* want you to trust him as a child trusts his parents.

Circle some characteristics of babies that can also be attractive in a Christian's life.

total dependence

wearing diapers

trust

crying much of the time

being stinky

loving using a pacifier

being cared for

Are you child-like in your faith? Do you find it easy to trust God to take care of you?

❀❀❀

Write out a prayer to him, asking him to strengthen your faith into total child-like trust.

❀❀❀

Dear Diary ...

We're talking a lot about humility in my Bible study group. I'm confused. Does being humble mean that you're weak? If so, I don't want it! Or does it mean acting like you don't really care when someone gives you a compliment? Hmmm.

I gotta get this figured out!

❀❀❀

Humble rhymes with *mumble*. And it's easy to think of a mumbler as a weak person—someone who's afraid to speak up. But *humble* also rhymes with *stumble*. And if we don't cultivate humility in our lives, we'll become prideful. Guess what pride does? It causes us to stumble.

Humility isn't weakness. But what is it? Underline the statements you think a humble person would make.

- "Hey, I was here first!"
- "That's okay. You can use it."
- "I'm sorry. I didn't mean step on your foot."
- "Get outta my way!"
- "Thanks! I *am* a pretty good singer."
- "Really? I'm glad you enjoyed the song! Thanks!"
- "Ooops! That was my fault."
- "Who do you think you are?"

Being humble is being able to admit it when you're wrong. It's also allowing someone else to go in front of you, not demanding your own way, and helping others shine.

Let's see what the Bible has to say about humility, okay? Read 2 Chronicles 7:4. What special things does God have in store for those who humble themselves?

❀❀❀

According to Luke 14:11, what will happen to the one who exalts herself (brags, boasts, tries to make herself look good)?

❀❀❀

Check out Luke 18:14, and write down what will happen to the one who humbles herself.

My Memory Verse

When pride comes, then comes disgrace, but with humility comes wisdom (Proverbs 11:2).

Hi, Diary!

Mom says I've been rationalizing a lot lately. So I go, "I don't even know what that means!" And she said it was like making excuses for stuff I know is wrong.

So I go, "Like when have I ever done that?"

And she gives me all these examples! It's like she remembers everything. She goes, "Well, remember that TV show you're not supposed to watch? When we saw you watching it last night, you said, 'It's just the last few minutes. It's going off right now.' You knew you weren't supposed to watch any of it, but you rationalized—you made an excuse for something you knew was wrong."

Okay. So she had me. Maybe I am rationalizing. How can I stop? I don't wanna go through life being one of those people who is always making excuses and doing stuff they shouldn't!

❋❋❋

Why do you think God hates rationalizing so much?

a. It's a hard word to spell.
b. There's usually deception involved.
c. He just likes to hate stuff.

Whenever someone rationalizes something, she usually has to lie, also. How would you feel if your teacher deceived you into thinking your history test would only have 10 multiple-choice questions, but it was actually filled with 100 essay questions?

Read the next few scenarios and decide who's rationalizing or deceiving.

1. Jill's having a party and has invited several girls. She knows your parents won't allow you to hang out with Samantha, but she really wants both of you to come. When you ask her if Samantha is going to be there, she replies, "Are you kidding? I know how your parents feel!"
   Is Jill rationalizing and being deceptive?
   ___ Yes ___ No

2. Your mom has planned a special birthday dinner for your dad tonight. Before you left for school this morning, she specifically told you not to eat anything when you came home from school. Late that afternoon, while working on your homework in the kitchen, you remember that you still have half a sandwich left from lunch. You eat it, thinking, *It's not really like I'm snacking—this is still lunch.* When your mom comes home from work and asks if you've eaten anything that could spoil your dinner, you reply, "Don't you trust me? I remember what you said this morning about snacking!"
   Are you rationalizing and being deceptive?
   ___ Yes ___ No

3. Mrs. Parsons said that everyone's homework assignment is due this morning. You were so busy celebrating your dad's birthday last night, you totally forgot! You didn't even *do* it! On top of that, you

left your textbook at home. After class you ask if you can bring it tomorrow?

"Did you complete the assignment?" Mrs. Parsons asks.

"I left it at home," you reply.

Are you rationalizing and being deceptive?

___ Yes ___ No

Check out 2 Corinthians 4:2 to find out what the apostle Paul is *not* using and write it here.

❀❀❀

Look up Jeremiah 7:4. What are we not supposed to trust?

❀❀❀

Are *you* struggling with deception? ___ Yes ___ No

Has it become easy for you to rationalize—to make excuses for things you know are wrong—and try to make yourself believe it's okay? ___ Yes ___ No

You already know that our heavenly Father loves to forgive his children. Is there anything you need to talk with him about right now?

Hey, Di!

I've been thinking a lot about this whole rationalizing thing lately. I'm just beginning to realize how easy it has become for me to be deceptive.

Yuck!

I don't wanna be this way. I wanna truly become God's girl! I wanna be a young woman of honesty and integrity and character.

❀❀❀

Ananias and Sapphira had it all worked out. It was the first big offering of the year, and they wanted to give big (to impress everyone), but not *too* big (because they wanted to fly to Acapulco for their wedding anniversary).

They had inherited some land and had thought about putting some rental property on it, but it was full of stickers (and right next to the West Avenue Home for juvenile delinquents), so they didn't think people would rent housing on it anyway.

They finally sold it and decided to give part of the money to the church and keep the rest of it for their trip and a set of matching motorcycles. They then reported to the church that their financial gift was the total amount they received from the sale.

"Whoa! You're donating 100 percent to the church?" Peter exclaimed.

"That's right," Ananias and Sapphira confirmed (through clenched teeth).

"You dirty, rotten scoundrels!" Peter screamed. (Okay, that wasn't exactly his wording—but he *did* let them know there was a high price to pay for *compromising*.) They both died instantly. (You can read the actual story in Acts 5:1–11.)

When someone rationalizes, he usually deceives as well. But there's another ingredient often found in the mix: compromise. Ananias and Sapphira compromised. First, they rationalized it would be okay to say they were giving more than they actually were. Then they deceived the apostle Peter by lying about it. The whole event was an act of compromise. God wanted them to give *everything;* yet they refused to give all. They compromised and gave only a portion.

Now, it's important to know there are two kinds of compromise—good and bad. Read the following scenarios and decide if each one is a good compromise or a bad one.

1. Sarah and Karri both wanted to use the computer during their 50-minute study hall at school. Sarah said, "Karri, even though we both want it for the whole period, let's split the time. You take the first 25 minutes, and I'll take the last 25 minutes." Did Sarah make a good compromise or a bad one? _____

2. Kassidy's mom gave her some extra allowance to vacuum the house for the office party they were having on Thursday evening. "I expect you to do a thorough job," her mom said. "Vacuum under the beds, in the corners—everywhere." Kassidy *did* vacuum the whole house—but she didn't vacuum behind the sofa. *No one will even see way back there,* she thought. *It doesn't matter.* Was Kassidy's compromise a good one or a bad one? _____

3. Ashley's volleyball coach had a doctor's appointment at 4:30. Practice usually didn't end until 5 P.M. "As you know, I have to leave early today," Coach Tompkins reminded the girls. "But I still want you to run 10 laps around the gym and work on drills until 5 P.M. I'll see you tomorrow."

   After Ashley and her team had run eight laps, she noticed it was 4:50 P.M. "Hey, if we're gonna take down the net and collect the balls, we better quit now," Ashley said.

   "But we haven't run 10 laps," Brittany panted. "And we still have three more drills to practice."

   "Yeah, but if we run the full 10 laps *and* practice the remaining three drills *and* put up the equipment, we won't get outta here till 5:15! I say we quit now and put up the equipment," Ashley countered. Was Ashley's compromise a good one or a bad one? _____

Write about a time you made a good compromise.

Now write about a time you made a bad compromise.

Write out a prayer asking God to help you make good compromises—without rationalizing or deceiving.

My Memory Verse

Do not imitate what is evil, but what is good. Anyone who does what is good is from God. Anyone who does what is evil has not seen God (3 John 11).

Hey, Di ...

I think I'm beginning to learn when it's okay to compromise and when it's not. I really wanna be someone who makes good choices. I wanna be the kind of girl that others admire. I want to do the right thing!

❀❀❀

Having a heart that wants to do right is a wonderful thing. In fact, it's a real blessing! If you find yourself wanting to do wrong more than you want to do right, ask God to change your heart.

Question: So if I ask God to change my heart, does that mean I won't blow it anymore?

Answer: No, you'll still blow it. You're human, remember?

Question: Then why ask God to change my heart?

Answer: Because he wants your heart's *desire* to always be right.

King David is sort of a Bible hero. (He's the one who killed Goliath the Giant, remember?) The Bible says that David was a man after God's own heart. He made plenty of mistakes (and you can read about them in the Old Testament), but when he asked God to change his heart, his desire was to do right.

Half the process of becoming God's girl—growing into a young lady who makes good compromises and refuses to rationalize and deceive—is simply having the desire to become all that God wants you to be.

Without a desire to make *good* compromises, you'll eventually begin to rationalize, deceive, and make *bad* compromises.

Read Mark 15:15. What dangerous compromise did Pilate make with the people?

❀❀❀

In 2 Corinthians 6:14, we're instructed to avoid relationships that compromise our faith. Read the Scripture and fill in the blanks.

"Do not be yoked _____ with _____. For what do righteousness and _____ have in _____? Or what fellowship can _____ have with _____?"

Find some brightly colored paper and some old magazines. Cut letters out of the magazine to spell these two words: "No Compromise." Glue the words on the paper and cut it to the size of a bookmark. Put it in one of your textbooks, and let it serve as a reminder that you're going to refuse bad compromises.

Dear Diary ...

I'm finding lots of stuff in the Bible about what happened when people rationalized and made bad compromises. I guess it all boils down to good choices = good consequences. Bad choices = bad consequences.

❀❀❀

You've probably heard of them—the World's Largest Backpacking Group. Well . . . that's what *I* like to call them. Maybe you're familiar with their *real* title: the Children of Israel. They were the huge group (more than 500,000) that followed Moses through the desert for 40 years. Eventually Moses died, and Joshua became their leader. We'll pick up the story from here, okay?

God had just given Joshua and his army (the World's Largest Backpacking Group) victory over the large city of Jericho. His instructions were clear: "No one take anything!"

Achan saw a small silver coin, a bathrobe, and a gold bar. Since no one was looking (and he really needed a new bathrobe), he stole the items and hid them in his tent.

Joshua later found the missing items and informed him of the high cost of compromise. Achan paid with his life.

All through the Bible, God speaks loud and clear on following his laws. When we fail to do it God's way, we're making bad choices; we're compromising. And bad choices equal bad consequences.

How much does it cost to live a life of compromise? The price is high. Death.

Though the wages (price tag) of sin is death, according to Romans 6:23, what does God want to give us . . . absolutely free?

❀❀❀

Achan assumed because no one saw him steal the items, no one would know. He forgot that God sees and knows everything!

Read Hebrews 4:13 and fill in these blanks.

"Nothing in all _____ is
hidden from _____ sight.
_____ is
_____ and
laid _____ before the eyes
of _____ to whom we must
give _____."

Dear Jesus,
Be Lord of my life. Use your Holy
Spirit to show me anything that's not pleas
ing to you.
Amen.

Dear Diary ...

I'm so excited that I'm learning more about God and growing closer to him. I don't ever wanna get tired of being a Christian. I wanna grow strong and deep—like some of the older people in my church who stand up and testify about all the cool things God has done for them over the years. Wow!

It's so easy to tell how strong they are in their faith just by the way they talk about God. I wanna be like that! I wanna grow strong spiritually.

❁❁❁

Wanting something and doing something about it are two different thing, aren't they? While it's great to *want* to run faster, you probably won't become a better athlete unless you actually practice running! Or if you want to become a better pianist, you gotta put time in on the keyboard, don't you?

It works the same way, spiritually. If you *want* to become a stronger Christian, you need to do something about it. But what can you do?

Well, thirteen-year-old Katie is into Bible-quizzing. "It forces me not only to *study* the Bible but *memorize* it as well." She stated that the discipline she was gaining from personal Bible study was also affecting the rest of her life in a positive way.

Courtney's spiritual life is enhanced another way. Her involvement in various church programs is strengthening the development of her gifts. She loves puppets and is excited to share how God is using this particular ministry to help her reach children.

And Megan is being discipled by an adult woman once a week. She says the regular meetings of discussing her week, sharing memorized Scripture and prayer requests is helping hold her accountable to what God wants to do in her life.

Have you ever seen reruns of the TV show *Growing Pains*? Kirk Cameron became a Christian after he started acting on that show. Guess what he did to help keep his mind on God's Word? He kept a notebook and Bible in his dressing room and began copying various chapters from the Bible—page after page after page.

What are some things *you* can do to grow spiritually?

1.
2.
3.

Look at 2 Thessalonians 1:3. What two things are mentioned in this verse as growing or increasing?

Check out 2 Peter 3:18. In which two areas does the apostle Peter tell us to grow?

❀❀❀

There are lots of things you can do to become spiritually stronger, but the main ingredient is simply spending time with God (reading the Bible, reading a devotional book—like this one—and talking with God—prayer).

Dear Diary ...

Rachel gets everything! I really wanted to be cheerleader this year. There was only one open spot, and guess who got it? Rachel! Last year, I wanted to be class treasurer but she was elected instead of me.

I am so totally sick of her!

Did you know ...

- If you can't see the license plate of the car in front of you at a stoplight, you're too close.
- A lot of sheep look like goats, and some breeds of goats look like sheep. Here's how you can tell them apart: Sheep's tails hang down, and goat's tails stand up.
- A grown rat can pass through a hole the size of a quarter.
- Your ring size is the same as your hat size.
- A red sky at sunset means that wind is on the way.
- After cracking your knuckles, you usually have to wait about 30 minutes before you can crack them again.
- A jealous person can't love others the way God wants her to.

Though all of the above are true, I hope the one you'll remember is the last one. Maybe you didn't make cheerleader this year, win the election, or get what Rachel did. Jealousy will *never* settle the score. It will only make you miserable.

Did you know that jealousy displeases the Lord? In fact, the apostle Paul calls jealousy an "act of the sinful nature." Let's check it out. Turn to Galatians 5:19–21 and jot down all the acts of sinful nature listed.

Now look at 2 Corinthians 12:20. Make a list of all the things that accompany jealousy in this verse.

Heavenly Father,
I confess I'm really jealous sometimes when other people get what I want. But I realize now that this isn't pleasing to you. I truly want to become all you want me to be. Will you forgive me for being jealous? Teach me how to rejoice when others do well.
I love you, Jesus.

Dear Diary ...

Marissa says if she doesn't get tickets to the Backstreet Boys concert, she'll die.

I said, "Marissa, those tickets are sky-high! How could you ever afford that?"

"I don't care," she said. "I'll do anything to get to that concert. It's the most important thing in my life!"

Oh, gimme a break. I wanted to say, "Get a life, Marissa!" But I just wished her luck instead.

❀❀❀

Can you imagine getting over 400,000 phone calls every month? When the singing group "New Kids on the Block" were at their peak, that's how many calls registered each month on their 900 line! Mail call was also a major experience, with over 30,000 fan letters being hauled in each week.

I imagine the numbers are pretty similar for the Backstreet Boys, NSync, 98°, and several other pop groups. Think for a second about the thousands of girls who were calling the NKOTB's 900 number at $2 per call and spending postage money on more than 30,000 letters every week! That's a lot of money, isn't it?

It feels good to be enthused and dedicated to something. It's exciting—especially when those around you are just as electrified by the cause as you are. The catch? When we throw ourselves so heavily into things of the world, it can go wrong very easily.

Everyone wants to belong to something, to be dedicated to something, to have someone to get all excited about. But when we put that much energy into temporary things we're setting ourselves up for major disappointment. When we put that much drive and commitment into eternal things, we're working for a lasting reward.

For a clue about the commitment that lasts, read Psalm 1:2. What kind of fan is described?

    a. One who's totally in love with God.
    b. One who loves to read the Bible.
    c. One who enjoys thinking about God's ways.

If you selected all three of the above, you're exactly right! Read the verse again, okay? What is this person meditating on?

How often does he meditate on it (or think about it)?

Wow! That's really being a fan of God, isn't it?! To always think about how we can follow him more closely means that God is on our mind

    a. at school.
    b. at soccer practice.
    c. during the day.
    d. as we're eating lunch.
    e. before we go to bed.

Again, if you selected all of the answers above, you're exactly right. To be saturated with God means we allow him to influence our thoughts all the time.

Psalm 1:3 says that a person who is a fan of God will be like what?

❀❀❀

What does that mean? A fan of God will

    a. be rich.
    b. be popular.
    c. have enough fruit to eat.
    d. have what she needs to live a life that pleases God.

Of course, D is the right answer. When we focus on God and follow him with all our heart, he gives us what we need to make decisions that please him.

Memorize Deuteronomy 6:5. Write it here.

My Memory Verse

Hey, Di!

I know God wants to help me with my problems, but sometimes it's just easier to get mad instead of praying about it. Like today. My little bro, Riley, borrowed my bike without asking me. Hey! It's not my fault his bike has a flat!

He borrowed my bike and took off with Jared. Well, they started racing on some dirt hills, and Riley ended up stripping my gears!

I'm so angry at him!

Okay, I know I should've prayed about it and let God help me through it, but instead I just screamed at Riley and Mom and Dad.

Oooh!

He's totally all over my nerves!

❋❋❋

Part of becoming God's girl is allowing him to help you become better and stronger through the tough times you face. Yes, it feels natural to scream and get even with the one who is hurting us, but the more you make yourself take the problem to God *first*, the more natural going to him will seem.

Write about a time you faced a hard time.

What did you do about it?

Let's see what the Bible has to say about hard times. Look up James 1:2–3 to answer this question. When we face trials, we are to be

a. joyful.
b. angry.
c. quiet.

According to the above Scripture, what do we have a chance to develop when our faith is tested?

❀❀❀

What's the biggest problem you're facing right now?

Write a letter to God asking for his direction.

Dear Diary ...

I feel like my life is totally falling apart! I bombed the history test. Meredith is making fun of me for being a Christian. Our dog is sick and at the vet's.

I've had it!

❀❀❀

Guess what? God understands your hurts! When you cry, he feels your tears. When your heart is breaking, his heart breaks also. He knows what it feels like to be left out and mistreated and misunderstood. God knows!

Look up 2 Corinthians 4:8–9 and complete this Scripture.

"We are hard _____ on _____ side, but not _____; perplexed, but not in _____; _____; but not _____; struck down, but not _____."

Check out 1 Peter 5:10. What has God called you to?

❀❀❀

What four things does he promise to do for you after you have suffered a little while?

❀❀❀

Now read 1 Peter 5:9. Who else is going through some of the same problems you're experiencing?

❀❀❀

My Memory Verse

Peace I leave with you; my peace I give you. I do not give to you as the world gives. Do not let your hearts be troubled and do not be afraid (John 14:27).

Dear Diary ...

Today at school we had an assembly. The guests were singers from another country. They were incredible! They wore colorful costumes and did these really cool dances. Everyone loved them.

I wish I could do what they're doing. Sometimes I wonder if I'll ever really make a difference in anyone's life.

❀❀❀

Y ou *can* be a powerful influence on someone's life . . . if you let God do the influencing *through* you. Ever heard the saying, "You're the only Bible some people ever see"? Christ wants to show his face through your life. That means being willing to eat with someone who's *not* the most popular kid in school—someone who's wearing Payless shoes instead of Reebok or Nike or some other expensive name brand; or the skinny kid with zits on his face.

That's exactly what happened with baseball's great Orel Hershiser. The former professional pitcher for the L.A. Dodgers says, "I was the skinny kid who always got picked on. I never had a very good self-image during my teen years.

"Since I was a good athlete, I did have respect from fellow athletes once we got onto the ball field. But that respect didn't carry over into the classroom or into the halls or even in the way I carried myself. It only showed up while I was on the field.

"I had slouchy shoulders, a small build—and to top it off—I wore glasses. And these were *not* cool-looking glasses!

"But I began to notice the consistency in a friend's life. He had something different. He just lived a consistent, Christ-like lifestyle. And the more I watched his life, the more I wanted what he had.

"A few years ago, a magazine did an article on us, called 'Influencing the Influencer.' He's living in Indiana, still walking with the Lord, and working in an ice cream factory."

Obviously, it's not looks, popularity, or accomplishments that God really cares about. It seems obedience is the key trait. When you walk in obedience to God, he's able to use you to influence others.

Read 1 Corinthians 9:22–23. The apostle Paul is talking about trying to find common ground with the people he meets. What are some things you may have in common with others your age whom you don't know well? (I'll get you started, you fill in the holes, okay?)

1. We all have homework.
2.
3.
4. We all have favorite TV shows.
5.
6. We all want friends.

List three things you do well. (I'll give you some ideas: Do you have good handwriting? Are you a good singer? Are you a good soccer player? Is it easy for you to meet new people?)

1.
2.
3.

How can you use the above things you do well to be a good influence on others?

❀❀❀

'Father God,
Help me not to be so concerned with my appearance and popularity. Help me to really focus on obeying you so that you can use me to make a positive difference in the lives of others.
Amen.

Diary ...

Me again.

Last summer at camp I made some exciting commitments to God. And I really felt that we were close, you know? I mean ... I was really a strong Christian.

But now?

I don't know. It's so hard at school. Sometimes I wish I could just live at camp. I don't think I'm as strong a Christian here as I am at camp.

❁❁❁

How *do* you keep the victory after leaving camp? No one lives on a continual spiritual emotional high. But we *can* be consistent in our walk with Christ. In times like these, it's great that we have the Bible to turn to! It's packed full of people who struggled with some of the same things we face.

Take Daniel, for instance. (You can find the story in the Old Testament in the book of Daniel.) As you read about his life, you may notice a pattern: Daniel was consistent because he *planned* to be consistent!

Can you imagine watching a football game being played by two teams with no strategy? It would be total chaos, wouldn't it? Every athlete needs a game plan. Guess what? It works the same way spiritually.

Daniel had a great strategy. Let's take a peek at his game plan, okay?

• *He surrounded himself with wholesome friends.* There were only three other devoted guys in his school. You've probably heard of them—Shadrach, Meshach, and Abednego. Of all the guys Daniel could have become friends with, he chose to hang with these godly young men. Wise choice!

It's hard to keep your spiritual fire burning if you're surrounding yourself with non-Christian friends. Yes, God wants us to reach out to those who are lost, but there's a difference in reaching out and forming really tight relationships.

Write down the names of your five closest friends.

How many of the above are Christians?

If you don't know any Christians at your school, pray that God will help you find them. If you have several non-Christian friends, start inviting them to church, and pray that they come to know Christ. In fact, why not pray for them right now? Go ahead. Write out your prayer in the space provided.

❀❀❀

Dear Diary ...

Guess who? Ha! Like anyone else would be writing in here, huh!

I know Elizabeth doesn't go to church anywhere. She's always talking about what she does over the weekend ... and it never includes church. So, I invited her to come with me next Sunday. She didn't say yes, but she did act interested.

I'm gonna pray she'll come. It would be sooooo cool if she'd become a Christian!

❀❀❀

Daniel maintained his spiritual victory by hanging out with Christian friends, but there was also another important part of his strategy. Let's take a peek at his life again, okay?

• *Daniel worked at maintaining a pure heart.* The Holy Spirit gives us the power to live holy lives, but it's not magic. Purity was important to Daniel. He was dedicated to a holy lifestyle. And guess what? His prayers were effective because he prayed with a pure heart! A pure heart produces a godly disciple.

Where are all the godly men and women today? Where are the prayer warriors? God is calling *you* to maintain your spiritual victory. Are you willing to do what's necessary to keep the fire burning?

What does the apostle Paul encourage you not to let happen in 1 Timothy 4:12?

There are five areas listed in the above verse in which we are to be an example. What are they?

❀❀❀

Check out 2 Timothy 2:22. What kind of heart does God want us to have when we call on him?

❀❀❀

What four things should we pursue (or go after) in the above verse?

❀❀❀

Lord,

I want to keep my spiritual victory. Help me to choose my friends wisely. And give me the desire to invite non Christians to church and see them come to know you. Through the power of your Holy Spirit, help me to maintain a pure heart. Make me a prayer warrior.

I love you, Jesus.

Dear Diary ...

Elizabeth finally went to church with me, and I really prayed hard that she would become a Christian. But today at school she said something that really surprised me. She goes, "I'm not ready to become a Christian yet. I know there are some things in my life that aren't right, and I'm not ready to give them up yet. Maybe someday, but not right now."

Wow. That's so sad! What if she dies before she gets around to giving her life to Jesus?

Well, I'm not giving up! I'm just gonna keep on praying for her, and I'm gonna keep loving her, and keep inviting her to church.

❀❀❀

It costs a lot to be a Christian. Yes, it's a free gift from God. But *following* him costs a lot. It costs our lives. God doesn't want just a little part of us, he wants *all* of us. That's what Christianity is all about—living in total surrender to his lordship.

You've probably heard of contemporary Christian recording artist Carman. Listen to what following God cost him.

"I was twenty years old when I became a Christian. I'd been playing drums, bass, guitar—whatever I could get my hands on, to get work. I found my audiences in the night-club world of Vegas and Jersey.

"But the day I got saved, I cut all my previous musical ties with the world. I just told everybody I was going to sing for the Lord. I soon realized I couldn't make a living off of Christian music. So I went to work digging holes for hot tubs. That's all I knew. I didn't know what I should do. All I knew was what I *shouldn't* do! Sometimes that's all you have to go on. You know that what you were doing wasn't good. So you just need to decide not to do those old things anymore and trust the Lord to provide an open door.

"Next, I earned a living by waxing and sanding fiberglass molds for septic tanks. It was terrible. I had all this fiberglass dust in my skin! I then got a job upholstering Denny's restaurants. I did that for almost five years. Then in 1981, the Lord began to open doors that led to full-time Christian music."

Mark the things someone might do before she becomes a Christian but would want to stop doing after inviting Jesus to control her life.

___Having a selfish attitude
___Using bad language
___Inviting people to church
___Carrying a Bible to school
___Watching movies and TV shows with bad language
___Disobeying parents

Carman gave up worldly music when he became a Christian. Are there things in your life that you think God wants you to give up to grow closer to him? What are they?

Dear Jesus,
I know the cost of following you is high.
You want all of me—not just part of me.
And, Jesus, I want you to have all of me!
Will you forgive me for hanging onto these
things? I give them to you right now.
With all my heart, I want to follow you,
Jesus.

Dear Diary ...

I'm gonna do it. It's tough, but I'm gonna do it. I'm not gonna listen to my favorite pop group anymore. I like their music, but they sing about having sex, and I know God doesn't want me to fill my mind with that.

❀❀❀

It was probably hard for Carman to give up playing for nightclubs. He was making good money. But when he decided to follow God, he walked away from all that.

It would've been easy for him to rationalize (flip back to page 143 for a reminder about what it means to rationalize). He could've said, "God's the One who gave me this musical talent. I *have* to earn a living, so why not continue playing the clubs? I'll still remain close to him."

But Carman had counted the cost. It meant severing (cutting off) the ties that would have eventually messed him up spiritually. The cost of discipleship (following Christ) involves severing our ties with those things of the world that trip us and slow us down from becoming all that God wants us to become.

Turn in your Bible to Titus 2:11–12. What from God brings salvation?

What are we to say no to?

❀❀❀

What three things describe the kind of lives we are supposed to live as Christians?

❀❀❀

According to Romans 12:2, what are we not supposed to do?

❀❀❀

God wants to transform your mind. Write down what you think that means.

What will you need to ask God to change in your life in order for you to be transformed?

Is there anything you need to give up (TV shows, rock music, attitudes, etc.)?

Diary ...

I know gossip is totally bad. I mean, we've talked about it in Sunday school. But this morning when Angela told me she heard that Kenny got suspended from school for smoking, I passed it on to Mallory. Only ... I added a little bit.

I said, "Kenny got suspended for smoking. Who knows what he was smoking!"

Anyway, by the end of the day everyone was talking about Kenny smoking marijuana and taking drugs.

I never said that. I just sort of made Mallory assume it could have been marijuana. And I knew she'd tell Chelsey.

Anyway, I feel terrible now. Why'd I have to be such a jerk and spread something that wasn't even true?

Did you know ...

- that a burglary happens every 10 seconds in the United States?

- that the risk of you dying this year in your bathtub or shower is one in a million?
- that your chances of getting rabies (and dying from them) in the United are less than one in 100 million?
- that you're more likely to die from an airplane falling on top of you than dying of rabies.
- that when you gossip, you risk ruining someone's reputation?

God is never pleased with gossip. In fact, it breaks his heart. Has anyone ever gossiped (spread unkind or untrue things) about you?

___ Yes ___ No

Circle the words that describe how you felt.

loved   lonely

angry

confused

happy   frightened

surprised

popular   rejected

grateful

ashamed

hurt   wonderful

excited

helpless

Let's see what the Bible has to say about gossip. According to Proverbs 13, what's the difference between a gossip and a trustworthy person?

What does a gossip do to close friends? (The answer is found in Proverbs 16:28.)

What things accompany gossip in 2 Corinthians 12:20?

❀❀❀

If you've been a gossip, right now would be a great time to ask God to forgive you. Will you write out your prayer here?

❀❀❀

My Memory Verse

Without wood a fire goes out; without gossip a quarrel dies down (Proverbs 26:20).

Dear Diary ...

I don't get it! I just wanna buy some power beads. So what's the big deal?

Marianne has like eight or nine power bracelets she wears every day. They're so cool. When I told Mom I wanted to use some of my baby-sitting money to buy some, she said I couldn't because they were New Age or something.

They're just beads. What's she talking about?

❀❀❀

You've probably seen lots of people wear a necklace with a cross on it. And you've seen people wearing WWJD bracelets ("What Would Jesus Do?"). And if they don't care about following Christ— if they don't love God—why are they wearing the necklace or the bracelet? It gives a false message.

Power beads have their beginnings in the Buddhist religion. Yes, Christians could wear them without believing in them . . . but why would they want to? It would send out the wrong message. People would see the beads and may assume that you believe in Buddha instead of Jesus Christ.

Oftentimes your non-Christian friends will do things or wear things that displease God. You'll be tempted to copy their behavior or their dress because you want to be accepted by them. It feels good to be "in," doesn't it?

But there are times when you'll simply need to be *different*. God doesn't want you to be *like* the world. He wants you to be a light shining in the darkness. In other words, he wants to influence others through your life that stands apart.

According to 1 Thessalonians 4:7, what did God *not* call us to be?

What kind of life does he call us to live?

Read Philippians 2:25. How can you be a shining star?

Dear Jesus,

Help me not to do something just because everyone else is. Teach me how to feel good about standing alone if I need to. I want to fit in, and I want to have friends. But I don't want to do anything that will compromise my relationship with you.

Amen.

We want to hear from you. Please send your comments about this book to us in care of the address below. Thank you.

Zonder**kidz** ™

Grand Rapids, MI 49530
http://www.zonderkidz.com

MEXICO

Baja California

Baja California Norte

◆

Baja California Sur

Automobile Club of Southern California

4

Cover:
A view of Land's End &
Mission Santa Rosalía de Mulegé
Page 2:
Sunset over Baja's Central Desert
Page 3:
Lovely handmade crafts are available throughout Baja

Although information presented in this publication has been carefully researched and was as accurate as possible at press time, the Automobile Club of Southern California is not responsible for any changes or errors which may occur. Readers should keep in mind that travel conditions in Baja California change rapidly. The Automobile Club is not responsible for the performance of any agency or service mentioned in this publication. It is wise to verify information immediately prior to your visit.

Only attractions or establishments that are approved by an Automobile Club of Southern California field representative may advertise. The purchase of advertising, however, has no effect on inspections and evaluations. Advertisements provide the reader with additional information which may be useful in selecting what to see and where to stay.

Additional advertisements (excluding attractions and establishments) for travel-related services may also be included in ACSC publications. Acceptance of these advertisements does not imply endorsement by ACSC.

♻ Printed on recycled paper

ISBN: 1-56413-322-2
Printed in the United States of America
Copyright © 1996 by Automobile Club of Southern California
Travel Publications Department
2601 South Figueroa Street, Los Angeles, California 90007

Table of Contents

8

BAJA CALIFORNIA

To many people, its very name carries an exotic connotation of ruggedness and adventure. Despite the long-standing popularity of its border towns and the fly-in fishing resorts near its southern tip, this 800-mile-long arid peninsula remained virtually unknown until recently. Geographically separated from the Mexican mainland and an insurmountable barrier to all but the hardiest overland travelers, the interior of Baja California resisted the large-scale intrusions of man for centuries.

But the peninsula's days of isolation are over. The completion of the paved Transpeninsular Highway (Mexico Highway 1) in late 1973 marked the beginning of a new era for Baja California. Once remote regions are now being drawn into the mainstream of Mexico's rapid economic development, and the population is increasing steadily. A ferry network and a microwave telephone system, along with the paved highway

A young couple performs the traditional ranchera-style dance.

extending the entire length of the peninsula, have established new and effective lines of communication. Increasing numbers of tourists have discovered the distinctive charms of Baja California: rugged desert and mountain landscapes, the deep blue waters of the Pacific and the Gulf of California, unique vegetation, Spanish missions, winter sunshine, lush palm oases, unspoiled beaches, remarkably good sportfishing and friendly people.

Detailed descriptions of Baja California's major highways are covered in several chapters in this book. The first and longest of these concentrates on **Mexico Highway 1**, a paved route extending from the U.S. border at Tijuana to Cabo San Lucas at the tip of the peninsula. Another chapter covers **Mexico Highway 5**, which runs along the Gulf of California coast from Mexicali to Puertecitos. Additional chapters

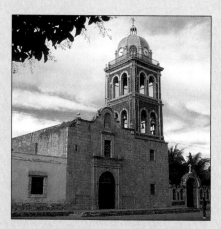

Mission Nuestra Señora De Loreto

cover **Mexico Highway 2**, **Mexico Highway 3** and **Mexico Highway 19**.

These route descriptions are divided into convenient sections. Each begins with a paragraph outlining the terrain, the route and general driving conditions, followed by a detailed mileage log that lists important landmarks and junctions, roadside facilities and points of interest. Driving times were computed under average driving conditions and are rounded off to the nearest quarter hour. Mileages were compiled with highly accurate survey odometers, but instruments can vary and the mileages may not agree exactly with those contained in the logs. *Towns that contain stores and facilities useful to the traveler are shown in bold print.* Also featured are maps and special sections on Baja California's major cities and towns.

With the completion of Mexico Highway 1, regular airline service, and the accompanying proliferation of new hotels, trailer parks and other

Colorful arts and crafts can be purchased from merchants and vendors in Cabo San Lucas.

tourist facilities, Baja California has become an accessible vacation destination for the average traveling family. At the same time, most of the peninsula has retained its essentially wild character, making it a continuing challenge for the avid off-road adventurer.

For quick reference, key places and roads connecting them are shown on the maps on pages 12 and 13. Heavy lines indicate Mexico Highways 1, 2, 3, 5 and 19; lighter lines denote side routes. A detailed index of all place names begins on page 268.

Sunset over tranquil Bahía de la Paz.

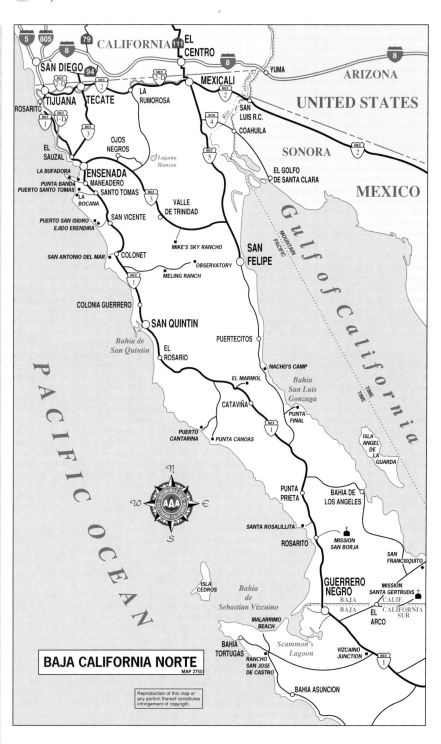

BAJA CALIFORNIA NORTE
MAP 2750

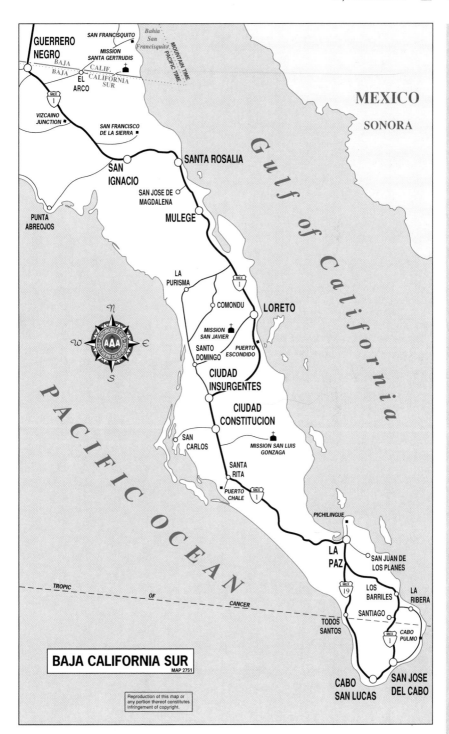

MEXICO

SONORA

Gulf of California

GUERRERO
NEGRO

SAN FRANCISQUITO

*Bahia
San
Francisquito*

MISSION
SANTA GERTRUDIS

*BAJA
BAJA*

CALIF.
CALIFORNIA
SUR

MOUNTAIN TIME
PACIFIC TIME

EL
ARCO

MEX
1

VIZCAINO
JUNCTION

SAN FRANCISCO
DE LA SIERRA

SANTA ROSALIA

SAN
IGNACIO

SAN JOSE DE
MAGDALENA

PUNTA
ABREOJOS

MULEGE

LA
PURISMA

MEX
1

COMONDU

LORETO

MISSION
SAN JAVIER

SANTO
DOMINGO

PUERTO
ESCONDIDO

CIUDAD
INSURGENTES

CIUDAD
CONSTITUCION

SAN
CARLOS

MISSION SAN LUIS
GONZAGA

SANTA
RITA

PACIFIC OCEAN

PUERTO
CHALE

MEX
1

PICHILINGUE

LA
PAZ

SAN JUAN DE
LOS PLANES

TROPIC   OF   CANCER

MEX
19

LOS
BARRILES

LA
RIBERA

SANTIAGO

TODOS
SANTOS

MEX
1

CABO
PULMO

BAJA CALIFORNIA SUR
MAP 2751

CABO
SAN LUCAS

SAN JOSE
DEL CABO

▼ *Showing The Way*

The key to an enjoyable, rewarding Baja California vacation is careful preparation. The *Baja California* book is a comprehensive guidebook designed to acquaint you with the peninsula's many attractions, as well as its major highways and interesting side routes. It includes important information on travel conditions and regulations for tourists, where to stay and eat, and a variety of other pertinent subjects. You will find it to be both a valuable trip-planning aid and a helpful day-to-day companion during your visit to Baja California. In addition, the Automobile Club of Southern California publishes a companion publication—the large, colorful *Baja California* map. Both should be used by those planning to visit the peninsula.

Geography

Baja California is a very elongated, irregularly shaped peninsula that extends about 800 miles southeastward from the Mexico-United States border. (Traveling Mexico Highway 1, which traverses the rugged peninsula, is a trip of about 1000 miles.) Varying in width from 30 to 145 miles, it is separated from the Mexican mainland to the east by the Colorado River and the Gulf of California (also known as the Sea of Cortez), while on the west it is bounded by the Pacific Ocean. Both coastlines are indented by numerous bays and coves, and many barren islands lie offshore. The backbone of the peninsula comprises a series of mountain ranges—notably the Sierra de Juárez, just below the U.S. border; the Sierra San Pedro Mártir, farther south; the Sierra de la Giganta, along the southern gulf coast; and the Sierra de la Laguna, in the extreme south. The highest point is 10,154-foot Picacho del Diablo, located in the rugged Sierra San Pedro Mártir between the Meling Ranch and San Felipe.

The topography of northern Baja California is similar to that of nearby Southern California. Most of Baja is classified as desert, but sharp regional differences exist. Chaparral-covered hills rise abruptly from the seashore and are dissected by numerous canyons and valleys. The northern mountains resemble California's Sierra Nevada in that they have gradual progressions of foothills on the west and steep eastern escarpments. The Mexicali Valley is part of a great rift that is a continuation of the Imperial Valley. South of the Colorado River Delta, this depression is submerged beneath the Gulf of California.

East of the mountains is an arid desert with scant plant life; some areas are almost devoid of vegetation. In contrast is the Mexicali Valley, where irrigated farmlands flourish on the rich alluvial soil deposited over the centuries by the Colorado River. Central Baja California, which extends from El Rosario to La Paz, is a true desert. The topography of the central desert is characterized by barren mountains separated by rocky valleys and sandy plains. Abrupt slopes rise from the shore of the Gulf of California, while the Pacific side of the peninsula is less

---

"The Rock Garden," with it's unusual geologic formations, is near Cataviña.

rugged. Two major lowlands, both near the Pacific coast, contrast with the sharply contoured landscape of much of the central desert. The Vizcaíno Desert near Guerrero Negro is a vast, sandy plain with little natural vegetation except saltbrush and scattered yucca válida. The Santo Domingo Valley (Magdalena Plain), farther south, is an important agricultural region, of which Ciudad Constitución is the center. Beginning near San Ignacio and spreading southward for more than 100 miles are extensive lava flows. Las Tres Vírgenes, three impressive volcanoes, sit side by side along Highway 1 south of San Ignacio, and the Sierra de la Giganta, a jagged mountain range also of volcanic origin extending from Santa Rosalía almost to La Paz.

The southern portion of the peninsula, from La Paz to Cabo San Lucas, lies within the tropics. It is part desert and part semiarid. The region south of La Paz is dominated by the Sierra de la Laguna mountains, which slopes downward from its 7000-foot crown toward both coasts.

Climate

The climate of northern Baja California is similar to Southern California. The semiarid coastal zone, from Tijuana to San Quintín, is mild, with summer highs in the 70s and 80s (Fahrenheit); temperatures rise a short distance inland. Winter temperatures are in the 60s during the day and the 40s at night. Fog is common during late spring and early summer. Most rainfall occurs during the winter and the total rainfall varies greatly from year to year. The average winter has more sunny days than cloudy days.

Depending on their elevation and the direction they face, the inland hills and mountains receive sporadically heavy rains and occasional snow. In the rain shadow east of the mountains, including the Mexicali Valley and the Gulf of California coast, is an arid landscape, often called the Sonoran Desert. It is characterized by mild, sunny winters and intensely hot summers, whose high temperatures may reach 110 to 120 degrees. Average rainfall is scant, about 3 inches.

The Central Desert of Baja California extends from about El Rosario in the north to Ciudad Constitución in the south; it merges with the Sonoran Desert along the gulf. Rainfall is very irregular, as violent thunderstorms may bring several inches, or a year may pass with hardly a drop of moisture. Winter temperatures are mild and pleasant; the air is clear and the sunshine is brilliant. The Pacific coast section remains mild in summer as far south as the Vizcaíno Peninsula, but the rest of the Central Desert has oppressive summer heat. The hot, dry air of interior places like San Ignacio is easier to bear than the often humid air of coastal locations such as Loreto.

The southern portion of the peninsula, from Bahía Magdalena to Cabo San Lucas, lies within the tropics. It is part tropical desert and part tropical semiarid, but it receives occasionally heavy rainfall as a result of tropical storms between August and early November. Every several years, southern Baja California is ravaged by a hurricane (on rare occasions hurricanes move to the northern coast of the gulf). Occurring more frequently are severe squalls, called *chubascos*. Rainfall in La Paz aver-

BAJA CALIFORNIA CLIMATE CHART

	January		February		March		April		May		June		July		August		September		October		November		December		Total Annual Rainfall
	Temp.*	Rainfall	Temp.	Rainfall	Temp.	Rainfall	Temp.	Rainfall	Temp.	Rainfall	Temp.	Rainfall	Temp.	Rainfall	Temp.	Rainfall	Temp.	Rainfall	Temp.	Rainfall	Temp.	Rainfall	Temp.	Rainfall	
Cabo San Lucas ...	64	–	66	–	68	–	70	–	73	–	79	–	81	0.4	82	1.6	81	2.5	79	1.2	72	1.2	68	0.8	7.7
Ciudad Constitución.	59	0.5	61	0.1	63	–	66	–	70	–	73	–	80	0.5	82	1.4	80	1.2	75	0.3	70	0.2	63	0.6	4.8
Colonia Guerrero ..	54	1.5	55	1.6	57	2.0	58	0.5	59	0.2	63	–	66	–	68	0.4	68	0.4	63	0.8	57	1.2	55	1.4	10.0
El Rosario	57	1.0	61	1.0	63	0.8	63	0.2	64	–	70	–	75	–	75	1.0	73	0.2	70	0.8	64	0.8	61	1.1	6.1
Ensenada	54	2.3	55	2.3	59	1.9	59	0.6	63	0.2	64	–	68	–	70	–	68	–	63	0.2	61	0.6	57	2.1	10.2
La Paz...........	63	0.4	63	–	64	–	70	–	73	–	81	–	82	0.2	84	1.2	82	2.4	77	0.8	70	0.8	63	0.4	6.2
Loreto	61	0.4	63	–	66	–	68	–	73	–	81	–	86	0.4	88	1.6	84	2.4	81	0.4	70	–	63	0.4	5.6
Mexicali	54	0.4	59	0.4	63	0.4	68	0.2	75	–	86	–	91	–	90	0.3	81	0.3	73	0.5	61	0.2	54	0.4	3.1
San Felipe.......	55	0.4	57	–	61	–	66	–	73	0.4	79	–	81	–	82	0.4	79	0.6	70	0.6	63	–	57	0.4	2.8
San Ignacio	57	0.4	61	0.4	63	0.4	64	–	72	–	75	0.4	81	0.4	82	0.4	79	0.8	73	0.4	64	0.4	57	0.4	4.4
San Vicente......	54	2.4	55	2.4	55	1.9	57	0.2	63	–	68	–	72	–	73	–	70	0.1	64	0.1	59	0.7	54	2.1	9.9
Tecate..........	50	2.4	52	2	53	2	55	0.4	59	0.3	66	–	72	–	72	–	70	–	64	0.2	57	1	52	1.9	10.2
Tijuana..........	55	2	57	2.4	59	2	61	0.4	66	–	68	–	73	–	73	–	72	–	66	0.4	63	1.2	57	1.8	10.2

*Temperatures are expressed in degrees Fahrenheit - Rainfall in inches. Figures represent official monthly averages.

ages 6 inches per year, San Antonio 16 inches. The most pleasant weather occurs from November to May, with highs in the 80s and lows in the 50s. Rain is rare during these months. Summers are quite hot, with highs from 100 to 110 degrees, except on the Pacific coast, which is a little cooler.

Vegetation

The unusual vegetation types of Baja California are directly related to its climates. The semiarid northwest corner, including the Pacific Coast, has wild grasses, chaparral brush and scattered oaks, as in neighboring Southern California. In the towns, palms and other subtropical trees have been planted. Wildflowers are visible along the rural roads in the springtime. Unlike most of the peninsula, the northern mountains have forests of pine and fir blanketing the upper slopes. In sharp contrast is the very arid Sonoran Desert east of the mountains. The natural vegetation generally consists of various low shrubs, along with smatterings of cardón cacti, ocotillo and mesquite; some areas are almost devoid of vegetation. A different landscape is found in the Mexicali Valley, where irrigated farmlands of cotton and grains flourish on the rich alluvial soil deposited by the Colorado River.

The Central Desert of Baja California has unique vegetation well adapted for survival in its harsh environment. Because of its geographical isolation, the Central Desert is home to many plant varieties that grow naturally nowhere else on earth. They include the giant cardón cactus, which resembles the saguaro of Arizona and Sonora; the yucca válida, a smaller cousin of California's Joshua tree; and

Cardón cactus

Blue palm tree

Cholla cactus

Elephant tree

the strange cirio, a tall, columnar botanical oddity which grows only in Baja California and Sonora. Other species, such as agave, cholla and barrel cacti, fan palm, ocotillo, palo verde, pitahaya (organ pipe) cactus and elephant tree, with its short, fat trunk, also have relatives in the southwestern United States. Date palms are found in scattered cases, but they are not native to the peninsula; most were planted by Jesuit missionaries during Baja California's colonial era. Along both coasts are dense thickets of mangrove—a common plant of the tropics.

Two major lowlands of the central desert, both near the Pacific coast, offer contrasting vegetation. The Vizcaíno Desert near Guerrero Negro is a vast, sandy plain with little natural vegetation except saltbrush and scattered yucca válida. The Santo Domingo Valley, farther south, is an important agricultural region, growing wheat, garbanzo and sorghum.

The vegetation of the southern portion of the peninsula reflects somewhat higher rainfall. Botanists classify the natural vegetation here as tropical desert and tropical thorn forest, consisting of thick stands of cardón, pitahaya, cholla and other cacti, along with numerous small trees and thorny shrubs. Higher elevations in the Sierra de la Laguna contain some subtropical forest. Cultivated plants include various tropical fruit trees, stately palms and bougainvillea with brilliant blooms of red, purple and orange.

Most of Baja's desert lands produce a rich variety of flora, considering the low precipitation. This is due to good soils, lack of frost and the occurrence of rainfall at different seasons of the year. Plants bloom at irregular times, following the occasional rains. On the average, however, wildflowers in the northern desert appear in the spring, and in the southern desert in the autumn.

Fauna

Baja California's wildlife is as diverse as the terrain. Each animal seeks out its preferred environment, be it chaparral, desert, mountain, canyon, valley, seashore, or any combination of these. The land mammals include mountain lions, big horn sheep, deer, wild boar (peccary), wild burros and many other smaller animals. Also seen on the Baja peninsula are a wide assortment of birds and reptiles. These include eagles, hawks, vultures and colorful songbirds in the bird family, and a variety of snakes and lizards in the reptile family.

Many of the world's larger marine mammals may also be seen visiting the coastline of Baja California. These include harbor seals, sea lions, porpoises, and Minke, humpback and gray whales. In order to bear their young in the warm waters of the region, the gray whale makes a yearly migration from northern waters, south along the North American coastline to the area around Guerrero Negro. The whales can be viewed from January through March.

Economy

For many years Baja California's economic base reflected its population

Wild burros roam the valleys near La Bocana.

A Guadalupe fur seal suns itself on a rock near Land's End.

centers, which were in the extreme northern and the southern sections of the peninsula.

Because of their proximity to the United States, the cities of Tijuana, Ensenada and Mexicali are the hubs of economic development in northern Baja California. Tijuana produces a variety of goods, including electronic components, clothing and auto parts. Mexicali is in the peninsula's most important agricultural region and also has light manufacturing. Ensenada is a busy seaport known for its fish canneries. Tecate, a smaller community along the border of California, is known for the production of beer. In the south, La Paz processes and ships farm products, and Ciudad Constitución has become a farm processing center. The most important industry of central Baja California is the salt-producing operation at Guerrero Negro. Tourism, however, remains Baja California's leading money maker.

Millions of tourists each year flock to the border towns and coastal resorts. While the Pacific coast is the focus of resort activity and tourism in the far north, the Gulf of California coast contains the most popular travel destinations south of Ensenada. La Paz and Los Cabos boast the plushest, best-known resorts, but San Felipe, Bahía delos Angeles, Mulegé and Loreto also draw thousands of visitors every year. Fishing is the number one lure here, but beautiful beaches and abundant

INTRODUCTION

year-round sunshine are also responsible for attracting tourists to the shores of the gulf.

Most of the central desert was sparsely inhabited until the 1960s, when agricultural development and tourism started to bring rapid growth to parts of this area.

Mexico's economic fluctuations have had relatively little impact on Baja California's economy, which has grown steadily over the past couple of decades.

Shopping

All of Baja is a duty-free zone, so shopping is popular with tourists. Stores offer substantial savings under U.S. prices on such imported merchandise as perfumes, jewelry, art objects,

Colorful rugs are among the finds in Cabo San Lucas; a ceramic crafts vendor just south of Rosarito shows his wares.

The street fair in La Paz is a great place to seek out those special gifts for friends back home.

cosmetics and textiles. Careful shoppers can also find good buys on Mexican-made articles. Besides the inexpensive souvenirs manufactured locally for the tourist trade, shops offer high-quality pottery, ceramics, guitars, blown glass, wrought iron furniture, baskets, silver and leather goods, sweaters, blankets, jewelry and works of Mexican art. Cities most oriented to foreign shoppers include Cabo San Lucas, Ensenada, La Paz, Loreto, Mexicali, Rosarito, San José del Cabo and Tijuana. Shops in other communities cater primarily to the local population.

U.S. residents may bring back, duty free, articles not exceeding $400 in retail value, providing they are for personal use and accompany the individual. For more information, refer to the *Tourist Regulations and Travel Tips* chapter, U.S. Customs Regulations section. U.S. Customs offices at border crossings have a number of pamphlets detailing regulations regarding the import of items purchased in Mexico.

Tourist Regulations & Travel Tips

A safe and enjoyable journey through Baja California will be greatly enhanced by knowing some of the basics of Mexican law and by understanding the day-to-day culture of Mexico. This knowledge will make it easier to interact with the Mexican people and authorities, as well as help to plan a trip to Baja California. The information in this chapter is designed to help make the reader a veteran Baja traveler.

Motorists can enter or leave Mexico at any of five points along the California-Baja California border: Tijuana (two places), Tecate, Algodones and Mexicali. There are two ports of entry at Tijuana. The one opposite San Ysidro, California, is open 24 hours. The other Tijuana crossing is at Otay Mesa, 5½ miles to the east, and it is open 6 a.m. to 10 p.m. Tecate is open daily from 6 a.m. to midnight. Algodones is open daily from 6 a.m. to 8 p.m. The crossing at Mexicali is open 24 hours. There is a new crossing for commercial traffic only, seven miles east of Mexicali, that is slated to open in 1996.

Tourist Regulations

Entering Mexico

Note: Mexican travel regulations are subject to change. Travelers to Baja California should always check with the Mexican consulate or other official agencies to verify current requirements.

U.S. and Canadian citizens who visit the border towns of Tijuana, Tecate, Mexicali, or any other location in Baja California provided the length of stay does not exceed 72 hours, can do so without having to obtain a tourist card. It is advisable to carry proof of citizenship even when traveling where tourist cards are not required. United States passports or birth certificates certified and issued by the federal, state, county or city government where the person was born are accepted. Naturalized U.S. citizens should carry a valid passport, a Certificate of Naturalization, or a Certificate of Citizenship issued by the U.S. Immigration and Naturalization Service; wallet-sized naturalization cards (form I-179) or other documents are not accepted. Citizens of Canada should have a valid passport or birth certificate.

For travel into the Baja California peninsula exceeding a 72 hour stay and mainland Mexico, two types of tourist cards (tourist entry forms) are issued; both are free. The single-entry card is valid for up to 180 days; the exact length of its term is determined

---

Auto Club trucks negotiating the road to La Purísima during the 1949 research expedition.

by the Mexican immigration official who validates the card. The second kind of tourist card, the multiple-entry card, permits unlimited entry into Mexico for a 180-day period; two front-view photographs are required. If a tourist card is not used within 90 days of its issue date, it becomes void. A tourist who overstays the time limit is subject to a fine.

Note: It is important to have tourist cards validated at the point of entry into Mexico.

Tourist cards can be obtained in the United States from Mexican consulates or the Mexican Government Tourism Office. In California, Mexican consulates are located in Calexico, Fresno, Los Angeles, Oxnard, Sacramento, San Bernardino, San Diego, San Francisco, San Jose and Santa Ana. The Mexican Government Tourism Office is in Century City; phone (310) 203-8191. Sometimes, offices of the Automobile Club of Southern California and the California State Automobile Association receive supplies of tourist cards from the Mexican government (these offices also distribute a detailed brochure about tourist cards). Airlines and travel agencies often provide tourist cards for their clients as well. They can also be obtained at the border from Mexican immigration authorities, but it is recommended that travelers acquire their tourist cards prior to leaving the United States.

Travelers obtaining a tourist card must fill in the necessary information and must have either a valid (current) passport or a birth certificate. Birth certificates must be certified and issued by the federal, state, county or city government where the person was born. Naturalized U.S. citizens must present a valid passport, a Certificate of Natural-

ization, or a Certificate of Citizenship issued by the U.S. Immigration and Naturalization Service; wallet-sized naturalization cards (form I-179) or other documents cannot be accepted. Citizens of Canada are required to have a valid passport or birth certificate. U.S. residents who are citizens of other nations must have a resident alien card and a passport. The original document presented as proof of citizenship must be carried into Mexico with the tourist card. Photocopies are not acceptable. The Tourist card must be certified by a Mexican immigration/customs official at the port of entry. The official can be found at the Immigration Office which bears the sign Servicios Migratorios.

Minors—Any minor (under 18 years) who plans to enter Mexico without both parents must also have a completed and notarized copy of the form "Permission for a Minor to Travel in Mexico," available at the Mexican Government Tourist Office. Sample forms can be obtained at any office of the Automobile Club of Southern California. According to Mexican officials, this is the only document that will be honored and it should be presented when applying for a tourist card. If a child's parents are divorced or separated, the signed form must be accompanied by the divorce or separation papers. If one parent is deceased, the death certificate must accompany the form in lieu of the deceased's signature; the surviving parent must still sign the form. If a child is under legal guardianship, the guardian(s) must sign the form and provide guardianship papers and, when applicable, death certificates for both parents.

Business Trips—U.S. citizens who desire to transact business of any kind in Mexico must obtain a business form by applying personally at a Mexican consulate. A 30-day form is free. For a one-year form the business traveler needs to show a passport and pay a fee that ranges from $73 to $119. Any person traveling on business without this form is subject to a fine.

Automobile Requirements

A free bilingual booklet, *Traveling to Mexico by Car,* offers detailed explanations about car permits; it is available at the Mexican Government Tourism Office in Los Angeles at 10100 Santa Monica Boulevard, Suite 224, Century City; phone (310) 203-8191. Another source of information is the Mexican Treasury Department; phone (800) 446-8277.

It is illegal for a foreign citizen to sell a motor vehicle in Mexico.

Car Permits—Car permits, or Temporary Vehicle Import Permits, are not required in Baja California **except** for vehicles being shipped to mainland Mexico aboard Baja California ferries. Motorists must, however, carry acceptable proof of vehicle ownership and a valid driver's license. In mainland Mexico a car permit and tourist card are required for the principal driver; passengers and alternate drivers need only the standard tourist card. (In Sonora, these documents are not necessary in San Luis and El Golfo de Santa Clara; they are needed when traveling on Mexico Highway 2 beyond Sonoíta.)

Car permits are issued at all points of entry into mainland Mexico. Both tourist cards and car permits are available in the same building or in nearby buildings. (Because of congestion at the Tijuana crossing, it is easier to obtain these documents at another point of entry.) The permits are free and valid for up to 180 days. Information sheets and application forms for car permits are available at any office of the Automobile Club of Southern California or the California State Automobile Association.

To acquire a car permit, motorists are required to have proof of U.S. citizenship (see the Entering Mexico section for acceptable documents), as well as the **original** current registration or a notarized bill of sale for each vehicle, including motorcycles. Although it is not officially recognized as proof of ownership, the vehicle's ownership certificate (also called vehicle title or, in California, pink slip) should be carried. Motorists whose vehicles are being purchased under finance contracts must obtain written notarized permission from the lien holder (bank, finance company, credit union, etc.) authorizing the applicant to take the vehicle into Mexico. No person may drive a vehicle owned by another person into mainland Mexico **unless the owner is present.** Individuals driving a vehicle registered in the name of the company for which they work must carry a **notarized affidavit of authorization.** Offenders are subject to confiscation of the vehicle or a heavy fine. The original and two photocopies of the driver's license and vehicle registration must be presented.

Only one car permit can be issued per person. For example, one person may not enter mainland Mexico or board a ferry in Baja California with both a motorhome and a motorcycle, even if he or she owns both vehicles. One of the vehicles must be registered to another person in the party, or a second person could obtain a car permit for the extra vehicle by using a notarized affidavit of permission from the owner. Under no circumstances can more permits be obtained than there are qualified drivers (18 years or older) in the party.

Crossing into the Mainland—A recent Mexican regulation, established in order to prevent theft or smuggling, calls for an additional procedure for visiting motorists who enter the mainland of Mexico or cross by ferry from Baja California to the mainland. The visitor must present a credit card—American Express, Diners Club, Master-Card, or VISA—along with a non-refundable fee of $11. The fee is paid to Banco del Ejercito, which has offices at all border crossings (at the Mexicali crossing, customs and the bank offices are open 24 hours). The motorist signs a declaration promising to return the vehicle to the United States. Failure to pay the fee with a credit card necessitates posting a bond (*fianza*), a more costly procedure with much paperwork.

Upon returning to the border the motorist gives back all documents to Mexican Customs. It is imperative to surrender all Mexican Government travel documents. Motorists failing to do so must return with them to the border. Otherwise, a large fine will be charged upon the next entry into Mexico.

Insurance—Mexican authorities recognize only insurance policies issued by companies licensed to transact insurance in the Republic of Mexico. Accordingly, motorists preparing to enter Mexico are strongly advised to purchase a separate policy issued through a Mexican-licensed company.

Mexican law differs from that in the United States. Persons involved in traffic accidents who cannot produce an acceptable policy may be held by the authorities regardless of the seriousness or type of accident, pending investigation. *Therefore, to be adequately protected, travelers must buy Mexican automobile insurance before crossing the border into Mexico. Note: In the event of an accident, a report should be filed with the Mexican insurance company before returning to the United States.*

AAA members may obtain this coverage at any office of the Automobile Club of Southern California. Policies are written by the day, with a discount for more than 30 days' coverage, and are issued immediately upon application. The member should call a touring representative in an Automobile Club district office to determine what specifications (vehicle ID number, accessories included on the vehicle, etc.) are needed so that the insurance policy may be accurately written. Low-cost automobile insurance providing one-day coverage within the city limits of Tijuana or Mexicali may be offered for sale in these border cities. Because such policies do not provide coverage for medical payments or for the driver's person and property, the Auto Club recommends that motorists purchase Mexican automobile insurance which provides more comprehensive protection.

The Auto Club also provides information on other travel insurance. A comprehensive travel plan is available which affords medical coverage, includes nonrefundable travel expenses in the event of delay or cancellation, and insures baggage and personal possessions. Also included is air passenger

insurance, which covers scheduled or charter flights.

Other Requirements

When taking a lot of expensive foreign-made items such as cameras, binoculars, etc., into Mexico, it is wise to register these articles with U.S. Customs before crossing the border, unless the original purchase receipts are in possession. This will avoid any question that they were purchased in Mexico, in which case duties would be assessed. Only articles having manufacturers' serial numbers may be registered.

Baggage—Occasionally, baggage is inspected in Baja California at police or military roadblocks (see Highway Travel section in this chapter).

Cameras—Tourists may take one still camera and one motion picture camera (8 mm or 16 mm) or video recording camera and a total of 12 rolls of film or videocassettes. Photography must not, however, be for commercial purposes. Tripods are allowed in most areas, but a special permit is required for their use in historic sites.

Citizens Band Radios—Mexico has legalized the use of citizens band radios by tourists, and three channels—9, 10 and 11—have been designated for visitors' use. Channel 9 is for emergencies; Channel 10 can be used for communications among tourists; Channel 11 is reserved for localization (directions and information). Permits are no longer required for CB radios. Any linear amplifier or other device that increases the transmission power to over five watts is prohibited.

Firearms—Guns are not permitted in Mexico except when brought into the

country during hunting season for the express purpose of hunting and when accompanied by the appropriate documents (see Hunting in *Recreation*).

Pets—It is advisable to leave dogs and other pets at home because of special inspections, health certificates and the possible refusal of hotel operators to allow pets in their establishments. If an animal is taken into Mexico, it must have both a veterinarian's vaccination certificate for rabies and the Official Interstate and International Health Certificate for Dogs and Cats (form 77-043). If the pet is out of the United States for over 30 days, its owner must present the rabies certificate when returning to the United States.

Trailers—A trailer measuring more than eight feet in width and 40 feet in length requires a special permit, obtainable only in Tijuana at the Federal Highway Police Road Office. Permits are issued at the discretion of the officials, since road conditions in much of Baja California make trailer travel prohibitive.

Returning to the United States

Proof of citizenship should always be carried along on trips to Mexico. It may be necessary to show this document to U.S. officials upon reentering the United States.

U.S. Customs Regulations

Each returning U.S. resident may bring back, duty-free, articles not exceeding $400 in retail value, providing they are for personal use and accompany the individual. This $400 exemption may be used only once in a 30-day period. Tourists returning from Mexico need not be absent from the United States for any minimum time to qualify for this exemption. U.S. Customs offices at border crossings have a number of pamphlets detailing these regulations. They also have information for the business traveler and persons returning with specialized products.

While away, tourists may send gifts not exceeding $50 in fair retail value to persons in the United States without payment of duty and taxes. As many gifts may be sent as desired, provided the total value of gift packages or shipments received by one person in one day does not exceed $50. The words "Unsolicited Gifts" and the value in large letters should be written on the outside of the package. Alcoholic beverages and tobacco products are not included in the privilege, nor are perfumes valued at more than $5. These bona fide gifts need not be included on the customs declaration nor within the customs exemption of returning travelers. Gifts accompanying a resident at the time of his or her return must be declared and included within an exemption.

Bringing certain agricultural products across the border is prohibited, including fresh fruits and vegetables, meats and poultry. One liter of liquor per adult (21 years and older) is allowed.

An increasing number of Americans are purchasing medications in Mexico for personal use. They may be brought in legally if the following regulations are observed. The medications must be declared to the U.S. Customs agent at the border. They have to be approved by the Food and Drug Administration for use in the United States. A written prescription from the physician must accompany the medication. The quantity is limited to a three-month personal supply.

Travel Tips

Currency

In 1993, Mexico adopted a new system of currency, sometimes known as *nuevos pesos*. The former currency, due to years of inflation, had denominations that numbered 1000 times the present coins and bills. Astronomical prices resulted. Under the new system, 100 centavos equal 1 peso. Coins come in denominations of 5, 10, 20 and 50 centavos and 1, 2, 5 and 10 pesos. Bills also come in 10 pesos and run in denominations of 20, 50, 100, 200 pesos, etc.

At the time of publication the exchange rate between Mexican and American currency was about 7.4 pesos to the dollar, with an individual peso worth about 14¢, but the exact value of the peso fluctuates slightly from week to week. In any case, travelers should expect rates to deviate depending on the time and place of a transaction. *Mexico uses the same symbol ($) to denote pesos as the United States uses for dollars.*

Although most Mexican Government agencies and many business establishments quote prices in pesos, U.S. dollars are readily accepted in tourist areas of Baja California. **Prices contained in this publication are listed in dollar equivalents as they were quoted at press time.** In the border cities, prices in Mexican money frequently carry the abbreviation "n.p." (*nuevos pesos*) and prices in American money, "dlls." (dollars).

Members traveling beyond the immediate border zone are strongly urged to

▼ *Baja California Cuisine*

When most people think of Mexican food, they think of meat, cheese and bean specialties such as enchiladas, burritos, quesadillas, tacos and tamales. While all of these are available in the Baja peninsula, there is much more to be found. With most of the peninsula in close proximity to major bodies of water—the Pacific Ocean on the west coast and the Gulf of California (also known as the Sea of Cortez) along the east coast—seafood specialties are quite common on most menus. Among the many species of fish that are caught and cooked in Baja are yellowtail, seabass, red snapper, dorado (mahimahi) and shark. Most menus do not specify the type of fish being offered and simply list it as pescado blanco (white fish)—in fact, almost any white-fleshed fish will do. There are numerous cooking methods used for serving up fish, but the most common is breaded and pan-fried.

Shellfish are also very popular on the Baja peninsula, especially with American tourists who can usually purchase a shellfish dinner for considerably less than they would pay in an American restaurant. A wide range of shellfish are cooked and served in the Baja peninsula, including lobster (*langosta*), crab (*cangrejo*), clams (*almejas*), scallops (*callos*), shrimp (*camarones*), abalone (*abulon*) and oysters (*ostiones*). They are cooked in a variety of tantalizing ways, from American-style to marinated in chili peppers.

convert at least some of their funds into Mexican pesos. While U.S. dollars have become commonly used at tourist-oriented businesses and in resort areas, they are frequently not accepted in locations distant from the border or away from major tourist destinations. Since travelers usually lose money each time they exchange currencies, a good rule to follow is this: if you pay in pesos, try to receive change in pesos; if you pay in dollars, attempt to receive your change in dollars.

With exchange rates in flux it is especially important to obtain a clear understanding about prices, whether in dollars or pesos, before making a purchase or agreeing to a service. Sales tax in Baja California (both states) is 10 percent. Usually included in the base price of goods and services, it occasion-

ally appears added to the bill. In Mexico, U.S. currency can be converted into pesos at some banks, which usually give the best exchange rates. Certain currency exchange firms on both sides of the border also offer good rates. All large towns in Baja California have banks, but business hours are slightly different from those of their U.S. counterparts: Monday through Friday most open at about 9 a.m., close between noon and 2 p.m. and reopen from 4 to 6 p.m.; they are closed on all Mexican holidays. Some banks will send and accept wired funds. Arrangements should be made through the bank and the local telegraph office.

Traveler's checks are accepted at most hotels and large tourist restaurants, and can be cashed at Mexican banks; they are not accepted at gasoline stations and most stores and restaurants. American credit cards—American Express, MasterCard, VISA and occasionally Diners Club—are accepted at some tourist establishments in Tijuana, Ensenada, Mexicali, La Paz and Los Cabos. They are not accepted in most of Baja California. Since business establishments in Baja California's more remote areas frequently keep very little cash on hand, smaller denomination traveler's checks and currency are more readily accepted. It is wise to have enough cash to cover several days' needs.

Facilities and Services

While it is generally advisable for travelers to bring everything they need into Mexico from the United States, Baja California does have facilities for those who need to obtain or replenish supplies. Most communities have small markets or general stores offering a limited selection of merchandise. Only in major cities and towns can travelers expect to find such items as clothing, pharmaceuticals, sporting goods, hardware and fuel for camp stoves. U.S.-style supermarkets are located in Tijuana, Rosarito, Mexicali, Tecate, Ensenada, Loreto, Ciudad Constitución, La Paz and Cabo San Lucas; prices average about the same as those in the United States.

Although the large cities and popular resorts in Baja California offer fine accommodations and many tourist facilities, smaller Mexican communities are distinctly different from their U.S. counterparts. Some have very few retail businesses and lack accommodations, restaurants, public rest rooms, telephones and auto repair facilities. In emergencies, however, townspeople are usually pleased to help travelers in any way they can.

Postal service extends throughout Baja California, but letters can take two or three weeks in transit—even when mailed from a town with scheduled air service. Telephone and telegraph terminals are now located in most towns on the peninsula; microwave telephone service is operational between San Ignacio and Cabo San Lucas, and northern Baja California has telephone lines that connect with those of the United States. In cases of emergency, travelers can send messages via government radio, which has terminals in most of the peninsula's communities.

Telephone numbers printed in this book include the international code 01152, the city code of two or three digits (shown in parentheses), and the local number of five or six digits. For local calls in Baja California you need to use only the five or six digits; these shortened numbers appear in all local advertisements and telephone directories. For example, the state tourism office in Ensenada has the local number 2-3000, which you use in that vicinity. To call from the United States, dial 01152 (617) 2-3000 (do not dial "1" before 01152).

Public telephones in Mexico are few in number, except in the larger cities. The price of making a call is low, requiring only one small coin.

Time Zones

The northern state of Baja California observes Pacific Standard Time, the same time as the state of California. Baja California Sur, the southern state, observes Mountain Standard Time. Its clocks are one hour ahead of California's throughout the year. Both Mexican states are on daylight-saving time from the first Sunday in April until the last Sunday in October.

Holidays

A number of major holidays are observed in Mexico. In addition, smaller communities may observe some religious feast days.

January 1
New Year's Day

February 24
Flag Day

March 21
Benito Juárez' Birthday

March-April
Palm Sunday
Easter Sunday

May
Labor Day

May 5
Cinco de Mayo

September 15-16
Independence Day

October 12
Día de la Raza

November 1
Presidential State of the Nation Address

November 20
Revolution Day

December 12
Feast of the Virgin of Guadalupe

December 25
Navidad

Language

Many Baja Californians speak at least some English—especially in the areas most frequented by tourists. Outside these areas, however, the number of bilingual residents decreases significantly. Very few gasoline stations beyond Ensenada have English-speaking employees; neither do most shops, stores, cafes, or even some hotels, trailer parks and government agencies. Some knowledge of Spanish is certainly helpful to the traveler. The tourist armed with a good English-Spanish dictionary, a basic Spanish phrase book and a little patience will do quite well in Baja California. Included in this guidebook's *Appendix* is a section entitled "Speaking of Spanish," which contains useful Spanish words, phrases and sentences, as well as a simple pronunciation guide. Don't be bashful about trying out your Spanish—the Mexican people are usually very patient and helpful with visitors who make an attempt to speak their language.

The Metric System

Mexico uses the metric system of weights and measurements. Speed limits are posted in kilometers and gasoline is sold by the liter. Knowledge of simple conversion factors for kilometers/miles and liters/gallons is essential, and may help prevent getting a speeding ticket or being overcharged at the gas pump.

Health Conditions and Medical Emergencies

Health conditions in Baja California are good, but tourists anywhere may react unfavorably to any change in their environment—particularly in their drinking water. Probably the best way to avoid the intestinal disturbance known as the *turistas* or "Montezuma's revenge" is to avoid overindulgence in food, beverages and exercise, and to

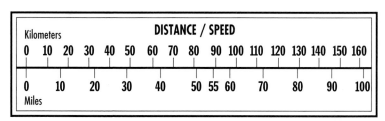

DISTANCE / SPEED

Kilometers																
0	10	20	30	40	50	60	70	80	90	100	110	120	130	140	150	160
0	10		20	30	40		50 55 60		70		80			90			100
Miles																

METRIC CONVERSION

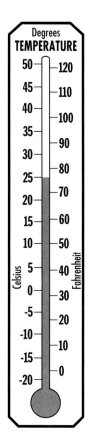

Degrees
TEMPERATURE

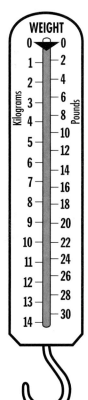

WEIGHT

CUSTOMARY		METRIC
One inch	=	2.54 centimeters
One foot	=	0.30 meters
One mile	=	1.61 kilometers
One quart	=	0.95 liters
One gallon	=	3.79 liters
One pound	=	0.45 kilometers
One psi*	=	6.89 kilopascals

METRIC		CUSTOMARY
One centimeter	=	0.39 inches
One meter	=	3.28 feet
One kilometer	=	0.62 miles
One liter	=	1.06 quarts
One kilogram	=	2.21 pounds
One kilopascal	=	0.145 psi*

*Pounds of force per square inch.

TEMPERATURE

To convert Fahrenheit to Celsius, subtract 32 from the Fahrenheit temperature, multiply by 5 and divide by 9; to convert Celsius to Fahrenheit, multiply by 9, divide by 5 and add 32.

LIQUID MEASURE

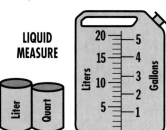

AIR PRESSURE

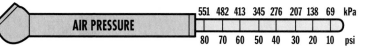

551	482	413	345	276	207	138	69	kPa
80	70	60	50	40	30	20	10	psi

get plenty of rest. Travelers should avoid tap water; fresh bottled water and good beer, soft drinks and juices are readily available. Choose carefully when selecting dairy products and fresh fruits and vegetables. It is interesting to note that Mexicans often contract a malady similar to the *turistas* when they visit the United States. Smallpox and other vaccinations are no longer necessary for entry into Mexico or reentry into the United States.

Baja California has good physicians and dentists, along with well-equipped hospitals, clinics and pharmacies, but they are found only in the largest cities and towns. Small towns may have clinics with limited facilities. The local Red Cross (*Cruz Roja*) can also be helpful. Since medical facilities are scarce elsewhere on the peninsula, travelers should carry first-aid kits and know how to use them. In case of emergency, help can be summoned via a government radio network, which is available for public use in most communities.

Travelers having emergencies anywhere in Baja California may contact the Binational Emergency Medical Committee, located in Chula Vista, at (619) 425-5080 (available 24 hours). This voluntary organization works with both Mexican and American authorities to help travelers stranded due to accident, illness, legal difficulty or lack of money.

In addition, emergency critical-care air transport service operates throughout Baja California with in-flight physicians and nurses. The following companies offer 24-hour emergency air service. Air-Evac International, located in San Diego, can be reached at (619) 278-3822, or from outside California at (800) 854-2569. Critical Air Medicine,

also in San Diego, may be contacted at (619) 571-0482, or toll-free within Mexico at 95 (800) 010-0268. Transmedic, in Ensenada, has phone numbers 01152 (617) 8-1400 and 8-2891.

Highway Travel

Baja California's paved highways are generally well signed and well maintained, although they are quite narrow by U.S. standards; the widths of Highways 1, 2, 3, 5 and 19 range from about 19 to 25 feet. Shoulders are nonexistent along many stretches, and turnouts are rare. In some areas the pavement has a rounded crown and rests on a raised roadbed; this makes careful steering important, because vehicles tend to drift to the right. High winds can also create driving difficulties, especially for operators of recreational vehicles, trucks and vehicles pulling trailers. Large, oncoming trucks and buses pose a real danger on hills and curves, because some drivers like to straddle the center line. Safe speeds for all vehicles are less than on most US highways: 40 to 50 m.p.h. on level terrain, 20 to 30 m.p.h. in hilly or mountainous areas. Driving at night should be strictly avoided. Cattle and other livestock commonly wander onto the asphalt at night for warmth, and have caused many serious accidents as a result. If night driving is necessary, the speed should be reduced drastically.

Travelers should be alert for occasional roadblocks of armed police or military personnel at which vehicles are searched for arms or drugs. Tourists should cooperate fully with the police, but afterward report any unfair treatment to the U.S. Consulate in Tijuana and the tourist assistance offices located in several cities. Visitors who

Road Signs

Mexico has officially adopted a uniform traffic sign system in which many signs are pictorially self-explanatory. Some of the most common appear below with Spanish-English definitions.

STOP

ESCUELA
School

PUENTE ANGOSTO
Narrow Bridge

GANADO
Cattle

CRUCE F.C.
Railroad Crossing

Yield Right of Way

CURVA PELIGROSA
Dangerous Curve

CAMINO SINUOSO
Winding Road

HOMBRES TRABAJANDO
Men Working

VADO
Dip
(across arroyo)

VADO
Dip
(across arroyo)

ZONA DE DERRUMBES
Slide Area

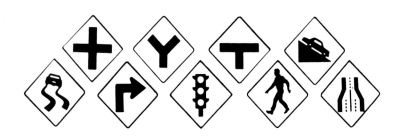

One Way

Two Way

Left Turn Only

Speed Limit

Keep to the Right

No Passing

NO VOLTEAR EN U
No U Turn

No Parking
8 a.m. to 9 p.m.

PROHIBIDO ESTACIONARSE
No Parking

One Hour Parking

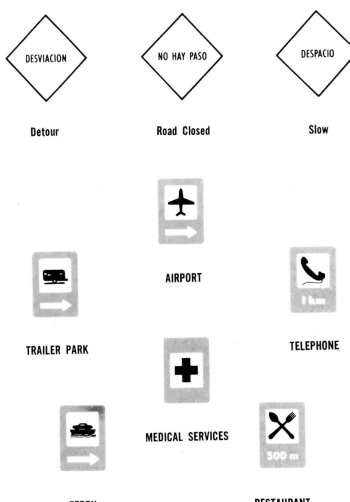

Detour

Road Closed

Slow

AIRPORT

TRAILER PARK

TELEPHONE

MEDICAL SERVICES

FERRY

RESTAURANT

GAS & MECHANICAL SERVICE

TOURIST REGULATIONS AND TRAVEL TIPS

encounter trouble or require emergency services while in Mexico should immediately contact the office of the State Tourism Department or, if there is no office nearby, notify local police. In Tijuana, Rosarito, Ensenada, Tecate, Mexicali and San Felipe, the following three-digit telephone numbers are operating: police 134, fire 136, Red Cross (medical) 132. Outside major cities, Mexican government authority rests with the *delegado,* an elected official who oversees all emergencies and civil or legal disputes; he can be found at the *delegación municipal* or *subdelegación.* In more isolated places, authority is usually vested in an appointed citizen who reports to the nearest *delegado.* Although crime is less a problem in Baja California than in the United States, travelers should take the usual common sense precautions against theft:

1. Lock the car at all times.

2. Avoid night driving whenever possible. When driving after dark, park only in well-lighted areas.

3. Carry as much cash as necessary, but use travelers checks whenever possible.

4. Money should not be carried all in one wallet or purse.

5. Keep a list of all travelers checks and credit card numbers.

6. Never leave valuables in the car or hotel room.

Gasoline

Gasoline is usually available along Baja California's major highways, but because local shortages sometimes occur, travelers are advised to keep their fuel tanks at least half full. This is especially important during long holiday weekends, when resort areas sometimes experience shortages. All gasoline sold in Mexico is distributed by *Pemex* (*Petróleos Mexicanos*)—the government-controlled oil monopoly. Pemex stations can be found in most cities and towns on the peninsula; the longest stretch of any paved highway without gasoline is the 84-mile section of Highway 1 between Mulegé and Loreto. In this book, very small towns and villages selling unleaded fuel at their gasoline stations have the words *magna sin* in their description. Diesel fuel is easier to find in Baja California than in the United States; the longest paved stretch between diesel outlets is the 96-mile stretch along Highway 19 from La Paz to Cabo San Lucas.

Road conditions in Mexico are not always excellent, as shown in this picture taken along Mexico Highway I south of Ensenada.

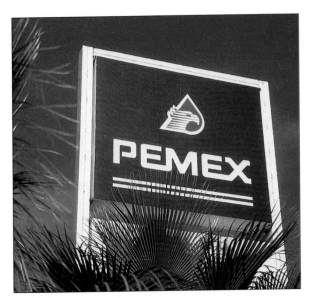

Most gasoline stations (PEMEX stations) can be located by their colorful signage.

The method used to establish octane ratings in Mexico differs from that used in the U.S. Consequently, higher ratings may appear on Pemex pumps. Premium grade unleaded fuel, called *magna sin,* has an octane rating of 92 and is dispensed from green pumps. Widely available from the border south to Ensenada and San Felipe and in the vicinity of La Paz and Los Cabos, it is rather scarce in the central part of the peninsula. Regular grade leaded fuel, called *nova,* is sold at all gasoline stations. It has an octane rating of 80 and comes from blue pumps. (Continued use of leaded gasoline in all but very old U.S.-made automobiles may damage the vehicles' catalytic converters.) Diesel fuel is sold from red pumps plainly marked "diesel," and is available at most stations that carry *magna sin.*

Some vehicles do not run well on Mexican gasoline, especially older ones that require high octane leaded fuel. The use of low octane fuel commonly causes pinging and preignition, conditions that can result in engine damage. If pinging or loss of power should occur, a gasoline additive may alleviate the problem. Mexican gasoline may occasionally contain water or other impurities. To prevent clogged fuel lines and carburetor jets, motorists should be prepared to clean or replace their in-line fuel filters if necessary while in Baja California. When gasoline is obtained in out-of-the-way locations (especially when it's pumped from drums), travelers occasionally filter the fuel through a chamois cloth.

At press time, fuel prices in pesos per liter were 1.31 for *nova,* 1.37 for *magna sin* and 1.06 for diesel. Converted into dollars and gallons, these figures equal about $0.73 for *nova,* $0.77 for *magna sin* and $0.59 for diesel. Some stations have been known to overcharge. It is a good idea to have a calculator handy to check the price charged. Be sure that the pump registers zeros when the attendant starts filling the tank.

The service provided at Pemex stations varies from one facility to the next. Generally, however, travelers should be prepared to check their vehicle's oil, water and air. Pemex attendants do not usually clean windshields, but if they do a small tip is expected. Motorists

The state-sponsored Green Angels patrol the highways and provide assistance to stranded motorists.

will find it convenient to carry paper towels and glass-cleaning fluid, as these products are not usually provided.

Emergency Road Service and Auto Repairs

The Green Angels, a government-sponsored group whose sole purpose is to provide free emergency assistance to tourists, regularly patrol Baja California's major highways, supposedly passing any given point at least twice a day. Their staff are mechanics (some bilingual) who carry limited spare parts and gasoline (provided at cost) and who can radio for assistance.

Before traveling in Mexico, the vehicle should be in top mechanical condition. Tires, including spares, should be inspected for tread wear and proper inflation, and all fluid levels should be checked. Brakes, batteries, shock absorbers, filters, pumps and radiators

all warrant special attention. The wise traveler will carry extra belts and hoses, as well as the tools needed to install them.

There are automobile dealerships in Tijuana, Mexicali, Ensenada, Ciudad Constitución and La Paz, and skilled mechanics can be found in most larger towns on the peninsula. But although competent mechanical help is relatively easy to find in Baja California, parts are not. The most prevalent makes of automobiles in Baja are Ford, Chevrolet, Dodge, Volkswagen and Nissan—parts for other makes are extremely scarce. Even in major cities, a breakdown can sometimes result in a considerable wait for parts. And in rural areas, while local mechanics are wizards at salvaging parts from junk cars and are adept at repairing vehicles of less than recent vintage, many are bewildered by the complexities of fuel injection, air conditioning, anti-smog devices and electronic ignition.

Backcountry Travel

When the paved Transpeninsular Highway was completed in 1973, Baja California became an accessible destination for virtually anyone with a car. Many off-road "purists" bemoaned the loss of what they regarded as their special domain. Their worries were unwarranted, however, because the "old" Baja California still exists, as any traveler who leaves the security of the pavement soon discovers. Despite the peninsula's rapid growth and development, most of its territory remains a wild, rugged frontier—a timeless land of vast, empty spaces, unspoiled beaches, lonely ranchos and roads that by and large are little better than mule trails. Baja California's backcountry is difficult to traverse and is definitely not for those seeking comfort and amenities. But for travelers with the proper vehicles and equipment, it offers beauty, solitude and adventure. To enter this fascinating realm is to leave the jet age behind and experience a region little touched by "civilization."

A journey into the remote reaches of the peninsula requires careful planning and preparation. Before leaving the pavement, travelers should let someone know where they are going and what is the planned return time. Tourists might consider traveling under the buddy system—with two or more vehicles in a caravan—and plan to be as self-sufficient as possible as facilities are extremely scarce. Enough extra gasoline to extend the vehicle's range by at least 50 miles should be taken, and if possible stored outside the vehicle. Five gallons of water per person should be carried, along with ample nonperishable food for two weeks' sustenance. A good first-aid kit is essential. A supply of plastic bags will protect cameras and other valuable items from the ever present Baja California dust. For a complete list of recommended equipment, see the "Suggested Supply Lists" section in the *Appendix.*

Although some of Baja's dirt roads are occasionally maintained and regularly traveled, others are seldom used tracks

Traversing backcountry roads is best accomplished using sturdy, high-clearance vehicles.

Baja's roads can take their toll on even the sturdiest of vehicles.

that are downright grueling. Even the "good" roads have bad stretches, and any unpaved route is only as good as its worst spot. Along many of the peninsula's back roads, the traveler can expect to encounter jarring, washboard sections, deep sand, hazardous arroyo crossings, precarious curves, rocks jutting upward from the surface and grades reminiscent of roller coasters. These roads can damage any vehicle. As a result, backcountry travel in Baja California calls for a specially prepared heavy duty rig, preferably one with four-wheel drive. It should be equipped for high clearance, with oversize tires, extra low gears, and protective steel pans beneath the engine, transmission and gasoline tank. Dual rear tires are not advisable because they do not easily fall into existing road tracks. As important as the proper vehicle is the driver who proceeds slowly and cautiously; to attempt to go too fast is to invite disaster.

There are few road signs in Baja California's backcountry—probably because local residents assume that anyone driving the back roads knows where to go. As a result, numerous unsigned junctions confront the motorist. In many cases, however, both branches leaving a fork soon rejoin one another. If an unsigned junction is reached, a good rule to follow is to choose the most heavily traveled fork; it will either be the correct route or will often lead to a ranch where directions can be obtained. Be sure to take along the Automobile Club of Southern California's *Baja California* map and check all junctions against those indicated. Remember, however, that odometers vary, and the mileages may disagree somewhat with those on the map.

Extensive off-pavement travel in Baja California involves camping out. When selecting camping equipment, keep in mind that high winds often whistle across the desert, and temperatures can be quite cool at night. Camping is allowed almost anywhere, but the bottoms of arroyos should be avoided, where flash floods sometimes occur. All trash that cannot be burned should be packed out. Wood for campfires is not abundant in the desert, but cactus skeletons make suitable fuel.

The prospective off-pavement explorer has a wide variety of routes and destinations from which to choose. Some of the most rewarding are described under the designation *Side Route* within the highway chapters. Travelers who are inexperienced in traveling the backcountry of Baja California should begin with one of the trips outlined in this book.

Tourist Assistance

Tourist Assistance/Protección al Turista provides assistance to visitors who experience legal difficulties with local businessmen or police. Offices throughout the peninsula are listed below. Tourist Assistance recommends the following steps to tourists who believe they have received inappropriate treatment by Mexican police: (1) Observe or ask for as many of the following as possible—the officer's name (most police wear nameplates), badge number, department (municipal, state, federal) and car number. (2) If there is a fine, go to the nearest police station to pay it and ask for a receipt. Traffic tickets received in Tijuana may be paid by mail from the United States. (3) Write out the complaint and mail it to the attorney general.

Ensenada *State Tourism Office on Boulevard Lázaro Cárdenas (Costero) at Calle las Rocas; phone 01152 (617) 2-3000*

La Paz *State Tourism Office, Paseo Alvaro Obregón at 16 de Septiembre; phone 01152 (112) 4-0100 or 4-0103*

Mexicali *State Tourism Office on Calle Calafia at Calzada Independencia; phone 01152 (65) 56-1172*

Rosarito *Boulevard Juárez and Calle Acacias; phone 01152 (661) 2-0200*

San Felipe *State Tourism building at Avenida Mar de Cortez and Calle Manzanillo; phone 01152 (657) 7-1155*

Tecate *State Tourism Office on the south side of the plaza; phone 01152 (665) 4-1095*

Tijuana *State Tourism Office in Plaza Patria on Boulevard Díaz Ordaz; phone 01152 (66) 81-9492*

The U.S. Consulate, in Tijuana on Calle Tapachula near Agua Caliente Racetrack, offers assistance to U.S. citizens traveling in northern Baja California. Travelers should report to the consulate any in-appropriate treatment they receive by Mexican police. Questionnaires concerning police mistreatment are available at the consulate. The consulate is open Monday through Friday 8 a.m. to 4:30 p.m.; call 01152 (66) 81-7400 during these hours. For after-hour emergencies call (619) 585-2000, or write to P.O. Box 439039, San Ysidro, CA 92143 U.S. In Baja California Sur, U.S. citizens can obtain help in Cabo San Lucas from the U.S. consular agent, located at Boulevard Marina y Pedregal No. 3. The phone is 01152 (114) 3-3566.

History

Before the arrival of the Europeans, Baja California was inhabited by numerous tribes of Indians. The main linguistic groups from north to south were the Yumans, Guaicura, Huchiti and the Pericu. While most of the tribes are now extinct, archeological evidence and the written histories of the early Europeans have shown that these Indians were hunter-gatherers. Their most enduring legacy has been the fantastic cave paintings and rock art that can be found along the length of the peninsula.

Following the conquest of central Mexico, rumors of great wealth to the west attracted the conquistador Hernán Cortés, who in 1535 sailed from the west coast of Mexico into present-day Bahía de La Paz. There he established a small colony, naming the bay and land Santa Cruz (modern La Paz). Due to supply shortages, the colony was abandoned in 1537.

Exploration of the peninsula's coastline was continued in 1539 by Francisco de Ulloa and in 1542 by Juan Rodríguez Cabrillo. In 1596 Sebastián Vizcaíno reestablished a colony at the site of Cortés' settlement and renamed the bay La Paz. This colony also failed due to a shortage of supplies. In 1602 Vizcaíno explored the Pacific Coast of the Californias, produced the first detailed maps of the area and established place names, most of which are still in use.

Continued rumors of great wealth in pearls attracted more Spaniards to the Gulf of California in the 17th century, although their efforts were rewarded with only moderate quantities of the semiprecious gems. Francisco de Ortega in 1628, Alonzo Gonzales in 1644, and Bernardo Bernal de Pinadero in 1663 were among those who came to the Gulf of California, but they added little in exploration and knowledge of Baja California.

In 1683, Isidro de Atondo y Antillón attempted to set up a colony at La Paz, but conflict with the Indians forced him to relocate to the site of modern San Bruno. An 18-month drought exhausted the provisions and he disbanded the colony in 1685. Along with him on this journey was Padre Eusebio Kino, whose urging resulted in renewed efforts 12 years later under the Jesuit religious order to convert the Indians to the Roman church.

On October 15, 1697, Padre Juan María Salvatierra landed on the east coast of the peninsula with six soldiers. He founded a mission at Loreto, which became the first permanent Spanish settlement in California, and for the next 70 years the Jesuits con-

---

Hiking up historic Cañon de Trinidad includes wading through pools of standing water.

HISTORY

▼ Baja California Pictographs

Scattered throughout the mountains and canyons of Baja California are thousands of figures (human, animal and unknown symbols) painted onto the rock walls. When the Spaniards arrived in the peninsula and saw these pictographs, they inquired as to the meaning of these mysterious drawings. The native inhabitants could only respond that they did not know the meaning of the figures, but that they had been left behind by a long-departed race of giants. Most of the pictographs (meaning painted figures) are found in the central section of the Baja peninsula, although there are many sites in the northern part of the peninsula as well.

Rock carvings in Cañon de Trinidad offer proof of early tribal Indian habitation on the peninsula.

Archaeological evidence from the pictograph sites, which include grinding stones, arrowheads, scrapers and carved bone, place the creators of the magnificent artworks between 5000 and 10,000 years ago. Some of the pictographs are done in only one color (red), while others are done in combinations of red and black. While the exact meaning and purpose can only be conjectured, they are generally believed to be related to hunting rituals.

Today these sites are protected by the Mexican government and it is illegal for anyone to visit them without being accompanied by an officially authorized guide. A list of authorized guides can be acquired from local civil authorities or sometimes from the front lobby at better hotels. These guides charge a fee for their services. Most of these sites are located in remote areas in rugged terrain. Some are so far off the beaten path that they require overnight pack trips with horse or burro to get there.

The uniqueness and mystery of these fascinating symbols more than offset the difficulty encountered in getting to them. One can't help but wonder if the native Indians who created these drawings had any idea that hundreds of years later the sketches would remain, intriguing visitors from other lands and cultures.

trolled Lower California. The Jesuits financed their own venture, with the Spanish government supplying only the soldiers.

The padres were brave, undiscouraged by the wild surroundings. They charted and explored the east and west coasts of the peninsula, and developed pioneer agricultural settlements. The mission fathers taught the Indians to cultivate the land. Grapes were grown and wine pressed to be exchanged for goods from Mexico. They founded 23 missions, 14 of which were successful; they instructed the Indians in religious matters and taught them useful arts; they made a network of trails connecting the missions, took scientific and geographical notes, and prepared ethnological reports on the native peoples.

But they were unable to conquer disease, and epidemics plagued the population. With thousands of Indians dying and many killed in revolts, the elaborate political and economic structure established by the Jesuits began to

weaken. Then, just as the priests were preparing to move north, enemies of the Jesuit order spread tales in Spain that the mission fathers were accumulating great wealth and power. Acting with dispatch, the Spanish government expelled the Jesuits from California in 1768.

Later that same year, 13 padres of the Franciscan Brotherhood, under the leadership of the small, energetic Padre Junípero Serra, landed at Loreto. A quick appraisal convinced them that their work lay in Alta (Upper) California near what is now San Diego, although they founded one mission on their way northward. In 1773 the Franciscans were succeeded on the peninsula by the Dominicans, who successfully carried on the establishment of the missions until the system was attacked by the Mexican government. In 1832 the Mexican government ordered the secularization of all missions and their conversion to parish churches. The Dominican missions in the north, however, were considered the only vestiges of civilization

Abandoned adobe ruins have been a part of Baja's landscape since the Spanish era.

In the 1930s, visitors had to travel ill-defined dirt roads across inhospitable terrain.

there and were retained until 1846. Some of the mission churches are still in use, while the ruins of others can be seen along the back roads of Baja California. A government sponsored program of mission restoration is currently in progress.

Far from the seat of government in Mexico City, Baja California soon became the forgotten peninsula—a haven for criminals, smugglers and soldiers of fortune. Lower California was a land torn by internal strife and poverty.

The Mexican-American War (1846-48)—which finally separated the Californias—created further turbulence, and there were hard feelings toward the new neighbor to the north. Moreover, investment of American capital in land and mines kept Mexico suspicious of U.S. intentions. The notorious filibuster William Walker only con-

Despite years of weathering and abuse, this highway sign, posted decades ago by the Automobile Club of Southern California, still serves Baja travelers.

firmed these suspicions when he invaded Lower California in a surprise attack and proclaimed himself president. Though he was soon relieved of his position, other rebels were quick to step into the gap. In 1911, in activity peripheral to the Mexican Revolution, Mexican Ricardo Flores Magón led the rebellion known as the Tijuana Revolution. Tijuana was successfully taken by the rebels, but Flores' inability to implement his theories caused the rebellion to fail. Thereafter, a succession of politically appointed governors maintained precarious rule over this troubled area.

Hidalgo, Carranza and Juárez, major political figures in Mexico's history, are memorialized in bronze in Ensenada's Plaza Civica.

Prohibition in the United States brought uncertain prosperity to the border towns. Americans entered Mexico in droves, seeking the pleasures of a more liberal rule. It was not until 1938 that Mexican President Cárdenas declared a "deep preoccupation" with the future of Lower California. Gamblers and undesirables were routed, and intense agrarian and educational reforms were instituted. In 1952, under the leadership of President Alemán, the northern part of Baja California officially became a state of Mexico, with an elected government in the state capital, Mexicali. The official name of this northern state is Baja California, although it is often referred to as Baja California Norte. In 1974 the southern half of the peninsula (below the 28th parallel) officially became Mexico's 30th state, Baja California Sur, with La Paz as its capital.

Each state is divided into *municipios* (municipalities), roughly equivalent to American counties. The state of Baja California, population about 2,200,000, is divided into *municipios* bearing the same names as its cities: Tijuana, Ensenada, Tecate and Mexicali. Baja California Sur, with a population of about 340,000, contains the *municipios* of Mulegé, Loreto, Comondú, La Paz and Los Cabos.

The last 20 years have seen great progress for Baja California. Surrounded by a huge supply of fish, lobster and shrimp, the arid peninsula is gradually yielding to man's efforts to make it a productive land. Through government assistance, farming cooperatives have sprouted. And with the completion of Mexico Highway 1, Baja California entered the modern era, growing and prospering as a mechanized land and a

Mexico Highway 1

Until 1973, the only way to reach the tip of Baja California by passenger car involved driving to Topolobampo or Mazatlán on the Mexican mainland, then crossing the Gulf of California by ferry to La Paz. Paved roads probed into the interior from the border and from La Paz, but they were separated by a vast, sparsely populated desert traversed by a rough, meandering track that could break even the sturdiest of off-road vehicles.

In late 1973, however, road crews working north and south at a feverish pace met near Rancho Santa Inés, completing the paving of a modern highway extending the entire length of the peninsula. Mexico Highway 1, Baja California's new lifeline, was named La Carretera Transpeninsular Benito Juárez (Benito Juárez Transpeninsular Highway) after one of Mexico's most revered heroes. The official dedication was made in December by then-President Luis Echeverría Alvarez in ceremonies held at the 28th parallel, near Guerrero Negro.

Designed to promote the peninsula's economic development, the paved highway allows for the movement of Baja California's internal commerce, and it has been an important stimulus for the peninsula's recent growth. It is no coincidence that in October 1974, less than a year after the completion of Highway 1, the territory of Baja California Sur became a full-fledged Mexican state.

To the tourist, the Transpeninsular Highway brings within reach the mountains and valleys of the north, the fascinating central desert and the beaches of southern Baja California. Convenient overland access to fine hunting and some of the world's best sportfishing is now available. Tourism has been further encouraged by the completion of government-financed hotels and gasoline stations along the highway. Automobile touring in Baja California, once a dream, is now a reality.

Crossing The Border

The San Ysidro-Tijuana border crossing, open 24 hours, is the world's busiest international gateway. While Mexico-bound tourists are normally waved through the border station without formality, travelers returning to the United States must stop for inspection. This can result in congestion, especially on weekends and holidays, when delays of more than two hours can occur. On weekdays, car-

The white sand beaches of Playas de Tijuana are minutes from the Mexican border.

MEXICO HIGHWAY 1

Border sea wall near Tijuana

pool lanes (for four or more persons) are open into San Ysidro.

Interstates 5 and 805 lead from San Diego directly to the international border. When approaching or returning from the border, particularly after dark, drivers should be alert for persons (undocumented immigrants) crossing the freeways. Visitors who wish to walk across the border will find ample pay parking on the U.S. side. Before driving into Mexico, drivers are encouraged to read the *Tourist Regulations and Travel Tips* chapter, and purchase Mexico automobile insurance.

Tourists wishing to drive to the border and cross into Tijuana on foot can find a number of parking lots on the U.S. side in San Ysidro. They are located near the border on Camiones Way (west of I-5) and at the end of San Ysidro Boulevard (east of I-5). Parking rates run $2 for a half-hour, but only $6-8 for 24 hours. Some lots provide security, others do not; inquire before parking. On the Mexico side, taxis and buses are available, or the visitor may continue walking a half mile to downtown Tijuana via a pedestrian bridge over the Río Tijuana. The Otay Mesa crossing is located just east of the Tijuana International Airport and just south of SR 905/Otay Mesa Road. It is open daily from 6 a.m. to 10 p.m. This border crossing is particularly useful for travelers returning from Mexico on weekends. Delays are not nearly as long as at San Ysidro, but on weekends and holidays motorists may have to wait an hour in line. From San Diego, the Otay Mesa crossing can be reached by taking SR 905 east from either I-5 or I-805 to Otay Mesa Road. Continue east for about four miles, following signs to the border.

From the south, the crossing is reached via a bypass which loops around southern and eastern Tijuana to Otay Mesa (both sides of the border are called "Otay Mesa"). Motorists approaching Tijuana from the south via Highway 1-D (the toll road) should exit onto Highway 1 at the Rosarito Norte interchange, then follow the highway, which is four-lane divided, 7½ miles to the bypass, named *Libramiento*. The motorist should watch for "La Mesa-Tecate-Mexicali" signs, then bear right onto the bypass and follow signs marked "Aeropuerto."

Although the bypass route is continuous in nature, it changes names several times between Highway 1-D and the Otay Mesa crossing. As the airport area is approached, signs in Spanish indicate the Otay Mesa border crossing (*Garita de Otay*) and separate lanes for heavy vehicles (*Vehículos Pesados*) and for light vehicles (*Vehículos Ligeros*), which include automobiles and recreational vehicles.

Tijuana

(See also *Lodging & Restaurants*.)

Pacific coast gateway to Baja California, Tijuana is the largest city (population 1,300,000) in the Baja peninsula and the fourth largest city in Mexico. The city is also the seat of government for the *municipio* (county) of Tijuana. The name Tijuana is believed to be derived from the Yuman Indian word *Ticuan* which means "near the sea." Originally centered in the river valley, the city has since expanded into the surrounding hills and canyons. The central commercial district lies just south of the San Ysidro border crossing, but due to the rapidly growing population and increased commercial investment, the city now parallels the United States border from Otay Mesa in the east to the Pacific Ocean on the west. The intermittent-flowing *Río Tijuana* (Tijuana River) traverses the central business district, crosses the international border, flows in a north-westerly direction and finally empties into the Pacific Ocean. Tijuana's climate brings mild summers (highs in the 80s Fahrenheit) and cool winters (highs in the 60s Fahrenheit). Night and morning fog occurs in the late spring and early summer.

Before the arrival of the Europeans, the area was inhabited by members of the Yuman-speaking Indian group. By the mid-19th century the region was home to a few isolated cattle ranches and in the 1870s the Mexican government built a customs house along the U.S.-Mexico border. Then in 1888 a short-lived gold rush in northwestern Baja California created an economic boom, and by 1889 the town of Tijuana was established. During the Mexican Revolution of 1910 revolutionary leader Ricardo Flores Magon and his followers

One of several traffic circles, called glorietas, along the Paseo de los Heroes in Tijuana at dusk.

(*Magonistas*) occupied Tijuana, but on June 22, 1911, Mexican federal troops defeated the Magonistas and retook the city. From 1920-1933 Prohibition, which prohibited the sale, manufacture and consumption of alcoholic beverages within the United States, provided an almost instant economy for Tijuana. Hollywood celebrities were among the flood of "thirsty" Americans seeking out the proliferating number of cantinas, gambling casinos and bordellos. With the repeal of Prohibition in the United States and the outlawing of gambling in Mexico, Tijuana experienced an economic depression. The Mexican government responded by declaring all of Baja California as an economic duty-free zone. Americans have since been crossing the border in search of retail bargains in ever-increasing numbers, providing Tijuana with a replacement source of tourism capital.

Tijuana has become a world-class city, known as well today as a center for international and domestic trade, manufacturing and commerce as it is for tourism. While there are still large areas of abject poverty, as there are in most major cities, Tijuana now boasts modern office buildings, new industrial and manufacturing complexes, an international airport, several universities, museums, libraries, shopping centers, sporting events, recreational facilities and much more. One of the sources of economic growth is the *maquiladoras*, manufacturing plants built with investment capital from businesses in foreign countries such as the United States, Japan, South Korea and others. Tijuana produces a wide variety of manufactured goods, including electronic components, automobile parts and clothing. Improved roadways and an updated transportation network within the city have helped facilitate the transition to a modern city. At the same time, vast numbers of workers and their families have relocated from the Mexican mainland—lured by the top minimum wage and one of the highest standards of living in Mexico, and proximity to the United States. All of these factors have combined to make Tijuana one of the fastest-growing cities on the North American continent. This has also provided the city with a large, educated, middle class economic base.

Tourism remains one of the major industries for Tijuana, and Mexicans attempt to cater to a wide range of interests. Tourists can find museums, historical sites, architectural monuments, bullfights, dog racing, jai alai games, *charreadas* (Mexican rodeos), shopping districts, restaurants and nightclubs. In general, the city exudes a warm welcome to visitors, with friendly and helpful people always willing to provide assistance.

Shopping

Probably the most popular tourist objective in Tijuana is shopping, partially due to the town's status as a duty-free port. U.S. currency is accepted virtually everywhere and some stores even accept U.S. credit cards. While English is spoken at most shops in the downtown area and at principal shopping centers, some knowledge of Spanish is helpful in other parts of the city. Mexican-made goods include tile, ceramics, wrought iron, leather goods, rugs, blankets, basketry, hand-made lace and an assortment of liquors.

The best known shopping area is the downtown district (Centro) on **Avenida Revolución**, where all types of retailers from Sanborn's department store to smaller stores and vendor

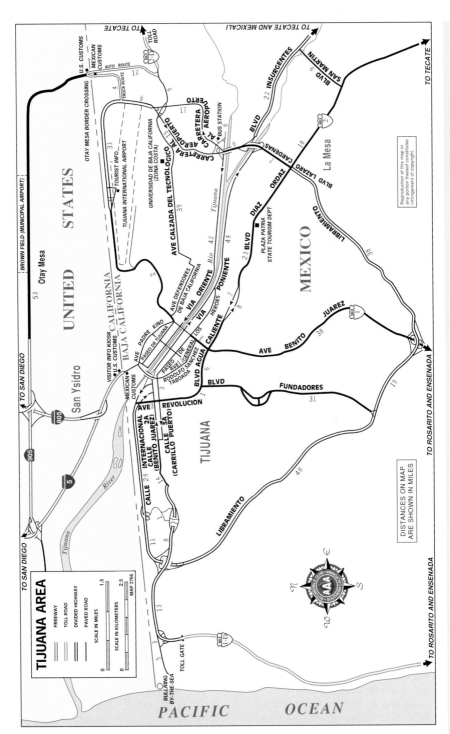

booths line the sidewalks and occupy the numerous arcades. Virtually every type of merchandise sold in Tijuana can be found along this street. **Avenida Constitución**, one block west of Avenida Revolución, has a good selection of shoe stores. These shops are popular with the local residents.

The **Mercado de Artesanías (Crafts Market)**, on Calle 2 between avenidas Negrete and Ocampo, contains a large number of booths selling a variety of crafts and clothing. The primary crafts are pottery and clayware.

Tijuana is well known for automotive work. In the downtown area is a district which specializes in **automobile services**; it is bordered by Calle 3, avenidas Ocampo and Pío Pico, and Calle 8. Shoppers here will find bargains on seat covers, painting and body work. Most auto shops have an English-speaking manager.

Plaza Río Tijuana, located on Paseo de los Héroes in the Río Tijuana district, contains large department stores such as Dorian's, Sears and Comercial Mexicana, numerous specialty shops, several restaurants, bakeries and a movie theater. Across the way is the **Plaza del Zapato (Plaza of Shoes)**, a mall that specializes exclusively in shoes and boots. Next door is the attractive **Plaza Fiesta**, built in the traditional colonial style; it features an assortment of eating and drinking establishments.

The colorful **Mercado Miguel Hidalgo**, at Paseo de los Héroes and Avenida Independencia across from the cultural center, is known primarily for fresh produce and other grocery items. There are also some arts and crafts stalls at this market.

Additional shopping can be found at the **Pueblo Amigo** on Vía Oriente a

half mile southeast of the border crossing, the **Plaza Patria** on Boulevard Diaz Ordaz in the La Mesa district, and along **Boulevard Agua Caliente**.

Dining

With a long and varied list of eating places, Tijuana has fare to please all tastes. The following are some of the better-known restaurants throughout the city. Some of the restaurants listed here are AAA approved; more information about these can be found in the *Lodging & Restaurants* chapter. Non-AAA-approved restaurants are also listed here as a service to visitors.

In the Downtown (Centro) district: **Bol Corona**, Avenida Revolución at Avenida 2, in the Plaza Revolución (Mexican food and varied menu); **Pedrins**, on Avenida Revolución across from the Frontón Palacio (seafood); **Sanborn's**, at Avenida Revolución and Calle 8 (varied menu); and **Tia Juana Tilly's**, on Avenida Revolución at Calle 7a (varied menu).

In the Río Tijuana district: **Las Espuelas**, in Plaza Río Tijuana shopping center (ranch atmosphere, varied menu); **Rívoli**, in the Hotel Lucerna, Paseo de los Héroes and Avenida Rodríguez (varied menu); **Guadalajara Grill**, Paseo de los Héroes and Avenida Diego Rivera (Mexican cuisine, steaks and seafood); **La Taberna de Infante**, on Avenida Diego Rivera between Paseo de los Héroes and Via Poniente (Mediterranean cuisine); and **Ochoa's Restaurant**, on Paseo de los Héroes 61, three blocks west of Hotel Lucerna (varied menu).

In the Agua Caliente district: **Bocaccio's**, near the Tijuana Country Club on Boulevard Agua Caliente 2500 (continental cuisine); **La Escondida de**

Tijuana, Calle Santa Mónica 1, about ¼ mile east of the racetrack (seafood, steaks and international cuisine); **Grand Bistrot Restaurante**, in the Hotel Fiesta Americana, on Boulevard Agua Caliente, just east of Avenida Rodríguez (French cuisine).

Nightclubs

After-dark entertainment in Tijuana includes such diverse activities as floor shows, dancing and various styles of live music. Visitors should be aware that many places maintain a strict dress code and require a cover charge. A few of the city's many popular night spots include **Tijuana Charlie's** in the Pueblo Amigo entertainment center on Paseo de Tijuana; **Tia Juana Tilly's**, by the Frontón Palacio on Avenida Revolución at Calle 7; **Wild Oh!**, on Paseo de los Héroes, just east of Avenida Cuauhtémoc; **Hard Rock Cafe**, on Avenida Revolución at Calle 2a; **Red Square**, at the intersection of Avenida Revolución and Calle 6a; and the lobby bar of the hotel **Plaza las Glorias**.

Points of Interest

CENTRO CULTURAL TIJUANA (TIJUANA CULTURAL CENTER) *Paseo de los Héroes and Avenida Independencia. 01152 (66) 84-1111 or 84-1132. Open daily 11 a.m. to 8 p.m. Museum: adults $2.40, children ages 11 and under, $1.20.* This ultramodern complex features an anthropology museum, a 1000-seat performing arts stage, the Omnitheater, an art gallery, gift shops and a restaurant. The museum contains archaeological, historical and handicraft displays. The performing arts hall offers a variety of musical and dramatic programs. **Omnitheater**, a spherical theater located in the Cultural Center, presents large-format three-dimensional films on various subjects. Gift shops offer books and handcrafted

The futuristic Tijuana Cultural Center houses a museum, a performing arts stage and the spherical Omnitheater.

▼ Quick Guide to Tijuana

Tourist Information Assistance

Secretaría de Turisma or **SECTUR (Mexican Government Tourism Office)** *Main facility on the third level of the Plaza Patria on Boulevard Díaz Ordaz (see* Tijuana Area *map). Open Mon. through Fri., 8 a.m. to 3 and 5 to 7 p.m., Sat. 9 a.m. to 1 p.m. Phone 01152 (66) 81-9492 or 81-9493; FAX 81-9579.* **SECTUR** *Second office on Calle 1 at Avenida Revolución. Open Mon. through Fri. 9 a.m. to 7 p.m., Sat. and Sun. 9 a.m. to 5 p.m. Phone 01152 (66) 88-0555.* SECTUR is an excellent source of tourist information with a very helpful staff. They also offer *Protección al Turista* (Tourist Assistance), which provides legal help for tourists who encounter problems while in Tijuana.

Camara Nacional de Comercio, Servicios y Turismo or **CANACO (National Chamber of Commerce)** *Calle 1 and Avenida Revolución, across the street from the SECTUR office. Open Mon. through Fri., 9 a.m. to 7 p.m.; phone 01152 (66) 85-8472.* Tourist information is provided, as well as information on accommodations, restaurants and retail outlets.

Comité de Turismo y Convenciónes de Tijuana (Tijuana Tourism and Convention Bureau) *On Paseo de los Heroes at Calle Mina. Open Mon. through Fri., 9 a.m. to 6 p.m. Phone 01152 (66) 84-0537.* General tourist information is available here.

The **United States Consulate** *Calle Tapachula 96, Colonia Hipodromo, near the Agua Caliente Racetrack. Open Mon. through Fri., 8 a.m. to 4:30 p.m., except U.S. and Mexican holidays. Phone 01152 (66) 81-7400. In case of an <u>emergency</u> involving a U.S. citizen, pertinent information may be left with the message service at (619) 585-2350.* Legal assistance, information on obtaining a visa and national disaster information is offered.

Newspapers

Several English-language tourist newspapers, including the *Baja Shopper, Baja Visitor* and the *Baja California News,* are distributed at tourist information centers, hotels and certain stores. In addition to advertisements, they contain information about tourist attractions in Tijuana and other parts of Baja California. The *San Diego Union* and the *Los Angeles Times* are sold at some newsstands and hotels. Tijuana has several Spanish-language dailies, including *El Heraldo, Baja California, El Mexicano* and *Novedades.* Newspapers from Mexico City are also available in Tijuana.

Radio and Television Stations

Due to its proximity to the United States, many California television and radio stations are received in Tijuana and northern Baja California. Tijuana also has several television stations of its own, as well as receiving television transmissions from Mexico City. Mexican radio stations feature a variety of music, including ranchera, mariachi, la banda and rock and roll.

Driving in Tijuana

Many visitors find their car to be the most convenient means of transportation, but the traffic in Tijuana can be a bit daunting. (Be sure to have Mexican auto insurance before driving across the border—see Automobile Requirements in the *Tourist Regulations and Travel Tips* chapter.) Many wide, through streets facilitate traffic flow, but outside of the main business districts the side streets are often unpaved and contain ruts and potholes. Speed bumps are common. The old downtown, referred to as *Centro,* including avenidas Revolución and Constitución and calles 2 and 3, can be very congested. Watch for the many one-way street signs. Traffic circles (*glorietas),* such as those found along Paseo de los Héroes and Paseo de Tijuana, often pose a challenge for visitors. When entering a traffic circle, bear right, then follow the flow of traffic counterclockwise. Patience and persistence will prevail. Some traffic lights in Tijuana resemble the old-fashioned American signals of the 1940s and 1950s and are not readily visible. Most parts of the city have street parking and most shopping malls

have free parking lots. The more congested parts of town, such as *Centro,* have a number of pay parking lots. Some visitors prefer to park on the San Ysidro (California) side of the border and then rent a car in Mexico. Several major American auto rental agencies have facilities in Tijuana.

Local Transportation

A typical taxi ride within town or from the border area costs anywhere from $4-8 on average, although sometimes bargaining can lower the fare. A price should be agreed upon before getting into the cab. There are also *taxis de ruta* (route taxis), operating along preset routes, that will pick up and drop off passengers anywhere along the line. These taxis are color-coordinated according to their route and have an average fare of 50¢.

City bus lines provide service to all parts of Tijuana, running frequently in the downtown area and on major thoroughfares. Like the route taxis, the city buses are color-coordinated according to their designated route. The basic fare is only about 25¢. (For bus travel between Tijuana and other parts of Baja California, see Bus Service in the Transportation section of the *Appendix.)*

goods for sale. The Tijuana Cultural Center was designed by the noted Mexican architect Pedro Ramírez Vásquez.

MEXITLAN *Calle 2 and Avenida Ocampo. 01152 (66) 38-4101; (619) 685-3628. Open all year, Tues. through*

Sun. 9 a.m. to 5 p.m. Adults $1.75; children ages 11 and under, free. This attraction contains an outdoor display covering a city block, featuring 200 scale models of the nation's greatest archaeological monuments, historic structures, cathedrals, churches, plazas, stadiums and other architectural treasures. Focusing mostly on mainland Mexico, the 1:25 scale replicas span four centuries of Mexican history. Mexitlan also has restaurants, snack bars and a souvenir shop. The models have working scale lights that are turned on during overcast days. Pedro Ramírez Vásquez, noted Mexican architect, designed Mexitlan. Free parking is available on the street level.

MONUMENTO DE LA FRONTERA (BOUNDARY MONUMENT) *Near the Pacific Ocean in Playas de Tijuana, north of the bullring.* At the fence separating Tijuana from Imperial Beach, California, lies the monument marking the western terminus of the Mexico-United States boundary. Bilingual plaques give the history of the border region.

MUSEO DE CERA (WAX MUSEUM) *Calle 1 near Avenida Revolución. Open Mon. through Fri. 10 a.m. to 7 p.m., Sat. and Sun. 10 a.m. to 8 p.m. Adults $1; children ages 5 and under, free.* Visitors are greeted by life-like figures from history, cinema and music, both Mexican and foreign. A few examples include Emiliano Zapata, Pedro Infante, Mahatma Gandhi, Mikhail Gorbachev, and the comedy team of Laurel and Hardy.

NUESTRA SEÑORA DE GUADALUPE CATHEDRAL *Calle 2 and Avenida Niños Héroes. Open from dawn til dusk.* The twin towers of this classic example of Mexican cathedral architecture rise majestically above the old downtown district. This is an active cathedral with daily worship services.

PARQUE TENIENTE VICENTE GUERRERO *Calle 3 at Avenida F.* This pleasant park is named in honor of Lt. Vicente Guerrero, who successfully led the federal troops against the revolutionary forces of Ricardo Flores Magon

in 1911. The Héroes of 1911 Monumento is dedicated to the defenders of Tijuana during the revolution.

Spectator Sports

BULLFIGHTS *The season runs from May through Sept. with July, Aug. and Sept. being the busiest months; held on selected Sun. at 4 p.m. Ticket prices range from $17 to $35 (the shaded side of the arena is always more expensive.) Tickets can be obtained from Five Star Tours, phone (619) 232-5049, and at the bullrings.* Some of the world's top matadors perform in Tijuana, with bullfights alternating between El Toreo and Plaza Monumental (Bullring-by-the-Sea).

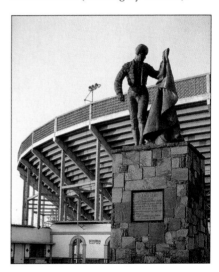

Bullring-by-the sea, Tijuana

El Toreo *2 miles east of downtown Tijuana on Boulevard Agua Caliente. 01152 (66) 86-1510.*

Plaza Monumental (Bullring-by-the-Sea) *6 miles west of downtown Tijuana via Hwy. 1-D. 01152 (66) 80-1808.*

CHARREADAS (MEXICAN RODEOS) *Most weekends from May through Sept. Events alternate among several charro*

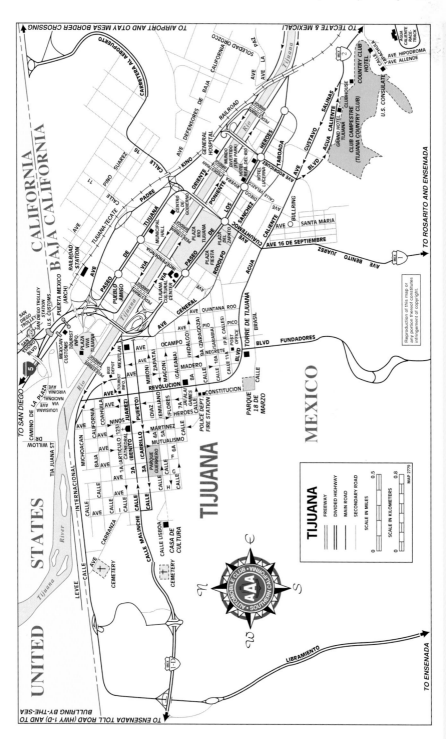

MEXICO HIGHWAY 1

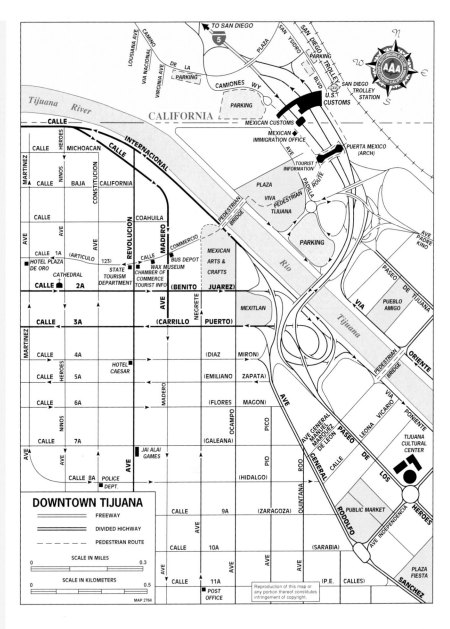

grounds in the Tijuana area. Most charreadas are free. For more information call
the Mexican Government Tourism Office
at 01152 (66) 81-9492. These colorful
equestrian events feature ornate costumes and festive music.

DOG RACING *Greyhounds race around
an oblong track in pursuit of a mechanized
prey in this fast-paced spectator sport.*

Caliente Racetrack *3 miles east of
downtown Tijuana off Boulevard Agua*

Agua Caliente racetrack

Caliente. (619) 231-1910. Greyhounds run nightly at 7:45 p.m. and on Sat. and Sun. at 2 p.m. General admission free. Turf Club Restaurant open Wed. through Fri. 7 to 11 p.m. Wagering on U.S. horse racing and professional sports teams can be made at the sports book windows.

JAI ALAI *Jai Alai is a fast-moving court game using a ball* and a long curved wicker basket strapped to the wrist.

Frontón Palacio On *Avenida Revolución at Calle 7.* 01152 (66) 85-2524 or *(619) 231-1910.* Mon. and Tues. at noon and Thur. through Sun. at 8 p.m. General admission ranges from $2 to $5; $20 admission to the *cancha club* (refundable with a wagering voucher).

The fast-paced game of jai alai is played on an indoor court.

MEXICO HIGHWAY 1
Distance Table

This table give distances between major points in Baja California both in miles and in kilometers; the italicized (upper) figures indicate miles, while the figures in regular type (lower) denote kilometers. All figures have been rounded off to the nearest whole mile or kilometer. To find the distance between two points, first find the northern point and read down the column below the name. Second, find the southern point and read across the column to the left of the name. The intersection of the two columns shows the distance. Note: Figures are based on the use of Mexico Highway 1-D (Toll Road) between Tijuana and Ensenada.

Distances shown as **miles / kilometers** (upper figure = miles, lower figure = kilometers).

	Tijuana	Ensenada	Colonet	San Quintín	El Rosario	Cataviña	Bahía de los Angeles Jct.	Guerrero Negro	San Ignacio	Santa Rosalía	Mulege	Loreto	Ciudad Constitución	La Paz
Ensenada	68/109													
Colonet	144/232	76/123												
San Quintín	187/301	119/191	43/69											
El Rosario	223/359	155/249	79/127	36/58										
Cataviña	299/481	231/372	155/249	112/180	76/122									
Bahía de los Angeles Jct.	364/586	296/476	220/354	177/285	141/227	65/105								
Guerrero Negro	444/714	376/605	300/483	257/414	221/356	145/234	80/129							
San Ignacio	532/856	464/747	388/624	345/555	309/497	233/376	168/271	88/142						
Santa Rosalía	577/928	509/819	433/697	390/628	354/570	278/449	213/344	133/215	45/73					
Mulege	615/990	547/880	471/758	428/689	392/631	316/510	251/405	171/276	83/134	38/61				
Loreto	699/1125	631/1015	555/893	512/824	476/766	400/646	335/541	255/412	167/270	122/197	84/136			
Ciudad Constitución	788/1268	720/1158	644/1036	601/967	565/909	489/789	424/684	344/555	256/413	211/340	173/279	89/143		
La Paz	922/1483	854/1374	778/1252	735/1183	699/1125	623/1005	558/900	478/771	390/629	345/556	307/495	223/359	134/216	
Cabo San Lucas	1059/1704	991/1594	915/1472	872/1403	836/1345	760/1226	695/1121	615/992	527/850	482/777	444/716	360/580	271/437	137*/221*

*Distance via Mexico Highway 19 is only 96 miles, 154 km.

◢ Travelogue

Tijuana to Rosarito via Old Highway 1

(15 mi., 24 km.; 0:45 hrs.)

Highway 1—the old road—is a toll-free highway leading from the international border at Tijuana to Ensenada. The route passes through a modern maze of interchanges, southeast along Paseo de los Héroes, then south at the Cuauhtémoc monument (follow signs marked "Ensenada" or "Rosarito"). The 11 miles between Libramiento and Rosarito are four-lane divided highway. After curving through commercial areas, then low hills and farmland, Highway 1 crosses the toll road just north of Rosarito.

00.0 Tijuana (U.S. border crossing).
01.9 Boulevard Agua Caliente (see *Highway 2*). Ahead to the left are the downtown bullring and the Agua Caliente Racetrack.
05.7 Interchange with Libramiento, a bypass that skirts the southern part of Tijuana.
07.2 La Gloria (San Antonio de los Buenos), a village with a Pemex station and a few stores.
15.4 Rosarito, town center.

Rosarito

(See also *Lodging & Restaurants* and *Campgrounds & Trailer Parks*.)

On a favored Pacific Ocean site fronting several miles of white sandy beach, Rosarito's mild semiarid climate is similar to that of coastal San Diego County. Also known as Rosarito Beach/Playas de Rosarito, the town is situated at the junction of divided Mexico Highways 1 and 1-D, both of which are four lanes from Tijuana. With its pleasant environment and proximity to Southern California, the town is one of the fastest growing in Baja California.

Rosarito's reputation as a vacation spot began in 1927 with the opening of the Rosarito Beach Hotel, the focus of recreational activities for many decades. The village became a destination for fly-in celebrities from the United States who sought seclusion. With the paving of the highway in 1930, a small stream of tourists started to travel the 15 miles south from the border to Rosarito's shores. Still a village in 1960, it has become a bigger boom town with each succeeding decade, with a current population of about 27,000. In the face of perpetual new construction, local leaders are

▼ Quick Guide to Rosarito

Tourist Information and Assistance

Rosarito Convention and Visitors Bureau *In the northern part of town, in Quinta Plaza. Open daily 9 a.m. to 5 p.m. 01152 (661) 2-0396; (800) 962-2252.*

Secretaría de Turisma or SECTUR (Mexican Government Tourism Office) *Avenida Juárez and Calle Acacias next to the police station. Open Mon. through Sat. 9 a.m. to 7 p.m., Sun. 10 a.m. to 6 p.m. 01152 (661) 2-0200.* They also offer *Protección al Turista*, which provides legal assistance to tourists in need.

MEXICO HIGHWAY 1

striving to preserve the community's relaxed uncongested atmosphere, so attractive to locals and visitors alike.

Visitors along the wide Avenida Benito Juárez pass some three miles of restaurants, souvenir shops, food markets, an open-air bazaar, real estate offices, hospitals and a gasoline station. Quinta Plaza, in the northern part of town, has a *Comercial Mexicana* discount store, restaurants, shops and a convention center.

A growing number of hotels and motels serve tourists, and luxurious condominiums keep rising along the waterfront. A large oil-fueled power plant north of town supplies electricity to Tijuana and Rosarito. Favorite pastimes are swimming and surfing in the ocean, and horseback riding along the beach or inland; bicycle and motorcycle races start and finish here. (The Rosarito-Ensenada 50-Mile Fun Bike Ride takes place every April and September, attracting throngs of visitors.)

▟ Travelogue

Rosarito to Ensenada via Old Highway 1
(50 mi., 82 km.; 1:15 hrs.)

South of Rosarito, Mexico highways 1 and 1-D run parallel to one another for 24 miles along the rocky Pacific shoreline. At La Misión the old highway turns inland, climbs onto a level plateau, then curves gradually down to the coast at San Miguel, where it joins the divided highway leading into Ensenada. **Caution: Speed berms on Boulevard Teniente Azueta just west of downtown Ensenada can damage vehicles if taken too fast.**

00.0	**Rosarito, town center.**
01.7	**Popotla,** a scattered seaside settlement with a large trailer park for permanent residents.
05.7	**Calafia Resort,** built on terraces overlooking the sea, has a popular restaurant and disco, a museum and a mobile home park with overnight accommodations.
06.6	**Las Gaviotas,** a residential subdivision overlooking the ocean.
13.0	**Cantamar,** an oceanside resort complex with a Pemex station, and **Puerto Nuevo,** a community with over 30 restaurants specializing in lobster.
23.8	**La Misión** is a quiet village located in a steeply walled valley. On the south side of the valley are the ruins of Mission San Miguel, founded in 1787. The highway climbs out of the valley past abrupt volcanic bluffs via a series of narrow switchback curves.
43.0	**San Miguel Village,** a beach camp at the junction of highways 1 and 1-D. The rocky beach here is popular with surfers.
44.4	**Junction with Highway 3,** which leads northward to Guadalupe and Tecate (see *Highway 3*). Just past the interchange is El Sauzal, a sprawling community with a large fish cannery.
48.0	**Junction.** Although Highway 1 swings inland here, the preferred route into downtown Ensenada (signed Centro) follows the coastline to the right.
50.4	**Ensenada,** at the intersection of boulevards Teniente Azueta and Lázaro Cárdenas.

Ceramic vendors south of Rosarito.

◪ Travelogue

Tijuana to Ensenada via Toll Highway 1-D
(68 mi., 109 km.; 1:30 hrs.)

The toll highway—a divided, fully access-controlled expressway—provides the fastest and safest route to Ensenada. Stopping along the highway is prohibited except in emergencies; call boxes are spaced along the expressway for travelers in distress. Many ramps offer access to seaside resorts and various points of interest. From the international border, follow the prominent "Ensenada Toll Road" (*Ensenada Cuota*) signs along Calle Internacional to Mexico Highway 1-D. This route parallels the border fence and bypasses much of Tijuana's congestion. Detours are common, however, and traffic is sometimes routed through downtown streets. Highway 1-D runs west to the first toll station at Playas de Tijuana, then turns south, following the scenic shoreline most of the way to Ensenada. **Caution: Speed berms on Boulevard Teniente Azueta just west of downtown Ensenada can damage vehicles if taken too fast.**

00.0 **Tijuana (U.S. border crossing).**

04.4 **Exit for Playas de Tijuana and Bullring-by-the-Sea. No toll is charged to this point.**

04.8 **Toll station, Playas de Tijuana (see Toll Rates table in this chapter).**

12.0 **Real del Mar, a resort complex with a hotel, tennis courts and a golf course.**

13.0 **Exit for San Antonio and Tijuana/Rosarito KOA.**

17.4 **Rosarito Norte interchange; junction with Highway 1 to Rosarito. (Although most tourists take this highway to Rosarito, the town is described**

MEXICO HIGHWAY 1

TOLL RATES, TIJUANA TO ENSENADA (in dollars)

Car, Motorcycle, Van, Pickup Truck	$ 4.10
2 Axles: Motorhome, Cargo Truck	$ 8.30
3 Axles: Vehicle with Trailer (Tourist or Commercial), Cargo Truck	$12.40
4 Axles: Vehicle with Trailer, Cargo Truck	$16.40

The toll collected at each of the three toll gates is one-third of the above totals.

previously in the log for Old Highway 1, which passes directly through Rosarito.)

20.8 Rosarito Sur interchange; junction with Highway 1. To the east rises the impressive Mesa de Rosarito.

21.1 Toll station, Rosarito.

32.1 Exit for Cantamar and Puerto Nuevo; junction with Highway 1. Puerto Nuevo (Newport) is a fast-growing community with a hotel and over 30 restaurants specializing in lobster.

40.0 Exit for La Fonda, site of a popular restaurant, and the village of La Misión, which is 2.9 miles beyond.

44.4 Exit for La Salina (see *Campgrounds & Trailer Parks*).

47.4 Exit for Bajamar, a resort development with houses, condominiums, a hotel, tennis and a golf course, the Bajamar Country Club.

51.1 El Mirador, a rest stop with restaurant. An overlook pro-vides a sweeping coastal panorama. At this point, Highway 1-D makes a sharp turn, which requires a reduction in driving speed. The next several miles are subject to slides.

57.7 Exit for Playa Saldamando campground.

60.4 Toll station, San Miguel.

60.9 Exit for San Miguel Village; junction with Highway 1. The last eight miles to Ensenada are on a toll-free divided highway.

62.3 Junction with Highway 3, which leads northward to Guadalupe and Tecate (see *Highway 3*). Just past the interchange is El Sauzal, a sprawling community with a large fish cannery. Many hotels, motels and trailer parks are located along the beach between here and Ensenada.

68.3 Ensenada, at the junction of boulevards Teniente Azueta and Lázaro Cárdenas.

ꙮ Ensenada ꙮ

(See also Lodging & Restaurants and Campgrounds & Trailer Parks.)

The third largest city in Baja California, Ensenada, meaning cove or small bay, occupies a lowland that slopes gradually downward from scrub-covered hills to the shore of lovely Bahía de Todos Santos. Thanks to its scenic setting, beautiful beaches, numerous duty-free shops, excellent sportfishing, abundance of fine accommodations and proximity to the United States, Ensenada is the peninsula's foremost summer resort. Hundreds of thousands of vacationers and weekend tourists flock to the city every year. The climate is very similar to that of San Diego, with mild, pleasant winters and sunny summers kept cool by refreshing sea breezes. Rainfall averages about 10 inches per year, most of which occurs from December through March.

With its protected harbor and modern dock facilities, Ensenada is also Baja California's leading seaport. It has become a major port of call for cruise ships. Some of the agricultural wealth of the Mexicali Valley is brought to Ensenada by truck, loaded onto ocean-going freighters and shipped to mainland Mexico and the Orient. Commercial fishing and seafood processing are other important contributors to the local economy; just west of the city is the largest fish cannery on Mexico's Pacific coast. Also in Ensenada is Bodegas de Santo Tomás—the nation's biggest winery.

In 1602, 60 years after Juan Rodríguez Cabrillo's voyage of discovery along the Pacific coast, Sebastián Vizcaíno sailed into the bay and was so enthralled by its beauty that he named it after all the saints—Ensenada de Todos los Santos. Lack of fresh water precluded the establishment of a permanent settlement for more than two centuries, but

MEXICO HIGHWAY 1

Ensenada is a growing metropolis.

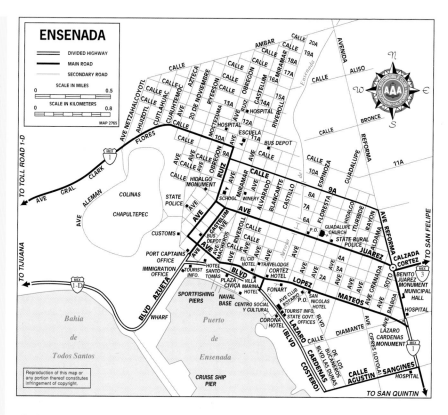

ENSENADA

DIVIDED HIGHWAY
MAIN ROAD
SECONDARY ROAD

SCALE IN MILES
0 — 0.5

SCALE IN KILOMETERS
0 — 0.8

MAP 2765

Reproduction of this map or any portion thereof constitutes infringement of copyright.

the bay was a frequent port of call for the treasure-laden Manila galleons and for the privateers who preyed on them, as well as for whaling ships and fur traders. In the early 19th century, ranchers moved into the area, and Ensenada became a supply point for the missionaries and pioneers trying to secure a foothold in Mexico's northern frontier. In 1870 gold was discovered at nearby Real de Castillo, and Ensenada boomed, soon becoming an important supply depot for the miners. In 1882 it was made the capital of the territory, and two years later it became headquarters for a land company organized to colonize a huge land grant covering much of the peninsula. Shortly after the turn of the century, however, the mines gave out, the land company

folded, the capital was moved to Mexicali, and Ensenada dwindled into a sleepy fishing village.

In the mid-1930s, two important factors combined to bring about a resurgence for Ensenada. First, agricultural reform and development in the Mexicali Valley created the need for a seaport to handle the export of farm products. And second, the completion of the paved highway from Tijuana permitted large numbers of American tourists to discover the area's rich recreational potential. Ensenada prospered and continues to grow; the city's population is about 230,000. Today it is the seat of government of the *municipio* of Ensenada, which extends south to the 28th Parallel and includes

▼ *Quick Guide to Ensenada*

Tourist Information and Assistance
Secretaría de Turisma or SECTUR (Mexican Government Tourism Office) *On Boulevard Lázaro Cárdenas (Costero) and Calle Las Rocas, next to the other state government buildings. Open Mon. through Fri. 9 a.m. to 7 p.m., Sat. 10 a.m. to 3 p.m., Sun. 10 a.m. to 2 p.m. 01152 (617) 2-3000 or 2-3022.* Protección al Turista (tourist assistance) provides legal assistance to tourists.

Tourist and Convention Bureau
A booth is located on Boulevard Lázaro Cárdenas near the western entrance to the city. Open Mon. through Sat. 9 a.m. to 6 p.m. and Sun. 9 a.m. to 2 p.m. Phone 01152 (617) 8-2411.

Newspapers
The English-language *Baja Sun* contains travel information, articles about Ensenada and other parts of Baja California, and numerous useful advertisements. California newspapers are available. The Spanish-language *El Mexicano* gives news of Ensenada and the state.

Radio and TV
Several American radio stations come in during the day, and more can be heard at night. Ensenada, of course, has its own radio stations. Radio Bahía Ensenada, 1590 AM, has an English/Spanish program on Saturday, 4 to 6 p.m. Most important hotels have satellite dish antennas to receive several American television stations, in addition to the Mexican channels.

Driving in Ensenada
Away from the heavily traveled arterial streets—those marked on the map with heavy black lines—Ensenada is not a difficult city for finding one's way; much of it is flat and laid out in a grid pattern. It is important, however, to watch for traffic lights and street signs; lights are often small and hard to see from a distance, and some streets are one way. In most of the city there is little problem parking on the street or in the local shopping centers, although in the business districts street parking is scarce and parking meters require Mexican coins.

Local Transportation
Taxi service is readily available downtown and at hotels. In Mexico the ubiquitous taxi driver soliciting customers is sometimes an annoyance to the tourist, but once hired, he is usually friendly and courteous. Be sure to agree on the fare before getting in.

Local bus service is offered at low prices for those who wish to ride to the outlying districts and who enjoy mixing with residents. Intercity buses follow both highways 1 and 1-D (the expressway) to Tijuana. Long-distance buses head south toward La Paz (see Bus Service in the Transportation section of the *Appendix*).

Ensenada's Bahía de Todos Santos hosts numerous cruise ships.

shoreline on both the east and west coasts of the state of Baja California.

Probably because of its dual position as both an important commercial center and a popular resort, Ensenada has two separate business districts. The downtown area, containing stores, banks, restaurants, cantinas and offices patronized primarily by local residents, is along avenidas Ruiz and Juárez. Tourist activity, on the other hand, centers on avenidas López Mateos and Lázaro Cárdenas (Costero), which are lined with motels, restaurants, nightclubs, sportfishing firms and dozens of shops catering to visitors.

Shopping

The city's easygoing, low-pressure atmosphere makes shopping in Ensenada an enjoyable experience for most tourists. In addition to the great savings on duty-free imported goods, Mexican-made items are also good buys. These include pottery, jewelry, baskets, ceramics, leather goods (jackets, sandals and purses), wrought iron furniture and embroidered clothing. Most shops have fixed prices. **Centro Artesenal/Mexican Hand Crafts Center**

is a large group of arts and crafts stores, located on Boulevard Lázaro Cárdenas (Costero) at Avenida Castillo.

In Ensenada along and near avenidas Ruiz, Juárez and Reforma, travelers can find many stores carrying a variety of consumer goods, including food, auto parts and camping supplies. The city also has many attractive supermarkets and discount stores.

Dining

Some of the restaurants listed here are AAA approved; more information about these can be found in the *Lodging & Restaurants* chapter of this book. Non-AAA-approved restaurants are also mentioned here as a courtesy to our readers.

Among Ensenada's better-known eating establishments are **Casamar**, on Boulevard Lázaro Cárdenas (Costero) 987 (seafood); **El Rey Sol**, in town at avenidas López Mateos and Blancarte (French and Mexican cuisine); **El Campanario**, in Hotel Misión Santa Isabel (varied menu); **Enrique's**, on Highway 1-D, 1½ miles north of town (Mexican and seafood specialties); **La Cueva de los Tigres**, on the beach three miles south of town via Highway 1 and gravel road (seafood, steaks and Mexican cuisine); the **Restaurant at Punta Morro** in the hotel of the same name (seafood and varied international cuisine); and **Viva Mexico Taquería** on Avenida López Mateos at Avenida Granada (tacos, steaks and carne asada). The widely known **Hussong's Bar**, on

Avenida Ruíz near López Mateos, has an old-fashioned rollicking cantina and a souvenir shop. In addition, Ensenada has many other large restaurants, plus numerous small cafes with reasonable prices.

Nightclubs

Ensenada is a lively place after dark. Many night spots and discos are found on or near Avenida López Mateos. The hotels Bahía, El Cid, La Pinta, Las Rosas and San Nicolás are well known for live entertainment and dancing.

Points of Interest

BODEGAS DE SANTO TOMAS *Avenida Miramar at Calle 7. 01152 (617) 8-2509. Wine tasting and tours daily at 11 a.m., 1 and 3 p.m. Tour charge $2.*

CENTRO CIVICO, SOCIAL Y CULTURAL *Boulevard Lázaro Cárdenas at Avenida Club Rotario.* Formerly called Riviera del Pacífico, this building once served as a glamorous resort and casino renowned for its impressive Mediterranean architecture. Now it is a cultural center with an art gallery, a museum and attractive gardens containing historic monuments and plaques. It is also a site for many local civic and social events.

CHAPULTEPEC HILLS *Via Avenida Alemán.* This attractive residential section overlooks the city and is an excellent vantage point for photographers. Another scenic viewpoint is the hill at Avenida Moctezuma and Calle 12.

MUSEO DE CIENCIAS DE ENSENADA *Avenida Obregón between calles 14 and 15. 01152 (617) 8-7192. Open Tues. through Fri. 9 a.m. to 5 p.m., Sat. and Sun. noon to 5 p.m. Admission 80¢.* This science museum features astronomy, oceanography and marine life exhibits for the region. A special exhibit stresses endangered animal species.

NUESTRA SEÑORA DE GUADALUPE *Calle 6 and Avenida Floresta.* Built in the Spanish Colonial style, this church's im-

A rainbow adds to the beauty of the Plaza Cívica in Ensenada.

MEXICO HIGHWAY 1

pressive twin towers make it one of the most prominent structures in Ensenada.

PLAZA CIVICA *Boulevard Lázaro Cárdenas (Costero) at Avenida Riveroll.* This landscaped court contains 12-foot-high busts of Mexican heroes Juárez, Carranza and Hidalgo. Nearby at Avenida Alvarado is the Naval Base, which at sunrise and sunset has colorful flag ceremonies with a drum and bugle corps. Horse-drawn carriages for sightseeing depart from here.

Vineyards are part of the beautiful scenery in Santo Tomás Valley.

▛ Travelogue

Ensenada to Colonet

(76 mi., 123 km.; 1:45 hrs.)

Leaving Ensenada, Highway 1 is an undivided four-lane road as far as Maneadero. It passes through commercial districts, then enters a coastal lowland where olives, vegetables and chili peppers are the principal crops. Beyond Maneadero, open countryside gives way to chaparral-clad slopes. The highway is quite narrow, and careful driving is essential. Thirty miles south of Ensenada, Highway 1 crosses the wide, beautiful Santo Tomás Valley, passing the vineyards of Mexico's largest winery. It then winds among steep hills and grassy valleys to San Vicente, where dairy and beef cattle graze. From here to Colonet, the landscape gradually becomes drier and less rugged.

00.0   **Ensenada, at the intersection of boulevards Teniente Azueta and Lázaro Cárdenas. Follow Lázaro Cárdenas south to its end, then turn left.**

01.9   **Junction with Highway 1, turn right.**

04.9   **El Ciprés, site of Ensenada Airport and a large military camp.**

06.9   **Turnoff to Estero Beach. The paved side road leads past several curio shops to a popular beach resort area. The sandy beaches and quiet waters of Bahía de Todos Santos are ideal for water sports.**

09.4   **Junction with road to Baja Country Club.**

10.6   **Maneadero, a community of about 30,000 people, at the junction with the paved road to Punta Banda (see Side Route to Punta Banda). This fast-growing agricultural market center has two Pemex stations, several small restaurants and many markets and other stores, including auto parts shops. Drivers should watch for unmarked speed bumps.**

21.6   **Ejido Uruápan, which offers camping, hunting and hot springs.**

26.5   **Junction with the gravel road to La Bocana and Puerto Santo Tomás (see Side Route to Puerto Santa Tomás).**

28.9 **Santo Tomás** (see *Campgrounds & Trailer Parks*), a village that has become well-known because of the domestic wine of the same name. A Pemex station (*magna sin*) and general store are located here. Ruins of Mission Santo Tomás are located just west of the trailer park.

45.6 Junction with the paved road to Ejido Eréndira (see Side Route to Ejido Eréndira).

51.9 A rough dirt road leads to the ruins of Mission San Vicente Ferrer, 0.6 mile to the west.

52.6 San Vicente, a busy farming center with a population of 6000. Facilities include two Pemex stations (*magna sin*), several stores, cafes, a motel, tire shops and an auto supply house.

75.6 Colonet, at the junction to San Antonio del Mar (see Side Route to San Antonio del Mar). Colonet, a center for farmers and ranchers in the area, offers a selection of goods and services.

🚙 Side Route
Maneadero to Punta Banda and La Bufadora
(14 mi., 23 km.; 0:30 hr.)
(See also *Campgrounds & Trailer Parks.*)

This short side trip is an ideal excursion for visitors to the Ensenada area and is a popular family outing for local residents.

From its junction with Highway 1, BCN 23 winds through olive orchards and cultivated fields for a few miles, then leads onto Punta Banda, the rocky peninsula that forms the southern end of Bahía de Todos Santos. Seven miles west of Maneadero is the turnoff to Baja Beach and Tennis Club, a private resort. Another mile west is a group of trailer parks and campgrounds on the shore of the bay;

La Bufadora is a natural sea spout, shooting ocean spray high into the air.

MEXICO HIGHWAY 1

La Jolla Beach Camp and Villarino Camp offer extensive camping facilities.

Beyond the trailer parks and campgrounds, the road has numerous curves and grades as it climbs to the summit of the peninsula and drops to the edge of a small rocky cove that is popular with skin and scuba divers. The road is badly potholed towards the end. Located here are three small restaurants and a shop offering diving supplies. Near the western tip of Punta Banda, the road ends at a parking lot (fee). From this point, steps lead to the main attraction of the trip—*La Bufadora*—a natural sea spout that shoots spray high into the air. Its most dramatic activity occurs during incoming tides. At the base of the steps are a bazaar and food stands.

Side Route

Santo Tomás to La Bocana and Puerto Santo Tomás
(15 mi., 24 km.; 1 hr.)

Visitors are attracted to this route by the scenic, rocky Pacific coastline. The graded road, suitable for sturdy passenger cars, follows the Santo Tomás Valley west to La Bocana, then winds along the coast northwest to Puerto Santo Tomás.

The road branches off Highway 1 at Ejido Ajusco, just north of Santo Tomás. After passing vineyards, fenced pastures and grain fields it follows the contours of the northern wall of the valley; an old route can be seen meandering along the sandy stream bed below.

The road reaches a junction at 15.6 miles. The fork to the left goes to a campground and a cement plant. The right fork leads to the tourist village of La Bocana de Santo Tomás, which offers rustic cabins with gas stoves and electricity, a small store, boats for rent and a small freshwater lagoon; a minimal charge is made for camping. The drive north from La Bocana offers good views of sharply eroded cliffs, offshore rocks and the rugged coastline. A number of attractive American vacation houses face the sea. The road has some rough spots as it approaches

The coastline along the Pacific at La Bocana is rugged and beautiful.

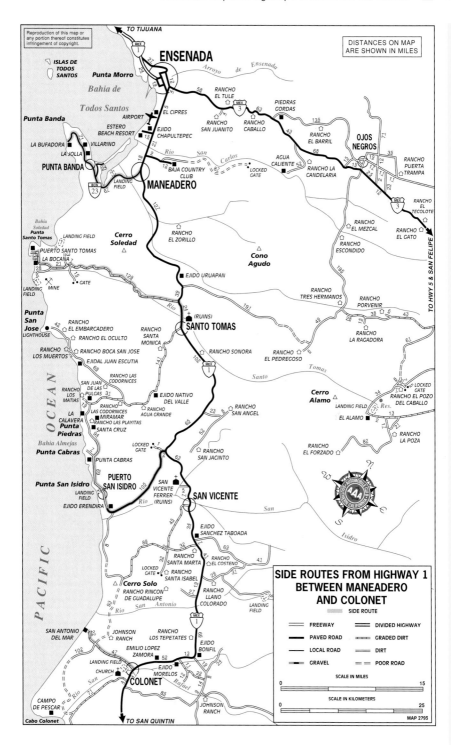

MEXICO HIGHWAY 1

TO TIJUANA

ENSENADA

DISTANCES ON MAP ARE SHOWN IN MILES

ISLAS DE TODOS SANTOS

Punta Morro

Bahia de

Todos Santos

Punta Banda

AIRPORT

EL CIPRES

ESTERO BEACH RESORT

EJIDO CHAPULTEPEC

LA BUFADORA

VILLARINO

LA JOLLA

PUNTA BANDA

LANDING FIELD

MANEADERO

Baja Country Club

RANCHO EL TULE

RANCHO SAN JUANITO

RANCHO CABALLO

PIEDRAS GORDAS

RANCHO EL BARRIL

OJOS NEGROS

RANCHO PUERTA TRAMPA

AGUA CALIENTE

LOCKED GATE

RANCHO LA CANDELARIA

RANCHO EL TECOLOTE

RANCHO EL MEZCAL

RANCHO EL GATO

RANCHO ESCONDIDO

Cerro Soledad

RANCHO EL ZORILLO

Cono Agudo

Bahia Soledad Punta Santo Tomas

LANDING FIELD

PUERTO SANTO TOMAS

LA BOCANA

MINE

GATE

EJIDO URUAPAN

RANCHO TRES HERMANOS

RANCHO PORVENIR

LANDING FIELD

Punta San Jose

LIGHTHOUSE

RANCHO EL EMBARCADERO

RANCHO EL OCULTO

RANCHO SANTA MONICA

(RUINS)

SANTO TOMAS

RANCHO SONORA

RANCHO EL PEDREGOSO

Cerro Alamo

LANDING FIELD

LOCKED GATE

RANCHO EL POZO DEL CABALLO

RANCHO LA RAGADORA

EL ALAMO

RANCHO LOS MUERTOS

RANCHO BOCA SAN JOSE

EJIDAL JUAN ESCUTIA

RANCHO LAS CODORNICES

SAN JUAN DE LAS PULGAS

EJIDO NATIVO DEL VALLE

RANCHO AGUA GRANDE

RANCHO SAN ANGEL

RANCHO LA POZA

RANCHO LOS MATIAS

LA CALAVERA

Punta Piedras

RANCHO LAS CODORNICES

MIRAMAR

RANCHO LAS PLAYITAS

SANTA CRUZ

LOCKED GATE

RANCHO SAN JACINTO

RANCHO EL FORZADO

Bahia Almejas

Punta Cabras

PUNTA CABRAS

PUERTO SAN ISIDRO

Punta San Isidro

LANDING FIELD

EJIDO ERENDIRA

SAN VICENTE FERRER (RUINS)

SAN VICENTE

EJIDO SANCHEZ TABOADA

RANCHO SANTA MARTA

RANCHO EL COSTENO

RANCHO SANTA ISABEL

LOCKED GATE

Cerro Solo

RANCHO RINCON DE GUADALUPE

Rio San Antonio

RANCHO LLANO COLORADO

LANDING FIELD

SAN ANTONIO DEL MAR

JOHNSON RANCH

RANCHO LOS TEPETATES

EJIDO BONFIL

EMILIO LOPEZ ZAMORA

LANDING FIELD

CHURCH

EJIDO MORELOS

COLONET

Rio San Rafael

JOHNSON RANCH

CAMPO DE PESCAR

Cabo Colonet

TO SAN QUINTIN

TO HWY 5 & SAN FELIPE

OCEAN

PACIFIC

SIDE ROUTES FROM HIGHWAY 1 BETWEEN MANEADERO AND COLONET

SIDE ROUTE

FREEWAY — DIVIDED HIGHWAY

PAVED ROAD — GRADED DIRT

LOCAL ROAD — DIRT

GRAVEL — POOR ROAD

SCALE IN MILES

0 — 15

SCALE IN KILOMETERS

0 — 25

AAA

MAP 2793

Puerto Santo Tomás, a small fishing village with rustic houses and campsites for rent. Trails suitable for motorcycles and four-wheel-drive vehicles crisscross the area.

🚙 Side Route

Highway 1 to Ejido Eréndira, Puerto San Isidro and Points North
(13 mi., 21 km.; 0:45 hr.)

The signed junction with the paved road to Ejido Eréndira is 6.9 miles north of San Vicente. From its junction with Highway 1 the road follows the east wall of a narrow, attractive tree-lined canyon, past chaparral-clad slopes similar to those of many parts of Southern California. About 6.4 miles from the main highway the road crosses a bridge as the canyon empties into a larger wider arroyo, which the road follows for 4.3 miles to a junction.

To the right is Ejido Eréndira, a farming community located just inland from the ocean. Facilities include two cafes, some stores and a Pemex station. Cabins, RV spaces and fishing boats are available for rent. Two miles beyond Ejido Eréndira the road reaches the beach, changes to a rough dirt surface, then turns northward and soon arrives in Puerto San Isidro, site of a government-operated oyster and abalone hatchery and a small cluster of dwellings overlooking the coast. The road continues northward along the rocky coastline for five miles to Punta Cabras, a collection of rustic beach homes and an electric plant under construction. There is little sandy beach along this stretch, but explorers will

enjoy the cliffs, the rock shelves jutting into the water and the many seawater spouts. North of Punta Cabras is a long sandy beach on crescent-shaped Bahía Almejas.

🚙 Side Route

Colonet to San Antonio del Mar
(8 mi., 12 km.; 0:30 hr.)

This partly graded dirt road, which leaves Highway 1 at a signed junction on the northern outskirts of Colonet, is in fairly good condition all the way to the coast and can be traveled in dry weather by all types of vehicles. It follows sparsely vegetated, gently rolling terrain for 4.3 miles. At this point there is a sweeping view of the coast before the road makes a brief, steep descent to the coastal lowland. At 4.7 miles is a junction with a dirt road to Johnson Ranch, 0.6 mile to the right. Proceed straight ahead for San Antonio del Mar. A number of beach houses and permanent trailers are located here and primitive campsites are available for a small fee. The beach area, backed by high dunes, is beautiful and affords good clamming and surf fishing.

◢ Travelogue

Colonet to Valle de San Quintín
(44.5 mi., 72.8 km.; 1 hr.)

South of Colonet the highway widens slightly as it crosses a level plateau dotted with occasional cultivated fields. After descending a steep hill into Camalú, Highway 1 reaches a flat, nearly featureless coastal plain. Approaching Colonia Guerrero, the motorist can glimpse the high Sierra San Pedro Mártir to the east; visible ahead are the ocean and the volcanic cones across Bahía de San Quintín. In this same area there is a narrow, reconstructed bridge over the Río Santo Domingo. Beyond Colonia Vicente Guerrero (see *Campgrounds & Trailer Parks*), the road runs in a straight line across level farmland to San Quintín.

00.0	Colonet, at the junction to San Antonio del Mar.
01.7	Junction with a good dirt road that leads to Cabo Colonet, site of a small fishing cooperative eight miles away.
07.8	San Telmo de Abajo, at the junction with an improved dirt road to San Telmo, Meling Ranch, the National Observatory and Mike's Sky Rancho (see Side Route to Meling Ranch).
18.4	Camalú, which has a Pemex station, clinic and a variety of supplies and services.
27.1	Colonia Vicente Guerrero (see *Campgrounds & Trailer Parks*) is a busy, fast-growing agricultural center. Facilities include a motel, a hospital, Pemex station (*magna sin*), telegraph and post office, stores and cafes.
27.5	Turnoff to Posada Don Diego and Mesón de Don Pepe trailer parks (tourist information is available at the latter).
41.5	San Quintín, a center for farmers and ranchers in the area, offers a variety of goods and services.
44.5	Lázaro Cárdenas, at the military camp.

▭ Side Route

Highway 1 to Meling Ranch
(31 mi., 50 km.; 1:45 hrs.)

Wide and graded most of the way to Meling Ranch, this road can be driven in a passenger car during dry weather. From the village of San Telmo de Abajo on Highway 1, about eight miles south of Colonet, the road winds between low, scrub-covered hills for 5.8 miles to the small village of San Telmo, which is picturesquely nestled in a small bowl-shaped valley. Beyond San Telmo the road passes Ejido Sinaloa and enters hilly country. At mileage 17.3 is the junction with a road on the left leading to Rancho Buenavista. The route to Meling Ranch now ascends a rocky arroyo, emerges onto a high ridge and winds through low hills to a junction at mileage 31.1. The turnoff for Meling Ranch is 0.4 mile ahead; the main road continues to the National Observatory.

Meling Ranch, also known as San José, is the product of a marriage uniting two pioneering families—the Melings and the Johnsons. Both families settled in northern Baja California in the early 1900s. The ranch house, rebuilt after the ranch itself was destroyed during the 1911 revolution, is a model example of the structures of that era. Today's 10,000-acre cattle ranch offers its guests comfortable accommodations, family style meals, a swimming pool and horseback riding; pack trips into Sierra San Pedro Mártir National Park can be arranged by reservation. A 3500-foot graded airstrip is just east of the ranch. The daily rate for two persons—room and meals—is $110. For information and reservations call (619) 758-2719 or write Apartado Postal 1326, Ensenada, Baja California, Mexico.

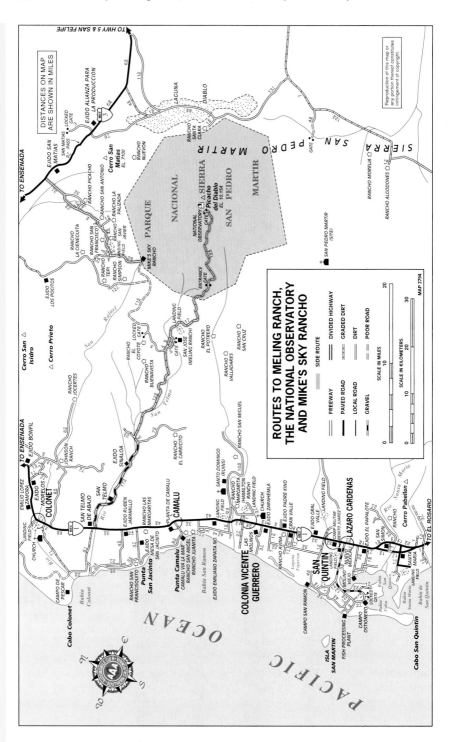

ROUTES TO MELING RANCH,
THE NATIONAL OBSERVATORY
AND MIKE'S SKY RANCHO

MAP 2794

MEXICO HIGHWAY 1

🚙 Side Route

Meling Ranch to the National Observatory
(30 mi., 48 km.; 1:15 hrs.)

The remarkably clear air atop the high Sierra San Pedro Mártir has prompted the Mexican government to build a modern astronomical observatory on a rounded summit 9000 feet in elevation, across from Picacho del Diablo, highest point on the peninsula. Thanks to the graded road built to aid construction of the observatory, visitors now have a chance to explore Sierra San Pedro Mártir National Park—a magnificent region of rocky peaks, forests of pine and fir, freshwater streams and mountain meadows. The graded road to the observatory is somewhat rough and steep, requiring high-clearance vehicles. Snow is a regular occurrence in winter, and the road can be impassable after heavy storms.

From the turnoff to Meling Ranch the road curves through rolling fields, then climbs steadily into the mountains. At beautiful forest-rimmed Corona de Abajo Meadow the road enters Sierra San Pedro Mártir National Park. No hunting is permitted in the park, but fishing, camping, hiking and backpacking are allowed. An entrance fee is sometimes charged at the gate for day use and overnight stays. Beyond the entrance station the road continues for 12.4 miles to a highway work station; from here visitors must walk the last mile to the observatory. The observatory is not open to the public, but near it is a viewpoint with a breathtaking panorama of Picacho del Diablo, the barren desert far below and the Gulf of California on the distant horizon. The return descent toward the west allows a view of broad ranges of hills extending to the Pacific Coast.

Valle de San Quintín
(See also *Lodging & Restaurants* and *Campgrounds & Trailer Parks*.)

The attraction of Bahía de San Quintín dates back to the late 19th century, when an English land company was authorized by the Mexican government to colonize the eastern shore of the bay. Crops were planted, and the colonists built a grist mill, a customs house and a pier. The enterprise was dependent on dry farming, however, and a prolonged drought caused the colony to fail. Evidence of the past can be seen at the Old Mill Motel, which contains some of the original mill machinery, and farther south along the bay where pier pilings march into the water. A re-creation of a pioneer farm, with buildings and equipment reminiscent of the early 20th century, is located a short distance east of the Old Mill Motel. Another reminder is a collection of wooden English crosses in the lonely, windswept cemetery.

Today, San Quintín has two faces. One, the San Quintín Valley, has a population of about 22,000 in an urbanized area strung out haphazardly for several miles along the highway. The valley's two commercial zones, San Quintín and Lázaro Cárdenas, serve as market centers for a developing agricultural region. The many businesses here cater primarily to local residents, but services are available to travelers as well. Facilities include long-distance telephones, a movie theater, a large new church, numerous shops, motels, restaurants, banks, two clinics, two Pemex stations, mechanics and auto parts houses. The surrounding farmland produces large quantities of barley, toma-

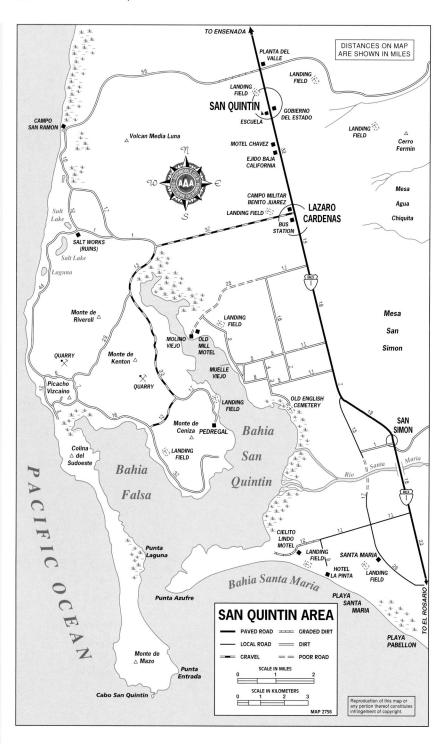

DISTANCES ON MAP
ARE SHOWN IN MILES

TO ENSENADA

PLANTA DEL
VALLE

LANDING
FIELD

LANDING
FIELD

SAN QUINTIN

GOBIERNO
DEL ESTADO

ESCUELA

LANDING
FIELD

CAMPO
SAN RAMON

Volcan Media Luna

MOTEL CHAVEZ

Cerro
Fermin

EJIDO BAJA
CALIFORNIA

Mesa

Agua

Chiquita

CAMPO MILITAR
BENITO JUAREZ

**LAZARO
CARDENAS**

LANDING FIELD

BUS
STATION

Salt
Lake

SALT WORKS
(RUINS)

Salt Lake

Laguna

Mesa

San

Simon

Monte de
Riveroll

LANDING
FIELD

MOLINO
VIEJO

OLD
MILL
MOTEL

QUARRY

Monte de
Kenton

MUELLE
VIEJO

Picacho
Vizcaino

QUARRY

LANDING
FIELD

OLD ENGLISH
CEMETERY

**SAN
SIMON**

Monte de
Ceniza   PEDREGAL

Bahia

Colina
del
Sudoeste

LANDING
FIELD

San

Bahia

Quintin

Rio   Santa   Maria

Falsa

CIELITO
LINDO
MOTEL

Punta
Laguna

LANDING
FIELD

SANTA MARIA

HOTEL
LA PINTA

LANDING
FIELD

Punta Azufre

Bahia Santa Maria

PLAYA
SANTA
MARIA

Monte de
Mazo

Punta
Entrada

PLAYA
PABELLON

Cabo San Quintin

P A C I F I C   O C E A N

TO EL ROSARIO

SAN QUINTIN AREA

	PAVED ROAD		GRADED DIRT
	LOCAL ROAD		DIRT
	GRAVEL		POOR ROAD

SCALE IN MILES

0   1   2

SCALE IN KILOMETERS

0   1   2   3

MAP 2756

toes, strawber-
ries, potatoes,
peppers and
other vegetables.

The other face of
San Quintín is
the nearby bay—
probably the
most popular
tourist destina-
tion between
Ensenada and
Mulegé. The
sheltered waters
of the U-shaped
inner bay separate

Tranquility settles over Bahía de San Quintín.

the cultivated fields of Valle de San
Quintín from a row of volcanic cones
to the west. Across a narrow sandspit to
the south is the outer bay, which is
more open to the winds and heavy surf
of the Pacific Ocean. Bahía de San Quintín is a seasonal paradise for sportsmen.
Black brant (a type of goose) migrate to
the area each winter and are popular
game. Good surf fishing and clam digging enhance the appeal of the beaches
along the shore of the outer bay. Fishing from boats is excellent in both parts
of the bay (see Fishing under Water
Recreation in the *Recreation* chaper).
The quiet waters of the inner bay provide a fine, protected anchorage for
small boats. Explorers with heavy-duty
vehicles can make the adventurous trek
to the western shore of the inner bay
and the Pacific beaches beyond, where
good primitive campsites can be found.

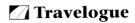 Travelogue

Valle de San Quintín to
El Rosario

(33 mi., 53.2 km.; 1 hr.)

Highway 1 narrows south of San Quintín. The road passes a group of roadside

communities and a series of cultivated
fields, then crosses a bridge spanning
the bed of the intermittently flowing
Río Santa María. Due to flooding, this
and several other bridges in the region
were reconstructed and may be narrow.
Thirty miles beyond San Quintín the
road turns sharply inland, soon reaching a summit from which there are
expansive views of the ocean and the
countryside to the northeast. From the
mesa, the highway drops into a wide
valley and enters El Rosario.

00.0   **Lázaro Cárdenas, at the military camp.**

01.4   **First turnoff to Bahía de San
Quintín. This dirt road leads
3.6 miles to the shore. A better
road follows.**

03.2   **Junction with the dirt road to
Muelle Viejo, the ruins of a
pier constructed by an unsuc-
cessful English colony, and to
the Old Mill Motel.**

07.9   **Junction with the paved road
to the Hotel La Pinta and the
Cielito Lindo Motel.**

09.0   **Turnoff on a dirt road to El
Pabellón RV Park.**

16.1   **Junction with the unmarked**

short dirt road to El Socorrito, a seaside village that offers sportfishing and scuba diving.

35.8 Rosario de Arriba, the primary settlement of El Rosario. The much smaller Rosario de Abajo, which contains the ruins of Mission Nuestra Señora del Rosario, lies about a mile west via a dirt road. The total population for both communities is about 4000. Before the completion of the Transpeninsular Highway and the peninsula's microwave telephone system, El Rosario was considered the last outpost of civilization in northern Baja California. It is now a quiet agricultural community and highway stop, with gasoline (*magna sin*), auto parts, restaurants (see *Lodging & Restaurants*), two motels and groceries. A museum containing a nice variety of items from northern Baja California is located on Highway 1 in the center of town. For entrance to the museum, inquire at Mamá Espinoza's Restaurant on the bend of the highway.

☑ Travelogue

El Rosario to Cataviña
(76 mi., 122 km.; 2 hrs.)

Leaving El Rosario, Highway 1 turns east and follows the wide, cultivated Arroyo del Rosario for a few miles, then crosses the valley and climbs into a region of low, deeply eroded hills. Soon the terrain begins to conform to the armchair traveler's notion of Baja, with cirio trees and giant cardón cacti appearing alongside the highway. With its blue skies, expansive views and abundance of unique vegetation, the Central Desert of Baja California is one of North America's most fascinating desert regions. After continuing southeast through ranges of hills and wide valleys, the highway enters a spectacular landscape of large boulder formations interspersed with dense thickets of cirio, cardón and other varieties of desert vegetation. Here Highway 1 crosses several deep arroyos that are subject to flash flooding. Many parts of the highway from El Rosario to south of Cataviña are rough and require very careful driving. In the heart of this

The boulder-strewn desert of central Baja, also known as the "rock garden," is home to the exotic cirio tree (on the left) as well as cardón cacti and other plantlife.

"rock-garden" zone are Cataviña and Rancho Santa Inés.

00.0   El Rosario.

04.8   A bridge carries Highway 1 across Arroyo del Rosario.

08.1   Cirio trees begin to appear, their weird forms reaching skyward in a profusion of

Cataviña provides the only accommodations for over 100 miles in either direction along Mexico Highway 1.

shapes. Aside from a small stand in Sonora on the Mexican mainland, these plants grow nowhere else in the world.

14.5   Junction with a good dirt road leading 39 miles to Punta San Carlos and a network of roads which provide access to several fishing camps.

31.3   Junction with a rough dirt road to Rancho El Cartabón.

38.3   Signed junction with an unpaved road to the adobe ruins of Mission San Fernando Velicatá, founded in 1769 by Father Junípero Serra, who went on to establish Alta California's chain of missions. Passenger cars can make this trip in dry weather.

39.8   El Progreso, which has a cafe. Once a busy construction camp, El Progreso is now all but abandoned.

46.8   Junction with the road to Santa Catarina and Punta Canoas (see Side Route to Puerto Catarina).

55.2   San Agustín, which consists of an abandoned government-built trailer park and a highway maintenance camp. From behind the camp a sandy road leads to Rancho San Agustín.

57.1   Junction with a good dirt road leading to El Mármol (see Side Route to El Mármol). Near the junction are two cafes.

59.4   Highway 1 now enters a region of impressive, boulder-strewn countryside. The Mexican government has created a park here, and the natural environment is protected by federal law.

74.1   Arroyo de Catavñacito, a deep arroyo with tall blue fan palms and occasional pools of water. The first elephant trees are seen near here, their short, fat trunks seemingly squatting among the boulders.

76.3   Cataviña (see *Lodging & Restaurants* and *Campgrounds & Trailer Parks*), set in the midst of "rock garden" scenery. A Pemex station, a market, two cafes and a mechanic's shop are on the

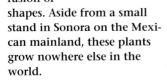

left; on the right is a government-built trailer park and the Hotel La Pinta, which sometimes sells gasoline (*magna sin*). Hikes over beautiful desert landscape may be taken in any direction from the village.

🚙 Side Route

Highway 1 to Punta Canoas and Puerto Catarina

(46 mi., 74 km.; 2:30 hrs.)

This trek, which descends through scenic desert to unspoiled Pacific shores, actually has two destinations. The branch to Punta Canoas is used to measure the mileage and time given above. This is a trip for seasoned, well-prepared adventurers in high-clearance, heavy-duty vehicles; four-wheel drive is desirable. There are no facilities so travelers should carry plenty of food, water and gasoline, and be prepared to camp out. Sites and experiences include rich displays of ocotillos, cardóns and elephant trees; remote Pacific beaches offer opportunities for clam digging, shell collecting, tidepool exploring and solitude. Surfers occasionally visit, lured more by lack of other surfers than by quality waves.

From its junction with the highway 5.6 miles southeast of Rancho Santa Cecilia (or 29 miles northwest of Cataviña), the road is graded and in

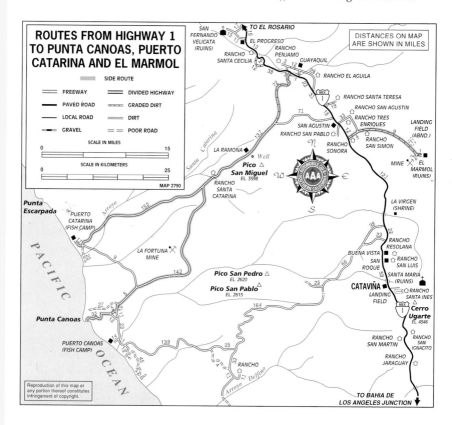

good condition for the first seven miles. Although its quality gradually deteriorates, a few sandy stretches present the only obstacles to passenger vehicles as far as Rancho Santa Catarina. This friendly settlement houses families who raise cattle and a few crops. Fresh water is available for washing and for radiators. After leaving the ranch the road climbs to a plateau. At mileage 20.9 is a junction. To the right, via 16.6 miles of rough road, is Puerto Catarina, once the shipping port for onyx from El Mármol. Bear left for Punta Canoas. The road becomes narrow and rough as it crosses the coastal hills. At mileage 40.2 is another junction; bear left. At mileage 41.9 is a fork. To the right the road leads 3.3 miles to Punta Canoas, site of a seasonally occupied fish camp. Campsites on a shelf high above the rugged coastline are plentiful.

🚙 Side Route

Highway 1 to El Mármol
(10 mi., 16 km.; 0:30 hr.)

The signed junction with the road to El Mármol is 2.2 miles southeast of San Agustín on Highway 1. The road is smooth, graded and easily passable during dry weather in any type of vehicle. After leaving the main highway, the road runs 0.4 mile to a junction with a remnant of the old peninsular road; on the right is a wooden corral and small gravel quarry. At mileage 0.9 the road passes a windmill and another corral, then veers to the right. After crossing open countryside that is sparsely covered with cacti and brush, the road flanks an abandoned airstrip, then enters El Mármol, 9.6 miles from Highway 1.

El Mármol was once an active onyx-mining concern, but a drop in the demand for onyx caused the camp to be abandoned in 1958. In 1993 limited mining began again. Blocks and chips of onyx lie strewn across the barren landscape alongside the quarry. A walk through the remains of the camp reveals the ruins of adobe buildings, a schoolhouse made of unpolished onyx, the carcasses of long-abandoned trucks and an interesting cemetery. Caution: several deep, uncovered wells present hazards; use care when walking here.

🚙 Travelogue

Cataviña to
Bahía de los Angeles Junction
(65 mi., 105 km.; 1:30 hrs.)

From Cataviña, the highway continues to lead southeast through interesting rock-strewn country. After crossing a narrow arroyo, the road climbs to a 2700-foot summit, then descends quickly to the edge of a dry lake. Beyond here the landscape becomes more barren as Highway 1 meanders through low hills, ascends a 2200-foot saddle and drops onto the basin of Laguna Chapala. This vast, desolate dry lake becomes a sea of mud following heavy rains. After crossing another range of low barren hills, the highway traverses a sandy plain to the junction with the road to Bahía de los Angeles. This region is a showcase for the typical vegetation of Baja California's central desert: cirio, cardón, cholla cactus, ocotillo, elephant trees and yucca válida.

00.0	Cataviña.
00.7	**Junction with the 0.8-mile paved road to Rancho Santa Inés, which offers a clinic, motel, campground, cafe, a**

paved airstrip and information for off-road explorers.

07.4 Rancho San Ignacito. In late 1973, road crews working north and south met here as they completed the paving of Highway 1. A small monument on the west side of the highway marks the spot.

18.6 El Pedregoso, a mountain composed entirely of jumbled boulders. Before the completion of the paved highway, this was an important landmark for peninsula travelers.

33.7 Laguna Chapala Junction. Here a graded dirt road, signed Calamajué, provides access to Bahía San Luis Gonzaga and other points along the northeastern shore of the peninsula. At the junction is a cafe.

34.5 Rancho Chapala. Stretching away to the east is the broad expanse of Laguna Chapala, with its bed of cracked clay.

50.8 Junction with a rough road to Campo Calamajué, a fish camp.

65.3 Junction with the paved road to **Bahía de los Angeles** (see Side Route to Bahía de Los Angeles). Here there is a highway patrol station. The junction is sometimes called Punta Prieta, although the original settlement bearing this name is eight miles to the south.

Side Route

Highway 1 to Bahía de los Angeles

(42 mi., 68 km.; 1 hr.)

(See also *Campgrounds & Trailer Parks*.)

This scenic seaside town is reached via a very rough paved highway. The road starts 8.4 miles north of Punta Prieta at a junction that has a Pemex station and a cafe. From this point it heads

A walk along the shore provides a magnificent vista of Bahía de los Angeles.

east across a sandy plain where the typical vegetation of Baja California's central desert is particularly abundant; it includes cardón, cholla and garambullo cacti, as well as cirio, ocotillo and yucca válida. Brightly colored wildflowers carpet the floor of the desert in early spring. Barren mountains are on the horizon.

Two tourists greet the day under a palapa at Bahía de los Angeles.

After about 10 miles, the road veers slightly to the right, passes through a gap in the mountains, then descends to the edge of a large dry lake. At mileage 28 is the signed junction with a rough dirt road to Mission San Borja; the road to the mission from Rosarito on Highway 1 is better and easier to drive. After a gentle downhill run through a canyon, the highway drops quickly to the shore of the Gulf of California.

With high, barren mountains as a dramatic backdrop to the west and several offshore islands jutting up from the deep blue waters of the gulf, Bahía de los Angeles is one of the beauty spots of Baja California. The bay, which is protected by 45-mile-long Isla Angel de la Guarda, offers a fine sheltered anchorage for boats. Sportfishing is excellent. Fishing trips can be arranged, and there are several launch ramps for private boats. Facilities include a paved airstrip, stores, restaurants, a bakery, three trailer parks, three motels and an inn. In the center of town are a plaza park, town hall,

and a museum that displays sea life and artifacts relating to the mining and history of the region. Isla Raza, a reserve for migratory waterfowl, is a bird-watcher's paradise. Dirt roads run both north and south of the town past vacation homes to remote beaches where good campsites can be found. In addition, a graded road winds southeastward from Bahía de los Angeles to remote San Francisquito.

🚙 Side Route

Bahía de los Angeles to San Francisquito

(81 mi., 130 km.; 3:45 hrs.)

A journey through scenic desert hills and valleys to a secluded bay on the Gulf of California (Sea of Cortez) is graded all the way. Because it is isolated, a motorist can travel great distances without seeing another automobile, so a fully equipped, sturdy high-clearance vehicle is a must. The road travels inland most of the way due to the rugged coastline. Numerous subtropical desert plants grow along

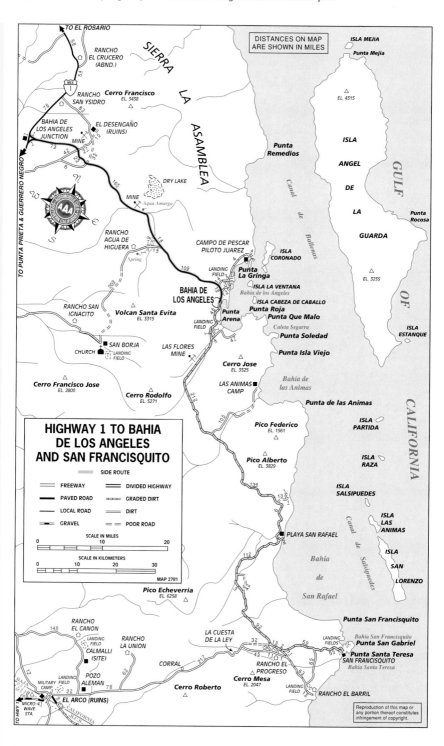

this route, especially cardón, elephant tree, ocotillo, cholla and sagebrush.

In the southern part of the village of Bahía de los Angeles the road turns right, then soon bears left. For several miles the bayshore, lined with houses and a trailer camp, is visible. Heading south between two mountain ranges, the road later climbs through hills. At 27 miles a side road goes north to Las Animas Camp, used by fishermen. Follow the large sign that points southeast toward Punta San Francisquito. The road now climbs through hills, then drops almost to Bahía San Rafael. Visible in the gulf are several small islands, and in the distance is the large Isla Tiburón. The road once more heads inland, climbs a steep grade, then gradually descends in an easterly direction toward the coast. At 68 miles is a junction; to the right is a road to El Arco. Turn left and drive 13 miles to San Francisquito. On the way two roads branch southeast to El Barril, a large cattle ranch that includes many Mexican ranchers and several American vacation homes. Keep left at each junction; the direction to the coast is mostly northeast.

On Bahía Santa Teresa, a small attractive bay with a long sandy beach, is the rustic fishing resort named Punta San Francisquito. It has cabañas, a restaurant and bar, electricity during the evening hours, fishing boats and an airstrip. Most guests arrive by airplane. About a mile north of the resort, on Bahía San Francisquito, is a beautiful cove sheltered by rugged headlands. Here is found a fish camp with a mechanic's shop. Camping is permitted for a small fee, and fishing is good.

◪ Travelogue

Bahía de los Angeles Junction to Guerrero Negro
(80 mi., 129 km.; 1:45 hrs.)

For the first 15 miles after leaving the Bahía de los Angeles junction, Highway 1 continues to cross a level, sandy plain. It then climbs into hilly country sparsely vegetated with cirio and elephant trees. Extra caution is required in this section, which is characterized by steep dropoffs, sharp curves and a narrow roadway. Near Rosarito, several flat-topped buttes dot the horizon to the east. Turning almost due south, the highway descends gradually onto the windy Vizcaíno Desert, one of the most desolate portions of the entire peninsula. Only hearty yucca válida and scattered clumps of saltbrush interrupt the uniformity of the sandy landscape.

00.0   **Junction to Bahía de los Angeles.**

08.4   **Junction with the short paved road to the village of Punta Prieta. A bustling construction camp during the paving of Highway 1, Punta Prieta is now a sleepy little hamlet. Facilities include a store, a cafe, a small military camp and a highway maintenance station. On the east side of the highway is a paved airstrip.**

18.3   **Brief view of the Pacific Ocean from a low summit.**

24.0   **Junction with a gravel road to Santa Rosalillita (see Side Route to Santa Rosalillita).**

32.3   **Rosarito, a village with a store, a cafe and a shrine. Rosarito also marks the junction with the dirt road to Mission San Borja (see Side Route to Mission San Borja).**

39.2 Junction with a dirt road leading north along isolated beaches for 18 miles to Santa Rosalillita. This area is popular with surfers.

42.7 Junction with a rough dirt road to El Tomatal.

49.4 Turnoff to Rancho San Angel.

59.0 Villa Jesús María, a farming village with a Pemex station (*magna sin*), two cafes and a small store. A paved road leads west to Ejido Morelos, a government-sponsored cattle-raising project, and Laguna Manuela, a lagoon with a fish camp and a sandy beach.

78.4 The 28th parallel separates the states of Baja California and Baja California Sur. Erected on the latitude line is a 140-foot-high steel monument in the form of a stylized eagle, commemorating completion of Highway 1 and the uniting of northern and southern Baja California—

a major milestone in the peninsula's history. On the west side of the monument are Hotel La Pinta and a trailer park. The 28th parallel also marks the boundary of the Pacific and Mountain time zones.

80.3 Junction with the paved road to the town of Guerrero Negro, two miles to the west.

🚙 Side Route

Highway 1 to Santa Rosalillita
(10 mi., 16 km.; 1 hr.)

A wide gravel road, negotiable in a passenger vehicle, now leads to the Pacific coast and the settlement of Santa Rosalillita. Leaving the highway 15.6 miles south of Punta Prieta the new road follows the shoulder of a wide arroyo, above the old road in the sandy wash below. At mileage 8.2 is a junction

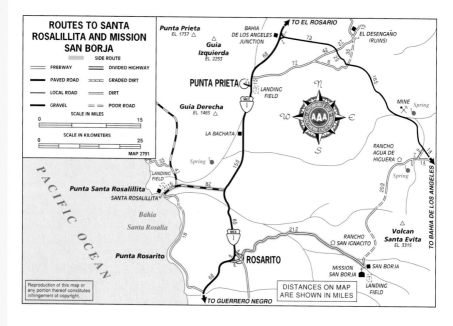

with a gravel road leading north that connects with the rugged road following the Pacific coast. The road crosses a dirt airstrip at mileage 8.4 and then loops down onto the beach and into Santa Rosalillita, 9.9 miles from High-

A visit to remote Mission San Borja, above and below, is a worthwhile trek for the properly equipped explorer.

way 1. Here a government-assisted fishing cooperative harvests abalone and other varieties of shellfish. There are no tourist facilities, but the nearby beaches offer excellent opportunities for shell collecting.

An alternate return route, which is not suitable for standard automobiles, leads south from Santa Rosalillita to several beautiful, isolated beaches. For 15 miles the road meanders along the coastline past beaches covered with small, smooth stones, volcanic rocks and pearly white turban shells. Surfing is good near the rocky points. At Playa Altamira, a good open camping spot, the road turns inland and runs about three miles to meet Highway 1 at a point 6.5 miles south of Rosarito.

 Side Route

Rosarito to Mission San Borja
(22 mi., 35 km.; 2 hrs.)

This, the best route to Mission San Borja, is totally unsuited to travel in a passenger car. There are no steep grades, but the single-track road has a high crown and numerous rough and rocky spots, calling for a sturdy high-

clearance vehicle. For those with the proper equipment the trip to this magnificent mission is well worth the time and effort. The road to San Borja begins in Rosarito, a village in the southern part of the state of Baja California.

Rosarito has a store and a cafe, and it should not be confused with the booming tourist town of Rosarito in the northern part of the state. The route bears right just past a small weather station and leads northeast through open desert past several flat-topped buttes. At mileage 13.6 is a junction; bear left. About two miles beyond the junction is Rancho San Ignacito, a large cattle ranch with a stone-walled corral and a deep well. Beyond the ranch the road makes a rough climb out of a small arroyo, then descends gradually to Mission San Borja, located in a broad valley at the base of high barren mountains.

Mission San Francisco de Borja was founded by the Jesuits in 1759, shortly before the order's expulsion from the New World. The stone church at San Borja was completed by the Dominicans in 1801. At one time the mission served more than 3000 Indians, but the diseases of the white man decimated the native population and the mission was abandoned in 1818. The mission is largely intact and has been restored by the Mexican government. Behind the church are several adobe ruins, including the remains of an irrigation system built by the mission friars. A few families live and farm nearby.

Another road leads north from the mission for 23 miles to a junction with the paved road connecting Highway 1 with Bahía de los Angeles. This road is even rougher than the one described previously; it is steep and narrow, with numerous rocky arroyo crossings.

Guerrero Negro

(See also *Lodging & Restaurants* and *Campgrounds & Trailer Parks*.)

Located in the midst of the vast Vizcaíno Desert, this hospitable community of about 11,000 residents plays a significant role in the economy of Baja California. Essentially a company town, Guerrero Negro is the world's leading producer of salt, according to the firm Exportadora de Sal. South of town are thousands of evaporating ponds, each about 100 yards square and from three to four feet deep when flooded with sea water. The desert sun evaporates the water quickly, leaving a residue of pure white, hard salt, which is scooped up by dredges and taken by trucks to a nearby wharf. The salt is then loaded by conveyor belt onto barges and carried to Cedros Island, where it is transferred into ocean-going freighters. Salt from Guerrero Negro is used in Mexico, the United States, Canada and Japan.

A wide variety of services and facilities are available in Guerrero Negro, including several motels and trailer parks, restaurants, stores, two Pemex stations, several auto parts houses, mechanics, markets, a hospital, banks and an airport.

During most of the year, Guerrero Negro offers little in the way of recreation, although good surf fishing can be found along the remote beaches to the north. In January, February and early March, however, nearby Scammon's Lagoon (*Laguana Ojo de Liebre*) is the destination of the spectacular run of gray whales, who migrate annually from the Bering Sea (see Fauna in *Introduction*).

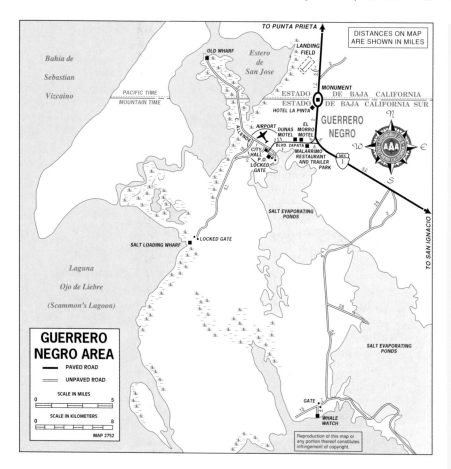

Good spots from which to see the whales are the old salt wharf, located seven miles west of Guerrero Negro via a dirt road, and the shore of Scammon's Lagoon, which has been designated a natural park by the Mexican government (see Side Route to Scammon's Lagoon).

Once an endangered specie, gray whales are now protected by the Mexican and American governments. The name "Guerrero Negro" is the Spanish translation of *Black Warrior*, an American whaling ship that was wrecked at the entrance to the lagoon in the late 19th Century.

Isla Cedros

Isla Cedros is a barren, rugged island situated about 55 miles west of the Guerrero Negro coastal area. Its inhabitants are supported mostly by a fish-packing plant. It also plays the role of transshipment point for the salt mined at Guerrero Negro, which has no deep-water harbor. Ocean-going ships load the salt for export at the port of Cedros (also called El Pueblo), where most of the population of about 6000 live.

Virtually untouched by tourism, Cedros has the character of a typical older Mexican coastal town. Facilities include restaurants, a bank, a church, taxis and a couple of low-priced inns. Visitors are able to find beaches, hire fishing boats and hike over trails to observe the unspoiled natural environment of most of the island. Cedros is accessible by a local airline, with flights leaving from both Ensenada and Guerrero Negro a couple times a week.

◪ Travelogue

Guerrero Negro to San Ignacio
(89 mi., 142 km.; 1:45 hrs.)

From the junction to Guerrero Negro, Highway 1 turns inland, heading southeast across the barren Vizcaíno Desert. Near the town of Vizcaíno, however, yucca válida, cardón cacti and dense thickets of low shrubs begin to appear alongside the highway. About 20 miles from San Ignacio, the road passes a group of flat-topped volcanic cones; the dark reddish-brown rocks in this region give further evidence of past volcanic activity. Finally, after winding through low, cactus-covered hills, the highway brings the traveler to the junction with the paved road to San Ignacio. Much of this section of Highway 1 is rough or narrow; drive with care.

00.0	Junction to Guerrero Negro.
05.6	Junction with the graded road to the shore of Scammon's Lagoon, signed *Laguna Ojo de Liebre* (see Side Route to Scammon's Lagoon).
17.1	Junction with the gravel highway to El Arco (see Side Route to El Arco).
45.4	Vizcaíno (sometimes called Fundolegal), with about 2000 inhabitants, has a Pemex station (*magna sin*), two motels,

an RV park, cafes, a market, a pharmacy and auto parts. A paved side road leads five miles to Ejido Díaz Ordaz (sometimes called Vizcaíno). This *ejido* is a major government-assisted farming cooperative. Water from deep wells has turned a section of forbidding desert into productive fields and orchards; principal crops include spices, cotton, figs, grapes and oranges. The *ejido* has a clinic, a market and a variety of small stores. Pavement on the side road ends after 16 more miles. From this point, the road is graded earth and leads onto the remote Vizcaíno Peninsula (see Side Route Loop Trip From Highway 1 Around the Vizcaíno Peninsula); this side trip is only for adventurous, well-prepared travelers with the proper vehicles and equipment.

52.4	A paved road leads to Ejido Emiliano Zapata, a large dairy-farming *ejido* or collective agricultural settlement.
57.4	Estación Microóndas Los Angeles, the first of 23 microwave relay stations along Highway 1 in Baja California Sur. The stations are closed to the public.
61.3	Junction with graded dirt road to San Francisco de la Sierra (see Side Route to San Francisco de la Sierra).
73.6	Junction with a graded dirt road to Punta Abreojos (see Side Route to Punta Abreojos). A cafe is located at the junction.

85.8   Junction with a 0.6-mile paved road to a good paved airstrip.

88.6   Junction with the 0.9-mile paved road to San Lino and Paredones, two villages on the outskirts of San Ignacio.

88.9   Junction with the 1.1-mile-long paved road to San Ignacio. Opposite the junction is a Pemex station offering *magna sin.*

🚙 Side Route

Highway 1 to Scammon's Lagoon (Laguna Ojo de Liebre)

(15 mi., 24 km.; 0:45 hr.)

From January through early March this side trip offers travelers an opportunity to see California gray whales, which make a 6000-mile annual migration from the Bering Sea to bear their young in the shallow waters of Scammon's Lagoon. This route also reveals a wealth of bird life, such as cormorants, herons and pelicans. *The second part of the route, about nine miles through salt company property, is open to the public from January 4 through March 30 only.* The dirt road to the southeastern arm of the lagoon branches off Highway 1 at a point 5.6 miles south of the turnoff to Guerrero Negro; the junction bears the signs "Laguna Ojo de Liebre" and "Parque Natural de la Ballena Gris/Gray Whale Natural Park." While it is wide and graded its entire length, the road is quite sandy for the first couple of miles and corrugated part of the way. During dry weather, however, a passenger car can make the trip if it is driven at a slow, even pace. After leaving Highway 1 the road passes several junctions, at some of

which are signs with a picture of a whale and an arrow pointing the way. The side roads in this area belong to Guerrero Negro's salt company and are closed to public use. A salt company checkpoint is 3.7 miles west; after this the road to Scammon's Lagoon crosses a levee between two evaporating ponds, where large salt dredges can occasionally be seen at work harvesting the salt. After another 10 miles the road comes to a small shack, which bears the sign "Parque Natural de la Ballena Gris/Gray Whale Natural Park." Sometimes admission of about $3 is collected. Just beyond the shack is a fork; the road to the left leads to the best beach from which to observe the massive marine mammals. Binoculars help, since the whales are usually some distance offshore. Tours in small boats are available during whale season for about $10 an hour. Overnight camping is permitted here, although no facilities have been installed.

🚙 Side Route

Highway 1 to El Arco

(26 mi., 43 km.; 1 hr.)

The road to El Arco, designated Mexico Highway 18, leaves Highway 1 at a well-signed junction located 17.1 miles southeast of Guerrero Negro. The highway is elevated, with a surface of gravel and broken pavement. There are no meals or lodging on this route nor those that follow it out of El Arco. Leading northeast from the junction the road runs through flat, barren terrain until mileage 6.6, when dense desert vegetation suddenly appears; cardón, yucca válida, elephant trees, cholla cacti and several brushy shrubs all grow in this "living desert." After continuing gently uphill for several

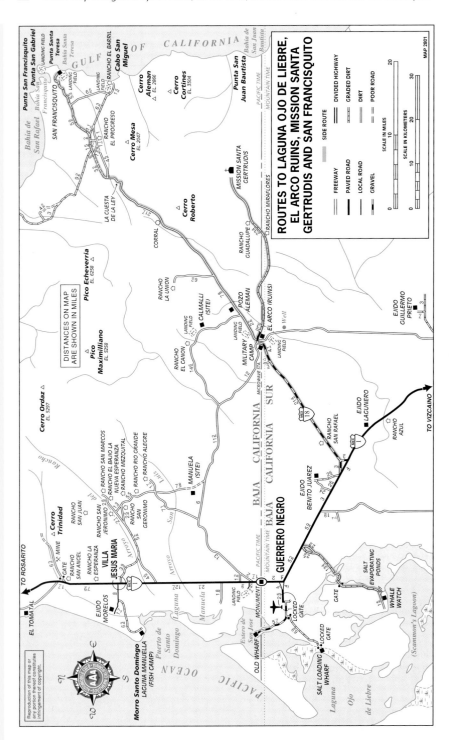

ROUTES TO LAGUNA OJO DE LIEBRE, EL ARCO RUINS, MISSION SANTA GERTRUDIS AND SAN FRANCISQUITO

miles, the road rounds a small range of steep, barren hills, then drops into El Arco.

El Arco is a small, scattered settlement situated about a mile north of the 28th parallel—the imaginary line dividing the states of Baja California and Baja California Sur. El Arco began as a gold-mining camp, and for many years was a waystop on old Highway 1. Now it is a peaceful if worn-looking community that serves as a center for the surrounding ranches. Within the village are a military camp, gasoline pumped from drums and a church. A little copper mining is done in the vicinity. A landing field is located just south of town. From El Arco, dirt roads lead to numerous points of interest.

This huge steel monument in the shape of a stylized eagle straddles the 28th parallel, dividing the states of Baja California and Baja California Sur.

🚙 Side Route

El Arco to Mission Santa Gertrudis
(23 mi., 37 km.; 1:30 hrs.)

Although this road is wide and graded for the first 17 miles and is in reasonably good condition for its entire length, an ordinary passenger car could have trouble clearing the high center crown and several rough spots. For the properly equipped explorer, however, this is a worthwhile side trip. The road to the mission begins where the paved road through El Arco makes a hard right turn and the pavement ends. Just beyond is a metal sign that at one time indicated the direction to the mission; veer right at this point. From El Arco the road traverses barren desert, passes two large cattle ranches, then meanders through an arroyo to Mission Santa Gertrudis.

Located in a narrow canyon, Mission Santa Gertrudis was founded by the Jesuits in 1752 and was an important supply center during the mission era. After the Jesuits were expelled from Baja California in 1768, the Dominicans arrived here and built the small stone church in 1796. Almost from the beginning, Santa Gertrudis was plagued by insufficient fresh water, and the local Indian population suffered greatly from diseases; the mission was finally abandoned in 1822. In addition to the chapel, which is still in use, the site contains several other stone ruins, including the remains of an irrigation system dating from the 18th century and a restored adobe belfry. A few ranchers now occupy the area.

🚙 Side Route

El Arco to San Francisquito
(48 mi., 77 km.; 2:30 hrs.)

The road to Bahía San Francisquito is generally good by off-road standards and is suitable for high-clearance vehicles. Until recently, however, four-wheel drive was necessary to make the trip because of the infamous grade known as La Cuesta de la Ley. This harrowing plunge, which dropped 400 feet in only 0.4 mile, has been regraded to accommodate most high-clearance vehicles. To locate the route, proceed northeast at the junction by the town hall in El Arco. After 2.3 miles, during which the road negotiates a steep narrow arroyo, the route passes through Pozo Alemán, which many years ago was an important gold-mining center but now looks like a ghost town. Beyond Pozo Alemán, the road traverses a flat plain, then enters a region of rocky arroyos dotted with huge cardón cacti. At mileage 7.9 a road leads left to Rancho La Unión; bear right. The road to the gulf now runs through a series of steep-sided valleys, then ascends a plateau. At mileage 29

La Cuesta de la Ley begins its descent. A major fork is located at mileage 34.9; to the right is Rancho El Barril, a privately owned cattle ranch, while the left branch leads to San Francisquito.

Punta San Francisquito is a rustic fishing resort located on Bahía Santa Teresa (San Francisquito). For details about this community, see Side Route to San Francisquito.

🚙 Side Route

Loop Trip From Highway 1 Around the Vizcaíno Peninsula

Because of the great distances involved and the remote nature of the territory, this trip is unique among Baja California's side routes. The trek onto the Vizcaíno Peninsula should be attempted only by serious off-road adventurers who are equipped to handle the worst that Baja California has to offer—isolation, poor roads, scarcity of fresh water, lack of facilities, frequent dust storms, desert heat and heavy coastal fog.

For the most part, the main routes are well signed, periodically maintained and fairly good by Baja California off-pavement standards. The main highway from Vizcaíno to Bahía Tortugas via Rancho San José de Castro may be traveled by well-supplied, light front-wheel-drive vehicles, but a sturdy high-clearance vehicle is recommended. The other roads on the peninsula contain bad spots that can trap or damage a passenger car or low-clearance vehicle. It is advisable to use the "buddy" system, with a caravan of two or more vehicles traveling together. Plenty of extra water, food and gasoline should be carried, and equipment should be checked against the Suggested Supply Lists in the *Appendix*.

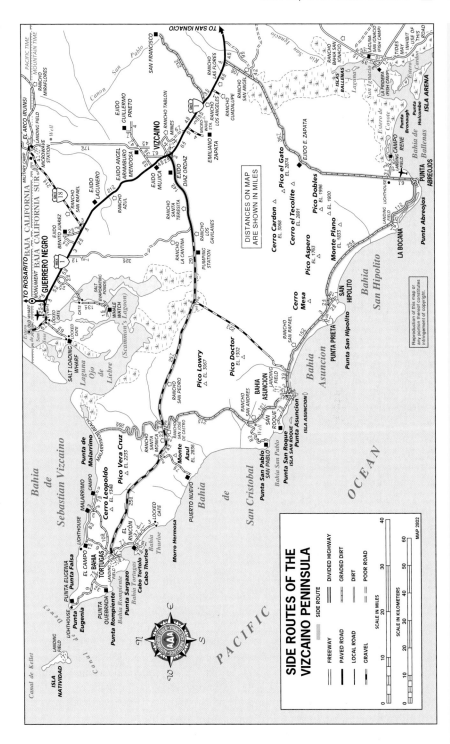

MEXICO HIGHWAY 1

SIDE ROUTES OF THE
VIZCAÍNO PENINSULA

For those prepared for the rigors of this journey, the remoteness of this huge hook protruding westward from the central spine of Baja California is the principal lure. Most of the Vizcaíno Peninsula has seen relatively little human intrusion. The desert scenery, though barren, is unusual and striking. Along the coast are attractive bays and coves, rugged headlands and miles of wide, beautiful beaches. Fishing and beachcombing are excellent.

The peninsula is not devoid of habitation. There are four fair-sized cannery towns, along with numerous small ranches and fish camps. But none of these settlements is prepared to cater to tourists, although the inhabitants are friendly and helpful. Meals, refreshments and limited supplies can be purchased in Punta Abreojos, La Bocana, Bahía Asunción and Bahía Tortugas. Gasoline, sometimes siphoned from drums, is relatively expensive, and unleaded *magna sin* is not always available. Overnight accommodations, where they exist, are extremely modest, but fine primitive campsites can be found throughout the peninsula (wood, however, is scarce).

From Highway 1, the traveler can enter the Vizcaíno Peninsula at Vizcaíno Junction (44.8 miles southeast of the Guerrero Negro turnoff) or at an unsigned junction 15 miles west of San Ignacio. The following route descriptions are organized as a loop beginning at Vizcaíno (Fundolegal); each segment of the loop is outlined in a separate subsection. Most of the mileages, driving times and route descriptions are based on an expedition made by an Auto Club research team; readers should keep in mind that conditions can change.

Side Route

Vizcaíno to Rancho San José de Castro
(72 mi., 116 km.; 5 hrs.)

This route onto the Vizcaíno Peninsula has a raised surface most of the way. It is a durable graded route, but is rather rough. Signs appear at most important junctions. Rancho San José de Castro is used here as a convenient route dividing point. The highway continues westward to Bahía Tortugas and is the lifeline between Highway 1 and that port. (The Bahía Tortugas description follows.) After Vizcaíno there is no fuel available until Bahía Tortugas, 103 miles away; Ejido Díaz Ordaz is the last chance for food or supplies of any kind.

Begin by taking the Vizcaíno turnoff from Highway 1 and following the paved road past the irrigated fields, orchards and vineyards of Ejido Díaz Ordaz. The pavement ends after 20 miles, and the graded road continues west across scrub-covered desert. After passing a group of small ranches the road goes through an area of salt flats.

At mileage 44.9 is a junction (signed) with another graded dirt road that heads southwest to join the coastal road 6.4 miles south of Bahía Asunción. At mileage 39.4 a dirt road, which belongs to the salt company and is frequently closed, leads northeast to Scammon's Lagoon and Guerrero Negro. West of this junction the new road begins to climb into low foothills. Elephant trees and cacti grow here, and the bay is occasionally visible to the right. Shortly, the road ascends into mountains, sometimes slicing abruptly through ridges, other times following natural gaps in the hills.

At mileage 70.6, the road reaches the hard-to-find Malarrimo Beach turnoff; it is on the right-hand side about .5 mile east of the San José de Castro sign. After another .5 mile, a dirt road on the left leads 1.3 miles south to Rancho San José de Castro, and connects to the older dirt road leading south to Bahía Asunción.

Rancho San José de Castro, a cattle ranch with a large spring, is also a residence for magnesite miners. There are no facilities for tourists, but cold drinks are sold and the friendly ranchers provide information and directions.

🚙 Side Route

Rancho San José de Castro to Bahía Tortugas
(31 mi., 50 km.; 2 hrs.)

West of the junction of the road to San José de Castro, the new road—bumpy in places—passes Rancho San Miguel, where cold refreshments are sold. At mileage 6.8 a dirt road veers off to the left 8.2 miles to Puerto Nuevo, a small fishing village.

At this point the new road heads through the mountains, sometimes cutting through them, other times following ridge contours. The scenery is fairly desolate on this stretch. At mileage 31.3 the new road drops out of the mountains and enters Bahía Tortugas.

With a population of more than 3000, Bahía Tortugas is the metropolis of the Vizcaíno Peninsula. The town, with its rows of pastel-colored dwellings, sits beneath barren hills on the north side of an almost circular bay, which is one of the finest natural harbors on Baja California's Pacific coast. Bahía Tortugas makes its living from the sea. A large cannery processes abalone,

shrimp and other marine products, many of which are trucked or flown to Ensenada. There is no fresh water in the area, and the town's supply must be brought in by ship or truck, or distilled from sea water in a small desalinization plant. Facilities include numerous stores and cafes, telegraph and radio communications, a medical center, an attractive church, rustic accommodations, a paved airstrip and a gasoline station. Prices are relatively high as all supplies must be hauled in over long distances. The town has an orderly progressive appearance and is a welcome stop for travelers. From Bahía Tortugas a dirt road runs 16.5 miles to Punta Eugenia at the western tip of the Vizcaíno Peninsula.

🚙 Side Route

Rancho San José de Castro to Malarrimo Beach
(27 mi., 44 km.; 2:30 hrs.)

The rough road to Malarrimo Beach takes off northward from the Vizcaíno Junction-Bahía Tortugas route, about .5 mile east of the Rancho San José de Castro sign. After winding through narrow steep-walled arroyos for several miles, it climbs onto barren but colorful mesas, then makes a steep rugged descent into a wide canyon, which it follows to the shore of the Pacific Ocean. This road is subject to periodic closures because of rock slides, washouts and other hazards.

Because of its position on the north-facing side of the Vizcaíno Peninsula, Malarrimo Beach is struck head-on by the prevailing currents of the North Pacific. As a result, it has been the dumping place for flotsam and jetsam from thousands of miles away, including giant redwood logs, World War II food tins, Japanese fishing floats, timbers from sunken vessels and trash thrown overboard from ships. Stories of cases of Scotch and other valuable items being found here are probably true, but Malarrimo has been pretty thoroughly picked over. Still, the careful beachcomber can make some interesting discoveries. The beach itself is very windy, and the best campsites are just inland near the mouth of the canyon. Driftwood for fires is abundant. Motorists should be cautious of quicksand in some areas along the beach.

🚙 Side Route

Rancho San José de Castro to Bahía Asunción

(35 mi., 56 km.; 1:45 hrs.)

The graded road to Bahía Asunción branches south from the Vizcaíno Junction-Bahía Tortugas route .5 mile west of the Malarrimo Beach turnoff; follow the signed road to the left 1.3 miles to San José de Castro, bear left, go 4.3 miles, then turn right (south) onto the dirt road to Bahía Asunción. The road climbs into a range of dark brown mountains, vegetated with cholla, pitahaya and garambullo cacti, along with agave, spiny shrubs and elephant trees. After crossing a saddle, the road descends onto a wide, sloping plain; the ocean is visible in the distance to the west. The road enters a shallow arroyo and follows the sandy bottom for 1.5 miles, then winds upward to a gap between a flat-topped volcanic butte and a range of barren hills. Later the road traverses low, chalk-colored hills, then runs southeast along the base of a volcanic mesa. It rounds the south end of the mesa and emerges onto a sparsely vegetated coastal plain. After dropping into a sandy arroyo, the road turns south and reaches Bahía Asunción at mileage 37.5.

Bahía Asunción is a windblown town of 1500 situated on a low peninsula opposite rocky Isla Asunción. Like Bahía Tortugas, Bahía Asunción is supported by the abalone and lobster trade and has a cannery that ships its products by truck to Ensenada and other towns. Facilities include rustic accommodations, gasoline (*nova* only), cafes, a pharmacy, small stores, a health center, a tiny movie theater, telephone and radio communications, a military camp and an airstrip. A graded road leaves town from behind the health center and runs 7.9 miles northwest along the coast to San Roque, a fishing village.

🚙 Side Route

Bahía Asunción to Punta Abreojos

(59 mi., 93 km.; 2 hrs.)

This is one of the easier legs of the loop trip around the Vizcaíno Peninsula. Although the road has a few sandy stretches, there are no steep grades and the surface is regularly graded. After leaving Bahía Asunción, the road parallels the curve of the shoreline along the edge of an arid coastal lowland, running about .5 mile inland from the beach most of the way. Several dirt roads provide access to the shore, which is littered with a variety of shells. Primitive campsites can be found all along the beach, but the wind is constant and wood is scarce. Shore fishing is excellent. At mileage 3.9 is a junction with the graded road that leads north to the Vizcaíno Junction-Rancho San José de Castro road. Eighteen miles from Bahía Asunción the road passes a small shrine, then reaches the junction with a dirt road to Punta Prieta, a fishing village. At mileage 21.7, a road branches right to San Hipólito, another fishing village.

To the north is Cerro Mesa, with its unusual magenta and green rock strata. The road continues to follow the coastline to La Bocana, reached by a turnoff at mileage 47.7. This cannery town of 800 has stores, cafes, a clinic, gasoline and mechanical assistance. Beyond La Bocana the road veers inland and skirts a shallow inlet. The surface from here to Punta Abreojos is smooth hard-packed dirt, which permits speeds of up to 50 mph and is a natural airstrip. South of La Bocana, at mileage 10.9, the road enters Punta Abreojos.

Punta Abreojos has another fishing cooperative with a cannery that sends abalone and lobster to the markets of the north. It sits on a sandy spit between the ocean and a salt marsh. Facilities in this village of 700 include a store, a cafe, gasoline drums, a telegraph office, radio communications and two lighthouses. Just north of Punta Abreojos is an airstrip.

Side Route

Punta Abreojos to Highway 1
(53 mi., 85 km.; 2 hrs.)

This is a long drive over barren, empty land on a wide, graded road. A carefully driven passenger car can make the trip without difficulty, but because some of the road has a jarring washboard surface, travel can be uncomfortable. Leaving Punta Abreojos, the route passes an airstrip, then swings north across level, barren desert. At mileage 6.1 is a signed junction with a road leading 3.1 miles to Campo René,

where rustic cabañas and windy campsites can be found on the beach. After skirting the southern flank of flat-topped Cabo Santa Clara Mesa, the road bears northeast across rolling, cactus-covered terrain. Visible to the west is a group of volcanic peaks rising from the desert. Approaching Highway 1 the road enters a "forest" of cardón cacti. To the south, some distance away, Laguna San Ignacio is visible. Highway 1 is reached at mileage 53, 15 miles west of San Ignacio.

Side Route

Highway 1 to San Francisco de la Sierra
(23 mi., 37 km.; 1:30 hrs.)

High mesas and deep canyons, a settlement inhabited by traditional ranchers, and trails that lead to Indian cave paintings are features of this isolated route. The road, partly graded with some rough sections, is suitable only for sturdy high-clearance vehicles.

At 27.6 miles northwest of San Ignacio, the route turns off Highway 1. After heading northeast over six miles of level desert, displaying cardón, yucca válida and ocotillo, the road makes a sharp, winding ascent onto a mesa. Southeast of the mesa a vast lonesome canyon may be viewed. Climbing more mesas and passing occasional ranches, the road comes to an abrupt descent at about 22 miles. The village of San Francisco is visible across the canyon. Winding down, then upward, the road reaches the village after 1.5 miles. The high country has barrel cactus, agave, occasional cirios and closely spaced brush. Temperatures are cooler; the climate has more rainfall and is classified as semiarid.

San Francisco de la Sierra (elevation 4500 feet) and vicinity are inhabited by Californios, descendants of Spanish ranchers who settled the interior highlands in the 1700s. Raising mules, horses and goats, they have to the present remained rather isolated from the mainstream of Mexican culture. The village has a school, church and small store; meals are available upon request. Mule trails lead from the village to cave paintings made by Indians several hundred years ago. The drawings are protected by the federal government and visitors must be accompanied by ranchers who are authorized guides. Pack trips to the paintings require three or four days. One small cave is located near the village, but even it requires a guide and a small fee is charged.

San Ignacio

(See also *Lodging & Restaurants* and *Campgrounds & Trailer Parks*.)

For the traveler who has motored through mile after mile of inhospitable terrain, the first view of San Ignacio is one of Baja California's great delights. A forest of date palms and one of the most charming towns on the peninsula are set in the bottom of a wide arroyo surrounded by arid desert. Northernmost of Baja California's major oasis communities, San Ignacio is an attractive, tranquil settlement of about 2000 inhabitants. Its thatched-roof dwellings and pastel-colored business structures are clustered around an imposing stone mission and a tree-shaded plaza.

The paved road leading from Highway 1 into San Ignacio passes over a small dam, impounding an underground river that emerges to the earth's surface here. It provides sustenance for an economy based on agriculture. Dates are the chief crop, but figs, oranges and grapes are also grown commercially. San Ignacio also serves as the market center for the isolated cattle ranches to the north and south. To the visitor, it offers hotels and trailer parks, cafes, gasoline, mechanical assistance, telephone service, supplies and an airstrip.

Before the arrival of European explorers, this was the site of a large Indian settlement. Seeing a fertile field for their work, the Jesuits founded a mission here in 1728 and planted the date palms that now cover the floor of the arroyo. After the expulsion of the Jesuits from Mexico, the Dominicans came to San Ignacio and built the present church, which was completed in 1786. Thanks to lava-block walls four-feet thick, it remains in an excellent state of preservation and still serves as a parish church.

In the rugged, remote mountains both north and south of San Ignacio are hundreds of mysterious cave paintings drawn by prehistoric Indians. Large figures of humans and animals in a variety of colors appear on high ledges and on the ceilings and walls of shallow caves. The origin, age and meaning of this rock art are unknown. One good road leads to the area, and arrangements for mule trips to many of these sites can be made at the hotels in San Ignacio.

South of San Ignacio a dirt road leads 30 miles to Laguna San Ignacio, a site for whale watching. From there a long graded dirt road travels 100 miles south along the Pacific coast to the agricultural oases of San José de Gracia and Ejido Cadeje and the large fishing village of San Juanico. Bahía San Juanico has beach campsites and good

San Ignacio, with its magnificent 18th-century mission, occupies a palm-lined arroyo surrounded by harsh desert terrain.

surfing. From here the road continues to Ciudad Insurgentes in the Santo Domingo Valley.

⬛ Travelogue

San Ignacio to Santa Rosalia

(45 mi., 73 km.; 1:15 hrs.)

Leaving the palm groves of San Ignacio behind, Highway 1 reenters arid countryside, winding through low hills toward Las Tres Vírgenes, a large mountain mass with three volcanic cones rising majestically above the surrounding desert. After skirting the base of the volcanoes, the road drops onto a cactus-covered plateau. At the end of the plateau is the steepest grade on the entire length of Highway 1; here the road drops via sharp switchbacks for

seven miles to the shore of the Gulf of California. (Drivers should exercise caution, watching particularly for trucks rounding the curves.) Then the highway turns south and follows the coastline for 4.7 miles to the junction with the main street of Santa Rosalía.

00.0	Junction with the paved road into San Ignacio.
08.8	Junction with a rough dirt road to Rancho Santa Marta, a departure point for mule trips to ancient Indian cave paintings in the rugged mountains north of San Ignacio.
24.0	Excellent viewpoint for Las Tres Vírgenes.
34.1	First view of the Gulf of California.
34.4	Beginning of a series of steep grades and tight curves, as the

The majestic Las Tres Virgines volcanoes rise above the surrounding desert.

highway plunges 1000 feet to the shore of the gulf.

40.6 The shore of the Gulf of California.

45.2 Junction with the main street of Santa Rosalía.

Santa Rosalía

(See also *Lodging & Restaurants* and *Campgrounds & Trailer Parks.*)

Santa Rosalía, with a population of 11,000, is a bustling city with narrow, congested streets and a businesslike atmosphere. It used to be a mining town, having been established in the 1880s by the French-owned El Boleo Copper Company. After discovering rich copper deposits here, the mining company imported Indian labor from Sonora, built a pipeline to bring water to the city and constructed a port to handle shipments of processed ore. Mining operations were very prosperous for several decades, but ore deterioration and low demand forced the closure of the mines in 1954. A few

efforts have been made since then to revive the industry.

With its row upon row of uniform frame buildings and its large smelters, Santa Rosalía looks like a company-owned mining town, quite different from any other town in Baja California. Even the church of Santa Bárbara seems incongruous, constructed of flat galvanized iron shipped in sections from France. The town consists of three sections, with two plateaus separated by a flat-bottomed arroyo. The northern plateau, with its many French-colonial buildings and its panoramic view of the smelter, is especially interesting. Commercial fishing boats are based in the small harbor, which also serves as the terminus for ferry service to Guaymas across the gulf (see *Appendix,* Transportation).

Santa Rosalía is the seat of government for the *municipio* of Mulegé, which also contains Guerrero Negro, San Ignacio and Mulegé. Although Santa Rosalía is not a tourist town, it does offer a variety of facilities, including overnight

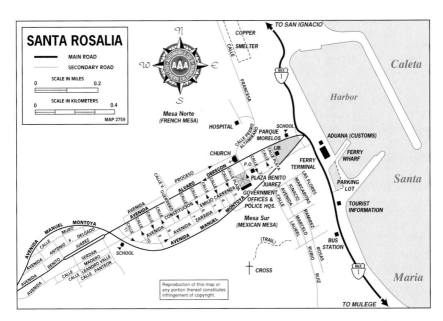

SANTA ROSALIA

— MAIN ROAD
— SECONDARY ROAD

SCALE IN MILES
0　　　　0.2

SCALE IN KILOMETERS
0　　　　0.4

MAP 2759

TO SAN IGNACIO

COPPER SMELTER

CALLE

FRANCESA

Mesa Norte
(FRENCH MESA)

HOSPITAL

CALLE PEDRO ALTAMIRANO

SCHOOL

PARQUE
MORELOS

ADUANA (CUSTOMS)

CHURCH

LIB.

CALLE PLAYA

FERRY
WHARF

PROGRESO

P.O.

FERRY
TERMINAL

PARKING
LOT

CALLE V. GUERRERO

ALVARO

OBREGON

PLAZA BENITO
JUAREZ

TOURIST
INFORMATION

AVENIDA

AVENIDA

CONSTITUCION

EMILIO CARRENZA

CALLE PLAZA

GOVERNMENT
OFFICES &
POLICE HQS.

LAS FLORES

MARGARITAS CALLE

ICNACIO

AVENIDA

Santa

ZARABIA

MONTOYA

Mesa Sur
(MEXICAN MESA)

RAMIREZ

MARCELO

LAUREL

MANUEL

MONTOYA

AVENIDA

AVENIDA

CALLE MURO

ANTONIO F. DELGADO

AVENIDA

JUAREZ

AVENIDA

AVENIDA

(TRAIL)

RUBIO

ROSAS

RUIZ

BUS
STATION

BENITO

SERDAN

SCHOOL

MADERO

CALLE (LEANDRO VALLE

CALLE PANTEON

Reproduction of this map or
any portion thereof constitutes
infringement of copyright.

✝ CROSS

TO MULEGE

Caleta

Harbor

Santa

Maria

accommodations, many stores and restaurants, an excellent bakery, a Pemex station, auto parts, mechanical service, banks, telephone and telegraph. Biblioteca Mahatma Gandhi, the public library at Calle Playa and Avenida Constitución, displays historical account ledgers from the mining company and photographs of past mining and shipping.

Santa Rosalía was developed by a French copper-mining company.

MEXICO HIGHWAY 1

◪ Travelogue

Santa Rosalía to Mulegé
(38 mi., 61 km.; 1 hr.)

From Santa Rosalía, Highway 1 heads south along the gulf shore for about four miles, offering excellent views of Isla San Marcos, where gypsum is mined and shipped to the United States. After swinging inland, the highway soon returns to the gulf, then turns inland again, passing through barren countryside before rapidly descending to Mulegé.

00.0   Junction with the main street of Santa Rosalía.

05.2   Junction with the 7.5-mile dirt road to Santa Agueda, a quaint farming village that produces papayas, mangos and dates, and has a spring that is the source of Santa Rosalía's water. Although graded its entire length, the road has a rough, washboard surface and a couple of bad spots that could damage a passenger car.

09.0   San Lucas, a fishing village situated on an attractive, palm-lined cove. Good camping beaches can be found both north and south of the village. A signed turnoff leads to San Lucas RV Park.

14.3   San Bruno, a village with an airstrip that has grown up around a fishing cooperative on the gulf shore, 0.8 mile from Highway 1.

17.5   Junction with the dirt road to San José de Magdalena (see Side Route to San José de Magdalena).

22.0   Entrance to the Santa Rosalía Airport.

25.6   A gravel road leading to **Punta Chivato**, site of a seafront hotel (see *Campgrounds & Trailer Parks*). Nearby are a good dirt airstrip, a cluster of vacation homes and a camping area on a sandy beach.

38.5   **Mulegé.** Turn left to enter the main part of town.

The prefabricated iron church, designed by A.G. Eiffel for the 1898 Paris World's Fair, was shipped in sections around Cape Horn to Santa Rosalía.

Punta Chivato boasts a seafront resort hotel.

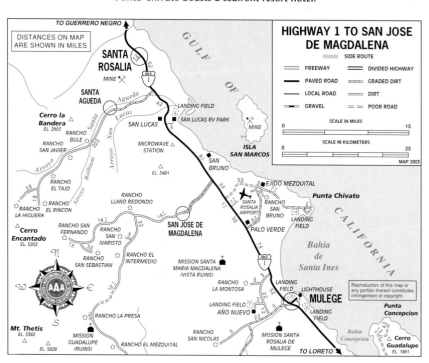

🚗 Side Route

Highway 1 to
San José de Magdalena

(9 mi., 15 km.; 0:30 hr.)

The short side trip to the picturesque old village of San José de Magdalena can be made in a standard passenger car. The road becomes rough past the village, however, and is only suitable for vehicles with high ground clearance. From a well-marked junction 17.5 miles south of Santa Rosalía on Highway 1, the graded dirt road branches west and traverses a sparsely vegetated plain for 3.5 miles. It then enters a range of barren foothills and negotiates a series of short, steep grades before dropping into a palm-lined canyon. After following the edge of the canyon past several ranches and an interesting cemetery, the road crosses a streambed and arrives in San José de Magdalena. This is an attractive oasis village with groves of stately palms, many colorful flower gardens and thatched-palm dwellings interspersed with concrete-block houses. Farming sustains the local economy; crops include dates, citrus fruits and several varieties of vegetables. San José de Magdalena dates back to Baja California's Spanish colonial days, when it was a visiting station of the Mulegé mission. Evidence of the village's history can be seen in the old stone walls running along the valley floor and in the ruins of a chapel built by the Dominicans in 1774. The Mission Guadalupe ruins can be reached by horseback from Rancho San Isidro, 10 miles southeast of San José de Magdalena.

༄ Mulegé ༄

(See also Lodging & Restaurants and Campgrounds & Trailer Parks.)

The oasis community of Mulegé is located near the bottom of a lushly vegetated river valley surrounded by barren hills. Its name is a contraction of Yuman Indian words meaning "large creek of the white mouth." The town, which has a population of about 5000, sits on the north bank of the Río Mulegé (Santa Rosalía) about two miles upstream from the Gulf of California. One of the oldest towns in southern Baja California, it began as a mission settlement in 1705. With its air of tranquility, abundance of date palms and many old-style houses, Mulegé exudes the atmosphere of a quiet, traditional town. Dates are the principal crop, but figs, oranges, bananas and olives are also grown here.

Since the completion of the paved Transpeninsular Highway, Mulegé has become a popular tourist destination. Its extensive facilities include hotels, trailer parks, restaurants, banks, markets, gift shops, a coin laundry, two Pemex stations, an auto supply store, mechanical assistance and a clinic. The downtown streets, although in good condition, are narrow and restricted to one-way traffic.

Points of Interest

MISION SANTA ROSALIA DE MULEGE *Just upstream from the bridge that carries Highway 1 across the river.* Founded in 1705 and completed in 1766, the mission has been restored with the help of the government and now functions as a church. Nearby, rocky steps lead up a hill that affords a bird's-eye view over the oasis. To reach the mission from town, go south on Calle Zaragoza (the longest north-south street in Mulegé), cross the river on a small bridge under the elevated highway bridge, turn sharply back to the right and follow a dirt road, first through palm groves then up a barren grade to the mission.

MUSEO DE MULEGÉ *On a hilltop overlooking the town.* A classic building that was formerly a federal prison now houses displays of the history of Mulegé and other places in Baja California Sur. It contains fine artifacts of Cochimí Indians and Mexican settlers,

The palm-lined banks of the Río Mulegé give the appearance of a tropical idyll.

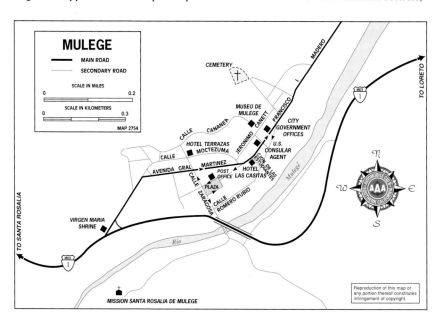

MULEGE

MAIN ROAD
SECONDARY ROAD

SCALE IN MILES
0   0.2

SCALE IN KILOMETERS
0   0.3

MAP 2754

CEMETERY

MADERO

TO LORETO

MEX 1

MUSEO DE MULEGE

FRANCISCO

CITY GOVERNMENT OFFICES

CALLE CANANEA

HOTEL TERRAZAS MOCTEZUMA

JERONIMO CANETT

U.S. CONSULAR AGENT

CALLE

MARTINEZ

AVENIDA GRAL

POST OFFICE

HOTEL LAS CASITAS

NICOLAS BRAVO

Mulegé

PLAZA

CALLE ZARAGOZA

CALLE ROMERO RUBIO

TO SANTA ROSALIA

VIRGEN MARIA SHRINE

Rio

MEX 1

MISSION SANTA ROSALIA DE MULEGE

Mision Santa Rosalía de Mulegé, founded by the Jesuits in 1705, has been extensively restored.

religious objects and paintings by local artists.

SANCTUARIO DE LA VIRGEN MARIA
At the west end of town. The shrine includes a panoramic painting of Mulegé.

🚩 Travelogue

Mulegé to Loreto
(84 mi., 136 km.; 2 hrs.)

Beyond the junction with Mulegé's main street, Highway 1 crosses the river and veers eastward toward the Gulf of California, then heads south through barren coastal hills. A dozen miles past Mulegé, the highway reaches the shore of beautiful Bahía de la Concepción, one of the scenic highlights of Baja California. For the next 25 miles, the road parallels the shore of the bay, providing a series of breathtaking panoramas of sparkling blue-green waters, volcanic islands and inviting campsites. From the head of the bay, Highway 1 climbs a low saddle, then emerges onto a long, sandy plain. The rugged backbone of the Sierra de la Giganta is visible to the west. Finally, after winding through scrub-covered hills, the highway drops to a coastal plain near the junction to Loreto. There is no gasoline available on this long stretch of highway.

00.0   **Junction to Mulegé.**

00.7   **Junction with a road leading to Mission Santa Rosalía de Mulegé.**

01.7   **Junction with the entrance road to the Villa María Isabel RV/Trailer Park.**

13.3   **Playa Santispac, a developed public beach on an attractive cove.**

14.6   Posada Concepción, a campground on the shore of Bahía Tordillo.

17.1   Rancho El Coyote, opposite a pair of lovely coves with enticing public beaches.

27.0   El Requesón, a small island connected to the shore by a sandspit. The narrow spit is a *playa pública.*

36.3   Junction with a lonesome dirt road that loops around the southern end of Bahía Concepción (see *Campgrounds & Trailer Parks*), then goes north along the eastern side of the bay for 36 miles to Punta Concepción. The road passes a few fish camps and much pristine desert. The last few miles are very rough.

45.7   Rancho Rosarito, a ranch in a small oasis.

46.8   Junction with a road across the Sierra de la Giganta to San Isidro, La Purísima, San Jose de Comondú and San Miguel de Comondú (see Side Route to La Purísima).

54.1   Junction with a scenic dirt road to San Juanico and Bahía San Basilio.

65.2   Junction with a dirt road to Rancho San Juan Londo, 0.2 miles from the highway in a palm grove. This is the site of a Jesuit *visita,* or visiting station, dating from 1705.

84.1   Junction with the paved road to Loreto.

🚙 Side Route

Highway 1 to Ciudad Insurgentes via La Purísima

(118 mi., 190 km.; 5 hrs.)

Because of their isolation, the Purísima and Comondú oases preserve a sense of an earlier era. A graded dirt road across the ruggedly scenic Sierra de la Giganta now leads from Highway 1 to the oasis villages of San Isidro and La Purísima. Wide and well-graded most of the way, the road is suitable for high-clearance vehicles.

The junction with the new road is 47 miles south of Mulegé (or 37 miles

Beautiful Bahía de la Concepción is famous for its fine camping beaches, excellent fishing and spectacular scenery.

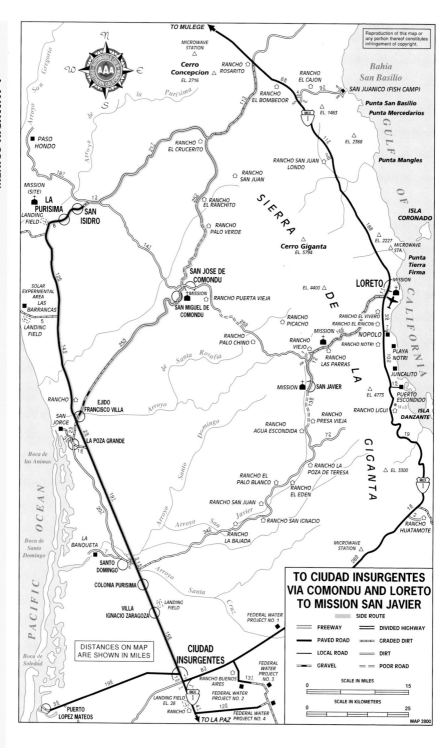

Reproduction of this map or any portion thereof constitutes infringement of copyright.

TO MULEGE

MICROWAVE STATION

Cerro Concepcion △ EL 2716

RANCHO ROSARITO

RANCHO EL CAJON

Bahia San Basilio

SAN JUANICO (FISH CAMP)

Punta San Basilio
Punta Mercedarios

RANCHO EL BOMBEDOR

MEX 1 EL 1463

EL 2368

Punta Mangles

RANCHO SAN JUAN LONDO

PASO HONDO

RANCHO EL CRUCERITO

RANCHO SAN JUAN

SIERRA

ISLA CORONADO

MISSION (SITE)
LA PURISIMA
SAN ISIDRO

LANDING FIELD

RANCHO EL RANCHITO

RANCHO PALO VERDE

Cerro Giganta EL 5794

EL 2227

MICROWAVE STA

Punta Tierra Firma

LORETO

MISSION

SOLAR EXPERMENTAL AREA
LAS BARRANCAS

LANDING FIELD

SAN JOSE DE COMONDU

MISSION
SAN MIGUEL DE COMONDU

RANCHO PUERTA VIEJA

EL 4400

DE

RANCHO EL VIVERO
RANCHO EL RINCON

NOPOLO

RANCHO NOTRI

PLAYA NOTRI

JUNCALITO

RANCHO PICACHO

MISSION

RANCHO PALO CHINO

RANCHO VIEJO

RANCHO LAS PARRAS

LA

MISSION
SAN JAVIER

EL 4773

PUERTO ESCONDIDO

RANCHO
EJIDO FRANCISCO VILLA

SAN JORGE

LA POZA GRANDE

RANCHO PRESA VIEJA

RANCHO AGUA ESCONDIDA

RANCHO LIGUI

Well

ISLA DANZANTE

Boca de las Animas

GIGANTA

EL 3300

RANCHO LA POZA DE TERESA

RANCHO EL PALO BLANCO

RANCHO EL EDEN

OCEAN

RANCHO SAN JUAN

RANCHO SAN IGNACIO

RANCHO HUATAMOTE

LA BANQUETA

SANTO DOMINGO

RANCHO LA BAJADA

MICROWAVE STATION

MEX 1

Boca de Santo Domingo

COLONIA PURISIMA

Santa Cruz

PACIFIC

VILLA IGNACIO ZARAGOZA

LANDING FIELD

FEDERAL WATER PROJECT NO. 1

Boca de Soledad

DISTANCES ON MAP ARE SHOWN IN MILES

CIUDAD INSURGENTES

FEDERAL WATER PROJECT NO. 3

TO CIUDAD INSURGENTES VIA COMONDU AND LORETO TO MISSION SAN JAVIER

SIDE ROUTE

FREEWAY	DIVIDED HIGHWAY
PAVED ROAD	GRADED DIRT
LOCAL ROAD	DIRT
GRAVEL	POOR ROAD

RANCHO BUENOS AIRES

FEDERAL WATER PROJECT NO. 2

LANDING FIELD EL 28

MEX 1

RANCHO

PUERTO LOPEZ MATEOS

FEDERAL WATER PROJECT NO. 4

TO LA PAZ

SCALE IN MILES
0   15

SCALE IN KILOMETERS
0   25

MAP 2800

north of Loreto) on Highway 1. The road winds through a series of narrow canyons, walled by steep volcanic bluffs. Vegetation is thick and consists of cardón, pitahaya, three varieties of cholla, palo adán, mesquite and dense underbrush. At mileage 11.3 is a junction: to the left is the road to San José de Comondú and San Miguel de Comondú; to the right is a seldom-used portion of the old La Purísima/San Isidro road. Proceed straight ahead. A mile beyond the junction, the road tops a low ridge via a rocky grade, then descends into a long, winding valley. The route meanders in and out of the valley, occasionally crossing sparsely vegetated hills of volcanic boulders, until at mileage 30.7 it reaches the rim of the La Purísima Valley. After dropping 700 feet to the valley floor via a series of steep switchbacks, the road becomes a palm-lined avenue with a stone aqueduct alongside. It passes orchards and cultivated fields before arriving in San Isidro at mileage 35.2. San Isidro, a community of 600 inhabitants, has a cafe, limited supplies, a telegraph, a clinic and a rustic motel. Three miles farther down the valley is La Purísima.

The oasis village of La Purísima sits amid groves of palms in the bottom of

After traversing many miles of rough road, the oasis of the Valle de la Purísima comes into view.

a deep valley that is walled in by high cliffs and surrounded by rugged, barren desert. Thanks to an irrigation system fed by spring water, the valley is intensively farmed and yields a variety of crops, including dates, mangos, grapes, citrus fruits, corn, beans and tomatoes. The town itself, with a population of about 700, has a well-worn look. La Purísima began in 1730, when a Jesuit mission was moved here from a site several miles away. The native Indian population was decimated by disease, and the mission was abandoned in

The municipal hall of the little town of La Purísima faces the town square.

1822; only stone ruins remain. The present village dates from the late 19th century, when the fertile valley was resettled by Mexican farmers—ancestors of today's friendly residents of La Purísima. Modest accommodations can be found here, along with gasoline, meals, limited supplies, a post office and a municipal office. Leaving La Purísima the road continues down the valley for another 3.5 miles to a junction. The right fork is a graded road running northward for 120 miles to San Ignacio; the route to Ciudad Insurgentes bears left here and climbs out of the valley onto a high mesa. Paved most of the way, it then heads southward, winding among barren rounded hills. Thirteen miles from the junction is a signed road to the fishing village of Las Barrancas, site of a joint German/Mexican solar energy project. At mileage 76.8 from Highway 1 (or 34.8 miles from La Purísima), the road arrives at Ejido Francisco Villa—a

dusty, windblown farming cooperative. Here the Comondú road angles in from the left, and a road to Poza Grande, another farming community, veers off to the right; proceed straight ahead for Ciudad Insurgentes. The road continues to run in a straight line through open desert punctuated by irrigated fields. Here on the Santo Domingo (Magdalena) Plain, farmers utilize water drawn from deep wells to transform a sandy desert into productive fields of wheat and other crops. About 22 miles past Ejido Francisco Villa is the junction with a 1.5-mile side road to Santo Domingo, a farming community with a store, a cafe and gasoline. Two miles farther is the junction with the road coming in from Loreto and Mission San Javier. Southward 15 miles farther lies the large farm market town of Ciudad Insurgentes. From Insurgentes a paved road leads 24 miles west to the fishing port of Puerto López Mateos.

꧁ Loreto ꧁

(See also *Lodging & Restaurants* and *Campgrounds & Trailer Parks*.)

Loreto enjoys a scenic setting in a grove of palms and other subtropical trees on the shore of the Gulf of California. The jagged peaks of the Sierra de la Giganta rise abruptly from the coastal plain, forming a dramatic backdrop to the west. Directly offshore is Isla del Carmen, site of a salt works that has operated since the Spaniards first settled. A branch road leads from Highway 1 to the center of Loreto, which is built around a picturesque central plaza and a graceful stone mission. On the shore of the gulf, Calle de la Playa and the *malecón* (sea wall) walkway have recently been refurbished and paved. A stroll along the malecón reveals impressive sights: crashing surf, pelicans and other birds diving for fish and a vista of azure waters and the rugged island beyond.

Despite its impressive mission church, Loreto gives little indication of the key role it has played in the history of Baja California. Loreto is the oldest permanent settlement in the Californias. It dates back to October 25, 1697, when the Jesuit padre Juan María Salvatierra arrived and founded Mission Nuestra Señora de Loreto. For the next 132 years, Loreto served as the capital of Baja California, as well as the commercial and military hub of the peninsula. It was the base from which Junípero Serra began the exploration and colonization of what is now California in 1769; on his journey northward he founded the chain of missions in Alta California. In 1829, after Loreto was devastated by a hurricane, the capital was moved to La Paz. After more than a century of peaceful slumber, Loreto has rebounded—thanks to its location

The **malecón** *in Loreto is an ideal place to relax.*

▼ *Quick Guide to Loreto*

Tourist Information and Assistance

Municipal Tourism Office *On the Plaza Cívica in the municipal hall.* Information and brochures about the region are available.

on Highway 1 and the discovery by sportsmen that fishing off Loreto was good even by Gulf of California standards. Since the completion of the paved highway in 1973, the warm waters of the area have attracted increasing numbers of anglers and tourists each year. Loreto Airport receives regular commercial flights from Los Angeles. FONATUR, a government-managed development group, has also targeted the Loreto area for a major tourist development, patterned after similar projects in Mexico at Can-

cún and Ixtapa. To date, FONATUR has assisted in developments in the town of Loreto and in resort facilities at Nopaló, five miles to the south. In addition a marina is being developed at Puerto Escondido (Puerto Loreto), 15 miles south of Loreto.

In this town of about 9000, fishing and tourism are the bulwarks of the local economy, with tourism playing an ever-increasing role. Facilities include a variety of hotels, trailer parks, numerous shops, two supermarkets, restaurants, a hospital, a bank, a coin laundry, Pemex station, mechanical service and auto parts. Typical Mexican articles for sale include shawls, women's clothing, pottery and leather crafts. In 1992 the city became the seat of government for the new *municipio* of Loreto.

Points of Interest

MISION NUESTRA SEÑORA DE LORETO *Center of town.* The current

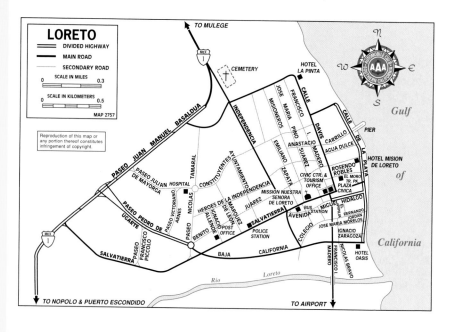

Loreto's historic municipal hall faces the Plaza Cívica.

building was completed in 1752. It has withstood numerous hurricanes, floods and earthquakes, and is still an active church after extensive restoration and remodeling.

MUSEUM *Next door to the mission. Open Mon. through Fri. 9 a.m. to 12:30 and 1 to 4 p.m. Admission $1.60.* Fascinating displays about missions, and horse and wagon equipment are presented in this museum.

PLAZA CIVICA *Avenidas Salvatierra and Francisco Madero, just east of the mission.* Laid out in traditional Mexican style, it faces the municipal hall, the tourism office and several stores.

▟ Travelogue

Loreto to Ciudad Constitución
(89 mi., 143 km.; 2 hrs.)

South of Loreto, the Sierra de la Giganta rises abruptly from the deep-blue waters of the gulf. For several miles, Highway 1 runs along the base of the reddish-brown mountains, following the dramatic coastline past fine beaches and offshore islands. Then the highway turns inland and climbs rapidly via sharp switchbacks. On approaching the summit, unusual hat-shaped mountain peaks are visible nearby. After the summit, the road begins a gradual descent along the edge of a deep canyon. Continuing southwest, the highway levels out onto the broad, gently sloped Santo Domingo (Magdalena) Valley. Though extremely arid, this sandy, cactus-covered lowland has developed into a major agricultural center—thanks to water from deep wells. Highway 1 passes several large farms and a pair of federal water projects before arriving in Ciudad Insurgentes, where it turns south and runs in a straight line along irrigated fields to Ciudad Constitución. Slow-moving vehicles are a common hazard in this final stretch; pass with care.

01.1   Junction with a rough dirt road to Mission San Javier (see Side Route to Mission San Javier). This road should only be attempted by sturdy high-clearance vehicles.

01.7   Junction with the paved road to Loreto's airport. Aero California flies here from Los Angeles. (See *Appendix*, Transportation Schedules section.)

05.2   Nopoló, site of a government-sponsored FONATUR resort complex, which is now being developed. Currently in operation are the Hotel Mercure El Cortés and a clinic.

10.0   A dirt road to Playa Notrí, a sandy beach.

▼ The Spanish Missions

In 1697, Father Juan Maria Salvatierra founded the first Spanish mission on the Baja California peninsula at Loreto. Father Salvatierra represented the Jesuit Order of the Roman Catholic Church, which had received permission from the Spanish Crown for the pacification of the native inhabitants and their conversion to the Roman Catholic faith. The Jesuits followed up this first mission with 19 more built during the period 1697-1767.

During this era of Jesuit control there were numerous Indian revolts. The most dangerous revolt occurred between 1734 and 1736, when the Pericu Indians of the Cape region succeeded in killing two of the missionaries and in burning three of the missions (Santiago, San Jose del Cabo and Loreto). A military force was dispatched from the Mexican mainland to quell the rebellion, which it did with brutal efficiency. In addition to this, epidemics of measles and small pox, brought to Baja by the Europeans, further decimated the native inhabitants, who had no natural immune system against these diseases. By 1767, when the Jesuit Order was expelled from Baja California for abuse of authority, the Indian population was a mere fraction of their original numbers.

The Baja California mission system was given over to the care of the Franciscan Order in 1768. They created only one mission in the Baja peninsula, San Fernando Velicata, in 1769. After that they turned their attention north to the more economically promising region of Alta California—the modern U.S. territory of California.

The Franciscans ceded administration of the Baja peninsula missions to the Dominican Order in 1773. Over the next 60 years, the Dominicans established nine more missions in Baja California, but the native population had become so small that the missions were no longer economically profitable. In 1832 all but the nine missions established by the Dominicans were secularized, and shortly afterwards these nine missions followed suit. By 1846 the mission era was over.

14.0 Junction with the short dirt road to Juncalito, a fishing village, where boats for sportfishing are available. The road continues beyond the village to a *playa pública*.

14.6 Posada Concepción, a campground on the shore of Bahía Tordillo.

15.2 Junction with the 1.5-mile paved road to Puerto Escondido (Puerto Loreto), a deepwater port once used for shipping products. This beautiful, nearly landlocked bay is slowly being developed by FONATUR. Tourist facilities include the Tripui Resort RV Park (see *Campgrounds & Trailer Parks*) and a marina with a boat ramp.

17.1 Rancho El Coyote, opposite a pair of lovely coves with enticing public beaches. 27.0 El Requesón, a small island connected to the shore by a sandspit. The narrow spit is a *playa pública*.

34.0 A steep, scenic dirt road leads southeast to Agua Verde, a fishing village on the Gulf of California. Campsites are available on nearby beaches.

44.6 Turnout overlooking a rugged canyon.

63.0 Entrance to Ley Federal de Aguas #1, a government-sponsored water project that provides fresh water for nearby farms. It has a large Pemex station.

67.5 Buenos Aires and Ley Federal de Aguas #2, a collection of prosperous-looking farms.

73.3 A red, white and green monument marks the junction with Ciudad Insurgentes, an agricultural settlement of about 12,000 with stores, cafes, two Pemex stations, banks, an auto parts store and mechanical assistance. The center of town is to the right. The main street continues north as a paved road for 66 miles, then as a graded dirt road following the coast for 139 more miles to San Ignacio; branches lead to San Javier, Comondú, La Purísima (see Side Route to La Purísima), and San Juanico, a very popular surfing area.

88.3 Entrance to the Ciudad Constitución airport. Ciudad Constitución, at the junction with the paved road (Mexico Highway 22) to San Carlos (see Side Route to San Carlos).

⊶ Side Route

Loreto to Mission San Javier
(23 mi., 37 km.; 2 hrs.)

The trip from Loreto to Mission San Javier is one of Baja California's most rewarding side routes. In addition to one of North America's most beautiful Spanish missions, it offers superlative mountain and canyon scenery. Sturdy, high-clearance vehicles should be used. The mission can also be reached from the Pacific side of the peninsula, but this approach is considerably longer and has many rocky arroyo crossings.

From a signed junction 1.1 mile south of the Loreto turnoff, the road leads westward from Highway 1 through low rounded hills for about six miles. It then begins a gradual winding climb into the rugged Sierra de la Giganta, following the steep wall of a deep arroyo. At mileage 9.5 there is a rocky section. The old road is visible meandering along the palm-studded floor of the canyon. A mile farther the road swings to the left, offering travelers an excellent view of the gaping canyon below and the blue Gulf of California in the distance. Rancho Las Parras, 12.2 miles from Highway 1, has a small stone chapel and groves of citrus and olive trees. Six miles beyond the rancho is a junction with a rough road to Comondú, 25.8 miles to the north. The road then gently winds for 4.4 miles through a narrow canyon to San Javier. The vegetation changes from desert to steppe (semiarid) because of the increased elevation. Local agriculture involves raising goats and cattle and growing olives, oranges and mangos.

Mission San Javier sits in the bottom of a deep valley beneath towering walls of dark gray stone. Surrounding the mission is the village of San Javier, which has a small store, cafe, telephone and a divided parkway instead of the usual plaza. The impressive mission is of a Moorish style that is dramatic in its simplicity; its stonework and ornamentation are considered outstanding. This was the second of Baja California's Jesuit missions, founded in 1699 but not completed until 1758. That a church of this size could be built in such a rugged, remote region and survive in such a fine state of preservation to the present day is truly remarkable.

Beyond the mission, the road continues to head southwest down the canyon, fording several arroyos and passing several small ranches. The canyon gradually widens into a broad valley, and irrigated farms appear along the road. Finally, 43.8 miles beyond San Javier, the road reaches the junction with the La Purísima/Ciudad Insurgentes route. This section takes almost three hours to traverse. From this point it is 15.5 miles to the junction with Highway 1 in Ciudad Insurgentes.

Mission San Javier, a beautifully preserved example of the Jesuit missions, still serves as a parish for local residents.

Rugged landscape is a distinctive feature of the state of Baja California Sur.

🚙 Side Route

Highway 1 to Ciudad Insurgentes via Comondú

(103 mi., 165 km.; 5 hrs.)

For the first 11.3 miles the route to Comondú is shared with the San Isidro/La Purísima road. Except for these first few miles, which are wide and graded, the road is narrow and winding with numerous steep, rocky grades. The trip to Comondú can be made with sturdy, high-clearance vehicles; however, the southern approach from Ciudad Insurgentes offers a much better road.

The unmarked junction with Highway 1 is 47 miles south of Mulegé and 37 miles north of Loreto. From the junction the road cuts a straight westward swath across open desert for five miles, then begins a gradual ascent through a steep-walled canyon. At mileage 11.3 is an unsigned, four-way intersection. Straight ahead is San Isidro and La Purísima; to the right is an abandoned road. For Comondú, turn left. The road now winds upward over grades of up to 15 percent to the summit of the Sierra de la Giganta; this section is passable by only the sturdiest of four-wheel-drive vehicles driven by experienced drivers. It then crosses a plateau, climbs another summit and descends through a rocky arroyo. After traversing low hills for several miles, the road comes to the edge of a deep canyon. Nestled far below in a forest of date palms is Comondú. Just ahead is a junction near a roadside cemetery. Straight on lies a new graded road to San Isidro and La Purísima. To the left the road drops sharply via a series of steep switchbacks to the valley floor, reaching San José de Comondú at mileage 36.

Comondú is really two villages: San José de Comondú and, two miles farther west, San Miguel de Comondú. The combined population of these twin oasis villages is about 600. Although the surrounding volcanic mesas are nearly devoid of vegetation, the floor of the valley is a seven-mile-long strip of green. Sufficient water from nearby springs nourishes crops of figs, grapes, dates, sugarcane and vegetables. In San José de Comondú, just left of the point where the road enters the village, is the site of a Jesuit mission moved here in 1737; one stone building still stands. The original bells, which date from 1708, hang from a standard alongside the church. San José also has a grocery store and a clinic. San Miguel has a worn look with many deserted buildings, but possesses an aura of historic charm. It has a general store that also sells gasoline (*nova* only). Meals may be ordered at a private home. Leaving Comondú a graded road winds down the canyon, which gradually opens up onto a wide, sparsely vegetated coastal plain. The road is wide, well-graded and easy to follow. About 25 miles beyond Comondú (or 61 miles from Highway 1) the road arrives at Ejido Francisco Villa, where it joins the La Purísima/Ciudad Insurgentes route.

Corn is one of the many crops grown in the agriculturally rich Santo Domingo Valley.

🚙 Side Route

Ciudad Constitución to San Carlos

(36 mi., 58 km.; 0:45 hr.)

The paved route to San Carlos (Mexico Highway 22) leaves Highway 1 in the northern part of Ciudad Constitución. After running alongside irrigated fields for seven miles it traverses gently undulating desert terrain, which is heavily vegetated with cardón, cholla, pitahaya and dense brush. After reaching the mangrove-edged shore of Bahía Magdalena, Highway 22 crosses a bridge and enters San Carlos, located on an irregular peninsula in the bay.

San Carlos (also known as Puerto San Carlos) is a port built to handle shipments of wheat, garbanzo and cotton grown in the Santo Domingo Valley. The port also has a commercial fishing fleet and packing plant (tuna and sardines). With a population of about 6000, it has developed some limited facilities for tourists, including several restaurants and cafes, three motels, a rustic campground, a public beach, several markets, a clinic and a Pemex station (*nova* and diesel). Visitors find recreation in fishing, boating and whale watching.

At a junction six miles west of Highway 1 on the San Carlos road is a paved road to Villa Benito Juárez.

From there a dirt road leads northwest for 28 miles to Puerto López Mateos. In this port, population 4000, whale-watching trips are offered in the winter. By taking this road and then traveling eastward from Puerto López Mateos to Ciudad Insurgentes, the motorist can make a loop trip through this interesting desert area.

Ciudad Constitución

(See *Campgrounds & Trailer Parks.*)

In the 1960s the Santo Domingo Valley (sometimes called Magdalena Plain) was opened to rapid agricultural development, and within two decades Ciudad Constitución grew from a village into a booming modern city. With a current population of about 48,000 it is the second largest population center in the state of Baja California Sur and the seat of government for the *municipio* of Comondú, which also includes

Ciudad Insurgentes. The region is extremely arid, but water trapped for centuries far beneath the earth's surface has been tapped by deep wells, transforming the desert into a checkerboard of attractive farms. The leading crops are wheat and garbanzo; also important are cotton, sorghum, alfalfa, corn and citrus fruits. Some farms also raise livestock. The agricultural products are shipped to the mainland from San Carlos, 36 miles to the west.

Ciudad Constitución is not oriented toward tourism, but offers extensive facilities including hotels, a trailer park, supermarkets, a large public market, large and varied stores, hospitals, banks, an ice house, coin laundries, automobile dealerships, Pemex stations, auto supply stores and auto repair shops. Among a large number of restaurants and cafes, Restaurant Sancho Panza in the Hotel Maribel offers a variety of fine Mexican dishes. Prices

Ciudad Constitución serves as a distribution center for the agricultural products of the Santo Domingo Valley.

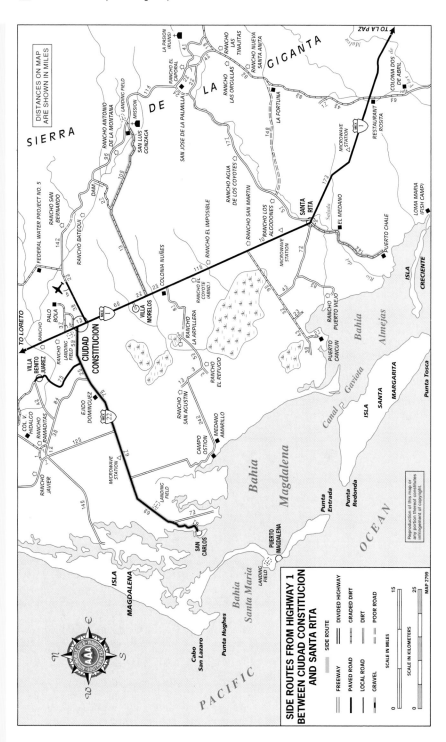

in Ciudad Constitución are lower than in the tourist towns.

◪ Travelogue

Ciudad Constitución to La Paz
(134 mi., 216 km.; 2:45 hrs.)

After leaving Ciudad Constitución, Highway 1 runs absolutely straight for more than 30 miles across virtually flat terrain. It then turns southeast and traverses a region of seemingly endless chalk-colored hills and mesas and deeply eroded gullies; numerous sharp curves present driving hazards in this section. Finally, at a high bluff marked by a tepee-shaped shrine, the Gulf of California and Bahía de La Paz come into view, with the city a cluster of white buildings on the far side of the bay. Descending rapidly, the highway soon reaches a wide, heavily vegetated coastal plain. After passing through the small bayside settlement of El Centenario, Highway 1 follows the curve of the bay into La Paz, capital of Baja California Sur.

00.0   Ciudad Constitución, at the junction with the highway to San Carlos.

01.5   Junction with the dirt road to Campestre La Pila, a large farm that contains a trailer park and a swimming pool.

07.9   Villa Morelos, a tiny farming community with a cafe.

10.1   Junction with the dirt road to El Ihuagil Dam and Mission San Luís Gonzaga (see Side Route to Mission San Luís Gonzaga).

14.0   Colonia Nuñes, another agricultural settlement. Highway 1 now leaves the region of irrigated farms and enters open desert.

35.6   Santa Rita, a village with a store, cafe and a church. At the north end of the village a dirt road branches west to Puerto Chale (see Side Route to Puerto Chale).

53.9   Junction with a mostly graded dirt road to a cattle and goat-raising region that includes the villages of San Pedro de la Presa, Las Animas and El Bosque. Winding along streams through the scenic Sierra de la Giganta, the road descends to San Evaristo on the gulf coast, 68 miles to the northeast.

Between Ciudad Constitución and La Paz, Mexico Highway 1 crosses open desert punctuated with chalk-colored mesas and buttes.

61.8 Las Pocitas, a village with a picturesque church, a clinic and a cafe. A graded road leads northeast to La Soledad and San Evaristo.

71.3 El Cien, a settlement with a Pemex station, highway department camp and a cafe.

83.9 Junction with the 12-mile dirt road to El Conejo, a wind-blown Pacific beach that is popular with surfers. Any high-clearance vehicle can make the trip.

99.8 A good graded dirt road to Conquista Agraria and the Pacific coast.

113.3 A summit with a sweeping panorama of Bahía de La Paz and the mountains beyond; a turnout leads to a tepee-shaped shrine. Highway 1 now begins a sharp descent.

123.9 Junction with a scenic paved road leading 24.7 miles north along the shore of Bahía de La Paz to the mining settlement of San Juan de la Costa. Phosphorus mined here is shipped by freighter to processing plants elsewhere in Mexico for use in the production of fertilizer. The town has gasoline and groceries. A graded dirt road follows the coast 45 miles farther north to the village of San Evaristo; its economy is based on fishing and salt evaporation and it has a protected cove. From there a road winds southwest through the Sierra de la Giganta and connects with Highway 1.

124.4 El Centenario, a small town of about 2000 inhabitants on the shore of the bay, has a Pemex station (*magna sin*). The sky-line of La Paz is visible across the water.

129.2 Chametla, a settlement at the junction with the 2.1-mile paved road to La Paz International Airport. Aero California and Aeromexico fly here from Los Angeles and Tijuana (see Air Service in *Appendix*, Transportation).

130.2 At the "Dove of Peace" monument, Camino a las Garzas veers to the right, providing a convenient bypass of central La Paz for motorists bound for the Los Cabos region.

133.5 La Paz, at the intersection of calzadas Abasolo and 5 de Febrero. Turn right here for Highway 1 south to Cabo San Lucas; straight ahead, the road along the bay's shore leads to downtown La Paz and to Pichilingue, the terminal for the Mazatlán and Topolobampo ferries (see *Appendix*, Transportation Schedules).

🚙 Side Route

Highway 1 to Mission San Luís Gonzaga

(26 mi., 42 km.; 2 hrs.)

This route is in generally good condition; however, a sturdy, high-clearance vehicle is needed. From Highway 1, at a point 2.2 miles south of Villa Morelos (10 miles south of Ciudad Constitución), turn east on the road marked Presa Ihuagil. After a mile, cultivated fields give way to native desert covered with cardón and a variety of brush. After 15 miles of flat terrain is the junction with a road leading west to Ciudad Constitución. Just beyond this is a dam, Presa Ihuagil, whose reservoir is only partially filled.

Take the right fork and follow the road along the top of the dam, then curve sharply to the right. The road on the second leg of the trip is rougher than on the first part, as it winds its way southeast over gently rolling land toward San Luis. Abundant vegetation includes cardón and cholla cacti. Several forks off the main road can cause confusion, and the route crosses several streambeds that can be troublesome during or after the occasional rains. For the last five miles ranches and grazing cattle are numerous. At mileage 23.7 is a roadside shrine.

Except for a modern school, the village of San Luis Gonzaga could be a museum piece from the past. The stone mission, founded in 1737, is still in use and has a colorful, well-kept interior. The mission and a companion building formerly used for living quarters face on a large square. Also facing the square are two other stone buildings—an abandoned store and a former public building that now serves as a kind of dormitory. Adjacent are several farm houses. Cattle ranching and date palms support the inhabitants.

🚐 Side Route
Santa Rita to Puerto Chale
(15 mi., 24 km.; 0:30 hr.)

This route, for the most part, is wide and graded. The road leaves the main highway just north of the village of Santa Rita and descends gently through barren countryside, passes the tiny hamlet of El Médano, then crosses an arroyo. Puerto Chale is a fishing village on mangrove-edged Bahía Almejas. The village has a market and a church. There are no tourist facilities, but fishing is excellent. Snook are said to lurk among the mangroves during winter, scallops are caught and the waters are good for diving.

❧ La Paz ❧
(See also Lodging & Restaurants and Campgrounds & Trailer Parks.)

L a Paz is picturesquely sandwiched between cactus-covered foothills and the curving shore of beautiful Bahía de la Paz—largest bay on the west side of the Gulf of California. Directly opposite the city is El Mogote, a narrow sandspit separating the main body of the bay from Ensenada de los Aripes, a shallow inlet to the west. Because of its location at the southeastern end of the bay, La Paz's shoreline faces northwest—a fact that becomes readily apparent during one of the city's magnificent sunsets. With its fine beaches, superlative sportfishing, numerous duty-free shops and abundance of tourist facilities, La Paz is fast becoming one of the top resorts on Mexico's west coast. The ideal time to visit La Paz is November through May, when days are warm and sunny and nights are cool. Summers can be uncomfortably hot, but often a welcome afternoon breeze known as the *coromuel* refreshes the city. Late summer to early fall is the rainy season. Rainfall is scant, varying from year to year, and most of it comes during short, violent tropical storms called *chubascos*.

La Paz has the longest history of any settlement in the Californias—and one

MEXICO HIGHWAY 1

of the most turbulent. The bay was discovered by a Spanish expedition in 1533, but the leader and several of his soldiers were killed by Indians shortly after landing. Two years later Hernán Cortés, the conqueror of Mexico, attempted to colonize the site of La Paz; supply problems, however, caused him to fail. The rich oyster beds in nearby gulf waters brought numerous seekers of wealth during the 17th century, and pearls from La Paz found their way into the Spanish royal treasury, but none of the colonies survived more than a short time. The task of colonization fell to the Jesuits, who

founded a mission here in 1720. The padres withstood a series of Indian uprisings, but after disease virtually wiped out the Indian population the mission was abandoned in 1749. Today the Cathedral of La Paz stands on its site. Not until 1811 did La Paz become a permanent settlement. In 1829, after Loreto was destroyed by a hurricane, the fledgling village of La Paz became the territorial capital. American troops occupied La Paz during the Mexican War and battles were fought in the streets of the city, but the soldiers returned to the United States after the treaty was signed. The notorious

William Walker also attempted a takeover, but he was quickly expelled.

After years of existence as a remote territory, Baja California Sur—one of Mexico's two newest states—has made rapid economic strides, with tremendous gains in population, productivity and tourism. As a result, La Paz has evolved from a sleepy little port into a vigorous, modern state capital. It is also the seat of government for the *municipio* of La Paz, which also encompasses Todos Santos. This jolt into the Mexican mainstream has not come without a few growing pains, such as the traffic snarls that occur daily in the narrow downtown streets. The current population numbers about 176,000. Still, there is something of a small-town atmosphere in La Paz, and the city retains touches of colonial grace and charm. Interspersed with contemporary structures and paved streets are colorful gardens, arched doorways and cobblestone sidewalks. Some businesses continue to observe the traditional siesta hour, closing their doors in the early afternoon. And on Sunday evenings, local residents join in the customary promenade along the palm-lined *malecón* (sea wall).

Shopping

La Paz is a free port and offers the careful shopper good buys on imported merchandise, as well as on Mexican handicrafts. Shops catering to tourists are clustered along **Paseo Alvaro Obregón** opposite the *malecón*. Bargains can also be found in small stores scattered throughout the downtown area just behind the waterfront. Handwoven cotton and woolen articles are made and sold at **Artesanía Cuauhtémoc/The Weaver**; it is located on Abasolo (Highway 1) between calles Jalisco and Nayarit. **Centro de Arte Regional**, on Chiapas at Calle Encinas, is a pottery workshop offering a variety of goods at reasonable prices.

Travelers who wish to replenish their supplies will find several large supermarkets, as well as many small grocery stores, bakeries and fruit markets. At the **Public Market** merchants sell a wide assortment of goods from individual stalls; it is located on Avenida Revolución de 1910 at Degollado. **La Perla de La Paz** is a downtown department store on Mutualismo offering a variety of high-quality merchandise. Other department stores include **Dorian's** downtown and **CCC**, with two stores near the state capitol and on Colima near Highway 1.

A favorite pastime for both locals and visitors alike is a leisurely stroll along the **malecón.**

▼ Quick Guide to La Paz

Tourist Information and Assistance

Secretaría de Turisma or **SECTUR** (Mexican Government Tourism Office) *On the Tourist Wharf at Paseo Alvaro Obregón and 16 de Septiembre (see map). Open Mon. through Fri. 8 a.m. to 8 p.m. 01152 (112) 4-0100 or 4-0103; another office for tourist information may be reached at 01152 (112) 4-0199.* The office is staffed by helpful bilingual personnel. The also offer Protección al Turista (tourist assistance), which provides legal assistance to tourists.

Newspapers

The *Baja Sun* is an English-language newspaper with recreational articles and advertisements covering the municipalities of La Paz and Los Cabos, plus additional material about the rest of Baja California. Several publications in English are for sale at the bookstore Librería Contempo on Agustín Arreolo near Paseo Alvaro Obregón. Two Spanish dailies in La Paz—*el Sudcaliforniano* and *Diario Peninsular*—serve the city and the remainder of Baja California Sur.

Radio and Television Stations

La Paz has several radio stations. XERT, 800 AM, has a varied selection of international music; 90.1 FM, *Radio Alegría,* presents traditional Mexican music. A few American radio stations come in at night. As in other parts of the Baja California peninsula, large hotels have satellite dishes which bring in several American TV stations in addition to the local channel and the national TV networks from Mexico City.

Driving in La Paz

Traffic flows smoothly on most of the long, straight streets of La Paz. Other than an abrupt terrace which rises from the bay, the city has level topography. To avoid being disoriented, drivers should closely follow the La Paz map, which reveals that the grid pattern of streets is oriented northeast-southwest. The old business section near the *malecón* (bay-front drive) has congested irregular streets and is better covered on foot. The city has several rental car agencies.

Local Transportation

La Paz has numerous taxis, especially along the *malecón* and near the hotels. Before getting in a cab, be sure to understand the fare to be charged. The rate for two miles is about $4, and from central La Paz to the airport (about eight miles) approximately $11. Local city buses run frequently to all parts of La Paz. The fare is only about 30¢. Bus riders should know some Spanish and understand the layout of the city. The central depot for local buses is by the public market at Revolución de 1910 and Degollado. Service to Pichilingue and Los Cabos is provided by Transportes Aguila at 125 Paseo Alvaro Obregón.

Long-distance travel is provided by Tres Estrellas de Oro bus lines to all other cities on the Baja peninsula;

the terminal is at Jalisco and Héroes de Independencia (see *Appendix,* Transportation section).

Ferry Transportation

Ferryboats, carrying passengers and vehicles to the mainland, sail out of Pichilingue, deep-water port for La Paz Grupo Sematur, the principal ferry company, has its ticket office on Guillermo Prieto at Cinco de May (see *Appendix,* Transportation section).

Dining

These restaurants are not all AAA approved but are shown as a convenience to travelers.

Well-known establishments include **Bermejo**, in Hotel Los Arcos (seafood, steak and Mexican dishes); **Kiwi**, on the beach near Paseo Alvaro Obregón and 5 de Mayo (seafood); **El Taste**, two blocks southwest of Hotel Los Arcos on Paseo Obregón (seafood and steaks); **Jardín Yee**, on Highway 1 about a mile southwest of the junction of Abasolo and 5 de Febrero (Cantonese cuisine); **Lapa de Carlos 'n Charlies**, on the waterfront at Paseo Obregón and de León (varied menu); **El Molino Steak House**, on the waterfront at Legaspy and Topete; **Hotel Plaza Real**, at Esquerro and Callejon La Paz in downtown (varied menu); **Samalú**, in southwest La Paz on Rangel, between Colima and Jalisco (seafood); **Caballo Blanco de La Paz**, 1½ miles southwest of downtown at Abasolo and Jalisco (steak and seafood); **La Terraza**, a sidewalk cafe in the Hotel Perla on Paseo Obregón (varied menu); and **Nuevo Pekín**, on Paseo Obregón, ¼ mile northeast of downtown La Paz (Chinese food).

Nightclubs

La Paz' nightlife is rather tame by resort standards, but the city does have a few establishments offering dancing and/or live entertainment. These include discotheques at the **Hotel Palmira** and the **Hotel Gran Baja**; the night club **La Cabaña**, on the lobby floor of the Hotel Perla; and **Quinto Patio**, on Alvaro Obregón near Bravo.

Offerings from street vendors include tasty snacks.

The center of La Paz' downtown district is the charming Plaza Constitución.

Points of Interest

BIBLIOTECA DE HISTORIA DE LAS CALIFORNIAS *North side of Plaza Constitución. 01152 (112) 2-0162. Open Mon. through Fri. 8 a.m. to 8 p.m. Free.* This library, occupying the old government center, has a display of vivid paintings about early Baja California Sur and a collection of books in Spanish and English about the history of Baja California and California.

BOAT TOURS *Tourist Wharf at Paseo Alvaro Obregón and 16 de Septiembre. 01152 (114) 3-3566 (SECTUR).* Several companies offer boat trips around Bahía de la Paz. Trips to Isla Espíritu Santo are available for those who wish to kayak around the island and enjoy its unspoiled natural environment. Some hotels and travel agencies also have information on boat tours.

DOVE OF PEACE MONUMENT *Junction of Hwy. 1 and Camino a las Garzas, the bypass to Los Cabos.* As a gateway to La Paz, the large contemporary sculpture bears an inscription which translates, "And if you want peace *(paz)*, I offer it to you in the sunny peace of my bay."

MUSEO DE ANTROPOLOGIA Y HISTORIA DE BAJA CALIFORNIA SUR *Ignacio Altamirano and 5 de Mayo. 01152 (112) 2-0162. Open Tues. through Fri. 8 a.m. to 6 p.m., Sat. 9 a.m. to 2 p.m. Donation.* This outstanding museum features exhibits on geology, geography, flora and fauna. Displays on anthropology explain Indian cultures with dioramas and replicas of cave paintings. History is covered through Spanish mission settlement, Mexican ranch life, and the struggle during the wars of independence. There is also a good book store.

NUESTRA SEÑORA DE LA PAZ *South side of Plaza Constitución.* This cathedral began as one of the original missions. Large bilingual plaques describe the history of the church and some of the early settlement of La Paz. Across Calle Revolución is an attractive plaza park.

TEATRO DE LA CIUDAD *Miguel Legaspy and Héroes de Independencia. 01152 (112) 5-0207.* The theater hosts a variety of performing arts and also contains an art gallery.

Side Route

La Paz to Pichilingue and Beaches to the North

(17 mi., 29 km.; 1 hr.)

The easy drive to Pichilingue and the beaches to the north make an enjoyable half-day excursion from La Paz. The paved road to Pichilingue (Mexico Highway 11) is a northward continuation of Paseo Alvaro Obregón—La Paz's bay-front thoroughfare. The road hugs the shore of Bahía de La Paz, offering fine views of cactus-covered hills, mangrove thickets and the clear, incredibly blue waters of the bay. Playa Coromuel, an attractive beach that is popular with La Paz residents, is 2.6 miles from Avenida 5 de Mayo, the last major street of the city. About a mile farther north are La Concha Beach Resort and El Caimancito, which has a public beach, a restaurant and the official governor's mansion. At Pichilingue, nine miles from La Paz, is the government-built ferry terminal used by the La Paz-Mazatlán and La Paz-Topolobampo ferries (see Transportation section in the *Appendix*). In addition to the ferry port facilities, Pichilingue has a commercial fishing fleet, warehouses and cafes.

The road has recently been paved to the beaches beyond Pichilingue. Just after the ferry terminal is Playa Pichilingue, another popular beach. A short distance farther north the road cuts inland, then a paved spur reaches the shore of Puerto Balandra, a lovely

Ferryboats to Mazatlán depart from La Paz' deep-water port at Pichilingue.

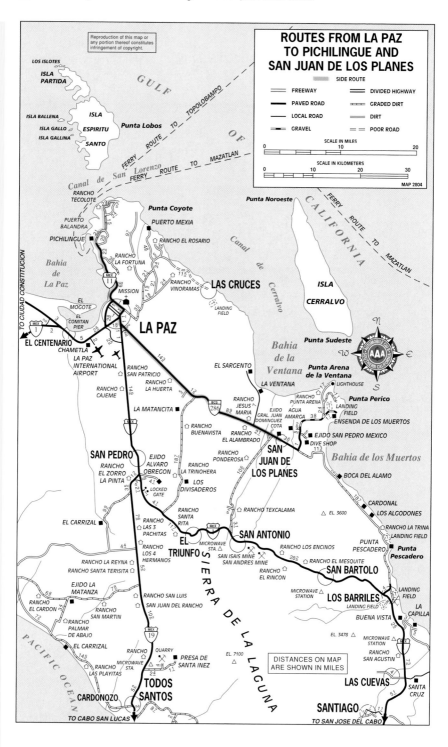

inlet that makes a good spot for a picnic. A trail leads up a hill to a viewpoint above the inlet. Past Puerto Balandra the road runs another mile to Playa Tecolote, an attractive *playa pública,* where pavement ends. A good dirt road lined with scenic desert plants turns east and follows the shoreline to a gravel mine and Playa Cachimba, eight miles northeast of Pichilingue. Surf fishing is reportedly good here. Visible offshore is 14-mile-long Isla Espíritu Santo, a destination for kayakers and wildlife observers.

🚙 Side Route

La Paz to San Juan de Los Planes
(29 mi., 45 km; 1:30 hrs.)

An excellent all-day excursion from La Paz, the side trip to Los Planes offers travelers a chance to visit a fast-growing agricultural region and to explore beautiful beaches that are seldom seen by tourists. After leaving Highway 1 at a well-marked junction on the southern outskirts of La Paz, a paved road signed "BCS 286" runs between rolling hills for nine miles, then climbs onto the northern shoulder of the Sierra de la Laguna. At mileage 11.9 is Rancho La Huerta, a long-established cattle ranch with a brick chapel, a small cemetery and a cafe. Beyond La Huerta the road passes turnoffs to several more ranches as it winds through countryside covered with cardón, cholla, pitahaya, copalquin (a small deciduous tree) and heavy underbrush. At mileage 15.9 the road reaches a summit; visible ahead are the cultivated fields of Los Planes, the blue expanse of Bahía de la Ventana, and barren mountainous Isla Cerralvo. From the summit the road makes a long, steady descent onto a level coastal plain, where it comes to a

junction at mileage 23.7. To the left a good graded road leads seven miles to El Sargento and La Ventana, fishing and ranching villages on the western shore of lovely Bahía de la Ventana. Continue straight ahead for Los Planes. At mileage 25.8 is an intersection with a new road on the right leading 14.8 miles to the village of San Antonio on Highway 1.

The route continues 3.2 miles farther to San Juan de Los Planes (or Los Planes, as it is commonly called), the center of a rapidly developing farming region. Water from deep wells irrigates fields of cotton, corn, chiles, tomatoes and beans. Los Planes is a friendly town of about 1000 with a cafe, three stores, telephone service, and a health center. The pavement continues past the center of town for a few miles en route to Ensenada de los Muertos (Deadman Bay), 13.4 miles to the northeast. Here is found a beautiful, curving bay with a small fish camp. Fine primitive campsites can be found here; fishing is excellent, and swimming is good. Punta Arena de la Ventana, directly opposite Isla Cerralvo on the eastern shore of Bahía de la Ventana, can be reached by backtracking two miles toward Los Planes, then turning right on a signed dirt road. This road leads past a cattle ranch, an airstrip and a group of salt-evaporating ponds to the isolated Hotel Las Arenas (closed at present) on the shore of the bay. North of the hotel is a lighthouse.

🏁 Travelogue

La Paz to Los Barriles
(65 mi., 105 km.; 1:45 hrs.)

After leaving the outskirts of La Paz, Highway 1 crosses level countryside with dense growths of cardón and pitahaya (organ pipe) cacti and various trees and shrubs. Just south of the village of San Pedro is the junction with Highway 19 to Todos Santos and Cabo San Lucas. At this point, the main highway bears left and climbs into the foothills of the Sierra de la Laguna. After passing through El Triunfo, the road descends to San Antonio in the bottom of a narrow valley. It then crosses another arm of the mountains and follows the course of a steep-walled canyon to San Bartolo. Emerging from the mountains, Highway 1 soon reaches Los Barriles on the shore of Bahía de Palmas, famous for its superlative sportfishing.

00.0   La Paz, at the intersection of Calzadas Abasolo and 5 de Febrero. To proceed south on Highway 1, take 5 de Febrero southeast for one mile to Carretera al Sur, then bear right.

01.4   Junction with the paved road (BC 286) to San Juan de los Planes (see Side Route to San Juan de los Planes).

16.0   San Pedro, a small community serving the surrounding farms and ranches.

19.0   Junction with Mexico Highway 19 to Todos Santos and Cabo San Lucas (see *Mexico Highway 19*).

32.3   El Triunfo, a picturesque mountain village with a cafe and a church. El Triunfo was once a rich gold and silver mining camp and at one time was the largest settlement in the south of Baja California. The mines closed in 1926, but with the increase in precious metal values, mining has resumed at some locations.

Numerous old buildings line the highway, and on a hill just south of the village are the remains of the old smelter. Handwoven baskets are for sale on the north side of the highway.

36.8   San Antonio, an attractive farming center located in the bottom of a deep arroyo. San Antonio's history also includes a mining boom. Facilities include groceries, eating establishments and gasoline. Past the junction with the village's main street, Highway 1 climbs sharply out of the canyon.

53.8   San Bartolo, a sleepy town strung out along a palm-lined canyon, produces guavas, oranges, avocados and other fruits. Groceries, local fruits and meals are available.

65.2   Junction with a dirt road signed "Ramal El Cardonal." This road leads 0.8 mile to another junction; the road to the left is nine miles of a rough and narrow but scenic coastal route to the resort community of **Punta Pescadero**. The road goes on to the village and resort of El Cardonal (see *Campgrounds & Trailer Parks*), to Boca del Alamo and farther northwest to San Juan de los Planes.

Just south of the junction is Los Barriles (see *Lodging & Restaurants* and *Campgrounds & Trailer Parks*), a rapidly growing tourist community on Bahía de Palmas with two hotels, two trailer parks, a Pemex station (*magna sin*), an

The coastline is scenic north of Punta Pescadero.

airstrip, cafes, markets, auto parts, a clinic and sportfishing boats.

📷 Travelogue

Los Barriles to San José del Cabo

(50 mi., 81 km.; 1:30 hrs.)

The highway skirts the coastline for a few miles, then crosses a long cactus-covered plain. The high Sierra de la Laguna looms dramatically to the west; cattle are frequently encountered on this section of highway. At San José del Cabo the road again reaches the shore of the Gulf of California (Sea of Cortez). Starting at Los Cabos Airport, the highway is four-lane divided all the way to Cabo San Lucas.

1.9 Junction with the entrance road of the Hotel Rancho Buena Vista.

4.4 Junction with a dirt road to the Hotel Buena Vista Beach Resort.

12.3 Junction with a paved road to La Ribera, then graded roads to Punta Colorada, Cabo Pulmo and Los Frailes (see *Side Route to Cabo Pulmo*). To the right is Las Cuevas, a quiet farming village with no tourist facilities.

17.4 Junction with the paved road to Santiago. This attractive agricultural community of about 4000 people sits on a pair of hills separated by a shallow palm-forested canyon. On the northern hill, 1.7 miles from Highway 1, is the town plaza, along with a Pemex station, an inn with a restaurant and several cafes and stores. Just beyond the southern hill is the Santiago Zoo, the only one in Baja California Sur, with a variety of wildlife native to Mexico.

19.4　The Tropic of Cancer, marked by a spherical concrete monument representing the 23.50 North Latitude parallel.

26.1　A Pemex station at the junction with the 1.7-mile paved road to Miraflores, a farming town known for its vegetables and cheeses. By the end of the paved road at the town entrance is a leather shop that does retail sales. Facilities in Miraflores include stores and cafes.

29.4　Junction with the graded dirt road to Caduaño, another small farming community. The town center is about a mile from the main highway.

36.3　Junction with a winding scenic road signed "Los Naranjos," which goes across the tree-covered landscape of the Sierra de la Laguna to El Pescadero and Todos Santos on Mexico Highway 19. Sturdy, high-clearance vehicles are necessary.

41.6　Santa Anita, a sleepy little town with a cafe and a small store.

43.3　Junction with the 0.9-mile paved road to Los Cabos International Airport (see *Appendix*, Transportation).

47.9　Santa Rosa, a rapidly growing community of about 3000, has a Pemex station, cafes and stores.

50.1　Junction with Calle Zaragoza, which leads to the center of San José del Cabo.

🚗 Side Routes

Highway 1 to La Ribera
(7 mi., 11 km.; 0:15 hr.),

Cabo Pulmo
(23 mi., 37 km.; 0:45 hr.) and

San José del Cabo
(80 mi., 129 km.; 4:30 hrs.)

With the longest seacoast extension of any side route in Baja California, this road follows along the East Cape (Cabo del Este). From a junction 11.6 miles south of Los Barriles on Highway 1, a paved road leads eastward past fields of hay and corn for 7.2 miles to La Ribera, a farming community of about 2000 with stores, a cafe, a trailer park and a Pemex station. From La Ribera a graded dirt road crosses rolling scrub-covered countryside for 4.8 miles to the Hotel Punta Colorada, situated atop a low bluff above a lovely beach. A little to the west a new paved road turns southeast, takes a more inland route over 10.5 miles of hilly terrain and reaches the gulf coast near La Abundancia, where it joins a graded dirt road that parallels the scenic shoreline to Cabo Pulmo. This village is a collection of thatched huts, two small seafood restaurants and a launch ramp on a picturesque tropical beach. Fishing and diving are said to be excellent here; offshore is a pretty coral reef.

The road south of Cabo Pulmo is wide and fairly good. It is passable for low-clearance vehicles, but a washboard surface requires sturdy autos. Fine open campsites are abundant along this section of coastline. Five miles past Cabo Pulmo is Los Frailes, a village named for the adjacent jagged promontory that forms the easternmost point of the Baja California peninsula. The vil-

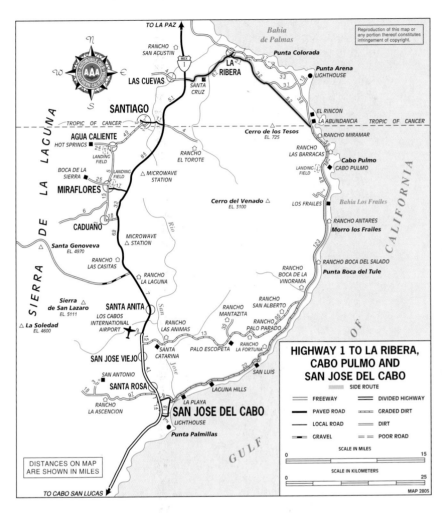

MEXICO HIGHWAY 1

HIGHWAY 1 TO LA RIBERA, CABO PULMO AND SAN JOSE DEL CABO

		SIDE ROUTE
FREEWAY		DIVIDED HIGHWAY
PAVED ROAD		GRADED DIRT
LOCAL ROAD		DIRT
GRAVEL		POOR ROAD

SCALE IN MILES

0   15

SCALE IN KILOMETERS

0   25

MAP 2805

DISTANCES ON MAP ARE SHOWN IN MILES

lage has vacation homes, trailers and a hotel. At mileage 55, beyond a wide sandy wash near Rancho Vinorama, is a junction with a graded road leading 24 miles southwest over the coastal foothills to Highway 1.

Ahead, the road continues to follow the coast past miles of beautiful beaches and a landscape that contains pitahaya and elephant trees. Three miles beyond the junction is a massive wild fig tree next to the road. Six miles later the rusting hulk of a large vessel may be

seen by walking down to the water's edge. Several miles farther the road swings inland, passes through densely vegetated terrain and climbs between two cone-shaped peaks to a low ridge that offers the first glimpse of San José del Cabo. Along the last few miles are new vacation homes at Laguna Hills and the fishing village of La Playa.

After crossing many roads on the outskirts of San José del Cabo, the road enters the center of town at mileage 80.0.

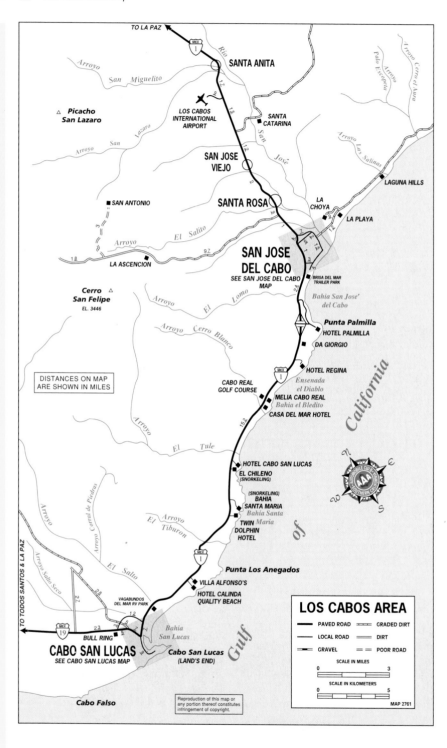

MEXICO HIGHWAY 1

TO LA PAZ

MEX 1

Río

SANTA ANITA

Arroyo

San Miguelito

Palo Escopeta

Arroyo Cerro el Aura

Arroyo

△ Picacho
San Lazaro

LOS CABOS
INTERNATIONAL
AIRPORT

SANTA
CATARINA

Arroyo Las Salinas

Lazaro

San

Arroyo

San

SAN JOSE
VIEJO

Jose

San

■ SAN ANTONIO

SANTA ROSA

LA
CHOYA

LAGUNA HILLS

El Salito

Arroyo

LA ASCENCION

SAN JOSE
DEL CABO

SEE SAN JOSE DEL CABO
MAP

LA PLAYA

BRISA DEL MAR
TRAILER PARK

Cerro △
San Felipe
EL. 3446

Arroyo

El

Lomo

Bahia San Jose'
del Cabo

Arroyo Cerro Blanco

Punta Palmilla

HOTEL PALMILLA

DA GIORGIO

DISTANCES ON MAP
ARE SHOWN IN MILES

MEX 1

HOTEL REGINA

Ensenada
el Diablo

California

CABO REAL
GOLF COURSE

MELIA CABO REAL

Bahia el Bledito

CASA DEL MAR HOTEL

Arroyo

El Tule

HOTEL CABO SAN LUCAS

EL CHILENO
(SNORKELING)

(SNORKELING)
BAHIA
SANTA MARIA

Bahia Santa
Maria

Arroyo Corral de Piedras

Arroyo

El Arroyo
Tiburon

TWIN
DOLPHIN
HOTEL

of

MEX 1

El Salto

Punta Los Anegados

VILLA ALFONSO'S

HOTEL CALINDA
QUALITY BEACH

Arroyo Salto Seco

VAGABUNDOS
DEL MAR RV PARK

TO TODOS SANTOS & LA PAZ

MEX 19

BULL RING

CABO SAN LUCAS

SEE CABO SAN LUCAS MAP

Bahia
San Lucas

Gulf

Cabo San Lucas
(LAND'S END)

Cabo Falso

LOS CABOS AREA

▬▬▬ PAVED ROAD	═══ GRADED DIRT
──── LOCAL ROAD	═══ DIRT
▬▬▬ GRAVEL	═ ═ POOR ROAD

SCALE IN MILES
0   3

SCALE IN KILOMETERS
0   5

MAP 2761

Reproduction of this map or
any portion thereof constitutes
infringement of copyright.

San José del Cabo

(See also Lodging & Restaurants and Campgrounds & Trailer Parks.)

At the spot where Highway 1 meets the Gulf of California, San José del Cabo occupies low hills and an attractive, narrow coastal lowland. Founded in 1730, its contrasting buildings suggest that it is an old settlement with much recent growth. Tropical agriculture—coconuts, mangos, spices and citrus fruits—plus fast-growing tourism have brought the population to about 11,000. San José del Cabo is the seat of government of the *municipio* of Los Cabos, which encompasses the East Cape and Cabo San Lucas.

The town center includes an attractive plaza park. Numerous stores and restaurants are open to the visitor, particularly along Calles Zaragoza and Mijares. The town also has auto parts, mechanical service and two hospitals. Immediately south of town, a new FONATUR resort development fronts directly on the beautiful beaches of the Gulf of California. To date, six large hotels are in operation, a golf course and a shopping center are open, and several condominium developments are finished.

Points of Interest

ESTERO DE SAN JOSE *End of Paseo San Jose, just east of Hotel Presidente Los Cabos.* The estuary of the Río San José is bordered by palm groves and is replete with aquatic plants. It is a protected sanctuary, home to a variety of birds. Facilities are being developed for visitors to hike along the shores and take boat rides.

This scenic lagoon at San José del Cabo sure looks inviting.

▼ *Quick Guide to San José del Cabo*

Tourist Information

Municipal Tourism Office *In San José's plaza park.* Information and printed materials about the Los Cabos region are available.

PLAZA PARK *Calle Zaragoza and Boulevard Mijares.* This small town square has the atmosphere of old Mexico. Facing the shaded plaza are the church, the tourism office and a monument to General José Antonio Mijares.

PALACIO MUNICIPAL/MUNICIPAL HALL *One block south of the plaza.* Dating from 1927, the traditional structure has offices that face on an interior patio.

The municipal hall is a prominent landmark in the city.

SAN JOSÉ CHURCH *West side of the plaza.* Founded in 1730, this active church has been rebuilt according to the original style. It has classic twin steeples.

📷 Travelogue

San José del Cabo to Cabo San Lucas

(21 mi., 34 km.; 0:30 hr.)

A recently completed four-lane expressway leads southwest to Cabo San Lucas, passing many hotels and

Yes, we have no bananas—and mangos, melons and other fruits and vegetables at the farmer's market in San José del Cabo.

restaurants, winding along the gulf through low, scrub-dotted hills, and occasionally offering tantalizing glimpses of beautiful beaches and azure waters. Several public beaches are accessible from the highway via side roads. Finally, just before arriving in Cabo San Lucas, travelers get the first view of Land's End (Finisterra), the tip of the Baja California peninsula. At the Cabo San Lucas wharf, 1059 miles from the U.S. border, Highway 1 ends.

00.0   Junction with Calle Zaragoza into San José del Cabo.

01.3   Junction with a palm-lined boulevard leading to the beach resort development marked *"zona de hoteles."*

01.8   Playa Tropical, site of Brisa del Mar Trailer Park. The highway swings to the southwest at this point.

03.8   Entrance road of the Hotel Palmilla resort.

06.7   On the north side of the highway is Cabo Real Golf Course. On the south side is Hotel Meliá Cabo Real.

11.0   Entrance road of the Hotel Cabo San Lucas.

12.8   Entrance road of the Hotel Twin Dolphin.

A craftsman tools leather in Miraflores.

15.4 Cabo del Sol golf club.

16.9 Junction with the paved road leading to the Cabo Bello development, which includes the Hotel Calinda Beach Cabo San Lucas. At this point, Land's End comes into view.

20.4 Cabo San Lucas, at the junction with Calle Morelos, which is the beginning of Mexico Highway 19 leading north to Todos Santos, San Pedro and La Paz. Boulevard Marina, on the left, leads to the waterfront.

26.1 A Pemex station at the junction with the 1.7-mile paved road to Miraflores, a farming town known for its vegetables and cheeses. By the end of the paved road at the town entrance is a leather shop that does retail sales. Facilities in Miraflores include stores and cafes.

29.4 Junction with the graded dirt road to Caduaño, another small farming community. The town center is about a mile from the main highway.

36.3 Junction with a winding scenic road signed "Los Naranjos," which goes across the tree-covered landscape of the Sierra de la Laguna to El Pescadero and Todos Santos on Mexico Highway 19. Sturdy, high-clearance vehicles are necessary.

41.6 Santa Anita, a sleepy little town with a cafe and a small store.

43.3 Junction with the 0.9-mile paved road to Los Cabos International Airport (see *Appendix*, Transportation).

47.9 Santa Rosa, a rapidly growing community of about 3000, has a Pemex station, cafes and stores.

50.1 Junction with Calle Zaragoza, which leads to the center of San José del Cabo.

Cabo San Lucas

(See also Lodging & Restaurants and Campgrounds & Trailer Parks.)

The town of Cabo San Lucas fronts a small harbor on the gulf side of the rocky peninsula that forms the southernmost tip of Baja California. The bay, which in the 16th and 17th centuries was a favorite hiding place for pirates who laid in wait for Spanish treasure ships, now serves as an anchorage for fishing boats and private yachts. Because of its renowned sport-fishing and the increasing popularity of its many luxury hotels, Cabo San Lucas has changed from a quiet, unassuming cannery village into an internationally known resort. From only 1500 inhabitants in 1970, the town has grown to about 12,000 at present.

Signs of this rapid growth are everywhere. Impressive condominiums spread over the hillside and the waterfront. A marvelous view of the waterfront and Land's End can be seen from the Hotel Finisterra or the Pedregal condominium zone on Camino del Mar. Facilities include trailer parks, many restaurants and cafes, markets, gift shops, shopping centers, Pemex stations, auto repairs and parts, and a marina. The once-busy ferry terminal at Cabo San Lucas is now idle; ferry service to Puerto Vallarta is suspended indefinitely.

The Hard Rock Cafe in Cabo San Lucas is popular with tourists.

Developments on Cabo San Lucas' harbor are quite impressive.

TO TODOS SANTOS

TO TODOS SANTOS

TO SAN JOSE DEL CABO

GREEN

EL FARO VIEJO TRAILER PARK

MIJARES

FELIX

HIDALGO

ROSARIO

ALIKAN

12 DE

OBREGON

CARRANZA

REVOLUCION

LOS CABOS INN

CONSTITUCION

5 DE MAYO

VICARIO

MENDOZA

MORELOS

ORTEGA

MORALES

OCAMPO

ABASOLO

MATAMOROS

ZARAGOZA

DE

20 DE NOVIEMBRE

LIBERTAD

NIÑOS HEROES

PARK

OCTUBRE

19

16

DE SEPTIEMBRE

LAZARO

BLVD

GUERRERO

MADERO

MARINA

PLAZA

CHURCH

SIESTA SUITES HOTEL

CAM. GRANDE

E. ZAPATA

J. O. DE DOMINGUEZ

CAMINO DEL MAR

TELEGRAPH OFFICE

HOSPITAL

16 DE SEPTIEMBRE

FARIAS

CARDENAS

POLICE STATION

POST OFFICE

EL

MEDANO

VILLA ALFONSO'S

PUEBLO BONITO RESORT

MELIA SAN LUCAS

MARINA

MARINA FIESTA RESORT HOTEL

HOTEL MAR DE CORTEZ

HOTEL HACIENDA

HOTEL PLAZA LAS GLORIAS

MARINA

MARINA

FONATUR

BLVD

SOLMAR

AVE

HOTEL FINISTERRA

SOLMAR SUITES RESORT

LANDS END

Bahia

San Lucas

CAM. DEL MAR

CAMINO DEL ANGEL

CAM. DEL PACIFICO

CAM DE LA LUNA

DEL

MAR

PACIFIC OCEAN

CABO SAN LUCAS

DIVIDED HIGHWAY

MAIN ROAD

SECONDARY ROAD

SCALE IN MILES

0   0.4

SCALE IN KILOMETERS

0   0.7

MAP 2762

Pristine beaches and warm waters are major attractions at Cabo San Lucas.

▼ *Quick Guide to Cabo San Lucas*

Tourist Assistance

U.S. Consular Agent *Boulevard Marina y Pedregal No. 3. 01152* *(114) 3-3566.* Offers assistance to U.S. citizens in the Los Cabos region.

Newspaper

Two informative newspapers which provide information and advertisements covering the Los Cabos region are the bilingual *El Tiempo Los Cabos Times* and the English-language *Baja Sun,* which also has material about the rest of the peninsula.

Radio Station

Radio 96 FM, Cabo Mil, plays a variety of fine international music.

Nightclubs

Cabo San Lucas vibrates at night. Many night spots and discos are located in the tourist area along boulevards Lázaro Cárdenas and Marina. Three popular ones with bizarre names are **Cabo Wabo**, **Squid Roe** and **The Giggling Marlin**.

Points of Interest

GALERIA EL DORADO *Boulevard Marina near Guerrero.* This arts and crafts store displays a nice collection of paintings and ceramics by local artists. Visitors are welcome to browse.

LAND'S END/FINISTERRA *The rocky, extreme southern end of the peninsula is situated at 22 degrees, 50 minutes north latitude.* Its rugged, wave-eroded rock formations, including The Arches/ *Los Arcos,* may be viewed from Highway 1 on the approach to Cabo San Lucas or from any slightly elevated spot in town. Land's End and its beaches may be reached by boat, or on foot by starting on the beach by Solmar Suites Resort and climbing over a rough rocky saddle. (This climb should be made only by those in good physical shape, traveling with a partner.)

Land's End is where the Gulf of California meets the Pacific Ocean.

Mexico Highway 2

The most direct route from Tijuana to Mexicali roughly parallels the U.S.-Mexico border. Starting in Tijuana the hilly terrain gradually rises in elevation, culminating in the steep and rugged Rumorosa Grade. Beyond the grade the terrain levels out into barren desert as it leads into Mexicali.

One of the two federal highways that connects Mexico Highway 1 and Mexico Highway 5, Mexico Highway 2 is the northernmost of the east-west connecting routes. It leads eastward from Tijuana to Tecate and Mexicali, then continues into Sonora, eventually connecting with Highway 15 to Mexico City.

Crossing the Border

The Tecate border crossing, which connects the village of Tecate, California, with Tecate, Baja California, gets relatively little use by tourists entering Mexico. For those returning to the United States from Ensenada and points farther south, however, it is a popular alternative to the crowded crossing at Tijuana. Delays are seldom encountered here by motorists in either direction. The border gates are open daily from 6 a.m. to midnight.

◪ Travelogue

**Tijuana to Tecate
via Highway 2**

(34 mi., 54 km.; 1 hr.)

Mexico Highway 2 starts in Tijuana as Boulevard Díaz Ordaz, passes through the bustling industrial and commercial zone of La Mesa, then crosses a dam and enters rural countryside that is evolving into an industrial district. Then the road climbs gradually into low rocky hills, past olive orchards, dairy farms and cattle ranches on the way to Tecate. Mexico Highway 2 is four lanes undivided to La Presa, then becomes a good two-lane road the rest of the way. Traffic is heavy in La Mesa, so Boulevard Insurgentes may be preferable. It is a divided road that starts in La Mesa, parallels Mexico Highway 2 for seven miles, then merges with it.

00.0   **Tijuana (San Ysidro border crossing). Proceed straight ahead and follow signs for Mexicali.**

03.9   **Caliente Racetrack. On the hills to the south is one of the city's most attractive residential neighborhoods.**

06.1   **Boulevard Lázaro Cárdenas, which goes northeast to**

Fishing boats awaiting sunrise at El Golfo de Santa Clara.

Boulevard Insurgentes, the central bus station and Tijuana Airport.

11.5 La Presa, the easternmost district in the Tijuana urbanized area.

11.8 Rodríguez Dam and lake, once the sole source of Tijuana's water supply. The road follows the top of the dam and is quite narrow.

15.4 El Florido, a large housing development; three miles farther is a dairy-farming village with the same name.

30.1 Rancho La Puerta, a nicely landscaped resort and spa specializing in physical fitness. It offers pleasant accommodations and strictly vegetarian meals.

33.6 Tecate, a friendly town clustered around a tree-shaded plaza. Mexico Highway 3 leads south from Tecate to El Sauzal and Ensenada (see description, *Mexico Highway 3*).

▨ Travelogue

Tijuana to Tecate via Toll Highway 2-D
(22 mi., 35 km.; 0:30 hr.)

Opened in 1992, this toll highway—a divided, fully controlled-access expressway—provides a fast alternative to Highway 2. It begins in the Otay Mesa district of Tijuana. After crossing the border, drive 1.2 miles straight south to the first main boulevard, then turn east (left). Follow Boulevard Industrial (Eje Oriente-Poniente) through Ciudad Industrial, the *maquiladora* (manufacturing) district. After about two miles the boulevard becomes the toll highway.

After passing sprawling urban housing developments, the expressway heads into rural landscape. At first it follows a narrow canyon where falling rocks are a possibility. Then it goes over rolling hills, passing occasional farms and ranches. After about 18 miles it enters the Tecate Basin, where Highway 2-D presently ends at the entrance to Tecate. This route is also called Autopista Tijuana-Mexicali, because it is the western section of a planned expressway that will, in the near future, link Tijuana with Mexicali. At press time, the expressway was still not open between Tecate and La Rumorosa, 41 miles to the east.

The toll road is lightly traveled because rates are quite high—$3.90 for cars, pickup trucks and vans; $7.80 for motor homes; and $9.70 for vehicles with trailers.

00.0 Tijuana (Otay Mesa).

03.6 Toll station.

16.1 Exit for Mexico Highway 2 and west entrance to Tecate.

21.8 Exit for Mexico Highway 3 and south entrance to Tecate.

Tecate

(See *Campgrounds & Trailer Parks*.)

Lacking proximity to any large population center in the United States, Tecate has never had much of a border town atmosphere. Instead, this pleasant city of about 50,000 is a typical Mexican community, where life centers around a tranquil tree-shaded plaza. At an elevation of 1690 feet, Tecate sits in a bowl-shaped valley surrounded by rocky hills; because of its inland location, the city has hot, dry summers and cool winters with occasional frost.

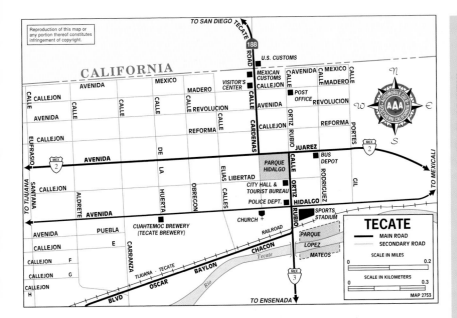

Tecate came into being in the late 19th century, when farmers and ranchers, attracted by its abundant water and fertile soil, settled the area. Tecate has long been a farm market center for a productive region that yields grapes, olives and grain. Industries—beer, instant coffee and *maquiladoras* (manufacturing plants)—have been growing in importance. Its diversified facilities and location at the junction of two major Mexican routes (Highways 2 and 3) have made Tecate a favorite stopover for travelers. Several accommodations can be found here, along with a variety of stores and restaurants, a hospital, Pemex stations, and auto parts and repairs. The city is the seat of government of the *municipio* of Tecate.

Points of Interest

PARQUE HIDALGO *On Avenida Juárez and Calle Ortiz Rubio.* The town plaza is an attractive retreat. An impressive monument to Benito Juárez is located at the northeast corner of the park.

▼ *Quick Guide to Tecate*

Tourist Information and Assistance
Secretaría de Turisma or **SECTUR (Mexican Government Tourism Office)** *1305 Callejón Libertad, on the south side of the plaza. Open Mon. through Fri. 8 a.m. to 7 p.m., Sat. and Sun. 10 a.m. to 3 p.m. 01152 (665) 4-1095.* Protección al Turista (Tourist Assistance) provides legal help for tourists who encounter problems while in Tecate.

CUAUHTEMOC BREWERY *Avenida Hidalgo and Calle Carranza. 01152 (665) 4-2011 (reservations). Beer garden open Tues. through Sat. 10 a.m. to 5 p.m. Brewery tours are given on Saturday mornings.* This is the brewery where popular Tecate beer is made.

MEXICO HIGHWAY 2

The colorful beer gardens enhance the setting of the Cuauhtémoc Brewery in Tecate.

◪ Travelogue

Tecate to Mexicali
(89 mi., 144 km.; 2:45 hrs.)

Continuing east from Tecate, Mexico Highway 2 begins a long, gradual climb onto a high plateau. It passes small farms and ranches, as well as several rustic resorts and campgrounds which are visited mainly by Mexicans. Near La Rumorosa, at an elevation of more than 4000 feet, the highway can become impassable after heavy snows, but these rarely occur. Just east of La Rumorosa is the Rumorosa (Cantú) Grade, one of the most spectacular mountain highways on the continent, where the road makes an abrupt switchback descent past strangely jumbled rock formations to the floor of the barren desert. Strong winds, slow-moving trucks and many sharp curves call for reduced speeds and careful driving in this 15-mile section;

passing can be difficult. After reaching the base of the grade, the highway skirts the vast bed of Laguna Salada, which since 1977 has held water. The road now sweeps through low hills, then enters the Mexicali Valley—one of Mexico's richest farming areas. Although Mexico Highway 2 bypasses the center of Mexicali, well-marked paved roads lead into the city.

00.0   Tecate, at the junction of Mexico highways 2 and 3.

13.6   Loma Tova, a village with a cafe.

21.2   Colonia El Hongo, a fast-growing farming community with cafes and stores. A partially paved road winds seven miles southwest to Hacienda Santa Verónica, a cattle ranch with a hotel and trailer park.

31.6   El Condor, a settlement with a Pemex station and restaurant, at the junction with a graded road to Laguna Hanson in the Sierra de Juárez.

41.0 La Rumorosa, elevation 4300 feet, located on a high boulder-strewn plateau. Facilities in the town include stores, cafes, a Pemex station (*magna sin*) and mechanical assistance. Just east of La Rumorosa, the highway begins its steep winding drop to the desert floor.

65.8 Junction with a graded dirt road along the edge of Laguna Salada to Cañón de Guadalupe. This lovely palm canyon is 27 miles south, then eight miles west. The road is suitable for passenger cars and small RVs. The canyon features hot springs, hot tubs, a small store and a developed campground; rates start at $15 per vehicle. For information call (714) 673-2670.

79.4 Colonia Progreso, a village with a large municipal building, a motel, restaurant and a Pemex station.

83.4 Junction with Calle Guadalajara, the shortest route to downtown Mexicali and the U.S. border. The sign says "Centro, Calexico."

88.9 Mexicali, at the traffic circle intersection of Mexico highways 2 and 5 (see *Mexico Highway 5*).

◪ Travelogue

Mexicali to La Rumorosa via Toll Highway 2-D
(31 mi., 50 km.; 0:45 hr.)

This expressway, the eastern part of the Autopista Tijuana-Mexicali, is at present open only to westbound (upgrade) traffic. Beginning at a Solidaridad monument 15 miles west of Mexicali, it crosses level desert floor, then winds up the steep Rumorosa Grade, paralleling old Mexico Highway 2. This two-lane one-way road has a very good surface, but be cautious on sharp curves and abrupt drop-offs. This part of Mexico Highway 2-D ends with a toll station at the top of the grade, next to the entrance to La Rumorosa. Just beyond the toll gate there are rest rooms. Tolls are high—$5.00 for cars, pickup trucks and vans; $10.10 for motor homes; and $15.10 for vehicles pulling trailers. Few vehicles choose to travel it. This route is a subject of controversy—the government is considering charging tolls on both highways, with old Mexico Highway 2 becoming one-way eastbound.

◪ Travelogue

Mexicali to San Luis R.C., Sonora
(41 mi., 66 km.; 1 hr.)

From the traffic circle on the southern outskirts of Mexicali, Mexico Highway 2 traverses an industrial area, then strikes out across the flat Mexicali Valley, one of Mexico's most important farming areas. Irrigated farms and small communities line the highway in this section. Cotton production, from field to gin, is in evidence. Also important are sorghum and hay crops. Although the highway has two lanes in each direction, motorists should be alert for slow-moving farm vehicles entering and leaving the roadway.

After crossing a toll bridge over the Colorado River, the highway enters the state of Sonora and the booming border town of San Luis R.C.

00.0   Mexicali, at the junction of highways 2 and 5.

06.0   Junction with a paved road to Ejido Puebla (stores, cafes, Pemex station) and the Cerro Prieto Geothermal Zone, site of a large geothermal electrical generating facility.

14.0   Double junction with BCN 1, a paved highway. To the left it goes to Mexicali International Airport. To the right it leads south past the farming towns of Nuevo León and Ledón, then intersects BCN 4, which turns eastward to Coahuila. From here, another paved road crosses into Sonora (see Side Route to El Golfo de Santa Clara, Sonora).

24.6   Bataques, which has a Pemex station.

27.4   Junction with a paved highway (BCN 2) to the agricultural center of Ciudad Morelos. Ten miles northeast on BCN 8 is the pleasant border town of Algodones. With a population of about 5000, Algodones has gasoline, a hotel, cafes, pharmacies, dentists, optometrists, souvenir crafts, a park and a state tourism office. Near Algodones is Morelos Dam, where irrigation water for the Mexicali Valley is taken from the Colorado River. From Andrade, at the international border, California State Route 186 takes the traveler to Interstate 8 at a point seven miles west of Yuma, Arizona.

38.3   Toll bridge (90¢ for cars and pickups) across the Colorado River, which forms the boundary between the states of Baja California and Sonora.

40.6   San Luis Río Colorado. "Río Colorado" is used to differentiate the city from other Mexican towns named San Luis. With a population of 135,000, the city thrives from agriculture (cotton and wheat), highway transportation and the international border trade. Tourist facilities are concentrated near the international border, which is 23 miles south of Yuma, Arizona. It has an attractive plaza park which is surrounded by businesses, a classic church and government buildings, including a state tourism office. From San Luis, Mexico Highway 2 heads eastward across barren desert to Mexico Highway 15, providing the fastest, most direct link between Southern California and the interior of Mexico. For travel on the mainland, car permits are required. Car permits can be obtained in San Luis at the international border (see *Tourist Regulations and Travel Tips*, Automobile Requirements section). Those traveling beyond San Luis should refer to the AAA *Travel Guide to Mexico.*

Side Route

Highway 2 to El Golfo de Santa Clara, Sonora

(81 mi., 129 km.; 3 hrs.)

Turn right at the junction with BCN 1, passing through the towns of Nuevo León and Ledón. Continue eastward along BCN 4 at the junction in Ledón. Gasoline (*magna sin*) and a few stores are at Ledón (Colonia Carranza). Crossing flat land planted in cotton, the road reaches Murguía, turns south, then eastward. Four miles past Murguía the highway crosses the Colorado River by means of a culvert. Due to irrigation demands, the river is usually a shallow narrow stream. After an occasional rain, however, the crossing may be flooded. (The highway formerly shared the railroad bridge to the north, but this route is closed for an indefinite time.) The last town in Baja California on this route is Coahuila, also called Colonia Nuevas. Drive slowly on the graded dirt streets. Turn left, cross the railroad and follow the signs to Sonora.

One hundred yards beyond the railroad, travelers enter the state of Sonora; there is no checkpoint. Sonora is on Mountain Time, and the urban area of Coahuila continues under the name of Luis B. Sánchez. The two towns constitute a sizeable farm market center, containing two Pemex stations (*magna sin*), auto parts, a clinic, and several markets and restaurants. After one more mile the road runs into state highway SON 40. A left turn leads north to San Luis, Sonora; a right turn leads southeast to El Golfo. After passing a secondary school and some farmland, the road to El Golfo comes to Riíto, a small agricultural center at the end of the cultivated area. Here are gasoline and diesel and a few stores. Between Riíto and El Golfo de Santa Clara are 43 miles of the barren Sonoran Desert, with no services. The only real settlement is El Doctor, a railroad work station with a few buildings and a rustic cafe. The highway is very flat and in good condition most of the way. The road becomes quite rough,

however, 12 miles southeast of El Doctor. Shortly before coming to the town the road smoothes out, curves and drops quickly to a small coastal basin. Pavement ends at the entrance to El Golfo.

Another route to El Golfo starts in the city of San Luis R.C., Sonora. From Mexico Highway 2, turn south on Calle 2, which becomes highway SON 40 to Riíto. From Riíto follow the route previously described to El Golfo.

El Golfo de Santa Clara is a fishing town of about 3000 residents, with a fish-processing plant, Pemex station (gasoline and diesel), a grocery store, a general store, a church and several cafes. The streets are sandy and cars can easily get stuck. The motorist should greatly lower tire pressure before driving these streets. Several shops advertise *"aire*/air" for refilling the tires later. The harbor has many fishing boats, large and small, that catch shrimp, clams and sierra. Arrangements can sometimes be made for sportfishing. The tidal range is great here at the head of the Gulf of California, with sandy beaches at high tide and mud flats exposed at low tide. Across the gulf the mountains of Baja California are visible.

A graded sandy road extends southeast of town, passing side roads to two RV parks and an area where signs announce a planned beach community. At 1.7 miles there is a large *playa pública* camping area (no facilities), backed by sand dunes, hills and a lighthouse. This spot is sometimes used by Americans with ATVs.

Mexico Highway 3

Mexico Highway 3 is actually comprised of two distinct sections of road, connected by a six-mile stretch of Mexico Highway 1-D (Ensenada Toll Road). The northern section connects Tecate with El Sauzal, which is the shortest link between Mexicali and Ensenada. The southern section runs from Ensenada to a junction with Mexico Highway 5 at a point about 31 miles north of San Felipe. Both of these routes are paved over their entire lengths.

🅰 Travelogue

Tecate to El Sauzal

(66 mi., 107 km.; 1:30 hrs.)

After leaving Tecate this two-lane highway climbs into a region of boulder-strewn, scrub-covered mountains and small upland valleys, some of which are under cultivation. Several sharp curves and steep grades in this section call for extra caution. On the southern third of the route the highway runs past olive orchards and miles of vineyards, through a level valley bordered by low hills to the junction with Mexico Highway 1 at El Sauzal. Because this is the shortest route from the farms of the Mexicali Valley to Ensenada's port, large trucks are sometimes encountered along this section of Mexico Highway 3.

00.0   Tecate, at the junction of Mexico highways 2 and 3.

01.8   Junction with Mexico Highway 2-D, the Tijuana-Mexicali Expressway.

05.7   Rancho Tecate, a resort with a golf course.

17.8   Valle de las Palmas, an agricultural community with gasoline (*magna sin*), stores and restaurants.

31.0   El Testerazo, a village with a cafe. To the west are prominent rocky peaks, 3000 to 4200 feet in elevation.

6.2   Domecq Winery; tours are given from Tuesday through Saturday, 9 a.m. to 1 p.m. At this point the highway enters a region containing extensive, well-maintained vineyards. A short distance north is L.A. Cetto Winery, which also conducts tours.

48.3   Guadalupe. Next to the elementary school are the ruins of Mission Nuestra Señora de Guadalupe (1834), last of the Baja California missions. Russian immigrants founded an agricultural community here early in the 20th century. Museo Comunitario del Valle de Guadalupe has a collection of pictures and artifacts about these Russian-Mexican settlers. This museum is located

---

Tree-lined Laguna Hanson lies in the heart of the Sierra de Juárez.

1½ miles west of the junction of Mexico Highway 3 and the main road into town. Hours are Wednesday through Sunday 9 a.m. to 4 p.m.; donation. Guadalupe and Francisco Zarco, an adjacent village, have two cafes, groceries, an inn and a clinic.

59.4 Villa Juárez, a town with a restaurant and a market. In the vicinity are new real estate developments.

66.1 El Sauzal, at the junction with Mexico Highway 1. Ensenada is six miles to the southeast.

⬚ Travelogue

Ensenada to El Chinero (Crucero La Trinidad), Junction with Highway 5

(123 mi., 198 km.; 3 hrs.)

Sometimes known as the Ensenada-San Felipe Road, this section of Mexico Highway 3 usually has a good paved surface. Together with Mexico Highways 1 (or 1-D), 2 and 5, this scenic route with very light traffic offers visitors an opportunity for an interesting loop trip through the northern portion of Baja California. The first 24 miles east of Ensenada are narrow and winding, as the highway climbs and crosses a range of chaparral-covered hills before dropping into wide green Valle de Ojos Negros—a productive farming and ranching center. Beyond the turnoff to the village of Ojos Negros, the pavement becomes wider. Heading south, then southeast, Mexico Highway 3 climbs through semiarid foothills to a plateau known as Llano Colorado. The landscape gradually becomes drier as the highway winds

through more hills and descends along the edge of Valle de Trinidad, an important agricultural development. After leaving the fields and cattle grazing lands of the valley, the highway follows a canyon called San Matías Pass, after which it drops to the floor of arid Valle de San Felipe. To the south the rugged face of the Sierra San Pedro Mártir is clearly visible, capped by Picacho del Diablo (elevation 10,154 feet), the highest point in Baja California. After crossing open desert bordered by low barren hills, Mexico Highway 3 meets Mexico Highway 5 at El Chinero, 32 miles north of San Felipe.

00.0 Ensenada, at the intersection of Avenida Benito Juárez (Mexico Highway 1), Avenida Reforma and Calzada Cortez. Follow Calzada Cortez eastward from the traffic circle.

08.1 El Gran 13, an amusement park with rides and playground equipment, a picnic ground, swimming pool and spa.

16.4 Junction with a 5.2-mile dirt road to Agua Caliente, a rustic tourist resort. This road should not be attempted in wet weather.

24.7 Junction with the paved road leading 1.2 miles to Ojos Negros, a farming and cattle-raising community with two markets and a nice park. Restaurant Oasis has tourist information. A graded road leads eastward from Ojos Negros to the Sierra de Juárez and Laguna Hanson (see Side Routes).

34.7 Junction with a signed road to Parque Nacional Constitución de 1857; the road from Ojos Negros is preferable.

This part of Mexico Highway 3 connects Ensenada with the eastern side of the Baja peninsula.

57.5　Héroes de la Independencia, a scattered settlement on Llano Colorado. The town has groceries, pottery stores, cafes, auto parts and a Pemex station (*magna sin*). A dirt road branches north to the ruins of Mission Santa Catarina, founded in 1797.

75.5　Junction with the short, paved road to Valle de Trinidad. This rapidly growing community is a farm market center of 3000 with stores, cafes, a bank, an ice house, schools, an unusual conical church, a mechanic, tire repair and a Pemex station.

86.2　Junction with a good dirt road to Mike's Sky Rancho, which is 22.5 miles to the south (see Side Route to Mike's Sky Rancho).

92.5　San Matías Pass, elevation 2950 feet.

95.9　Junction with a dirt road leading first to *ejidos* Villa del Sol and Colonia San Pedro Mártir, then southeast to San Felipe. This rugged route passes close to the base of the Sierra San Pedro Mártir; Cañón El Diablo, 20 miles south of the junction, is where many climbers begin the difficult ascent of Picacho del Diablo.

123.4　El Chinero (Crucero la Trinidad), junction with Mexico Highway 5 (see *Mexico Highway 5*). At the junction is a government-built restaurant and picnic area. About 0.7 mile south of the junction is a Pemex station (*magna sin*) and a cafe.

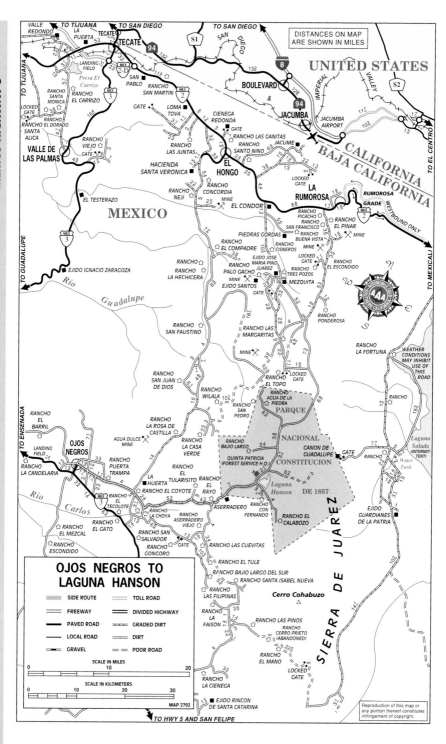

DISTANCES ON MAP ARE SHOWN IN MILES

UNITED STATES

CALIFORNIA

BAJA CALIFORNIA

MEXICO

TO TIJUANA

TO GUADALUPE

TO ENSENADA

TO EL CENTRO

TO MEXICALI

PARQUE NACIONAL CONSTITUCION DE 1857

SIERRA DE JUAREZ

OJOS NEGROS TO LAGUNA HANSON

SIDE ROUTE	TOLL ROAD
FREEWAY	DIVIDED HIGHWAY
PAVED ROAD	GRADED DIRT
LOCAL ROAD	DIRT
GRAVEL	POOR ROAD

SCALE IN MILES
0   10   20

SCALE IN KILOMETERS
0   10   20   30

MAP 2792

TO HWY 5 AND SAN FELIPE

🚙 Side Route

Ojos Negros to Laguna Hanson
(27 mi., 43 km.; 1:45 hrs.)

This unpaved side route offers visitors a chance to explore the high plateau country of the Sierra de Juárez—a land of cool mountain air and thick forests of ponderosa pine. In the heart of this rugged region is a Mexican national park highlighted by Laguna Hanson, a small, intermittent lake surrounded by tall pines, unusual rock formations and excellent primitive campsites. Another attraction of this trip is solitude; despite its fine scenery and its proximity to the international border, the park gets very few tourists.

Laguna Hanson can be reached from El Cóndor, west of La Rumorosa on Mexico Highway 2, but the preferred route—usually accessible in dry weather by passenger cars—begins at Ojos Negros, 25 miles east of Ensenada via Mexico Highway 3 and a paved spur road. From the end of pavement in Ojos Negros, turn right onto a wide graded road running eastward toward the mountains. For the first few miles the road passes Puerta Trampa and other prosperous farms and ranches, then enters brush-covered foothills. At mile 7.9 is a major junction; bear right here. Beyond the junction the road begins to climb steadily, but there are no steep grades. After another eight miles the road leaves the chaparral belt and traverses forests of ponderosa pine. At mileage 20.4 is another important junction; bear left. From this point the route swings north and enters Aserradero, a village of wooden buildings; the road leaves Aserradero ahead to the left. Just beyond the village the road crosses the southern boundary of Parque Nacional Constitución de 1857. Four miles beyond Aserradero is Laguna Hanson. Park regulations prohibit hunting, but camping is permitted. From Laguna Hanson, the road continues northward for another 37 miles, eventually meeting Mexico Highway 2 at a junction just west of La Rumorosa.

🚙 Side Route

Highway 3 to Mike's Sky Rancho
(23 mi., 37 km.; 1:30 hrs.)

This route to a secluded backcountry lodge begins at a signed junction at a point 10.7 miles southeast of Valle de Trinidad. Sturdy high-clearance vehicles are necessary. The first half of the trip is over a dirt road rising gradually over semiarid landscape. Cerro San Matías (elevation 7100 feet) is visible to the east. The road becomes rougher and more winding as it approaches a junction at mileage 13.8. Here is found a 6000-foot graded airstrip that belongs to Mike's. A rough road to the right goes to Ejido Los Pocitos. Bear left to continue 8.2 miles farther over rough surface to the ranch.

Mike's Sky Rancho rests on a knoll overlooking Arroyo San Rafael, a wooded valley flanked by steep, brush-covered mountains. The ranch offers motel-type accommodations for about $25, family-style meals, a swimming pool, horseback riding, sycamore-shaded campsites and information about trips into the rugged country to the east. The small stream that flows through the valley yields occasional catches of small rainbow trout. Hunters can go after deer, rabbit, quail and mountain lion.

Mexico Highway 5

From Mexicali—the bustling capital city of the state of Baja California—Mexico Highway 5 leads southward past the verdant patchwork of one of Mexico's most productive agricultural regions, then crosses open desert backed by rugged, barren mountains.

The route has a good paved surface to San Felipe, a resort town on the shore of the Gulf of California (Sea of Cortez), and for a short distance beyond. Between Punta Estrella and Puertecitos the road is paved but rough. From Puertecitos a graded but bumpy road extends farther south to Bahía San Luis Gonzaga. An ambitious highway construction project calls for the paving of the entire San Felipe-to-Bahía Gonzaga road sometime in the near future. This would bring rapid development to a region which, until very recently, was inaccessible to most tourists. The highway would also provide an alternate route for those who wish to travel from the California border south to the central desert region. Ample accommodations and facilities can be found in Mexicali and San Felipe, while rustic lodging, eating and camping facilities are scattered along the gulf coast. Fishing in the Gulf of California is excellent.

Crossing the Border

California State Route 111 leads through the Imperial Valley town of Calexico to the international border at Mexicali. The border crossing at Mexicali is open 24 hours a day. Scheduled to open by summer of 1996 is a new border crossing, located seven miles east of Mexicali, serving commercial traffic only.

Mexicali

(See also *Lodging & Restaurants*.)

Mexicali is unique among Mexico's large border cities in that its size and economic well-being do not result from either its proximity to the United States or its ability to attract tourist dollars. Instead, this mushrooming metropolis of about 775,000 owes its prosperity and phenomenal growth to its position as capital of the state of Baja California, and as the seat of government of the *municipio* of Mexicali, which extends south to San Felipe. It is

This imposing state government monument is located in Mexicali.

also the hub of one of Mexico's most important agricultural regions. Many tourists pass through Mexicali en route to San Felipe or to the Mexican mainland, but relatively few pause to examine this bustling, interesting city.

In the early 20th century Mexicali developed as a farm market center, and in 1915 it became the capital of the territory of Baja California Norte. For a couple of decades legalized alcohol and gambling and land speculation attracted visitors from across the border. In the late 1930s, under the leadership of Mexican president Lázaro Cárdenas, the fertile land of the Mexicali Valley was distributed among Mexican farmers and collective agricultural colonies, called *ejidos*. Also, the flow of irrigation water from the Colorado River was guaranteed by international treaty. These factors contributed to the economic bases of farming and industry.

Water has been the key to Mexicali's growth. The Mexicali Valley is extremely arid—the pleasant winters and torrid summers bring only about three inches of rain per year, not enough to exploit the rich, silt-laden soil deposited throughout the centuries by the Colorado River. So Mexico developed an elaborate irrigation complex tied to Morelos Dam, on the Colorado River just south of the border. The result is an agricultural empire in the midst of the desert, served by a proud city with modern commercial and industrial complexes, palm-lined boulevards, lush parks and quiet residential neighborhoods with neatly manicured shrubs and gardens. Permeating present-day Mexicali is a distinct aura of growth and vitality.

A good example of this vitality is the new Centro Cívico-Comercial de Mexicali—an innovative center for government and commerce along Calzada Independencia in the central part of the city. Included in this ambitious urban development are municipal, state and federal government offices, three hospitals, the bus terminal, a bullring, movie theaters, hotels, restaurants, private offices and shopping centers.

Shopping

The largest commercial area of Mexicali is the **border business district**, located in a rough rectangle bounded by avenidas Cristóbal Colón, Alvaro Obregón, the Río Nuevo and Calle C. This typical Mexican commercial district contains shops and restaurants catering to the tourist trade, along with businesses oriented to local consumers. Articles for sale that appeal to tourists include pottery, wrought iron, leather goods, blankets, silver, jewelry and works of art.

Other important, newer commercial strips spread southward along **calzadas López Mateos, Justo Sierra** and **Benito Juárez**. Plaza Cachanilla is an impressive shopping mall 1.7 miles from the border on the northeast side of López Mateos. Neon signs on these streets present an impressive spectacle after dark. A growing business district is the **Centro Cívico-Commercial**, near the government center.

Dining

Mexicali has a long list of fine Mexican and international eating places. A few of them are **9 Dragones**, on Calzada Benito Juárez just south of Lázaro Cár-

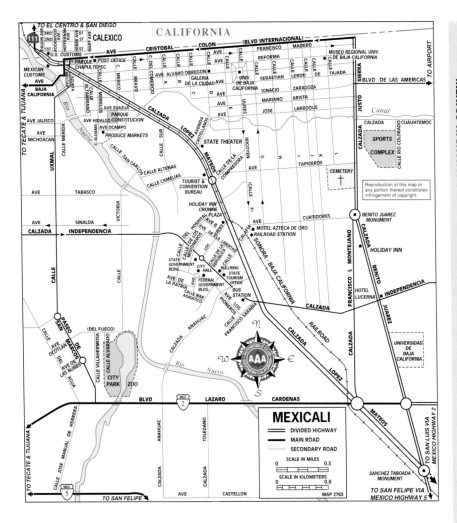

denas, in the Plaza Mandarín (Chinese cuisine); **Sakura** on Calzada Francisco Montejano and Boulevard Lázaro Cárdenas (Japanese food); **Rívoli** in Hotel Lucerna (varied menu, including steak and seafood); **Los Arcos** on Calle Calafia near the bullring (seafood); **El Vaquero** in Centro Cívico-Commercial on Avenida de los Héroes near Calzada Independencia (steak, carne asada); **Los Búffalos**, in the Plaza Cachanilla shopping center (ranch-style cooking); and **El Sarape** in the border business district on Calle México between Colón and Madero (Mexican food).

Nightclubs

Numerous piano bars and discotheques lie within walking distance of the international border. Live entertainment and dancing are offered at hotels **Lucerna** and **Holiday Inn** on Calzada Benito Juárez, and at **Forum Discotheque** at Calzada Justo Sierra and Avenida Reforma.

▼ *Quick Guide to Mexicali*

Tourist Information and Assistance

Secretaría de Turismo or SECTUR (Mexican Government Tourism Office) *Located near the corner of Calle Calafia and Calzada Independencia in the Centro Cívico-Comercial. Open Mon. through Fri. 8 a.m. to 7 p.m., Sat. 9 a.m. to 3 p.m., and Sun. 9 a.m. to 1 p.m. 01152 (65) 56-1072 or 56-1172.* Protección al Turista (Tourist Assistance) provides legal help for tourists who encounter problems while in Mexicali.

Mexicali Tourist and Convention

Bureau *On Calzada López Mateos at Calle Camelias. Open Mon. through Fri. 9 a.m. to 7 p.m.; Sat. 9 a.m. to 3 p.m. 01152 (65) 57-2376 or 57-2561.* General tourist information is provided.

Newspapers

Mexicali has no English-language newspaper, but tourist brochures in English are available at the tourism offices. The AAA-approved hotels in town often have California newspapers. There are two Spanish-language newspapers: *La Voz de la Frontera* and *Novedades de Baja California.*

Radio and Television Stations

Many California radio stations are received all through northern Baja California. Among the several Mexicali stations, XED at 1050 AM broadcasts a rich variety of traditional folk music. A few American television stations are received, along with the Mexicali stations.

Driving in Mexicali

Before crossing the border into Mexicali, be sure to obtain Mexican auto insurance (see Automobile Requirements in the *Tourist Regulations and Travel Tips* chapter). Tourists driving in Mexicali find wide, flat streets, many of which are one way. Unfortunately, many streets lack signs. Mexicali has no expressway bypass like Tijuana, but three wide boulevards—calzadas López Mateos, Justo Sierra and Benito Juárez—usually allow traffic to move through the city at moderate speeds. Traffic circles, or *glorietas*, found along these boulevards pose a challenge for new visitors. When entering a traffic circle, drivers should bear right, then follow the flow of traffic counterclockwise. It is important to watch for traffic lights and street signs; lights are often small and hard to see from a distance. Stop signs are sometimes not very noticeable.

Parking is scarce in the business district near the border and around the government center, but it does not pose a problem in other parts of the city. Visitors planning to shop in the border business district should park on the Calexico, California, side and walk across. Most of the tourist-oriented stores are within a few blocks.

Local Transportation

Traveling a few miles in town by taxi costs about $6, although sometimes bargaining can lower the fare. It is wise to agree on the price before getting into the cab.

As in other large Baja California cities, Mexicali bus fare is extremely cheap. Riders should know a little Spanish, have an idea of the city's layout and not mind traveling in old coaches. For long-distance travel, Mexicali is an important departure point for bus and train lines to Mexico City.

Points of Interest

CITY PARK/BOSQUE DE LA CIUDAD *Avenida Ocotlán (del Fuego) and Calle Alvarado, in southwest Mexicali. 01152 (65) 55-2833. Open Tues. through Fri. 9 a.m. to 5 p.m., Sat. and Sun. 9 a.m. to 5 p.m. Admission $1.* The park, most easily approached from the north along calles Victoria and Alvarado, contains a zoo, a museum of natural history, a picnic area and a children's playground.

GALERIA DE LA CIUDAD *1209 Avenida Alvaro Obregón between calles D and E. 01152 (65) 53-5044. Open Mon. through Fri. 9 a.m. to 8 p.m. Free admission.* Housed in what was formerly the state governor's residence, the art gallery features works of Baja California painters, sculptors and photographers.

GLORIETA MONUMENTS The traffic circles on Mexicali's main boulevards contain impressive monuments. Crosswalks lead to the landscaped islands where the monuments stand.

MUSEO REGIONAL UNIVERSIDAD DE BAJA CALIFORNIA *Avenida Reforma and Calle L. 01152 (65) 54-1977. Open Tues. through Fri. 9 a.m. to 6 p.m., Sat. and Sun. 9 a.m. to 2 p.m. Free admission.* This fine museum contains

These proud military cadets participate in a public ceremony in Mexicali.

comprehensive exhibits on geology, rocks and minerals, anthropology of American Indians, and the missions and ranches of early Baja California.

STATE THEATER/TEATRO DEL ESTADO *Calzada López Mateos, 1½ miles south of the U.S. border. 01152 (65) 54-6418.* Plays, musicals and dance presentations are featured here. The Mexicali Convention and Tourist Bureau also has programs and schedules.

Spectator Sports

BULLFIGHTS Plaza de Toros Calafia *Calle Calafia in the Centro Cívico-Comercial. 01152 (65) 57-0681.* Bullfights are held every autumn and sometimes in spring.

CHARREADAS (Mexican Rodeo) Charro Grounds *3⁷⁄₁₀ miles east of Calzada Justo Sierra on Carretera a Compuertas (the road to the airport).* There is no set schedule for these colorful equestrian events, but charreadas average once a month during the winter and spring, usually on Sunday and major Mexican holidays.

 Travelogue

Mexicali to San Felipe

(124 mi., 198 km.; 2:30 hrs.)

The most direct route to San Felipe follows Calzada López Mateos from the international border to Mexico Highway 5. Upon leaving the Mexican port of entry, turn right and follow Calzada López Mateos in a southeasterly direction to the traffic circle at the intersection with Mexico Highway 5. An alternate route, popular in previous years, follows Avenida Francisco I. Madero eastward to Calzada Justo Sierra, which leads south to Mexico Highway 5. Motorists returning to the United States from Mexicali must approach the U.S. Customs facility along Avenida Cristóbal Colón, a one-way westbound street immediately

Bullfights are held in the Plaza de Toros Calafia in Mexicali.

south of the international border. After leaving Mexicali, the highway skirts the western edge of one of Mexico's most productive farming regions for about 30 miles. To the southwest is the imposing mountain wall of the Sierra de los Cucapá.

Plumes of steam, visible to the east, rise from the Cerro Prieto geothermal electric plant. (Mexico is one of the world's leading producers of geothermal electricity, and some of this electricity is exported to the United States.) Mexico Highway 5 then continues southward through extremely arid desert. After about 45 miles, the road runs atop an 11-mile-long earthen levee while crossing an arm of the intermittent lake, Laguna Salada. Then it passes through the Sierra Pinta, whose dark volcanic basalt hills have an otherworldly appearance. As the highway nears San Felipe, the high Sierra San Pedro Mártir, capped by 10,154-foot Picacho del Diablo, is visible to the west. On the outskirts of San Felipe the flat, straight highway bends toward the gulf, passing under big white gateway arches.

The dry lake bed of Laguna Salada, 50 miles south of Mexicali along Mexico Highway 5, is a harsh contrast to the nearby Gulf of California.

00.0   Mexicali (U.S. border crossing).

03.0   Junction with Calzada Independencia.

04.1   Junction with Calzada Lázaro Cárdenas.

05.1   Traffic circle at Sánchez Taboada Monument. Bear right, then take the right fork, which heads south.

05.7   Junction with Mexico Highway 2 west to Tecate and Tijuana (see *Mexico Highway 2*).

07.7   A paved road branches west to Club Deportivo Campestre de Mexicali, which has a golf course and other sports facilities.

25.2   Junction with the paved road to the farming communities of Zakamoto and Ejido Nayarít.

26.1   La Puerta, a roadside farming center with a Pemex station (*magna sin*), cafe and store.

29.3   Junction with highway BC 4, a paved route that crosses the Mexicali Valley to Coahuila (Colonia Nuevas) and continues to El Golfo de Santa Clara on the Sonora side of the gulf (see Side Route to El Golfo de Santa Clara).

37.0   Campo Sonora, the first of several rustic trailer camps along Río Hardy.

38.3   Río del Mayor, a village with an Indian museum. Located by the police station, it is called Museo Comunitario, Centro Cultural Cucapá.

44.2 At this point, the highway, elevated by a levee, sets out across the southern end of Laguna Salada.

71.2 La Ventana, which has a Pemex station and café.

92.7 El Chinero (Crucero la Trinidad), junction with Mexico Highway 3, which leads westward to Valle de Trinidad and Ensenada (see *Mexico Highway 3*). At the junction is a government-built restaurant and picnic area. About 0.7 mile south of the junction is a Pemex station (*magna sin*) and a café.

111.0 A dirt road branches left to Campo Don Abel, the first of a string of rustic trailer camps on the gulf shore north of San Felipe. Facilities in these camps are usually modest.

114.8 A graded one-mile road to El Paraíso/Pete's Camp, a long-established popular camp with tent and RV spaces, showers, a disposal station and a restaurant-bar.

123.6 San Felipe, at the junction of Mexico Highway 5 and Avenida Mar de Cortez.

🚐 Side Route

Highway 5 to El Golfo de Santa Clara, Sonora

(69 mi., 112 km.; 2:30 hrs.)

This route encompasses rich agricultural land in the Mexicali Valley, the Sonoran Desert and a picturesque fishing town on the Gulf of California. Just beyond El Faro, 26 miles south of Mexicali on Mexico Highway 5, turn east on state highway BC 4 where the sign points to Colonia Nuevas. (State highways are not usually indicated on signs, but the abbreviation is printed on occasional roadside posts.) This paved highway leads across pasture land and grain fields to Ejido Durango, a farm village with gasoline.

At mileage 10 is Ledón (Colonia Carranza), which has gasoline (*magna sin*) and a few stores. Crossing flat land planted in cotton, the road reaches Murguía, turns south, then eastward. Four miles past Murguía the highway crosses the Colorado River by means of a culvert. Due to irrigation demands the river is usually a shallow narrow stream. After an occasional rain, however, the crossing may be flooded. (The highway formerly shared the railroad bridge to the north, but this route is closed for an indefinite time.) The last town in Baja California on this route, 21 miles east of Mexico Highway 5, is Coahuila, also called Colonia Nuevas. Drive slowly on the graded dirt streets. Turn left, cross the railroad and follow the signs to Sonora.

One hundred yards beyond the railroad, travelers enter the state of Sonora; there is no checkpoint. Sonora is on Mountain Time, and the urban area of Coahuila continues under the name of Luis B. Sánchez. The two towns constitute a sizeable farm market center, containing two Pemex stations (*magna sin*), auto parts, a clinic and several markets and restaurants. After one more mile the road runs into state highway SON 40. A left turn leads north to San Luis, Sonora; a right turn leads southeast to El Golfo. After passing a secondary school and some farmland, the road to El Golfo comes to Riíto, a small agricultural center at the end of the cultivated area. Here are Pemex facilities and a few stores.

HIGHWAY 5 TO EL GOLFO
DE SANTA CLARA, SONORA

SIDE ROUTE

FREEWAY — DIVIDED HIGHWAY
PAVED ROAD — GRADED DIRT
LOCAL ROAD — DIRT
GRAVEL — POOR ROAD

SCALE IN MILES
0 — 10 — 20

SCALE IN KILOMETERS
0 — 10 — 20 — 30

MAP 2780

DISTANCES ON MAP
ARE SHOWN IN MILES

Between Riíto and El Golfo de Santa Clara are 43 miles of the barren Sonoran Desert, with no services. The only real settlement is El Doctor, a railroad work station with a few buildings and a rustic cafe. The highway is very flat and in good condition most of the way. The road becomes quite rough, however, 12 miles southeast of El Doctor. Shortly before coming to the town the road smoothes out, curves and drops quickly to a small coastal basin. Pavement ends at the entrance to El Golfo.

Another route to El Golfo starts in the city of San Luis R.C., Sonora. From Mexico Highway 2, turn south on Calle 2, which becomes highway SON 40 to Riíto. From Riíto follow the route previously described to El Golfo.

El Golfo de Santa Clara is a fishing town of about 3000 residents, with a fish-processing plant, Pemex station, a grocery store, a general store, a church and several cafes. The streets are sandy and cars can easily get stuck. The motorist should greatly lower tire pressure before driving these streets. Several shops advertise *"aire*/air" for refilling the tires later. The harbor has many fishing boats, large and small, that catch shrimp, clams and sierra. Arrangements can sometimes be made for sportfishing. The tidal range is great here at the head of the Gulf of California, with sandy beaches at high tide and mud flats exposed at low tide. Across the gulf the mountains of Baja California are visible.

A graded sandy road extends southeast of town, passing side roads to two RV parks and an area where signs announce a planned beach community. At 1.7 miles there is a large *playa pública* camping area (no facilities), backed by sand dunes, hills and a light

house. This spot is sometimes used by Americans with ATVs.

San Felipe

(See also *Lodging & Restaurants* and *Campgrounds & Trailer Parks*.)

This major winter resort and fishing center occupies a site where the shimmering waters of the Gulf of California lap against the shores of a forbidding desert. Clearly visible across the sandy coastal plain to the west is the steep eastern wall of the Sierra San Pedro Mártir—highest range on the peninsula. The town itself is nestled beneath 940-foot-high Punta San Felipe, a rugged headland that provides a partial shelter for boats and forms the northern end of shallow Bahía San Felipe. From this point, the shore of the bay makes a crescent-shaped dent in the coastline, then swings southeastward in a line of wide, attractive beaches to Punta Estrella, 12 miles distant. An interesting natural phenomenon here is the extreme tidal range, which can

---

▼ *Quick Guide to San Felipe*

Tourist Information and Assistance

Secretaría de Turismo or **SECTUR (Mexican Government Tourism Office)** *On Avenida Mar de Cortez at Manzanillo. Open Mon. through Fri. 9 a.m. to 6 p.m., Sat. and Sun. 9 a.m. to 2 p.m. 01152 (657) 7-1155.* Protección al Turista (Tourist Assistance) provides legal help for tourists who encounter problems while in San Felipe.

Peaceful San Felipe is a mecca for American college students.

reach more than 20 feet; this makes boating a tricky proposition for those without experience in these waters.

San Felipe is a friendly community of about 15,000, with modest dwellings, sandy side streets and little vegetation. The wide variety of facilities include numerous hotels and trailer parks, markets, bakeries, restaurants, bars, launch ramps, banks, clinics, auto mechanics and two Pemex stations. Curio shops sell a great variety of goods, including blankets, shawls, shoes, beach wear, shirts and pottery. Mexico Highway 5 ends at Avenida Mar de Cortez, which parallels the shore and forms the main street of town; its many businesses cater to local residents and tourists alike.

Although nomadic fishermen were attracted to this area as early as the mid-19th century, San Felipe did not become a permanent settlement until the 1920s. Large-scale fishing began in earnest during World War II, and the completion of the paved highway from Mexicali in 1951 brought a surge of American sports enthusiasts. In the years that followed, San Felipe gradually evolved from a sleepy fishing village into a popular resort. Rapid expansion during the 1980s, with the addition of many new hotels, condominiums and trailer parks, is continuing in the 1990s. The recently modernized airport has gained international status.

November through April is the ideal time to visit San Felipe. Days are usually warm and sunny, and nights are refreshingly cool. Summers, however, can be unbearably hot, with daytime temperatures sometimes exceeding 115 Fahrenheit. Rainfall is less than two inches per year. U.S. vacation periods (Washington's Birthday, Easter week, Memorial Day, Labor Day, Thanksgiving, etc.) are extremely crowded, and accommodations, trailer parks and even beach campsites are likely to be jammed. San Felipe tends to attract a somewhat unruly brand of tourist, and annoyances caused by motorcycles, dune buggies and loud parties are common during holiday periods. Litter is also a problem. The town is relatively peaceful the rest of the year.

Points of Interest

VALLE DE LOS GIGANTES *13½ miles south of town center, then about 3 miles southwest on a sandy road.* There is no sign pointing to this attraction, but look for one that points in the opposite direction to Colonia Gutierrez Polanco. The title of this place translates "Valley of the Giants," and this cluster of very large cardón cacti has specimens more than 100 years old. Sturdy high-clearance vehicles should be used on this road.

VIRGIN OF GUADALUPE SHRINE *Situated on a hilltop just north of San Felipe.*

A panoramic view of the town and the coastline is offered. Adjacent is a lighthouse (not open to visitors).

◤ Travelogue

San Felipe to Puertecitos

(52 mi., 83 km.; 2 hrs.)

This route through rapidly developing and changing territory has been paved as far as Puertecitos. Plans call for additional paving south to Bahía San Luis Gonzaga sometime in the future. Some of the pavement on the southern end of this route is rough, ranging from broken surfaces to large potholes.

Punta San Felipe is a rugged backdrop for the modern lighthouse on the bay.

The first eight miles run close to the bay through part of San Felipe's resort area, with a number of hotels, campgrounds and condominiums; more are under construction. The pavement is good on this first section, but drifting sand is a problem in a few spots; drive with caution to avoid skidding. The remaining 44 miles follow a route a little inland from the Gulf of California, with turnoffs leading to numerous campos that contain small communities of American and Canadian vacation homes and trailer camps. As yet, virtually no facilities exist for motorists on this long section. Along the route, the terrain changes very little; level to rolling countryside is interspersed with low, barren hills. Ocotillo, mesquite, cholla cactus and smoke trees are the most common forms of vegetation, although a few elephant trees and cardón cacti may be seen.

00.0	Junction of Mexico Highway 5 and Avenida Mar Caribe (street name for the beginning of the route.)
00.5	Junction with a graded road which also leads to Puertecitos; in the past this inland route was the preferred road for some travelers.
00.9	Entrance to Hotel Las Misiones and Mar del Sol RV Park.
01.4	Entrance to the commercial harbor.
05.5	Junction with the paved road to San Felipe International Airport.
07.3	La Hacienda, a condominium development.
09.7	Turnoff to Faro Beach and Punta Estrella, at the southern end of Bahía San Felipe.
13.5	An unsigned sandy road leads southwest to Valle de los

Exceptionally low tides are common at Puertecitos.

Gigantes, a group of very large cardón cacti. In the opposite direction a sign points to Colonia Gutierrez Polanco.

19.0   A sandy spur road leads 2½ miles to Laguna (Rancho) Percibú, a growing community of American beach houses, a campground and a restaurant.

25.4   Turnoff to Campo Santa María, a large collection of trailers and vacation homes.

28.2   The village of Ejido Delicias, with a clinic and a small store. On the beach opposite are a lighthouse and Campo El Vergel, a large settlement.

40.7   Junction with the inland road leading north toward San Felipe.

51.6   Puertecitos, overlooking a small bay. At the northern entrance is a municipal delegation and a small Mexican community called Ejido Matomí. Most of Puertecitos, however, is inhabited by Americans who lease their homes and trailer sites from the owners of the land. Facilities include a motel, a cafe and bar, a small general store, a Pemex station (not always open) and an airstrip. Arrangements can be made for camping, cabaña rentals, fishing boats, trailer rentals and boat launching. Fishing is good outside the shallow bay, which becomes dry during extreme low tides. The short road branching to the southeast point of the bay passes a rocky footpath leading to natural hot springs; depending on the tide, three separate pools are filled with water of varying temperatures.

⬛ Travelogue

Puertecitos to Bahía San Luis Gonzaga

(45 mi., 72 km.; 4 hrs.)

Long notorious as one of Baja California's roughest routes, this graded dirt road along the Gulf of California was greatly improved in 1987. The surface is rough washboard, however, and sturdy high-clearance vehicles are recommended. Carry adequate emergency equipment, as this is a lonely stretch of road. Vegetation is sparse along this arid route, but interesting rocks can be seen in shades of orange, red and brown. Much of the road has been realigned, but motorists can see the former tortuous, rocky route alongside. Between 11 and 19 miles the road crosses several hills, with spectacular views of canyons and the gulf. The treacherous Huerfanito Grade is now bypassed. Between Nacho's Camp and Punta Bufeo are numerous signs advertising undeveloped campsites and lots for sale. The road here is level, running close to shore. For the last six miles it crosses sandy arroyos and passes among hills before reaching the shore of the bay.

Bahía San Luis Gonzaga, not to be confused with the mission of the same name in Baja California Sur, is a beautiful, pristine body of water. Although the landscape is barren, Bahía Gonzaga typifies an isolated, peaceful seaside spot in Baja California, with brilliant sun by day and a million stars by night.

00.0	Puertecitos.
04.8	Campo La Costilla, a small private camp at the edge of an attractive cove, where the natural slope of the beach makes

Bahía San Luis Gonzaga's beauty is relatively unspoiled.

an excellent launch ramp. Refreshments can be purchased here.

11.6   The first of many good camping spots along the rocky gulf shore.

17.7   Nacho's Camp, a group of homes owned by Americans.

20.0   San Juan del Mar, a growing beach settlement with an airstrip.

35.1   Campo Salvatierra, an abandoned private campground with several good primitive camping spots.

37.8   Junction with the road to Las Encantadas.

39.4   Junction with a 1.3-mile dirt road to Campo Punta Bufeo, a collection of homes owned by Americans and an airstrip. Refreshments and simple meals are available.

42.5   Junction with the 0.9-mile road to Papa Fernandez'

camp, located on Bahía San Luis Gonzaga. The resort offers meals, refreshments, boats and motors for rent, and occasionally gasoline and oil. The level grassy field to the west makes a good natural airstrip. Fishing is excellent.

▧ Travelogue

Bahía San Luis Gonzaga to Highway 1
(39 mi., 63 km.; 2 hrs.)

With careful driving, this graded dirt road can be traveled by passenger cars and small RVs. After passing the shore of Bahía San Luis Gonzaga near Punta Willard, the route comes to the junction for Punta Final, on the southern end of the bay. For the first few miles after the bay, the road ascends through gently sloping desert terrain where wildflowers form carpets of color during early spring. Then the road enters a range of hills containing numerous elephant trees. Just beyond a rocky canyon with a winding road is Rancho las Arrastras. A short distance past the ranch, the route forks to the left and then meets a road leading southwest to Mexico Highway 1.

00.0   Bahía San Luis Gonzaga, at the junction to Papa Fernandez.

02.6   Rancho Grande, a water purification/ice plant and a campground. A 1.6-mile side road leads to Alfonsina's Camp, located on a narrow sandspit facing the bay. Facilities include a small hotel, a campground, a restaurant, an airstrip and gasoline. Vacation homes line the sandspit next to the camp.

Fishing at dawn in Gonzaga Bay.

11.7 Junction with the road to Punta Final, a private beach community.

22.0 Rancho las Arrastras de Arriola, which has radiator water and cold drinks.

26.0 Junction with the road leading 13 miles southwest to Mexico Highway 1. It joins the highway just north of Laguna Chapala, 33.7 miles south of Cataviña. From the junction, turn right for Mexico Highway 1. A left turn leads east, then north to Hermenegildo Galiana and to Campo Calamajué on the gulf.

Mexico Highway 19

Mexico Highway 19 forms part of a loop with Mexico Highway 1 in the extreme southern portion of the peninsula. Travel time between La Paz and Cabo San Lucas is about one hour shorter on this route than via Mexico Highway 1. Mexico Highway 19 is paved over its entire length.

⊿ Travelogue

Highway 1 to Todos Santos

(32 mi., 51 km.; 0:45 hr.)

This route leaves Mexico Highway 1 at a point 19 miles south of La Paz, and offers the possibility of a scenic loop trip from La Paz to Cabo San Lucas and back. Since 1986, when it became completely paved, Mexico Highway 19 has been the most direct route between La Paz and Cabo San Lucas. It is about an hour (and 30 miles) shorter than Mexico Highway 1, the old traditional route. From its junction with Mexico Highway 1 the road leads southward across flat, cactus-covered countryside toward Todos Santos.

00.0	**Junction with Mexico Highway 1, just south of the village of San Pedro.**
06.0	**Club Campestre El Carrizal, a local country club with a pool and a restaurant.**
26.5	**Signed road to Presa de Santa Inéz, a dam.**
31.8	**Todos Santos, town center.**

Todos Santos

(See also *Campgrounds & Trailer Parks.*)

With its red brick buildings and wide streets, Todos Santos is still a tranquil town, despite the increasing impact of tourism. Almost directly on the Tropic of Cancer, this town of about 6000 inhabitants is laid out on a small, rolling coastal plain called the Valle del Pilar, a couple of miles from the Pacific Ocean shore.

Founded in 1733 as a mission settlement, Todos Santos remained a village until the latter 19th century. At this time ample supplies of underground water were tapped to develop agriculture, especially sugar cane. When the sugar market collapsed in recent times, farmers diversified into growing vegetables, mangos, coconuts, papayas and other tropical fruits. Fishing also contributes to the economy. Ruins of sugar mills may be seen on Avenida Juárez about a block south of the ISSTE general store, and at El Molino Trailer Park.

Facing the pleasant plaza are the church, Nuestra Señora del Pilar (suc-

---

Todos Santos has many fine shops offering a wide variety of wares.

The central plaza in Todos Santos includes a theater.

cessor to the early mission); a theater; the town hall; and Restaurant Santa Fé (Italian dishes and seafood). An excellent museum, Casa de la Cultura, is located near the center of town at Calles Topete and Pilar. It contains materials on the history of Baja California Sur and Mexico, as well as items that reveal Todos Santos' civic pride. Several buildings in town bear plaques honoring noted residents who fought in various struggles for Mexican independence. Hotel California, built in 1926, exhibits a Mexican colonial style. It is on Calle Juárez, a block west of the plaza. Todos Santos has markets, restaurants, a bank, medical clinics, a Pemex station and a park. For visitors

there are three hotels and two trailer parks. A lighthouse stands at Playa Punta Lobos, an attractive beach two miles west of town.

 Travelogue

Todos Santos to
Cabo San Lucas
(45 mi., 72 km.; 1:30 hrs.)

Beyond Todos Santos, Mexico Highway 19 parallels the coastline over rolling terrain and provides access to some of Baja California's most beautiful, unspoiled Pacific beaches. Many of these are *playas públicas* (public beaches) and are notable for good surfing.

00.0 Todos Santos, town center.

01.7 Junction with a dirt road to Playa Punta Lobos, used by fishermen and also a popular picnic spot with local residents.

03.6 El Pescadero (see *Campgrounds & Trailer Parks*), a farming and fishing town of 1500 located just east of the highway. Several dirt roads lead from the pavement to the center of town, where stores and cafes ring a small plaza. El Pescadero is a junction with a road leading across the Sierra de la Laguna to Mexico Highway 1, five miles north of Santa Anita.

7.5 Junction with a good dirt road to Playa Los Cerritos, a wide, beautiful beach with a private trailer park and public beach camping.

14.9 Colonia Elías Calles, a small farming community surrounded by fields and orchards. Several nice beaches lie just to the west.

26.8 Rancho Migriño, a cattle ranch.

42.2 Junction with a dirt road to Cabo San Lucas airstrip.

44.5 Cabo San Lucas, at the junction with Mexico Highway 1.

Recreation

The very soul of Baja is in enjoying the rugged outdoors. The pristine coastline lends itself very well to aquatic activities such as surfing, sailboarding, surf-fishing, snorkeling, scuba diving and swimming. Ocean waters offer prime sportfishing opportunities. For those less energetically inclined, Baja's beautiful beaches provide an opportunity for sunbathing and beachcombing. The peninsula's rugged terrain is a hunter's paradise and also offers scenic vistas for aspiring photographers.

There is little in the way of formalized recreational activities such as those commonly found in the United States, although major resorts in Baja offer some planned activities, such as golf. The availability of recreational equipment is limited throughout most of Baja California, so travelers are advised to bring those items with them from home.

Golfing

Considering the nature of recreation in Baja California, a surprising number of golf courses exist, most of them located in the major cities or operated by resort hotels.

Information for the following listings was provided by the courses to the Automobile Club of Southern California for publication. The semi-private courses may have restrictions on public play ranging from members and guests only to liberal reciprocal agreements with members of other courses; please contact the course directly for

details. Reservations are advised at most courses.

Bajamar

BAJAMAR OCEANFRONT GOLF RESORT Semi-private

21 miles north of Ensenada, off Hwy. 1-D at Jatay exit. Phone 01152 (61) 55-0152. Fees include mandatory golf cart: Mon. through Thu. $45; Fri. through Sun. $55.

The course is 18 holes. Par 71, 4696 yards, 115 slope, 69.0 rating. Clubhouse, locker room, golf shop, power carts, rental clubs, driving range; tennis, swimming; restaurant; cocktails.

Cabo San Lucas

CABO DEL SOL GOLF CLUB Public

5 miles northeast of Cabo San Lucas off Hwy. 1. Phone 01152 (114) 3-3149; (800) 637-2226. Fees include mandatory golf cart: hotel guests $80-110; nonhotel guests $105-135.

The course is 18 holes. Par 72, 5843 yards, 116 slope, 66.8 rating. Profes-

A view of the golf course at Bajamar.

RECREATION

At Cabo San Lucas the golf course is right on the beach.

sional, golf shop, power carts, rental clubs; snack bar.

CABO SAN LUCAS COUNTRY CLUB Semi-private

On east edge of Cabo San Lucas, just north of Hwy. 1. Phone 01152 (114) 3-4653; (800) 854-2314. Fees include mandatory golf cart: 18 holes $99, 9 holes $62.

The course is 18 holes. Par 72, 6135 yards, 132 slope, N/A rating. Professional, golf shop, rental clubs, driving range.

PALMILLA GOLF CLUB Public

5 miles northeast of Cabo San Lucas off Hwy. 1. Phone 01152 (114) 8-8525; (800) 637-2226. Fees inlcude mandatory

golf cart: hotel guests $65-95, nonhotel guests $90-120.

The course is 18 holes. Par 72, 5673 yards, 110 slope, 66.5 rating. Professional, golf shop, power carts, rental clubs; snack bar.

Ensenada

BAJA COUNTRY CLUB Semi-private

9 miles south of Ensenada via Hwy. 1, then 1 mile east. Phone 01152 (617) 3-0303. Fee includes mandatory golf cart: $34.

The course is 18 holes. Par 72, 6820 yards, 119 slope, N/A rating. Locker room, power carts, professional, golf shop, rental clubs, driving range; coffee shop; cocktails.

RECREATION

Loreto

CAMPO DE GOLF LORETO Public

In Nopaló, just south of the Loreto Inn. Phone 01152 (113) 3-0788. Fee: $22.

The course is 18 holes. Par 72, 6400 yards, N/A slope, N/A rating. Power carts, professional, golf shop, rental clubs; coffee shop.

Rosarito

REAL DEL MAR Semi-private

5 miles north of town center off Hwy. 1-D (toll highway). Phone 01152 (66) 13-3401. Fees: Mon. through Thu. $43; Fri. through Sun. $49.

The course is 18 holes. Par 72, 5949 yards, 122 slope, 67.8 rating. Professional, clubhouse, golf shop, locker room, driving range; tennis; snack bar; cocktails.

San José del Cabo

CAMPO DE GOLF SAN JOSÉ Public

Off Boulevard Mijares, situated among the condominiums and hotels in the resort area. Phone 01152 (114) 2-0905. Fees: 9 holes $15.

The course is 9 holes. Par 35, 2879 yards, N/A slope, N/A rating. Professional, clubhouse, locker room, golf shop, power carts, pull carts, rental clubs; snack bar; cocktails.

Tijuana

CLUB SOCIAL Y DEPORTIVO CAMPESTRE (TIJUANA COUNTRY CLUB) Semi-private

3 miles east of downtown Tijuana via Boulevard Agua Caliente. Phone 01152 (66) 81-7855. Fee includes mandatory golf cart: $20.

The course is 18 holes. Par 72, N/A yards, N/A slope, N/A rating. Clubhouse, power carts, professional, golf shop, rental clubs; restaurant, coffee shop, snack bar; cocktails.

Hunting

Most of the hunting on the peninsula is in the north, in the state of Baja California. Several species of squirrel populate the region, as well as peccary, bobcat, fox, coyote, jack rabbit and cottontail. Ducks are found in the lagoons and marshes along both coasts; black brant are plentiful in San Quintín Bay; quail, pheasant and dove are found throughout the state. Although mule deer and desert bighorn sheep inhabit some areas in Baja California, they are scarce and special permits are required to hunt them. Hunting seasons vary according to species, but most open seasons occur between September and the end of February.

Hunting in Baja California requires a special-purpose visa, a consular certificate, a Military Gun Permit, a hunting permit and during the hunt the presence of a licensed outfitter's assistant. In addition to the above, when hunting for mule deer or desert bighorn sheep, a contract with a licensed Mexican organizer must be purchased. It is advisable to contact an American organization that specializes in hunting in Mexico to obtain the documents and to make arrangements with a Mexican contract organizer.

Weapons are forbidden in Mexico unless they are brought into the country during hunting seasons for the express purpose of hunting. Only two sporting firearms and 50 rounds of ammunition for each are permitted.

RECREATION

Military and .22 caliber rimfire weapons and all pistols are prohibited. Bow and arrow hunting requires a special permit.

Standard Licensing Procedure

1. **CONSULAR CERTIFICATE** This document is issued by all Mexican Consulates. Applicants must present a letter of good conduct from their local police department or sheriff's office vouching for their moral character, plus two color, front-view passport-size photographs. The consular certificate is not a hunting permit—it is merely an authorization for the hunter to enter Mexico in this capacity, and is also required when applying for a Military Gun Permit. It will contain a description of each firearm, including kind, make, serial number, caliber or gauge and number of cartridges. The hunter needs a consular certificate for each state within Baja California.

2. **HUNTING PERMITS (LICENSES)** Hunters must purchase permits for each Mexican state in which they intend to hunt and for each bird or animal they intend to hunt. Hunting permits are issued in the names of individual hunters and are not transferable. Each permit is only valid for the current season and in the state for which it was issued.

All the paperwork necessary for hunting in Baja California may be handled by the Southern California organization listed below. They also furnish information on hunting conditions and government regulations (which are subject to change). Depending on the types of mammals or birds hunted, the total cost of all the permits ranges

from about $350 to $500. For information about the specific services offered, contact the Mexican Hunting Association, 6840 El Salvador Street, Long Beach, CA 90815; phone (310) 430-3256; FAX (310) 430-9584.

Water Recreation

Boating

Anyone planning to operate a private boat in Mexican waters, regardless of size or construction, must first obtain a Mexican Boat Permit issued by the Mexico Department of Fisheries. Permits are sold on a yearly basis and are valid for 12 months from the date of issue. Fees for permits are based on the length of the craft: under 23 feet, $18.60; 23 feet to 29 feet 11 inches, $37.20; 30 feet and over, $55.80. (These fees are subject to change; the Mexico Department of Fisheries office can provide current fees.)

Obtain applications for Mexican Boat Permits and submit the completed forms to the Mexico Department of Fisheries at 2550 5th Avenue, Suite 101, San Diego, CA 92103-6622; (619) 233-6956. The office is open Monday through Friday 8 a.m. to 2 p.m.

Boat permit applications must include a copy of the boat's registration document. The boat registration document has to be shown before applying for a boat permit. Fees must be paid by cashier's check or money order for the exact amount due to Oficina Recaudadora de Pesca (personal checks are not accepted). For mail orders, include a stamped return envelope.

Fishing

The Gulf of California is widely considered to offer the world's finest fishing.

Kayaking is popular at Bahía de la Concepción.

Virtually every popular saltwater species—including marlin, sailfish, roosterfish, cabrilla, dorado (mahi-mahi), sierra, yellowtail, sea bass, wahoo and bonito—can be found here. Favorite gulf fishing areas are Bahía de los Angeles, Cabo San Lucas, the East Cape, La Paz, Loreto, Mulegé with nearby Bahía Concepción, and San Felipe. On the Pacific Ocean side, Ensenada calls itself the "yellowtail capital of the world" and San Quintín Bay offers a variety of species.

Licenses

Any nonresident alien must possess a valid Mexican Sportfishing License before fishing in Mexican waters. This license covers all types of fishing and is valid anywhere in Mexico. Everyone aboard private boats in Mexican waters must have a fishing license regardless of age and whether or not they are fishing. Licenses for people fishing on commercial sportfishing boats are normally provided by the boat operators. A fishing license is also officially required for underwater fishing and free diving.

Fishing licenses are issued for periods of one week, one month and one year, effective at 12:01 a.m. on the starting date specified on the license application. Fees for licenses are $11.35 for one week, $17 for one month and $22.70 for one year. (These fees are subject to change; the Department of Fisheries office can provide current fees.) Mexican fishing licenses are not transferable, and each license must include the person's full legal name, home address and telephone number.

Obtain applications for Mexican Sport-fishing Licenses and submit the completed forms to the Mexico Department of Fisheries at 2550 5th Avenue, Suite 101, San Diego, CA 92103-6622; (619) 233-6956. The office is open Monday through Friday 8 a.m. to 2 p.m.

Applications must be accompanied by a cashier's check or money order for the exact amount due, payable to Oficina Recaudadora de Pesca (personal checks are not accepted). For mail orders, include a stamped return envelope.

The Mexico Department of Fisheries also has offices in Mexico (Oficina de Pesca), but travelers are advised to obtain fishing licenses before crossing the border.

Daily Bag Limits and Other Regulations

Each fisherman is permitted to catch up to 10 fish per day, with no more than five fish of the same species. In addition, anglers are subject to the following limits: no more than one billfish (marlin, sailfish or swordfish) and two tarpon or halibut. In brackish waters anglers are permitted to take up to 20 perch and 20 carp per day. Once the permitted limit has been bagged, all further catches must be released.

Except when skin or scuba diving, fish must be taken by angling with a hand-held line or a line attached to a rod. The use of nets (except handling nets), traps, poisons or explosives is prohibited. Skin and scuba divers may fish only with hand-held spears or band-powered spear guns. It is illegal to sell, trade or exchange the fish caught. Fish can be eviscerated and filleted, but a patch of skin must be left to permit identification. The taking of abalone,

lobster, shrimp, pismo clams, cabrilla, totuava, oysters and sea turtles is prohibited by Mexican law. Anyone wishing to purchase any of these species to take into the United States must first obtain a form from the Mexico Department of Fisheries; only the Oficina de Pesca located within Mexico provides this form. All purchases of these species must be made at designated public markets or fishing cooperatives.

U. S. Customs Regulations

Sportfishers may bring into the United States only fish for personal consumption. Shellfish, except for lobster and shrimp, are prohibited. The number of fish must not exceed the Mexican bag limit. Fish transported across the border can be eviscerated but must be identifiable; usually the head, tail or a patch of skin left intact will suffice. Anyone bringing fish into the United States will be asked by customs officials to present a valid Mexican fishing license or a Mexico Department of Fisheries form covering the purchase of the fish. More information can be obtained by contacting the United States Fish and Wildlife Law Enforcement Agency at (619) 661-3130.

Sites for Fishing

Sportfishing the waters off the coast of the Baja peninsula can be a rewarding and memorable experience. The following list some of the better known fishing areas. Fish listed at each locale represent only the more common or sought-after species. Most fish migrate over great distances and make only seasonal appearances at some locations. As an example, marlin and sailfish can be found at the southern cape all year but travel north only during the sum-

FISHING QUALITY PROFILE

Fish	Pacific				Gulf							
	Ensenada	San Quintin	Bahia Tortugas	Cabo San Lucas	San Felipe	Puertecitos	San Luis Gonzaga	Bahia de L.A.	Mulege	Loreto	La Paz	Las Cruces to Punta Palmilla
Albacore	6-10	6-10	6-10									
Barracuda	4-10	4-10									8-11	
Black marlin												6-10
Black sea bass			6-10									
Bluefin tuna		4-10									6-10	
Corvina					3-9	5-8	3-9	2-6	5-10	4-10	1-10	
Crevalle								4-10			4-10	4-10
Grouper						4-10	4-10	4-10	4-10		5-7	4-10
Marlin	6-9	6-9		2-7				6-9	5-7	5-6		4-6
Needlefish											5-9	5-8
Rockfish	10-4	10-4										
Roosterfish						6-9		11-2		10-3	4-10	7-9
Sailfish				6-9				5-6	5-7	6-7	6-11	4-11
Sea bass						6-10	6-9		5-10			
Seatrout					4-10							
Sierra					5-9					10-4	10-6	4-7
Skipjack												5-7
Snapper									4-10	4-10	4-10	4-10
Snook								5-10				
Swordfish				6-9								
Tuna				5-9								
Wahoo				6-9	11-4	11-3				1-3	4-12	6-10
White sea bass	4-10	4-10	4-10									
Yellowfin Tuna											4-12	4-5
Yellowtail	4-10	4-10	4-10	4-5		5-10	5-10	4-5		10-6	12-5	4-5

This chart indicates *best fishing months*, not legal seasons. Numbers refer to months in sequence; 6-10 is June through October. The availability of any particular kind(s) of fish varies.

Fishing, Cabo San Lucas style

mer months when the water is warmer. Fishermen should check in advance to make sure a particular fish is in season.

BAHIA DE LOS ANGELES The bay, which is protected by 45-mile-long Isla Angel de la Guarda, offers a fine sheltered anchorage for boats. Sportfishing is excellent with corvina, dorado, grouper, roosterfish and yellowtail found in the waters around the nearby islands. Marlin and sailfish are occasionally hooked in the deeper waters farther offshore. Fishing trips can be arranged, and there are several launch ramps for private boats.

CABO SAN LUCAS AND SAN JOSE DEL CABO Sportfishing is the top

attraction for many visitors in this region. Located at the convergence of the warm waters of the Gulf of California and the cooler Pacific waters, the southern cape offers excellent fishing throughout the year. These include dorado, grouper, marlin, sailfish, skipjack, snapper, swordfish, tuna and wahoo. Sportfishing cruisers usually cost $285 to $385 per day; skiffs (*pangas*) cost about $160 per day.

ENSENADA Sportfishing for albacore, barracuda, halibut, marlin, rockfish, sea bass and yellowtail is excellent. Arrangements for sportfishing trips can be made at the sportfishing piers off Boulevard Lázaro Cárdenas and at some shops on Avenida López Mateos.

Rates for charter fishing cruisers vary depending on size of craft and number of passengers; rates start at about $250 per day. Open-party boats start at $35 per person. In addition, surf fishing is good along the sandy beaches and rocky shorelines both north and south of the city.

LA PAZ Many popular saltwater species are found in the waters off La Paz, including dorado, marlin, needlefish, roosterfish, sailfish, sierra and yellowtail. Cruisers, which rent for about $250 to $350 per day, are available through many hotels. Skiffs (*pangas*) average $180 per day for two persons.

LORETO Famous for roosterfish, Loreto's offshore waters hold virtually every major game species that inhabits the Gulf of California, including corvina, dorado, grouper, sailfish, sierra, snapper and yellowtail. Because fishing is good in the hot season, Loreto attracts as many visitors in summer as the rest of the year. Boat trips may be arranged to Isla Coronado for clam digging and observing large numbers of sea lions and pelicans.

MULEGE Sportfishing in the Gulf of California and in nearby Bahía Concepción is excellent, and fishing trips can be arranged at any of Mulegé's hotels. The many species found in these waters include corvina, dorado, grouper, marlin, roosterfish, sailfish, sea bass, sierra, snapper, snook and yellowtail. The beach, two miles northeast of town, can be reached by following an extension of Calle Madero, a good dirt road, along the river.

SAN FELIPE The gulf waters off San Felipe yield corvina, grouper, sea trout, sierra and white sea bass. Sportfishing rates vary, with skiffs (*pangas*) ranging from $30 to $45 per person, per day

(for one to five passengers); six-day open-party trips on large boats are about $600 per person. Boats are available from several dealers along Paseo de Cortez, the central waterfront drive.

SAN QUINTIN The waters of Bahía de San Quintín offer a paradise for sportfishing. Among the fish found are corvina, barracuda, halibut, marlin, rockfish, sea trout and yellowtail. Although the fish are comparable in size and species to those found in Southern California waters, the bay offers both an abundance of fish and a relative lack of anglers. The daily costs for fishing boats (with guide) are about $150 for skiffs (*pangas*) and $225 to $335 for cruisers. Good surf-fishing and clam digging enhance the appeal of the beaches along the shore of the outer bay.

Surfing and Sailboarding

Surfing along the Pacific coast of the Baja peninsula has become popular. Over the past 20 years, thanks in part to the opening of the Transpeninsular Highway (Mexico Highway 1), more and more surfers have been riding the waves south of the border. Larger waves occur in the summer, but the surfing is considered good throughout the year. Among the more notable locations are Santa Rosalillita, Punta Abreojos, San Jacinto and Islas de Todos Santos.

Both the Pacific Coast and the Gulf of California have seen a marked increase in **sailboarding** activities. Sailboarders (also known as windsurfers) can find a wide range of conditions, from relative calm to big waves and heavy winds. While there are many great areas for sailboarding, the more well-known

RECREATION

This surfer takes the waves near Playa Punta Lobos.

include Santa Rosalillita, Bahía de Los Angeles, Punta Chivato and the southern cape (including Cabo San Lucas and San José del Cabo).

Snorkeling and Scuba Diving

Snorkeling is best done in the lower half of the Gulf of California where the warm, clear water provides a window on the tropical marine life. The colorful and unique sealife includes such species as starfish, feather dusters, coral, moray eels, angel fish, purple wrasse, and the ever-present sergeant-major fish. Popular snorkel ing sites include the waters off Punta Chivato, Mulegé and Cabo San Lucas.

There are many excellent **scuba diving** locations along both coasts of Baja California. The Pacific Coast waters are more turbulent and thus are recommended for more experienced divers. The abundant sea life includes whales, dolphins, lobsters, seals, sea lions, sharks, sea turtles and many game fish. In the warmer and calmer waters of the Gulf of California, the marine life becomes more exotic and includes manta rays, hammerhead sharks, dolphins and a variety of colorful tropical fish.

A meditative approach to water recreation in Cabo San Lucas.

Appendix

Transportation

The information included in this chapter is provided solely as a service to our readers, and no endorsement of any service by the Automobile Club of Southern California is implied or intended. Because the schedules of most operators change frequently, detailed listings and fares are given. If you plan a bus trip to Baja California, contact the bus company or companies for a list of departures; air schedules and fares can be obtained either from the individual carriers or at any Auto Club Travel Agency office.

Air Service

Since flight schedules change on a frequent basis, they are not listed in this publication. Carriers listed below operate either within Baja California or between California and Baja California. Current schedules and fares can be obtained from the airlines' ticket offices or any Auto Club Travel Agency office. The Auto Club is not responsible for discontinuance of any flight or service.

Aero California *(310) 322-2644, (800) 237-6225.* Operates daily flights from Los Angeles to Loreto, La Paz and Los Cabos Airport (San José del Cabo), and from Tijuana to La Paz.

Aeromexico *(800) 237-6639.* Operates daily flights from Los Angeles to La Paz; it also flies from Tijuana to La Paz.

Air L.A. *(310) 215-8234, (800) 933-5952.* Flies daily from Los Angeles to Tijuana.

Alaska Airlines *(800) 426-0333.* Flies daily from Los Angeles and San Diego to Los Cabos.

Mexicana Airlines *(310) 646-7321, (800) 531-7921.* Flights on Tuesday and Friday through Sunday from Los Angeles to Los Cabos.

Bus Service

Domestic

The Central de Autobuses *(Central Bus Terminal) 01152 (66) 21-2911 or 21-2982.* Located in the La Mesa district on Boulevard Lázaro Cárdenas at Boulevard Alamar in eastern Tijuana.

Autotransportes de Baja California **(ABC)** and **Tres Estrellas de Oro** *01152 (66) 84-1407. The trip to La Paz lasts about 24 hours and the fare is about $56 one way.* Regular passenger service is offered in Baja California between Tijuana, Ensenada, San Felipe and Mexicali. From Mexicali there are connections for Mexico City and the interior. The same two lines also run from Tijuana to Baja California Sur. The old bus terminal located in downtown Tijuana at Calle Comercio and Avenida Madero serves some small local companies. Passengers arriving here by Greyhound bus can obtain inexpensive transportation on one of these small local buses to any business section of Tijuana.

International

Greyhound Lines *In Los Angeles call (800) 231-2222 or (213) 629-8402; in*

San Diego call (619) 239-3266. Fares to Tijuana from Los Angeles are $15 one way, $29 round trip. From San Diego the fares are $4 one way, $7 round trip. Fares to Calexico from Los Angeles are $22 one way, $39 round trip. Frequent departures leave from downtown terminals in both Los Angeles and San Diego to Tijuana. Some buses let off passengers in Tijuana at the old downtown terminal; others go to the Central Bus Terminal (for addresses see the preceding description under "Domestic").

Five Star Tours *(619) 232-5049. Round-trip fare is $8.* Service from San Diego to Tijuana. Six buses leave daily from the San Diego's Amtrak Depot at Broadway at Kettner Boulevard and go to the Mexicoach Terminal near the Jai Alai stadium on Avenida Revolución between calles 6 and 7. Five Star Tours also provides bullfight trips.

Mexicoach *Round-trip tickets are $2.* Many buses run daily from the trolley station in San Ysidro to the Mexicoach Terminal in Tijuana.

San Diego Trolley *(619) 233-3004. Trolleys operate from 5 a.m. to 1 a.m., with 15-minute service most of the time; maximum one-way fare is $1.75.* Daily rail service runs between downtown San Diego and the international border at San Ysidro.

Car Rentals

A few American rental agencies allow customers to drive their vehicles into Mexico; others may arrange rentals with affiliated companies in Mexico. Check with individual companies for their policies. Car rental agencies are located in the larger cities and at the airports in Baja California. Auto rentals are much more expensive in Mexico than in the United States.

Ferry Service and Schedules

The ferry system, a vital transportation link between Baja California and Mexico's mainland, carries both vehicles and passengers. Formerly owned and operated by the Mexican government, the ferry system was sold in 1989 to a private Mexican company, Grupo Sematur. Rates under the new owner have increased substantially, but service has improved. In the past, motorists often had difficulty obtaining reservations.

Motorists planning to ship their vehicle to the mainland must obtain a car permit. Permits are available at border crossings. **Note: applicants for car permits must present the original current registration or a notarized bill of sale for each vehicle; copies and temporary papers are not accepted.** (See *Tourist Regulations and Travel Tips*, Automobile Requirements.)

Ferry reservations may be made by telephone from the United States or within Mexico, but some knowledge of Spanish is necessary. Most travelers prefer to make reservations in person at the ferry offices. Reservations should be made at least a week in advance, and a month in advance during holiday periods, although some people report getting a reservation on short notice.

Pets are permitted on the ferries when accompanied by the appropriate health certificates which have been visaed by a Mexican Consul (see *Tourist Regulations and Travel Tips*).

Ferry Ticket Offices

La Paz *On Guillermo Prieto at Cinco de Mayo, 2 blocks southeast of Plaza Constitución. 01152 (112) 5-3833 or 5-4666.*

Open Mon. through Fri. 7 a.m. to 1 p.m. and 4 to 6 p.m., Sat. and Sun. 8 a.m. to 1 p.m. Ferry information may also be obtained at the State Tourism Office; 01152 (112) 2-5939. The ferry terminal is located at Pichilingue, the deep-water port for La Paz, 10 miles north of the city.

Santa Rosalía *Located in the terminal building on Hwy. 1 just south of the main entrance into the city. 01152 (115) 2-0013 or 2-0014.*

The Cabo San Lucas to Puerto Vallarta ferry is no longer operating.

Ferry Routes

Within Mexico, ferry information may be obtained by calling the toll-free number 91 (800) 696-96. Each ferry contains a telephone, cafeteria and medical assistance.

La Paz-Mazatlán *Ferries depart from both ports Sun. through Fri. at 3 p.m. (Sat.* *sailings during holiday periods). Sailing time is about 19 hours.*

La Paz-Topolobampo (Los Mochis) *Ferries depart from La Paz Wed. through Mon. at 8 p.m. They leave Topolobampo on Mon. through Sat. at 9 a.m. Sailing time is about nine hours.*

Santa Rosalía-Guaymas *Ferries depart from Santa Rosalía on Wed. and Sun. at 8 a.m. They leave Guaymas on Tues. and Fri. at 8 a.m. Sailing time is about eight hours.*

Tours

As a result of the increasing popularity of Baja California as a tourist destination, many tour operators offer organized tours of the peninsula. These include cruises, air tours, bus tours and even a four-wheel-drive tour. The Automobile Club of Southern California's Travel Agency can handle bookings on most tours; call or visit any Travel Agency office for details.

FERRY RATES (shown in dollars)

	PASSENGER CLASS				VEHICLE TYPE				
	Salon (Padded seats)	Tourist (Roomette with washbasin and bunks for four persons)	Cabin (Beds and bath for two persons)	Special Cabin (Beds, lounge and bath for two persons)	Car, Small Truck, and Van		Car or Truck with Trailer		Motor-home
ROUTE					up to 16.4 feet (5 meters)	16.5 to 21.3 feet (5 to 6.5 meters)	up to 29.5 feet (9 meters)	29.5 to 55.8 feet (9 to 17 meters)	over 16.4 feet (5 meters)
La Paz-Mazatlán	18	37	55	73	134	175	242	457	228
La Paz-Topolo-bampo	12	(not included on this route)			82	106	148	278	140
Santa Rosalia-Guaymas	12	24	(not included on this route)		94	124	170	321	161

Speaking Spanish

This section lists some of the Spanish phrases and sentences which are most useful to visitors in Baja California. A basic knowledge of the language may be helpful. Many of the Baja Californianos who deal with tourists speak English; those who don't are glad to help you along with your attempts at their language. Spanish is not difficult to pronounce. A study of the following pronunciation rules will be sufficient to make yourself understood.

Pronunciation

The pronunciation of the Spanish language presents few difficulties. The spelling is almost phonetic; nearly every letter has one sound which it retains at all times.

Vowels

A pronounced as in *father.*

E pronounced as in *bed.*

I pronounced as in pizza.

O pronounced as in *hold*

U pronounced as in *junior.*

Diphthongs

Spanish diphthongs are pronounced as very swift elisions of the component vowels equally stressed.

ue as in weh   *fuente*

au as in English ouch   *gaucho*

Consonants

Consonants do not differ materially from the English. The few differences can be summarized as follows:

C is pronounced with a soft sound before *e* and *i*. Otherwise it has a *k* sound.

cinco   SEEN-ko.

G is like a strong English *h* when it precedes *e* and *i*. In all other cases it is like English *g* in go.

gente   HEN-te.

H always silent.

J pronounced like a strong English *h*.

LL pronounced like the English *y*.

caballo   kah-BAH-yo

Ñ combination of *n* and *y*.

niño   NEEN-yo

Qu pronounced like *k*.

Z is always pronounced like the English *s*.

Accent or Stress

1. When a word ends in a vowel, *n* or *s*, the stress falls on the next to the last syllable.

hombre   OM-bre

hablan   AH-blan

estos   ES-tos

2. When the word ends in a consonant other than *n* or *s*, the stress falls on the last syllable.

hablar   ah-BLAR

3. In some cases an accent mark will be found over a vowel. This does not change the pronunciation of that vowel, but indicates that the stress falls on that syllable.

gramática   gra-MAH-ti-ca

corazón   cor-a-SOWN

Words and Phrases

Note: Nouns in Spanish are either masculine or feminine, and there are two words meaning "the": *el* is used before masculine nouns, *la* before feminine nouns. The plural of *el* is *los*, of *la* is *las*. After words given on these pages the gender is indicated by (m.) for masculine, (f.) for feminine. For instance, say *el* hotel and *los hoteles; la posada* and *las posadas*. The word *"usted,"* meaning *"you,"* is usually abbreviated *Ud. or Vd.* An adjective also agrees in gender with the noun it modifies. For example, *el hombre pequeño*—the small man; *la camisa roja*—the red shirt. In most cases, the adjective follows the noun.

Language

Do you understand English?
¿Entiende Ud. el inglés?

I do not speak Spanish.
No hablo español.

Yes, sir; no, madam.
Sí, señor; no, señora.

Very little
Muy poco; (or) poquito

I do not understand.
No entiendo.

Do you understand me?
¿Me entiende Ud.?

Please speak slowly.
Por favor hable despacio.

I wish to speak with an interpreter.
Quisiera hablar con un intérprete.

What are you saying?
¿Qué dice?

Polite Phrases

Good morning.
Buenos días.

Good afternoon.
Buenas tardes.

Good night.
Buenas noches.

Goodbye.
Adiós; hasta la vista.

Thank you.
Gracias.

Yes, very good.
Sí; muy bueno.

Please.
Por favor.

Excuse me.
Perdóneme.

I am very sorry.
Lo siento mucho.

To Explain Your Needs

I need; we need.
Necesito; necesitamos.

I would like to telephone.
Quisiera telefonear.

I am hungry; we are hungry.
Tengo hambre; tenemos hambre.

I am thirsty; we are thirsty.
Tengo sed; tenemos sed.

I am cold; we are cold.
Tengo frío; tenemos frío.

I am warm; we are warm.
Tengo calor; tenemos calor.

I am tired; we are tired.
**Estoy cansado (a);
estamos cansados.**

I am sick; we are sick.
**Estoy enfermo (a);
estamos enfermos.**

The child is sick; tired.
**El niño (la niña) está enfermo (a);
cansado (a).**

Directions

north/**norte**
south/**sur**
east/**este**
west/**oeste**

(Note: In some addresses, east is **oriente**, abbreviated **Ote.**; west is **poniente**, abbreviated **Pte.**)

Numerals

1	**uno**
2	**dos**
3	**tres**
4	**cuatro**
5	**cinco**
6	**seis**
7	**siete**
8	**ocho**
9	**nueve**
10	**diez**
11	**once**
12	**doce**
13	**trece**
14	**catorce**
15	**quince**
16	**diez y seis**
17	**diez y siete**
18	**diez y ocho**
19	**diez y nueve**
20	**veinte**
21	**veinte y uno**
30	**treinta**
40	**cuarenta**
50	**incuenta**
60	**esenta**
70	**setenta**
80	**ochenta**
90	**noventa**
100	**ciento**
200	**doscientos**

Days and Time

Sunday/**domingo**

Monday/**lunes**

Tuesday/**martes**

Wednesday/**miércoles**

Thursday/**jueves**

Friday/**viernes**

Saturday/**sábado**

today **hoy**

tomorrow/**mañana**

yesterday/**ayer**

morning/**la mañana**

noon/**el mediodía**

afternoon/**la tarde**

tonight/**esta noche**

night **la noche**

last night/**anoche**

midnight/**a medianoche**

What time is it?
    ¿Qué hora es?

It is one o'clock.
    Es la una.

It is ten minutes past two.
    Son las dos y diez.

It is a quarter past three.
    Son las tres y cuarto.

It is a quarter of five.
    Es un cuarto para las cinco.

It is 25 minutes of six.
    Son veintecinco para las seis.

It is half past four.
    Son las cuatro y media.

Useful Adjectives

bad/**malo**

beautiful/**hermoso**

cheap/**barato**

clean/**limpio**

cold/**frío**

difficult/**difícil**

dirty/**sucio**

early/**temprano**

easy/**fácil**

expensive/**caro**

fast/**rápido**

good/**bueno**

high/**alto**

hot/**caliente**

kind/**benévolo, bondadoso**

large/**grande**

low/**bajo**

late/**tarde**

long/**largo**

polite/**cortés**

sharp/**agudo**

Spanish words and phrases are useful in a variety of settings: checking into a hotel in Todos Santos; stopping for coffee in Puerto Nuevo; fixing a flat on the road to San Felipe; and shopping in Cabo San Lucas.

short/**corto**

slow/**lento**

small/**pequeño**

ugly/**feo**

unkind/**despiadado, duro**

Colors

white/**blanco**

pink/**rosa**

black/**negro**

blue; dark blue/**azul; azul obscuro**

gray/**gris**

green; light green/**verde; verde claro**

brown/**café**

purple/**morado**

red/**rojo; colorado**

yellow/**amarillo**

At the Border

passport
pasaporte

tourist card
tarjeta de turista

age
edad

marital status
estado civil

single
soltero (m.); soltera (f.)

married
casado (m.); casada (f.)

widowed
iudo (m.); viuda (f.)

divorced
divorciado (m.); divorciada (f.)

profession; occupation
profesión; ocupación

vaccination card
certificado de vacuna

driver's license
licencia de manejar

car owner's title (registration)
título de propiedad (registración)

year of car
modelo (o año)

make (Ford, Mazda, etc.)
marca

license plate and state
placa y estado

chassis and motor number
número de chasis y motor

number of doors
número de puertas

number of cylinders
número de cilindros

number of passengers
número de pasajeros

On the Road

kilometer/**kilómetro (m.)**

highway/**carretera (f.)**

road/**camino (m.)**

street/**calle (f.)**

avenue/**avenida (f.)**

boulevard/**bulevar (m.)**

block/**cuadra (f.)**

corner/**esquina (f.)**

left side/**lado izquierdo (m.)**

right side/**lado derecho (m.)**

Show me the road to...
Enséñeme el camino a...

How far is...?
¿Qué tan lejos está...?

Can we get to ...before dark?
¿Podemos llegar a ...antes del anochecer?

Is this road dangerous?
¿Es peligroso este camino?

Is that road in good condition?
¿Está en buen estado aquel camino?

Is it paved or is it a dirt road?
¿Está pavimentado o es de tierra?

Go straight ahead.
Siga adelante.

Turn to the right; left.
Vuelta a la derecha; izquierda.

What city, town, is this?
¿Qué ciudad, pueblo, es éste?

Where does this road lead?
A dónde conduce este camino?

In Case of Car Trouble

I want to ask you a favor.
Quiero pedirle un favor.

I need a tow truck.
Necesito una grua.

My car has broken down.
Se me ha descompuesto el carro.

My lights don't work.
Mis faros no funcionan.

The starter does not work.
El arranque no funciona.

I have run out of gasoline.
Se me acabó la gasolina.

Is there a gasoline station near here?
¿Hay una estación de gasolina cerca e aquí?

Is there a garage near here?
Hay un garage cerca?

Please send someone to repair my car.
Por favor mande a alguien a componer mi carro.

May I go with you to get a mechanic?
¿Puedo ir con usted a conseguir un mecánico?

Have you a rope to tow my car?
¿Tiene una soga para remolcar mi carro?

Do you want to help me push the car to one side of the road?
¿Quiere ayudarme a empujar el carro a un lado del camino?

Do you want to help me change a tire?
¿Quiere ayudarme a cambiar una llanta?

Do you want to be my witness?
¿Quiere ser mi testigo?

Arriving in Town

Is English spoken here?
¿Se habla inglés aquí?

Where is the center of town?
¿Dónde está el centro de la ciudad?

Where is X Street, X Square, the X Hotel?
¿Dónde está la Calle X, la Plaza X, el Hotel X?

May I park here?
Puedo estacionarme aquí?

Please direct me to the nearest post office.
Por favor diríjame a la oficina de correos mas cercana.

Where can I find a policeman, a hair dresser, a doctor, a drug store?
¿Dónde puedo hallar un policía, una estética, un médico, una farmacía?

Where is the police station, the chamber of commerce?
Dónde está la comisaría, la cámara de comercio?

Where can I find road maps, post cards, American newspapers?
¿Dónde se pueden hallar mapas de caminos, tarjetas postales, periódicos norteamericanos?

Please direct me to the railroad station, the bus station.
Por favor diríjame a la estación del ferrocarril, al terminal del autobús.

How often does the bus go by?
¿Que tan seguido pasa el autobús (camión)?

Does the bus stop here?
¿Para aquí el autobús?

Could you recommend a good restaurant; a good small hotel; a first class hotel?
¿Puede Ud. recomendar un buen restaurante; un buen hotel pequeño; un hotel de primera clase?

I wish to telephone, to telegraph, to cable.
Quiero telefonear, telegrafiar, cablegrafiar.

I wish to change some money.
Quiero cambiar dinero.

What is the rate of exchange?
Cuál es el tipo de cambio?

I want to cash a check.
Quiero cambiar un cheque.

At the Hotel

hotel/**hotel (m.)**

inn/**posada (f.)**

apartments/**apartamentos (m.)**

room/**cuarto (m.)**

furnished room/**cuarto amueblado**

bedroom/**recámara (f.)**

pillow/**almohada (f.)**

blanket/**cobija (f.)**, **manta (f.)**

air conditioning/**aire acondicionado**

kitchen/**cocina (f.)**

bathroom/**cuarto de baño (m.)**

towel/**toalla (f.)**

wash cloth/**toalla chica (f.)**

soap/**jabón (m.)**

dining room/**comedor (m.)**

ice water/**agua con hielo (m.)**

hot water/**agua caliente (m.)**

elevator/**elevador (m.)**

stairway/**escalera (f.)**

key/**llave (f.)**

office/**oficina (f.)**

manager/**gerente (m.)**

maid/**camarista (f.)**

office employee/**empleado de oficina (m.)**

bellboy/**maletero (m.)**

porter/**mozo de servicios (m.)**

guest/**huésped (m.)**

I want a single room, with bath.
Deseo un cuarto sencillo, con baño.

I want a room for two; with twin beds.
Deseo un cuarto para dos; con camas gemelas.

I want two connecting rooms.
Deseo dos cuartos comunicados.

A front room; a back room.
Un cuarto al frente; al fondo.

A quiet room.
Un cuarto tranquilo.

On the lower floor; upper floor.
En el piso bajo; piso alto.

Will you have the baggage brought
up? ...down?
**Quiere Ud. hacer subir ...bajar el
equipaje?**

We are leaving tomorrow.
Partimos mañana.

We are staying several days ...just
tonight.
**Nos quedaremos aquí unos pocos
días ...solamente esta noche.**

What is the price (rate)?
¿Cuál es el precio (la tarifa)?

What is the minimum rate?
Cuál es el precio mínimo?

Do you accept checks in payment?
Acepta Ud. cheques en pago?

I want my bill, please.
Quiero la cuenta, por favor.

Have you hot running water?
¿Hay agua corriente y caliente?

The shower doesn't work.
La regadera no funciona.

Is there a garage?
Hay garage?

Where is the ladies' room, men's
room?
**Dónde está el baño (lavabo) de
damas, de caballeros?**

Where is the barber shop?
¿Dónde hay una peluquería?

Please send these clothes to the laundry.
**Hágame el favor de mandar esta
ropa a la lavandería.**

Please clean and press this suit.
**Hágame el favor de limpiar y
planchar este traje.**

I want it today; tomorrow.
Lo quiero hoy; mañana.

Please call me at six o'clock.
**Hágame el favor de llamarme a
las seis.**

Please forward my correspondence to
this address.
**Por favor reexpida mi correspon-
dencia a esta dirección.**

Do you want to prepare a lunch for us
to carry with us?
**¿Quiere Ud. prepararnos un
almuerzo para llevárnoslo?**

At the Garage

How much is gasoline per liter?
**¿Cuánto cuesta el litro de
gasolina?**

Fill up the gasoline tank; the radiator.
**Llene el tanque de gasolina;
el radiador.**

Give me five, ten, fifteen, twenty liters.
**Deme cinco, diez, quince, veinte
litros.**

Check the oil; change the oil.
Vea el aceite; cambie el aceite.

Please lubricate the car; wash the car.
**Favor de lubricar el carro; lavar el
carro.**

Please tighten the brakes; adjust the
brakes.
**Favor de apretar los frenos; ajustar
los frenos.**

Please tune the engine; change the
sparkplugs.
**Favor de poner al punto (afinar) el
motor; cambiar las bujías.**

My tire has a puncture. Can you repair
the tube?
**¿Mi llanta tiene un agujero. Puede
reparar la cámara?**

The tire is flat.
La llanta está desinflada.

The horn is not working.
La bocina no funciona.

Put water in the battery.
Ponga agua en la batería.

The battery needs charging.
La batería necesita carga.

Please put another bulb in this head-lamp.
Favor de reemplazar el foco de este faro.

The gasoline tank is leaking.
El tanque de gasolina está gote-ando.

The gas line is clogged.
La tubería de gasolina está tapada.

The engine heats.
El motor se calienta.

The exhaust is choked.
Está obstruido el tubo de escape.

The steering gear is out of order.
La dirección está descompuesta.

The radiator leaks.
El radiador gotea.

The clutch slips.
El embrague resbala.

There is a short circuit.
Hay un cortocircuito.

The windshield wiper does not work.
El limpiavidrios del parabrisa no funciona.

The taillight does not work.
El faro trasero no funciona.

Please clean the windshield.
Favor de limpiar el parabrisa.

When will the repairs be finished?
¿Cuándo terminará la reparación?

How much do I owe you?
¿Cuánto le debo?

At the Restaurant

Please bring me the menu.
Favor de traerme el menú.

I like my meat rare (well done).
Quiero la carne tierna (bien cocida).

Please bring me the check.
Favor de traerme la cuenta.

breakfast/**desayuno (m.)**

lunch/**almuerzo (m.)**

dinner/**comida (f.)**

supper/**cena (f.)**

knife/**cuchillo (m).**

fork/**tenedor (m.)**

spoon/**cuchara (f.)**

cup/**taza (f.)**

glass/**vaso (f.)**

napkin/**servilleta (f.)**

bill/**cuenta (f.)**

tip/**propina (f.)**

Bread

bread/**pan (m.)**

crackers/**galletas (f.)**

toast/**pan tostado (m.)**

Fruit

apple/**manzana (f.)**

avocado/**aguacate (m.)**

banana/**plátano (m.)**

dates/**dátiles (m.)**

figs/**higos (m.)**

fruit/**fruta (f.)**

guava/**guayaba (f.)**

lemon/**limón (m.)**

lime /**lima (f.)**

nuts/**nueces (f.)**

olives/**aceitunas (f.)**

orange/**naranja** (f.)

peach/**durazno** (m.)

pineapple/**piña** (f.)

strawberries/**fresas** (f.)

Vegetables

beans/**frijoles** (m.)

beets/**betabeles** (f.)

cabbage/**repollo** (m.); **col** (f.)

corn/**maíz** (m.)

lettuce/**lechuga** (f.)

onion/**cebolla** (f.)

peas/**chícharos** (m.)

potatoes/**papas** (f.)

rice/**arroz** (m.)

string beans/**tejotes** (m.)

sweet potatoes/**camotes** (m.)

tomatoes/**tomates** (m.)

vegetables/**legumbres** (f.)

Meat, Pork, Poultry, Eggs, Fish

sausage/**chorizo** (m.)

meat/**carne** (f.)

beef/**carne de res** (f.)

beefsteak/**biftec** (m.) **filete** (m.)

veal/**ternera** (f.)

lamb/**carne de carnero**

lamb chops/**chuletas de carnero**

roast/**asado** (m.)

pork/**carne de puerco**

ham/**jamón** (m.)

bacon/**tocino** (m.)

chicken/**pollo** (m.)

egg/**huevo** (m.)

fried/**frito**

soft-boiled/**tibio**

hard-boiled/**cocidos duro**

scrambled/**revueltos**

duck/**pato** (m.)

turkey/**guajolote** (m.); **pavo** (m.)

abalone/**abulón** (m.)

clam/**almeja** (f.)

fish/**pescado** (m.)

scallops/**callos** (m.)

shrimp/**camarónes** (m.)

lobster/**langosta** (f.)

Beverages, Liquors

beer/**cerveza** (f.)

brandy/**aguardiente** (m.)

champagne/**vino de champaña** (m.)

cocktail/**coctel** (m.)

coffee/**café** (m.)

with cream/**con leche**

without cream/**sin leche**

gin/**ginebra** (f.)

milk/**leche** (f.)

rum/**ron** (m.)

tea/**té** (m.)

water/**agua** (m.)

whiskey/**whiskey** (m.)

wine/**vino** (m.)

Desserts

cake/**pastel** (m.)

candies/**confites; dulces** (f.)

custard/**flan (f.)**

ice cream/**helado (m.)**

Miscellaneous

butter/**mantequilla (f.)**

cheese/**queso (m.)**

flour/**harina (f.)**

honey/**miel de abejas (f.)**

pepper/**pimienta (f.)**

salad/**ensalada (f.)**

salt/**sal (f.)**

sauce/**salsa (f.)**

soup/**sopa (f.), caldo (m.)**

sugar/**azúcar (m.)**

Suggested Supply Lists

The items included in the following lists will help make a trip to Baja California safe and enjoyable. Two lists are shown: the first, for all trips, lists items that should be taken on any trip down the peninsula; the second, for backcountry travel, is more extensive and necessary only for those planning extended off-road and camping trips. Travelers should use their own discretion in deciding which items to include. It is better, however, to take along too much than too little, if there is room in the vehicle. All items on the first list should also be included in preparation for backcountry trips.

All Trips

For vehicles ...

Air filters

Brake fluid

Flares

Fuses (check amperage)

Motor oil

Power steering fluid

Tools

Water (5 gal. for radiator)

Window cleaner

For people ...

Can opener

Canteen

Dark glasses

Drinking water and cups

First aid kit

Flashlight and batteries

Insect repellent

Keys (extra, for car)

Paper towels

Salt tablets

Skin lotion

Sun block

Sunburn cream

Sun shade

Toilet tissue

Trash bags

Backcountry Trips

For vehicles ...

Alternator brushes

Baling wire

Battery cables

During the 1973 research trip, Auto Club personnel check out equipment and vehicles at Rancho Santa Inés. (Auto Club Historical Photo)

Bolts and nuts (assorted sizes)

Chamois (for straining gasoline)

Duct tape

Electric fuel pump

Electric tape

Fittings (gas lines)

Fire extinguisher

Gaskets (head, fuel pump)

Gasoline cans (two, 5-gal.)

Gasoline filter (in-line)

Grease

Hammer (heavy)

Hoses and clamps (radiator)

Hydraulic jack (small sand-support board)

Ignition coil(s)

Ignition module

Lug wrench

Radiator sealant

Spare tires (extra)

Spark plugs

Tire inflator

Tow rope

Tube repair kit

Universal joints

Valve cores

Water cans (two, 5-gal.)

Wire (10-gauge electrical) and
Wire connectors

For people and camps ...

Blankets

Camp cook set

Camp knives

Chairs (folding)

Cleanser

Compass

Cots

Crowbar

Detergent (liquid)

Dishes

Eating utensils

First aid kit (large)

Flashlight (large)

Fly swatter

Fuel (stove and lantern)

Funnels (small and large)

Gloves (leather)

Grate (for cooking)

Hatchet

Lantern (extra mantles)

Matches (wooden)

Netting (mosquito)

Notebook

Pail or bucket

Pens and pencils

Portable toilet

Radio (portable, short-wave or CB)

Rags

Rope (small)

Scrub brush

Shovels (folding)

Signal mirror

Sleeping bags

Snake bite kit(s)

Soap (freshwater and saltwater)

Stove

Table (folding)

Tarpaulins

Tent

Toilet paper

Towels (bath, face)

Trash bags (large and small)

Wash cloths

Water purification tablets

Lodging & Restaurants

Accommodations in Baja California are diverse, ranging from small motels to luxurious seaside resorts. Many of the peninsula's resorts and certain hotels in major cities have all the services and facilities normally associated with first-class hotels in the United States. Tourists in Baja California should remember, however, that no matter where they are staying, they are in a foreign country, and there may be a different, more relaxed approach to service and housekeeping. If travelers keep this in mind, their visits will be more enjoyable.

Lodging and Restaurants lists hotels, motels, and resorts in Baja California operating as of April 15, 1996. Properties are listed alphabetically under the nearest town, with lodging facilities first and restaurants second. The location is given from the center of town or from the nearest major highway.

AAA-rated lodging and restaurant properties listed in these pages have been inspected at least once in the past year by a trained representative of the Automobile Club of Southern California. In surprise inspections, each property was evaluated according to AAA's extensive and detailed requirements for approval. These requirements are reflective of current industry standards and the expectations of the traveling public. Less than two-thirds of the lodging establishments open for business are listed in AAA publications.

Many listings include AAA's esteemed "diamond" rating, reflecting the overall quality of the establishment. Many factors are considered in the process of determining the diamond rating. In lodging properties, the facility is first "classified" according to its physical design—is it a motel, a hotel, a resort, an apartment, etc. Since the various types of lodging establishments offer differing amenities and facilities, rating criteria are specific for each classification. For example, a motel, which typically offers a room with convenient parking and little if any recreational or public facilities, is rated using criteria designed only for motel-type establishments—it is not compared to a hotel with its extensive public and meeting areas, or to a resort with its wide range of recreational facilities and programs. The diamonds do, however, represent standard levels of quality in all types of establishments.

This book also lists accommodations which are not AAA-rated, but nearly attain AAA standards. In these cases, the ◆ symbol will be missing from the listing. Wherever the inclusion of non-rated hotels, motels and resorts occurs, they are listed as a courtesy and convenience to readers. No endorsement is implied or intended.

The number of lodgings listed in this chapter is limited in the following towns: Ciudad Constitutión, Loreto, Mulegé, Santa Rosalía and Tecate. Information about hotels and motels in these towns may be obtained at state tourism offices throughout the peninsula and in the tourist newspaper *The Baja Sun*. These sources also mention other hotels in the larger cities of Baja California. The names of some additional hotels and motels are also mentioned in the highway route logs of this book.

There is no charge for a property to be listed in ACSC publications. Many AAA-approved lodgings and restaurants, however, choose to purchase display advertising. These display ads sometimes provide additional information about popular features of the establishment.

Nearly all lodging and restaurant facilities accept credit cards as forms of payment for services rendered. The following symbols are used to identify the specific cards accepted by each property.

AE	American Express
CB	Carte Blanche
DI	Diners Club
MC	MasterCard
VI	VISA

Some lodgings and restaurants listed in Auto Club publications have symbols indicating that they are accessible to individuals with disabilities. The criteria used in qualifying these listings are consistent with, but do not represent the full scope of, the Americans with Disabilities Act of 1990. AAA does not evaluate recreational facilities, banquet rooms or convention and meeting facilities for accessibility. Individuals with disabilities are urged to phone ahead to fully understand an establishment's facilities and accessibility. Facilities accommodating handicapped travelers are largely unavailable in Baja California. The Automobile Club recommends contacting the lodging establishment directly should a traveler have special needs.

Lodging

The following accommodations classifications may appear in this book.

Bed & Breakfast—Usually a small establishment emphasizing personal attention. Individually decorated guest rooms provide an at-home feeling and may lack some amenities such as TVs, phones, etc. Usually owner-operated with a common room or parlor where guests and owners can interact during evening and breakfast hours. May have shared bathrooms. A continental or full hot breakfast is included in the room rate.

Complex—A combination of two or more kinds of lodgings.

Cottage—Individual bungalow, cabin or villa, usually containing one rental unit equipped for housekeeping. May have a separate living room and bedroom(s). Parking is usually at each unit.

Country Inn—Similar in definition to a bed and breakfast. Offers a dining room reflecting the ambience of the inn. At a minimum, breakfast and dinner are served.

Hotel—A multistory building usually including a coffee shop, dining room, lounge, room service, convenience shops, valet, laundry and full banquet/meeting facilities. Parking may be limited.

Lodge—Typically two or more stories with all facilities in one building. Located in vacation, ski, fishing areas, etc. Usually has food and beverage service. Adequate on-premises parking.

Motel—Usually one or two stories; food service, if any, consists of a limited facility or snack bar. Often has a pool or playground. Ample parking, usually at the guest room door.

Motor Inn—Usually two or three stories, but may be a high-rise. Generally has recreation facilities, food service and ample parking. May have limited banquet/meeting facilities.

Apartment—Usually four or more stories with at least half the units equipped for housekeeping. Often in a vacation destination area. Units typically provide a full kitchen, living room and one or more bedrooms, but may be studio-type rooms with kitchen equipment in an alcove. May require minimum stay and/or offer discounts for longer stays. This classification may also modify any of the other lodging types.

Condominium—A destination property located in a resort area. Guest units consist of a bedroom, living room and kitchen. Kitchens are separate from bedrooms and are equipped with a stove, oven or microwave, refrigerator, cooking utensils and table settings for the maximum number of people occupying the unit. Linens and maid service are provided at least twice weekly. This classification may also modify any of the other lodging types.

Historic—Accommodations in restored, pre-1930 structures, reflecting the ambience of yesteryear and the surrounding region. Rooms may lack some modern amenities and have shared baths. Usually owner-operated and provides food service. Parking is usually available. This classification may also modify any of the other lodging types.

Resort—May be a destination unto itself. Has a vacation atmosphere offering extensive recreational facilities for such specific interests as golf, tennis, fishing, etc. Rates may include meals under American or Modified American plans. This classification may also modify any of the other lodging types.

Suite—Units have one or more bedrooms and a living room, which may or may not be closed off from the bedrooms. This classification may also modify any of the other lodging types.

A property's diamond rating is not based on the room rate or any one specific aspect of its facilities or operations. Many factors are considered in calculating the rating, and certain minimum standards must be met in all inspection categories. If a property fails approval in just one category, it is not diamond rated. The inspection categories include housekeeping, maintenance, service, furnishings and decor. Guest comments received by ACSC may also be reviewed in a property's approval/rating process.

These criteria apply to all properties listed in this publication:

- Clean and well-maintained facilities
- Hospitable staff
- Adequate parking

- A well-kept appearance
- Good quality bedding and comfortable beds with adequate illumination
- Good locks on all doors and windows
- Comfortable furnishings and decor
- Adequate towels and supplies
- At least one comfortable easy chair with adequate illumination

Lodging ratings range from one to five diamonds and are defined below:

◆—Good but unpretentious. Establishments are functional. Clean and comfortable rooms must meet the basic needs of privacy and cleanliness.

◆◆—Shows noticeable enhancements in decor and/or quality of furnishings over those at the one-diamond level. May be recently constructed or an older property. Targets the needs of a budget-oriented traveler.

◆◆◆—Offers a degree of sophistication with additional amenities, services and facilities. There is a marked upgrade in services and comfort.

◆◆◆◆—Excellent properties displaying high levels of service and hospitality, and offering a wide variety of amenities and upscale facilities, inside the room, on the grounds and in the common areas.

◆◆◆◆◆—Renowned for an exceptionally high degree of service, striking and luxurious facilities, and many extra amenities. Guest services are executed and presented in a flawless manner. Guests are pampered by a very professional, attentive staff. The property's facilities and operations set standards in hospitality and service.

Room rates shown in the listings are provided by each establishment's management for publication by the Automobile Club of Southern California. During special events or holiday periods rates may exceed those published and special discounts or savings programs may not be honored. High-season rates are always shown; off-season rates are listed if they are substantially lower than the rest of the year. Rates are for typical rooms, not special units, and do not include taxes or service charges. A 10-percent sales tax is imposed on all hotel, restaurant and nightclub bills. Some establishments, particularly in the Los Cabos region, add a service charge of 10 to 20 percent to room bills; it is typically a gratuity fee used in lieu of tipping, but this may not always be the case. Upon check in, be sure to understand what additional charges, if any, will be added to the bill.

Some hotels quote prices in pesos, others in dollars. All prices listed in this book are given in dollar equivalents. All establishments accept dollars; however, you can sometimes get a better price by paying in pesos. When making reservations, be sure to have a clear understanding of the price you will pay.

In addition to the dates for which the rates are valid, each rate line lists the prices quoted for one person (abbreviated 1P) and for two persons (2P); the two-person rate may be for either one or two beds. Figures following these abbreviations are the price(s) for the specified room and occupants. Most rates listed are European plan, which means that no meals are included in the rate. Some lodgings' rates include breakfast [BP] or continental breakfast [CP]. A few properties offer the American Plan [AP], which includes three meals, or a Modified American Plan [MAP], which offers two meals, usually breakfast and dinner. Most establishments also provide a per-person rate applicable to the third or more individuals staying in the same room or unit; this rate is added to the two-person rate listed in the rate line.

Many properties welcome children in the same room with their parents at no additional charge. There may be charges for additional equipment, such as roll-aways or cribs.

All bathrooms have a combination tub and shower bath unless noted otherwise. Since nearly all establishments have telephones and color TV, only the absence of any of these items is noted in the listing. Check-in time is shown only if it is after 3 p.m.; check-out time is shown only if it is before 10 a.m. Service charges are not shown unless they are $1 or more, or at least 5 percent of the room rate. If the pet acceptance policy varies within the establishment, no mention of pets is made. A heated pool is heated when it is reasonable to expect use of a pool. Outdoor pools may not be open in winter.

Reservations are always advisable in resort areas and may be the only way to assure obtaining the type of accommodations desired. Deposits are almost always required. Should plans change and a reservation needs to be canceled, travelers should be aware of the amount of notice required to receive a refund of the deposit. The price of accommodations should be confirmed at the time the reservations are made. Always request a written confirmation from the hotel, motel or resort. Due to the slowness of Baja California mail service, all correspondence should be sent at least six weeks in advance. In the hotel mailing addresses, *BC* is the abbreviation for the state of Baja California and *BCS* stands for the state of Baja California Sur. Some properties have reserved rooms for nonsmokers; guests should look for the ⊘ symbol in the listing and be sure to request a smoke-free room both when making a reservation and upon registration.

Restaurants

Restaurants listed in this publication have been found to be consistently good dining establishments. In metropolitan areas, where many restaurants are above average, listings include some of those known for the superiority of their food, service and atmosphere, and also those offering a selection of quality food at moderate prices (including some cafeterias and family restaurants). In smaller communities the restaurants considered to be the best in the area may be listed.

The type of cuisine featured at a restaurant is used as a means of classification for restaurants. There are listings for Steakhouses and Continental cuisine as well as a range of ethnic foods, such as Chinese, Japanese, Italian and yes, American. Special menu types, such as early bird, a la carte, children's or Sunday Brunch, are also listed. Something about each restaurant's atmosphere and appropriate attire is mentioned where possible. The availability of alcoholic beverages is shown, as well as entertainment and dancing.

Restaurant ratings are applied to two categories of operational style: full-service eating establishments, and self-service, family-dining operations such as cafeterias or buffets.

◆—Good but unpretentious dishes. Table settings are usually simple and may include paper place mats and napkins. Alcoholic beverage service, if any, may be limited to beer and wine. Usually informal with an atmosphere conducive to family dining.

◆◆—More extensive menus representing more complex food preparation and, usually, a wider variety of alcoholic beverages. The atmosphere is appealing and suitable for either family or adult dining. Service may be casual, but host or hostess seating can be expected. Table settings may include tablecloths and cloth napkins.

◆◆◆—Extensive or specialized menus and a more complex cuisine preparation requiring a professional chef contribute to either a formal dining experience or a special family meal. Cloth table linens, above-average quality table settings, a skilled service staff and an inviting decor should all be provided. Generally, the wine list includes representatives of the best domestic and foreign wine-producing regions.

◆◆◆◆—An appealing ambience is often enhanced by fresh flowers and fine furnishings. The overall sophistication and formal atmosphere visually create a dining experience more for adults than for families. A wine steward presents an extensive list of the best wines. Smartly attired, highly skilled staff is capable of describing how any dish is prepared. Elegant silverware, china and correct glassware are typical. The menu includes creative dishes prepared from fresh ingredients by a chef who frequently has international training. Eye-appealing desserts are offered at tableside.

◆◆◆◆◆—World-class operation with even more luxury and sophistication than four-diamond restaurants. A proportionally large staff, expert in preparing tableside delicacies, provides flawless service. Tables are set with impeccable linens, silver and crystal glassware.

Buena Vista

Lodging

HOTEL BUENA VISTA BEACH RESORT ◆◆ Resort
On shore of Bahía de Palmas, ¼ mile east of Hwy 1.
Phone 01152 (114) 1-0033; FAX (114) 0133.
US reservations: 100 W 35th St, Ste V, National City, CA 91950. (619) 425-1551, (800) 752-3555.

All year	1P $65	2P $80

XP $15. 10% service charge. 30-day cancellation notice. Meal plans available. Resort on hillside overlooking the sea. 60 units. Shower baths, coffee makers; no phones, TV. 2 pools, whirlpools, beach, scuba diving, kayaking, tennis, horseback riding. Fishing trips arranged in cruisers and pangas. Pets allowed in designated rooms. Dining room open 6-11 am, noon-3 pm, 7-9:30 pm; cocktails, bar. MC, VI. Smoke detectors.

Cabo San Lucas

Lodging

HOTEL CALINDA QUALITY BEACH CABO SAN LUCAS   ◆◆ Resort Motor Inn
3½ miles east on Hwy 1. Mail: Apdo Postal 12, Cabo San Lucas, BCS, Mexico.
Phone 01152 (114) 3-0044; FAX 3-0077.
US reservations: (800) 228-5151.

4/8-8/31	1P $ 92-114	2P $ 92-114
9/1-12/19	1P $ 80-103	2P $ 80-103
12/20-4/7	1P $120-140	2P $120-140

XP $15. 3-day cancellation notice. Spectacular location on bluff overlooking ocean with a view of Land's End. 2 stories. 125 units. Coffee makers. Pools, whirlpools, swimming beach, tennis, rental kayaks, scuba/snorkeling. Fishing arrangements. Valet laundry. Gift shop. No pets. Meeting rooms. Dining room; 7 am-11 pm; cocktails; bar. AE, MC, VI.

CLUB CABO MOTEL RESORT   Motel
3 miles east of town center; turn south off Hwy 1 on road to Club Cascadas. Mail: Apdo Postal 463, Cabo San Lucas, BCS, Mexico.
Phone 01152 (114) 3-3348.

All year	1P $ 40- 60	2P $ 40- 60

XP $5-10. 8 units. Motel-type rooms in RV park. Shower baths; most with cooking facilities; courtesy phone available. Pool, whirlpool.

HOTEL FINISTERRA   ◆◆◆ Resort Complex
Located at southernmost tip of Baja California peninsula. Mail: Apdo Postal #1, Cabo San Lucas, BCS, Mexico.
Phone 01152 (114) 3-0000, (714) 476-5555, (800) 347-2252; FAX 01152 (114) 3-0192.

All year	1P $ 89-122	2P $ 99-132

XP $20. 10% service charge. 7-day cancellation notice, 30 days for holiday periods. Spectacular location overlooking Land's End. Rooms with ocean or bay view. Large pool area surrounded by tropical gardens. 197 units; 6 luxury suites with fireplace. Cable TV, movies, radios, coffee makers, combination or shower baths, private balconies; some efficiencies. 3 pools, whirlpools, health club, massage, beach, scuba diving, snorkeling, tennis, horseback riding. Fishing trips arranged. No pets. Dining room open 6:30 am-9:30 pm; cocktails, lounge, entertainment. AE, MC, VI. ⊘ **(See ad page 225.)**

MARINA FIESTA RESORT HOTEL   ◆◆◆ Condominium Hotel
On east side of marina at Marina Lotes. Mail: Marina Lote 37, Cabo San Lucas, BCS, Mexico.
Phone 01152 (114) 3-2689; FAX 3-2688.
US reservations: (800) 332-2252.

All year	1P $140-170	2P $140-170

LODGING & RESTAURANTS

XP $25. 3-day cancellation notice. 5 to 7 stories. 115 units; 1- and 2-bedroom suites $240-375; penthouse suite $400. Cable TV, movies, refrigerators, kitchens & untensils; some shower baths. Pool, whirlpools, exercise room, boat ramp, marina. No pets. Restaurant; 6 am-10 pm; cocktails. AE, MC, VI.

MELIA SAN LUCAS ◆◆◆ Resort Hotel
On the shore 2 blocks east of Bl Marina (Hwy 1). Mail: El Medano s/n, Cabo San Lucas, BCS, Mexico.
Phone 01152 (114) 3-444, (800) 336-3542; FAX 01152 (114) 3-0422.

4/8-12/20	1P $169-229	2P $169-229
12/21-4/7	1P $181-241	2P $181-241

XP $40. 10% service charge. 3-day refund notice. Pueblo-style hotel overlooking the harbor and Land's End. 187 units. Refrigerators. Pools, beach, boating, sailboarding. Fishing trips arranged. No pets. Restaurant; 5 am-11 pm; cocktails.

MISIONES DEL CABO ◆◆◆ Condominium
3 miles east on Hwy 1. Mail: KM 6 Carr Transpeninsular, Cabo San Lucas, BCS 23410, Mexico.
Phone & FAX 01152 (114) 3-2899.
US reservations: (800) 524-5104.

5/1-10/31	1P $148	2P $148-230
11/1-4/30	1P $170	2P $170-230

10% service charge. 7-day cancellation notice. At the beach with a view of Land's End. 3-6 stories. 40 1- & 2-bedroom units with full kitchen. No phones. Pool, swimming beach. No pets. Snack bar, bar. Restaurant nearby. AE, MC, VI.

HOTEL PLAZA LAS GLORIAS Hotel
Part of a large complex that includes condominiums and a shopping center, between Bl Marina and the harbor. Mail: Bl Marina s/n Lotes 9 y 10, Cabo San Lucas, BCS 23410, Mexico.
Phone 01152 (114) 3-1220; reservations (800) 342-2644.

All year	1P $ 80-130	2P $ 90-155

XP $15. 287 units. Cable TV; some refrigerators. Pool, fishing. 2 restaurants; 7 am-11 pm; cocktails.

PUEBLO BONITO RESORT ◆◆◆ Resort Hotel
3 blocks south of Hwy 1 on El Médano. Mail: Apdo Postal 460, Cabo San Lucas, BCS, Mexico.
Phone 01152 (114) 3-2900, (800) 442-5300; FAX 01152 (114) 3-1995.

4/15-12/21	1P $160-195	2P $160-195
12/22-4/14	1P $200-235	2P $200-235

XP $30. 10% service charge. Beachfront hotel on Cabo San Lucas Bay. 141 units. Cable TV, movies, efficiencies. Pool exercise room, beach, scuba diving, snorkeling, boating. Fishing trips arranged. No pets. 2 restaurants; 7 am-10 pm.

SIESTA SUITES HOTEL ◆◆ Suite Hotel
Downtown on Calle E Zapata at Hidalgo. Mail: Apdo Postal 310, Cabo San Lucas, BCS, Mexico.
Phone & FAX 01152 (114) 3-2773.
US reservations: 8966 Citation Ct, Alta Loma, CA 91737. Phone & FAX (909) 945-5940.

All year   1P $ 41- 50   2P $ 41- 50

XP $10. 15-day cancellation notice. 15 units. Shower baths, kitchens with utensils; some air conditioning, radios, TVs; no phones. No pets.

SOLMAR SUITES RESORT ◆◆◆ Resort Complex
Located on the southernmost tip of the peninsula.
Phone 01152 (114) 3-3535; FAX 3-0410.
US reservations: Box 383, Pacific Palisades, CA 90272. (310) 459-9861, (800) 344-3349.

6/1-10/31   1P $135-190   2P $135-190
11/1-5/31   1P $150-205   2P $150-205

XP $22-36. 10% service charge. 7-day cancellation notice. All-suite hotel on the beach. Expansive grounds and pool area. Most rooms face the Pacific Ocean. 90 units; Roca suites and condominiums available. Cable TV, movies, honor bars, coffee makers, safes, patio or private balconies. 3 pools, whirlpool, beach, diving, snorkeling, tennis. Fishing trips on cruisers. Restaurant open 6:30 am-10 pm; cocktails, entertainment, poolside bar. AE, MC, VI.

Restaurants

ALFONSO'S RESTAURANT ◆◆◆ Continental
In the Plaza Bonita shopping center on the marina.
Phone 01152 (114) 3-2022.

$15-22. Open 11:30 am-10 pm. Intimate dining inside or on the marina patio. Attentive service.

CARLOS 'N CHARLIE'S ◆ Mexican
On Bl Marina 20.
Phone 01152 (114) 3-1280.

$7-14. Open noon-midnight. Varied menu. Cocktails. AE, CB, DI, MC, VI.

CASA RAFAEL'S ◆◆◆ Continental
Between Bl Lázaro Cárdenas and the bay on El Médano.
Phone 01152 (114) 3-0739.

$18-35. Open 6-10 pm. Mexican Colonial house with quaint dining room and patio features international cuisine. Cocktails. MC, VI.

DA GIORGIO ◆◆ Italian
3 miles northeast of town center, then ½ mile south, adjacent to Misiones del Cabo.
Phone 01152 (114) 3-2988.

$6-16. Open 8 am-11 pm. Open-air palapa on hillside with view of Land's End. Seafood and pasta. Cocktails, bar. AE, MC, VI.

GALEON ITALIANO RESTAURANT   ◆◆ Italian
½ mile south of town center on Bl Marina across from the wharf.
Phone 01152 (114) 3-0443.

$8-21. Open 4-11 pm. View of the bay and the town. Pasta, veal and seafood.
Cocktails, bar. MC, VI.

PEACOCKS RESTAURANT   ◆◆ Continental
Two blocks southeast of Hwy 1 on Paseo del Pescador.
Phone 01152 (114) 3-1858.

$12-21. Open 6-10 pm. European cuisine. Cocktails, bar.

ROMEO Y JULIETA RISTORANTE   ◆◆ Italian
¼ mile south of town center at entrance to Pedregal condominium district.
Phone 01152 (114) 3-0225.

$7-19. Open 4-midnight. Quaint hacienda atmosphere. Pasta, pizza and seafood.
Cocktails. MC, VI.

SALSITAS   ◆ Mexican
At the marina in Plaza Bonita shopping center.
Phone 01152 (114) 3-1740.

$7-12. Open 7 am-11 pm. Indoor and outdoor seating with variety of Mexican
dishes. Cocktails. AE, MC, VI.

THE TRAILER PARK RESTAURANT (LA GOLONDRINA)   ◆ Mexican
One block southeast of Hwy 1 on Paseo del Pescador.
Phone 01152 (114) 3-0542.

$13-32. Open Tue-Sun 4-10 pm. Popular patio setting at a historic trading post.
Mexican style cooking with a selection of seafood, chicken and beef.

Cataviña

Lodging

HOTEL LA PINTA   ◆ Motor Inn
On Hwy 1, 1 mile north of Rancho Santa Inés. Mail: Apdo Postal 179, San Quintín, BC,
Mexico.
No phone.
US Reservations agent: Mexico Condo Reservations, 5801 Soledad Mountain Rd, La
Jolla, CA 92037. (619) 275-4500, (800) 262-4500.

All year   1P $60   2P $65

XP $10; maximum 4 persons per room. 3-day cancellation notice. Spanish-style
hotel in scenic rock-strewn area. 28 units; suite $125. Shower baths; no phones.
Pool, recreation room, playground. No pets. Dining room, 6 am-10 pm; cocktails,
bar. MC, VI. (See ad page 229.)

El Rosario

Restaurant

MAMA ESPINOSA'S ◆ Mexican
In the center of town on Hwy 1.

$4-10. Open 6 am-9 pm. Historic restaurant and home of Doña Anita. Serves lob ster, fish and beef dishes in the Baja tradition.

Ensenada

Lodging

BEST WESTERN CASA DEL SOL MOTEL ◆ Mo
At avs López Mateos and Blancarte. Mail: Apdo Postal 557, Ensenada, BC 22800, Mexico.
Phone 01152 (617) 8-1570; FAX 8-2025.
US Reservations agent: (800) 528-1234.

All year | 1P $53 | 2P $58

XP $8. 3-day cancellation notice. 48 units. Cable TV, shower baths; some air con ditioning, kitchens. Pool. Small pets accepted. Restaurant, bar, gift shop adjacent. AE, MC, VI.

BEST WESTERN EL CID MOTOR HOTEL ◆ Motor Inn
At Av López Mateos 993. Mail: Apdo Postal 1431, Ensenada, BC 22800, Mexico.
Phone 01152 (617) 8-2401; FAX 8-3671.
US reservations: Box 786, Chula Vista, CA 91910. (800) 352-4305.

Fri-Sat 6/1-8/31	1P $65	2P $65-86
Sun-Thu 6/1-8/31	1P $38	2P $52-65
9/1-5/31	1P $38	2P $38-52

3-day cancellation notice. Attractive Spanish styling. 52 units; suites available. Cable TV, radios; some shower baths, private balconies. Pool. Fishing trips arranged. No pets. Dining room and coffee shop; Tue through Fri 7 am-10 pm, closed Mon; cocktails, lounge. **(See ad below.)**

HOTEL CORAL & MARINA RESORT ◆◆◆ Resort Hotel
2 miles north of Ensenada on Hwy 1-D. Mail: Carr Tijuana-Ensenada Km 103, No 3421 Zona Playita, Ensenada, BC 22860, Mexico.
Phone 01152 (617) 5-0000; FAX 5-0005.
US Reservations agent: (619) 523-0064, (800) 946-2746.

All Year 1P $135-220 2P $135-220

XP $15. All-suite resort hotel overlooking the bay and marina. 147 units; Master and Presidential suites $285 to $450 for 4-6 persons; 11 efficiencies. Cable TV, movies, private balconies or patios. 2 pools (1 indoor), wading pool, whirlpools, sauna, steambaths, health club, boating, sailing, marina, charter fishing, 2 lighted tennis courts. Gift shop, conference facilities. Dining room; 7 am-11 pm. AE, DS, MC, VI. Wheelchair accessible rooms available.

CORONA HOTEL ◆ Motor Inn
At Bl Lazaro Cardenas No 1442 (Bl Costero) across from Riviera del Pacifico Building. Mail: 482 W San Ysidro Bl, Ste 303, San Ysidro, CA 92173 USA.
Phone 01152 (617) 6-0901; FAX 6-4023.

Fri-Sat 1P $ 50 2P $ 65
Sun-Thu 1P $ 38 2P $ 46

XP $8. 3-day reservation cancellation notice. 4 stories. 93 units. Color TV, movies, balconies. Pool. No pets. Restaurant; 7 am-10 pm; cocktails; bar. AE, MC, VI.

DAYS INN ◆ Motel
Just north of Av Blancarte on Av López Mateos. Mail: Av López Mateos 1050, Ensenada, BC 22800, Mexico.
Phone 01152 (617) 8-3434, (800) 422-5204.

5/1-8/31 1P $ 47-51 2P $ 47-51
9/1-4/30 1P $ 37-41 2P $ 37-41

XP $6. 3-day cancellation notice. 66 units. Color cable TV, movies; some shower baths. Pool, whirlpool. No pets. AE, MC, VI.

ENSENADA TRAVELODGE ◆◆ Motor Inn
At Av Blancarte 130, near Av López Mateos. Mail: 4492 Camino de la Raza, Ste ESE-118, San Ysidro, CA 92173.
Phone 01152 (617) 8-1601, (800) 578-7878.

All year 1P $ 53-60 2P $ 58-75

XP $8; family rates available. 3-day cancellation notice. 52 units; suites available. Cable TV, movies, radios, shower baths, honor bar. Heated pool, whirlpool. No pets. Restaurant open 7:30 am-11 pm; cocktails, bar. AE, MC, VI. **(See ad page 232.)**

ESTERO BEACH RESORT HOTEL ◆◆ Resort Complex
8 miles south of city center via Hwy 1 and graded side road. Mail: Apdo Postal 86, Ensenada, BC, Mexico.
Phone 01152 (617) 6-6230; FAX 6-6925.

5/1-9/10	1P ...	2P $48-82
9/11-4/30 Fri-Sun	1P ...	2P $38-72
9/11-4/30 Mon-Thu	1P ...	2P $28-62

XP $6. 3-day cancellation notice. Beach-front resort complex on attractive grounds. 106 units; suites $250-285. Cable TV, shower or combination baths; many private patios or balconies. Beach, tennis, recreation room, archaeological museum, gift shop, boat ramp, boat rentals, water-skiing, fishing, horseback riding. No pets. Restaurant; 8 am-10 pm; cocktails. MC, VI.

HACIENDA LAS GLORIAS ◆◆◆ Resort Complex
At Bajamar Golf Resort, 21 miles north of Ensenada off Hwy 1. Mail: 416 W San Ysidro Bl, Ste #L-732, San Ysidro, CA 92173 USA.
Phone 01152 (615) 5-0151; FAX 5-0150.
US reservations: (800) 265-2418.

Fri-Sat	1P $ 85	2P $85
Sun-Thu	1P $ 65	2P $65

Children ages 12 and under stay free. 2-night minimum stay on weekends. 3-day reservation cancellation notice. 2 stories. 81 units; 1-bedroom suites with kitchens $120-130. Mexican Colonial-style buildings. Color TV, movies, safes. Heated pool, whirlpool, sauna, 18- and 9-hole golf courses, pro shop, tennis. No pets. Restaurant; 7 am-10 pm; cocktails; bar. AE, MC, VI.

LODGING & RESTAURANTS

HOTEL LA PINTA ◆◆ Motor Inn
At Av Floresta and Bl Bucaneros. Mail: Apdo Postal 929, Ensenada, BC 22800, Mexico.
Phone 01152 (617) 6-2601.
US reservations agent: Mexico Condo Reservations, 5801 Soledad Mountain Rd, La
Jolla, CA 92037. (800) 262-4500; (619) 275-4500.

Fri-Sat	1P $ 60	2P $ 65	
Sun-Thu	1P $ 40	2P $ 45	

XP $10. 3-day cancellation notice. 52 units. Cable TV, shower baths. Pool. No
pets. Restaurant; 7:30 am-10 pm. MC, VI. **(See ad page 229.)**

LAS ROSAS HOTEL & SPA ◆◆ Motor Inn
4 miles north on Hwy 1. Mail: Apdo Postal No 316, Ensenada, BC 22800, Mexico.
Phone 01152 (617) 4-4310; FAX 01152 (617) 4-4595.

All Year	1P $101-108	2P $101-112

XP $22; children under 12 $16. 2-night minimum stay weekends. 7-day reservation cancellation notice; no refunds. Located on a bluff with spectacular oceanfront view. 2 stories. 31 units; suites $128-139. Color TV, shower baths, private
balconies. Pool, whirlpool. Fee for tennis, racquetball, gym, sauna, massage. No
pets. Restaurant 7 am-10 pm; cocktails, bar. MC, VI.

HOTEL MISION SANTA ISABEL ◆ Motor Inn
At Bl Lázaro Cárdenas and Av Castillo No 1100. Mail: Box 120-818, Chula Vista, CA
91912 USA.
Phone 01152 (617) 8-3616; FAX 8-3345.

Fri-Sat	1P $ 55	2P $ 60- 70
Sun-Thu	1P $ 50	2P $ 55- 65

XP $10. 3-day reservation cancellation notice. 3 stories. 58 units; junior suites
$80-87. Colonial-style architecture. Color TV, movies, shower baths. Pool. No
pets. Meeting rooms. Restaurant; Mon-Sat 7 am-11 pm, Sun 8 am-4 pm; cocktails;
bar. AE, MC, VI.

HOTEL PARAISO LAS PALMAS ◆ Motor Inn
In southeast part on Calle Agustin Sangines 206. Mail: 445 W San Ysidro Bl, Ste 2507,
San Ysidro, CA 92173 USA.
Phone 01152 (617) 7-1701; FAX 7-1701 ext 402.

All year	1P $ 50	2P $ 50

XP $5. 3 stories. 70 units; suites $68. Color TV, shower baths; no air conditioning. Pool, whirlpool. No pets. Restaurant; 7 am-11 pm; cocktails; bar. AE, MC, VI.

PUNTA MORRO HOTEL SUITES ◆◆ Suite Motor Inn
On oceanfront, 3 miles north of town center off Hwy 1. Mail: Box 434263, San Diego,
CA 92143 USA.
Phone 01152 (617) 8-3507; FAX 4-4490.
US reservations: (800) 526-6676.

Fri-Sat	1P $ 68-86	2P $ 68- 86
Sun-Thu	1P $ 58-69	2P $ 58- 69

2-night minimum stay weekends. 7-day reservation cancellation notice. 3 stories. 24 units; 2-bedroom suites for up to 4 persons, $95-116; 3-bedroom suites for up to 6 persons, $130-156; suites with kitchens and 3 studios with refrigerators. Patio or balcony, TV, movies, shower baths, fireplace. Pool, whirlpool. No pets. Restaurant; Mon-Fri 7 am-10 pm, Sat from 8 am, Sun from 9:30 am; cocktails; bar. AE, MC, VI.

HOTEL SANTO TOMAS   Motel
On Bl Lázaro Cárdenas (Costero) at Av Miramar. Mail: Bl Lázaro Cárdenas 609, Ensenada, BC, Mexico.
Phone 01152 (617) 8-1503.

Fri-Sat	1P $54	2P $58
Sun-Thu	1P $50	2P $54

XP $4. 3-day reservation cancellation notice. 3-story motel. 80 units. Cable TV, shower baths. No pets.

Restaurants

BRONCOS STEAKHOUSE   ◆ Steakhouse
At Av López Mateos 1525.
Phone 01152 (617) 6-4900.

$8-15. Open 8 am-10:30 pm. Old west atmosphere with menu featuring a variety of steaks and seafood. Cocktails. AE, MC, VI.

CASINO ROYAL RESTAURANT   ◆◆◆ French
Southeast of main hotel row at Bl Las Dunas 118, near Bl Lázaro Cárdenas.
Phone 01152 (617) 7-1480.

$10-23. Open noon-midnight. Elegantly decorated mansion style building. Cocktails. MC, VI.

EL REY SOL RESTAURANT   ◆◆◆ French
½ mile south of town center on Av López Mateos at Av Blancarte.
Phone 01152 (617) 8-1733.

$9-19. Open 7:30 am-11 pm. French and Mexican cuisine. Cocktails, bar. AE, MC, VI. **(See ad page 232.)**

ENRIQUE'S RESTAURANT   ◆ Mexican
On Hwy 1-D, 1½ miles north of town center.
Phone 01152 (617) 4-4061.

$5-14. Open 8 am-11:30 pm. Closed 1/1, 9/16, 12/25. Mexican food, steaks and seafood. Cocktails. MC, VI.

HALIOTIS   ◆◆ Seafood
On Calle Delante (Agustín Sanginés) 179, ½ mile east of Hwy 1.
Phone 01152 (617) 6-3720.

$5-16. Open Wed-Mon 12:30-10:30 pm. Seafood, chicken and beef. Cocktails. AE, MC, VI.

LA EMBOTELLADORA VIEJA RESTAURANTE　◆◆◆ Continental
North of the downtown area at Calle Miramar 666 at the Santo Tomás Winery.
Phone 01152 (617) 4-0807.

$7-18. Open noon-11 pm. Fine dining in a room once used to age wines. Extensive wine list. MC, VI.

PALMIRA AT CANTAMAR RESTAURANT　◆ American
21 miles north of town center, adjacent to Hwy 1-D at Km 46.
Phone 01152 (661) 4-1203.

$7-17. Open Mon-Thu noon-9 pm; Fri noon-10:30 pm; Sat & Sun 8 am-midnight. Indoor and outdoor dining with a selection of Pacific Rim cuisine. Cocktails.

Guerrero Negro

Lodging

HOTEL EL MORRO　Motel
1 mile west of Hwy 1 on east edge of town. Mail: Apdo Postal 144, Guerrero Negro, BCS 23940, Mexico.
Phone 01152 (115) 7-0414.

All year　1P $26　2P $27-31

XP $4. Modest motel. 32 units. Fans, shower baths; no air conditioning, phones. Restaurant; noon-10 pm; bar.

HOTEL LA PINTA　Motor Inn
On Hwy 1 at the 28th parallel. Mail: Guerrero Negro, BCS 23940, Mexico.
Phone 01152 (115) 7-1301.
US reservations agent: Mexico Condo Reservations, 5801 Soledad Mountain Rd, La Jolla, CA 92037. (800) 262-4500; (619) 275-4500.

All year　1P $60　2P $65

XP $10; 4-person maximum per room. 3-day cancellation notice. Single-story hotel near Paralelo 28 monument. 29 units. Shower baths, 2-bed rooms; no air conditioning, phones. No pets. Dining room; 7 am-10 pm; cocktails, bar. Trailer park adjacent. **(See ad page 229.)**

Restaurant

MALARRIMO RESTAURANT　◆ Seafood
1 mile west of Hwy 1 on east edge of town.
Phone 01152 (115) 7-0250.

$4-15. Open 7:30 am-10:30 pm. Seafood and Mexican specialties; bar; museum, tourist information. Cocktails.

LODGING & RESTAURANTS

La Paz

Lodging

ARAIZA INN PALMIRA   ◆ Motor Inn
1½ miles north on Carr Pichilingue. Mail: Apdo Postal 442, La Paz, BCS 23010, Mexico.
Phone 01152 (112) 2-4000; FAX 2-3727.
US reservations: (800) 929-2402.

All year   1P $60   2P $60

XP $7. Across from by on attractive tropical grounds. 3 stories. 120 units. Shower
baths, coffee makers. Pool, wading pool, tennis, playground, fishing/tour arrangements. No pets. Gift shop. Conference center. Restaurant; 7 am-10:30 pm. AE,
MC, VI.

CABAÑAS DE LOS ARCOS   ◆◆ Motel
*Opposite the malecón, at Paseo Alvaro Obregón and Rosales. Mail: Apdo Postal 112, La
Paz, BCS 23000, Mexico.*
*Phone 01152 (112) 2-2744, FAX 5-4313; (714) 476-5555 or (800) 347-2252; FAX
(714) 476-5560.*
US Reservations: 18552 MacArthur Bl, Ste 205, Irvine, CA 92715.

All year   1P $55   2P $60

XP $10. 7-day cancellation notice. Four-story hotel wing and 16 bungalows in
tropical garden setting. 52 units. Cable TV, movies, radios, coffee makers, shower
baths. Pool. Fishing trips arranged. No pets. Restaurant and bar at Hotel Los
Arcos, ½ block away. AE, MC, VI.

CASA LA PACEÑA BED & BREAKFAST   Bed & Breakfast
On Bravo 2 blocks from La Paz Bay. Mail: Apdo Postal 158, La Paz, BCS 23000, Mexico.
Phone 01152 (112) 5-2748.

11/15-6/30 [CP]   1P $25-30   2P $30-35

Open 11/15 to 6/30. 5-day cancellation notice. 3 units. Radios, shower baths, bay
view, TV in common room; no phones. Pets.

CLUB EL MORRO   ◆◆ Suite Motor Inn
1 mile north on Carr Pichilingue. Mail: Apdo Postal 357, La Paz, BCS 23010, Mexico.
Phone 01152 (112) 2-4084; FAX 5-2828.

All year   1P $40-70   2P $40-70

3-day cancellation notice. Moorish-style buildings on colorfully landscaped
grounds across from bay. 2 stories. 21 units, most with kitchens. Shower baths.
Pool, whirlpool, barbecue, kayak rentals. Pets allowed in designated rooms.
Restaurant; 8 am-11 pm; cocktails, bar. AE, MC, VI.

LA CONCHA BEACH RESORT   ◆◆ Resort Complex
*3 miles northeast on Carr Pichilingue. Mail: Apdo Postal 607, La Paz, BCS 23010,
Mexico.*
Phone 01152 (112) 1-6161, (800) 999-2252; FAX 01152 (112) 1-6218.

| 8/1-9/30 | 1P $ 70 | 2P $ 70 |
| 10/1-7/31 | 1P $ 85 | 2P $ 85 |

XP $15. 3-day cancellation notice. On attractive shaded grounds at the bay. 3-6 stories. 119 units. Shower baths, refrigerators, balconies. Pool, whirlpool, swimming beach, boating, windsurfing, scuba diving, snorkeling, charter fishing, kayak rental, exercise room. No pets. Conference center. Restaurant; 7 am-10:30 pm; cocktails, bar. AE, MC, VI.

CROWNE PLAZA RESORT ◆◆◆ Suite Hotel
3½ miles west of town via Hwy 1 at Marina Fidepaz. Mail: Apdo Postal 482, La Paz, BCS 23094, Mexico.
Phone 01152 (112) 4-0830.
US reservations: Holiday Inn (800) 227-6963.

| All year | 1P $100-120 | 2P $100-120 |

XP $10. On the bay. 2 stories. 54 units; 2-bedroom suites $170 for 4 persons. Refrigerators, coffee makers, wet bar. 3 pools, whirlpool, sauna, steam bath, beach, squash court, exercise room. Fishing trips, watersports and tours arranged. Restaurant; 7 am-11 pm; cocktails, bar. AE, MC, VI.

HOTEL LOS ARCOS ◆◆ Hotel
Opposite the malecón, facing La Paz Bay, at Paseo Alvaro Obregón and Allende. Mail: Apdo Postal 112, La Paz, BCS, Mexico.
Phone 01152 (112) 2-2744; (714) 476-5555, (800) 347-2252; FAX (714) 476-5560, 01152 (112) 5-4313.
US Reservations: 18552 MacArthur Bl, Ste 205, Irvine, CA 92715.

| All year | 1P $ 72-75 | 2P $ 75-80 |

XP $10-15. 7-day cancellation notice. Colonial-style hotel. 130 units; suite $85-100. Cable TV, movies, radios, coffee makers, shower baths. Pool, sauna (fee). Fishing trips arranged. No pets. Coffee shop, 7 am-10 pm; dining room, 7 am-11 pm; cocktails, bar. AE, MC, VI. **(See ad page 225.)**

HOTEL MARINA ◆◆ Hotel
1½ miles north on Carr Pichilingue. Mail: Apdo Postal 34, La Paz, BCS 23010, Mexico.
Phone 01152 (112) 1-6254; FAX 1-6177.
US reservations: (800) 826-1138.

| All year | 1P $ 75 | 2P $ 75 |

XP $10. 3-day cancellation notice. On the bay and marina. 5 stories. 92 units; suites with efficiencies and kitchens, $120-150. Some shower baths. Pool, whirlpool, lighted tennis court, dock, marina, fishing/diving/snorkeling trips arranged. No pets. Restaurants; 7 am-11 pm; cocktails, bar. AE, MC, VI.

HOTEL MEDITERRANE Lodge
On Allende ½ block from Paseo Alvaro Obregón. Mail: Allende 36-B, La Paz, BCS 23000, Mexico.
Phone & FAX 01152 (112) 5-1195.

| All year | 1P $ 40 | 2P $ 45 |

XP $5. 5-day cancellation notice. Mexican/European style villa. 6 units. Radios, shower baths; some air conditioning, refrigerators; no phones. VCR library. Whirlpool. Fishing trips arranged. Restaurant adjacent. AE, MC, VI.

Restaurants

EL TASTE ◆◆ Mexican
½ mile southwest of town center on Paseo Alvaro Obregón at Juárez.
Phone 01152 (112) 2-8121.

$4-14. Open 8 am-midnight. Overlooks the malecón and the bay. Mexican cuisine including beef and seafood. Cocktails. MC, VI.

LA PAZ - LAPA DE CARLOS 'N CHARLIES ◆ Mexican
On Paseo Alvaro Obregón at 16 de Septiembre.
Phone 01152 (112) 2-6025.

$4-$10. Open noon-11 pm. Palapa and patio dining across from bay. Mexican cuisine, including steaks and seafood. Cocktails. MC, VI.

LA PAZTA ◆◆ Italian
On Allende ½ block from Paseo Alvaro Obregón, near Hotel Mediterrane.
Phone 01152 (112) 5-1195.

$5-7. Open Wed-Mon 4-10 pm. Trattoria featuring fresh, made-to-order pasta, and Swiss dishes and fondues. AE, MC, VI.

LOS VITRALES ◆◆ Mexican
At Paseo Alvaro Obregón and Pineda in Vista Coral Plaza.
Phone 01152 (112) 3-3737.

$4-7. Open Tue-Sun 8 am-11:30 pm. Traditional Mexican cuisine from various regions. Cocktails. Coffee house adjacent.

Loreto

Lodging

DIAMOND EDEN AN ALL INCLUSIVE RESORT ◆◆ Resort Hotel
Formerly Hotel Mercure El Cortes. At Nopoló, 8½ miles south via Hwy 1 and paved road to beach. Mail: Bl Mision de Loreto, Loreto, BCS 23880, Mexico.
Phone 01152 (113) 3-0700, FAX 3-0377; (800) 858-2258.

All year [AP] 1P ... 2P $190-210

XP $95-155. Age restriction, 18 years & older. Rates include all meals, beverages, taxes, gratuity & most recreational services. 14-day cancellation notice. Modern 3-story hotel on beach with attractive landscaping. Most rooms have private patios and ocean view. 140 units; 1- and 2-bedroom suites, $110-150. Shower baths. 2 pools, beach, tennis, golf, fishing, scuba diving, boating, sailboarding. No pets. Restaurant; 7 am-10 pm; cocktails, bar. AE, DI, MC, VI.

HOTEL LA PINTA Motor Inn
On beach, 1 mile north of town plaza. Mail: Apdo Postal 28, Loreto, BCS, Mexico.
Phone 01152 (113) 5-0025.
US reservations agent: Mexico Condo Reservations, 5801 Soledad Mountain Rd, La Jolla,
CA 92037. (800) 262-4500, (619) 275-4500.

All year   1P $48-60   2P $ 50-65

XP $12; 4-person maximum per room. 3-day cancellation notice. Spacious rooms. 49 units. Shower baths, private patios; no phones. Pool, beach. Fishing trips and golf arranged. No pets. Dining room; 6:30 am-10 pm; cocktails, bar. MC, VI. **(See ad page 229.)**

HOTEL OASIS Motor Inn
On shore of Loreto Bay, ½ mile south of town plaza. Mail: Apdo Postal 17, Loreto, BCS
23880, Mexico. Open noon to 11 pm. Closed 12/25.
Phone 01152 (113) 5-0112.

4/1-10/31 [AP]   1P $79   2P $110
11/1-3/31   1P $49   2P $ 60

XP $20. 30-day cancellation notice. Set in palm grove. 35 units. Spacious rooms. Shower baths, 2 double or 3 single beds; some patios. Pool, beach, tennis. Fishing trips arranged in cruisers and pangas. Dining room; 4:30-11 am, 12:30-3 and 6:30-8:45 pm; cocktails, bar.

Restaurant

EL NIDO STEAKHOUSE ◆◆ Steak & Seafood
At town entrance 1 mile east of Hwy 1 on Salvatierra 154.
Phone 01152 (113) 5-0284.

$5-15. Open noon-10:30 pm. Closed 12/25. Ranch atmosphere. Cocktails. MC, VI.

Los Barriles

Lodging

HOTEL PUNTA PESDACERO ◆◆ Resort Motor inn
7½ miles north of Hwy 1 on an unpaved rd. Mail: Apdo Postal 362, La Paz, BCS 23000,
Mexico.
Phone 01152 (114) 1-0101; FAX 1-0669.
US reservations: (800) 426-2252.

All year   1P $90   2P $ 90

XP $25. 15% service charge. 15-day cancellation notice. Secluded resort on picturesque bluff. 21 units; also 2- to 4-bedroom villas. Shower baths, refrigerators, coffee makers; no phones. Pool, swimming beach, boat and canoe rentals, scuba diving, snorkeling, charter fishing, tennis. No pets. Gift shop. 3500-ft paved landing strip, unicom 122.8. Dining room; 6:30-9:30 am, 1 pm lunch seating, 7 pm dinner seating; prix fixe meals; cocktails, bar. AE, MC, VI.

Restaurant

TIO PABLO'S BAR & GRILL   ◆ American
½ mile east of Hwy 1 in town.

$4-14. Open 8 am-10 pm. Casual palapa and patio dining with a variety of dishes prepared American and Mexican style.

Mexicali

Lodging

ARAIZA INN MEXICALI   ◆◆ Motor Inn
At Bl Benito Juárez 2220, 5 miles southeast of border crossing. Mail: 233 Pauline Av, #947, Calexico, CA 92231 USA.
Phone 01152 (65) 66-1300; FAX 6-4901.

All year   1P $50   2P $50-56

XP $5. 172 units; suites $64 for 2 persons. Cable TV, radios. Pool, 1 lighted tennis court. No pets. Facilities for meetings. Restaurant and coffee shop open 7 am-midnight; cocktails, bar, entertainment. AE, MC, VI.

HOLIDAY INN CROWNE PLAZA   ◆◆◆ Hotel
5 miles southeast of border crossing, on Av de los Héroes #201, Mexicali, BC 21000, Mexico.
Phone 01152 (65) 57-3600, (800) 465-4329.

All year   1P $59-72   2P $59-72

XP $20. 3-day cancellation notice. Family plan available. 8 stories. 158 units. Cable TV, movies, radios. Pool. 2 restaurants; 6 am-midnight; cocktails & bar. AE, MC, VI. Smoke detectors.

HOTEL LUCERNA   ◆◆◆ Motor Inn
At Bl Benito Juárez 2151, 5½ miles southeast of border crossing. Mail: Box 2300, Calexico, CA 92231 USA.
Phone 01152 (65) 66-1000, (800) 582-3762.

All year   1P $57   2P $60

XP $10. Beautifully landscaped grounds. 175 units. Cable TV, radios, refrigerators; some shower baths, private balconies. 2 pools, tennis. No pets. Meeting rooms available. 2 dining rooms (see Mezzosole Restaurante Italiano) and coffee shop; 7 am-2 am; cocktails, bar, nightclub, gift shop. AE, DI, MC, VI.

Restaurant

MEZZOSOLE RESTAURANTE ITALIANO   ◆◆◆ Italian
At Bl Benito Juárez 2151 in the Hotel Lucerna.
Phone 01152 (65) 66-1000.

$9-16. Open Mon-Sat 5 pm-midnight. A small elegant dining room overlooking the pool. Cocktails. AE, DI, MC, VI.

Mulegé

Lodging

RESORT HOTEL SAN BUENAVENTURA Resort Hotel
25 miles south of Mulegé via Hwy 1, at Km 945 on Bahía Concepción. Mail: Apdo Postal 56, Mulegé, BCS, Mexico.
Phone 01152 (115) 3-0408.

| All Year | 1P ... | 2P $50- 60 |

20 units. Shower baths. Beach, fishing, charter service and concrete boat ramp. Restaurant; 7 am-8 pm.

Restaurant

LAS CASITAS ◆ Mexican
In the hotel of the same name in center of town.
Phone 01152 (115) 3-0019.

$4-11. Open 7:30 am-10 pm. Attractive patio setting. Mexican cuisine, specializing in beef and seafood. Features Fri evening fiesta buffet with mariachi band. Cocktails.

Rosarito

Lodging

BRISAS DEL MAR MOTEL Motor Inn
In center of town on Bl Benito Juárez 22. Mail: Box 1867, Chula Vista, CA 91912 USA.
Phone 01152 (611) 2-2547, (800) 697-5223; FAX (619) 685-1246.

Fri-Sat 10/1-5/31 &		
6/1-9/30	1P $ 53-63	2P $53- 63
Sun-Thu 10/1-5/31	1P $ 43-63	2P $43- 63

3-day cancellation notice. 2-story motel. 66 units. Cable TV. Pool, playground. No pets. Restaurant; 7 am-10:30 pm; cocktails.

HOTEL FESTIVAL PLAZA ◆ Hotel
In center of town on Bl Benito Juárez at Calle del Nogal. Mail: Mex #410, Box 439060, San Diego, CA 92143 USA.
Phone 01152 (661) 2-2950, (800) 453-8606.

Fri-Sat 5/1-9/30	1P ...	2P $61-110
Sun-Thu 5/1-9/30	1P ...	2P $50-100
Fri-Sat 10/1-4/30	1P ...	2P $50- 80
Sun-Thu 10/1-4/30	1P ...	2P $40- 80

XP $17. 1 block from beach; ocean-view rooms. 8-story hotel. 120 units; 7 casitas, $88-127. Cable TV, shower baths. Amusement park; pool, whirlpools. Cafeteria, restaurant, bar; nightclubs; 8 am-midnight. MC, VI.

LODGING & RESTAURANTS

LAS ROCAS HOTEL AND SUITES ◆◆ Motor Inn
6 miles south of town on Hwy 1. Mail: Box 189003 HLR, Coronado, CA 92178 USA.
Phone 01152 (661) 2-2145, 2-2140, (800) 733-6394.

Fri-Sat 10/1-5/31 &			
6/1-9/30	1P $ 70-150	2P $ 70-150	
Sun-Thu 10/1-5/31	1P $ 49- 99	2P $ 49- 99	

XP $10. 8-day cancellation notice. Hotel on a bluff overlooking the ocean. 74 units. Cable TV; some refrigerators, microwaves, fireplaces, ocean-view balconies. Pool, whirlpool, tennis. No pets. Restaurant; 7:30 am-10:30 pm; cocktails. AE, MC, VI.

OASIS RESORT ◆◆ Resort Motor Inn
On Hwy 1-D, 3 miles north of town; southbound exit El Oasis, northbound exit San Antonio. Mail: Box Box 158, Imperial Beach, CA 91933 USA.
Phone 01152 (661) 3-3253, (800) 462-7472; FAX 01152 (661) 3-3252.

Fri-Sat 3/15-10/1	1P $109	2P $109
Sun-Thu 3/15-10/1	1P $ 99	2P $ 99
Fri-Sat 10/2-3/14	1P $ 65	2P $ 65
Sun-Thu 10/2-3/14	1P $ 55	2P $ 55

XP $10-15; discounted rates for children. 3-day reservation cancellation notice. Master & deluxe suites $150-275. All-suite resort and RV park on the beach. Color TV, movies, refrigerators. 3 pools, whirlpools, sauna, beach, putting green, exercise room, tennis. Convention facility. No pets. Restaurant; 7 am-11 pm; cocktails; bar. MC, VI.

ROSARITO BEACH HOTEL & SPA ◆ Resort Hotel
In south part of town on Bl Benito Juárez, facing the Pacific Ocean. Mail: Box 430145, San Diego, CA 92143 USA.
Phone 01152 (661) 2-0144, (800) 343-8582; FAX 01152 (661) 2-1125.

Fri-Sat 9/6-11/30 &			
7/23-9/5	1P $ 89-129	2P $ 89-129	
Sun-Thu 9/6-11/30	1P $ 69-129	2P $ 69- 99	

XP $15. 3-day cancellation notice. 280 units; suites. Cable TV, shower baths; some air conditioning, private balcony. 2 pools, 3 whirlpools, beach, racquetball, basketball, tennis. No pets. Facilities for meetings. 2 restaurants; 7:30 am-9 pm; buffet with live music Fri and Sat evenings; cocktails, 2 bars; gift shop. MC, VI. **(See ad page 243.)**

Restaurants

CHABERTS RESTAURANT ◆◆ French
In south part of town on Bl Benito Juárez at Rosarito Beach Hotel.
Phone 01152 (661) 2-0144.

$8-16. Open 5 pm-midnight. July-Aug closed Tue, Sep-June closed Mon-Fri. An elegant dining room located in a former mansion. Cocktails. MC, VI.

EL NIDO STEAKHOUSE   ◆◆ Steak & Seafood
At Bl Benito Juárez 67.
Phone 01152 (661) 2-1431.

$7-16. Open 8 am-midnight. Closed 9/16 and 12/25. Ranch atmosphere featuring mesquite-broiled steaks & seafood. Cocktails.

LOS PELICANOS   ◆◆ Steak & Seafood
On the beach at Calle Ebano 113.
Phone 01152 (661) 2-1757.

$7-16. Open 8 am-midnight. Closed 9/16. Cocktails. MC, VI.

San Felipe

Lodging

MOTEL EL CAPITAN   Motor Inn
On Av Mar de Cortez, corner of Manzanillo across from State Tourism office. Mail: Box 1916, Calexico, CA 92232 USA.
Phone 01152 (657) 7-1303.

Fri-Sat	1P $45	2P $45
Sun-Thu	1P $36	2P $36

XP $5. 2-person rates good for up to 4 persons. 3-day cancellation notice. 40 units. Shower baths; some color TV, radios. Pool. Sailboat charters arranged. Restaurant open 7 am-10 pm; bar.

PLAYA BONITA   Condominium Motel
1 mile north of town center via Av Mar de Cortez.
Phone 01142 (657) 7-1215.
US reservations: 475 E Badillo St, Covina, CA 91723. (818) 967-8977.

3/1-10/31	$80
11/1-2/28	$65

XP $15. $10 charge for linen & towels located in trailer park at the beach. 2 stories. 8 1-bedroom suites with cooking facilities, sleep up to 6 people. Swimming beach.

SAN FELIPE MARINA RESORT   ◆◆◆ Resort Motor Inn
3 miles south of town on road to airport. Mail: 482 W San Ysidro Bl, Ste 175, San Ysidro, CA 92173 USA.
Phone 01152 (657) 7-1568, 7-1455.
US reservations: (619) 558-0295, (800) 777-1700

All Year	1P $95-200	2P $95-200

XP $20. 3-day cancellation notice. On the beach overlooking the bay. 59 units; master suite and villas, $330-500 for 6-8 persons. Cable TV, radios, balcony or patio, walk-in showers, most with full cooking facilities and utensils. 2 pools (1 indoor, heated), sauna, steam room, exercise equipment, beach, 2 lighted tennis courts. Restaurant; 7 am-11 pm, cocktails, lounge. AE, MC, VI. **(See ad page 245.)**

Restaurant

EL NIDO STEAKHOUSE   ◆◆ Steakhouse
¼ mile south of town center on Av Mar de Cortez.
No phone.

$8-16. Open Thu-Tue, 2-11 pm. Closed Wed. Ranch atmosphere. Features steaks and seafood. Cocktails.

San Ignacio

Lodging

HOTEL LA PINTA   Motor Inn
1 mile west of Hwy 1, on entrance highway leading to town plaza. Mail: Apdo Postal 37, San Ignacio, BCS 23943, Mexico.
Phone 01152 (115) 4-0300.
US reservations agent: Mexico Condo Reservations, 5801 Soledad Mountain Rd, La Jolla, CA 92037. (619) 275-4500, (800) 262-4500.

All year	1P $60	2P $65

XP $10; 4-person maximum per room. 3-day cancellation notice. Spanish-style, single-story hotel set in palm grove with rooms facing interior patio. 28 units.

Shower baths, 2-bed rooms; no phones. Pool, recreation room. No pets. Dining room; 7 am-10 pm; cocktails, bar. MC, VI. **(See ad page 229.)**

San José del Cabo

Lodging

CASA DEL MAR ◆◆◆ Resort Motor Inn
7 miles west of town at Cabo Real. Mail: KM 19.5 Arr Transpeninsular, San José del Cabo, BCS 23400, Mexico.
Phone 01152 (114) 4-0030, (800) 221-8800; FAX 01152 (114) 4-0034.

6/1-10/31	1P $150	2P $165
11/1-5/31	1P $220	2P $230

XP $25. 3-day cancellation notice. Attractive colonial-style building at the ocean. 2 stories. 31 units. Whirlpool bathtubs, refrigerators, safes. Pool, wading pool, whirlpool, beach, golf course. No pets. Restaurant, see separate listing. AE, MC, VI.

FIESTA INN ◆◆ Motor Inn
On beach, 1½ miles west of town. Mail: Apdo Postal 124, San José del Cabo, BCS 23400, Mexico.
Phone & FAX 01152 (114) 2-0793, (800) 343-7821; FAX 01152 (114) 2-0480.

4/14-12/21	1P $ 68-83	2P $ 68- 83
12/22-4/13	1P $ 77-94	2P $ 77- 94

XP $20. 3 stories. 153 units with patio or balcony. Pool, bicycle rentals, horseback riding, scuba/snorkeling/fishing arrangements. Gift shop. Meeting rooms. Restaurant; 7 am-10 pm. AE, MC, VI.

HOWARD JOHNSON PLAZA SUITE HOTEL RESORT ◆◆◆ Resort Hotel
¼ mile east of town, just off Hwy 1 on Paseo Finisterra. Mail: Apdo Postal 152, San José del Cabo, BCS, Mexico.
Phone 01152 (114) 2-0990, (800) 654-2000; FAX 01152 (114) 2-0806.

4/16-11/30	1P $ 70-110	2P $ 70-110
12/1-4/15	1P $ 90-130	2P $ 90-130

7-day cancellation notice. Mexican Colonial and Moorish-style buildings surrounding courtyard and pool. 4 stories, no elevator. 172 units; hotel rooms and 1- to 3-bedroom suites with kitchens. Pool, exercise room. Fee for golf, tennis, scuba/snorkeling/fishing arrangements. No pets. Gift shop. Meeting room. Restaurant; 7 am-10:30 pm; cocktails, bar. AE, MC, VI.

HUERTA VERDE BED & BREAKFAST ◆◆◆ Bed & Breakfast
3 miles north of town along Hwy 1, then 1 mile east on Las Animas Atlas. Mail: Las Animas Atlas, San José del Cabo, BCS 23400, Mexico.
Phone & FAX 01152 (112) 8-8511.
US reservations: (303) 831-5162; FAX (303) 431-4455.

All year [BP]	1P $ 85-135	2P $ 85-135

3 rooms and 5 suites, individually decorated. Tropical gardens in a secluded hillside setting. Shower baths; some refrigerators. Pool. Hiking. Additional meals by arrangement.

LA JOLLA DE LOS CABOS ◆◆◆ Condominium Hotel
3 miles west of town center on Hwy 1. Mail: Apdo Postal 127, San José del Cabo, BCS, Mexico.
Phone 01152 (114) 2-3000; FAX 2-0546.
US reservations: (800) 455-2226.

4/16-11/30	1P $105-142	2P $105-250
12/1-4/15	1P $122-168	2P $122-290

XP $15. 10% service charge. 3-day cancellation notice. On the beach. 3 to 6 stories. 55 units; studios, 1- and 2-bedrooms with kitchens. Some shower baths, refrigerators, coffee makers. Pools, whirlpools, saunas, steam rooms, exercise room, massage, lighted tennis courts. No pets. Gift shop. Restaurant; 7 am-10:30 pm; cocktails, bar. AE, MC, VI.

MELIA CABO REAL BEACH & GOLF RESORT ◆◆◆ Resort Hotel
On Hwy 1, 7 miles west of town. Mail: Carr a Cabo San Lucas, Km. 19, San José del Cabo, BCS, Mexico.
Phone 01152 (114) 4-0000, (800) 336-3542.

4/19-12/19	1P $137-182	2P $137-182
12/20-4/18	1P $180-300	2P $180-300

XP $40. 10% service charge. 15-day cancellation notice. Spacious ocean-front grounds. 309 units. Movies, VCPs. Pool, whirlpool, golf, tennis, scuba diving, snorkeling, fishing trips arranged. 2 restaurants, 2 coffee shops; 7 am-11 pm; 24-hour room service; cocktails. AE, MC, VI.

POSADA REAL LOS CABOS ◆ Motor Inn
On beach, 1½ miles west of town. Mail: Apdo Postal 51, San José del Cabo, BCS 23400, Mexico.
Phone 01152 (114) 2-0155, (800) 528-1234; FAX 01152 (114) 2-0460.

4/1-11/30	1P $ 55	2P $ 55
12/1-3/30	1P $ 75	2P $ 75

XP $10. 3-day cancellation notice. 3 stories. 150 units. Shower baths; most ocean view. Pool, wading pool, shirlpools, tennis, bicycle rental, scuba/snorkeling/fishing arrangements. No pets. Gift shop. Meeting rooms. Restaurant; 7:30 am-10:30 pm; cocktails, bar. AE, MC, VI.

PRESIDENTE LOS CABOS FORUM RESORT ◆◆◆ Resort Hotel
On beach 1¼ miles west of town. Mail: Apdo Postal 2, San José del Cabo, BCS 23400, Mexico.
Phone 01152 (114) 2-0211, (800) 327-0200; FAX 01152 (114) 2-0232.

All year [AP]	1P $245	2P $260

XP $45. Rates include all meals and beverages. 240 units; suite available. 10% service charge. 3-day cancellation notice. Movies, shower baths. Pool, tennis, scuba diving, snorkeling, boat rentals, fishing trips arranged. No pets. Dining room and coffee shop; 7 am-10 pm; cocktails, bar, disco. AE, CB, DI, MC, VI. ⌀

TROPICANA INN ◆◆ Motor Inn
*On Bl Mijares just south of town plaza. Mail: Bl Mijares 30, San José del Cabo, BCS
23400, Mexico.*
Phone 01152 (114) 2-0907; FAX 2-1580; FAX in USA (510) 939-2725.

5/1-12/20	1P $ 50	2P $ 50
12/21-4/30	1P $ 61	2P $ 61

XP $10; children ages 11 and under free. 7-day cancellation notice. Attractive
Mexican style. 2-story motel. 40 units. Cable TV, coffee makers, showers. Pool.
No pets. Restaurant; 8 am-11 pm; cocktails. AE, MC, VI.

WESTIN REGINA RESORT—LOS CABOS ◆◆◆◆ Resort Complex
*On Hwy 1, 6 miles southwest of San Jose del Cabo. Mail: Apdo Postal 145, San Jose del
Cabo, BCS 23400, Mexico.*
Phone 01152 (114) 2-9000; FAX 2-9010.
US reservations: (800) 228-3000.

All year	1P $195-290	2P $195-290

XP $25. $2.50 daily service charge per room. High-rise hotel, water-themed landscape blended with dramatic architecture creating a window to the sea. Suites
available. Air conditioning, color TV, phones, combination baths, honor bar,
safes, private balconies. 3 pools, whirlpool, beach, tennis, fitness center. Fishing
trips and golf arranged. No pets. Restaurants, cocktails.

Restaurants

ARRECIFES ◆◆◆ Continental
In the Westin Regina Resort.
Phone 01152 (114) 2-9000.

$15-26. Open Wed-Mon 6-11 pm. Closed Tue. Spectacular ocean-view setting.
Creative dishes with an artful presentation. Cocktails. AE, MC, VI.

CASA DEL MAR RESTAURANT ◆◆◆ Mexican
7 miles west of town at Cabo Real.
Phone 01152 (114) 4-0030.

$10-30. Open 7-11 am, noon-4, 6:30-10:30 pm. Regional dishes in an elegant set-
ting. Cocktails. AE, MC, VI.

DA GIORGIO RESTAURANT ◆ Italian
5 miles west on Hwy 1 near Hotel Palmilla on a hill overlooking the gulf.
Phone 01152 (114) 2-1988.

$7-12. Open noon-10 pm. Cocktails, bar. AE, MC, VI.

DAMIANA ◆ Mexican
East side of town plaza at Bl Mijares No 8.
Phone 01152 (114) 2-0499.

$7-16. Open 9 am-11 pm. Patio and inside dining with Mexican and seafood cui-
sine. Cocktails, bar. MC, VI.

LA CONCHA BEACH CLUB SEAFOOD RESTAURANT   ◆◆ Seafood
7 miles west on Hwy 1, on the beach at Cabo Real.
No phone.

$7-15. Open 11:30 am-9 pm. Dining under palapas at beachside, specializing in fresh seafood with a limited selection of beef and chicken entrees. Cocktails.

TROPICANA BAR & GRILL   ◆ Mexican
On Bl Mijares just south of town plaza.
Phone 01152 (114) 2-0907.

$4-18. Open 8 am-11 pm. Hacienda and patio dining featuring Mexican and European entrees. Cocktails. AE, MC, VI.

San Quintín

Lodging

HOTEL LA PINTA   Motor Inn
2½ miles west of Hwy 1 via paved road to outer San Quintín Bay. Mail: Apdo Postal 168, Valle de San Quintín, BC 22930, Mexico.
Phone 01152 (616) 5-2878.

US reservations agent: Mexico Condo Reservations, 5801 Soledad Mountain Rd, La Jolla, CA 92037. (800) 262-4500, (619) 275-4500.

All year   1P $60   2P $65

XP $10; 4-person maximum per room. 3-day cancellation notice. 58 units. Attractive Spanish-style, beach-side hotel. Movies, shower baths; some 2-bed rooms, balconies; no air conditioning, phones. Beach, fishing, tennis. No pets. Dining room; 7:30 am-10:30 pm; cocktails, bar. MC, VI. **(See ad page 229.)**

OLD MILL MOTEL   Motor Inn
On eastern shore of inner San Quintín Bay, 4 miles west of Hwy 1 via unpaved road.
Mail: Apdo Postal 90, Valle de San Quintín, BC, Mexico.
Phone (619) 428-2779, (800) 479-7962; FAX (619) 428-6269.
US Reservations: 223 Via de San Ysidro, Ste 7, San Ysidro, CA 92173.

All year   1P $30-60   2P $30-60

XP $8. 2-day cancellation notice. Motel on site of old grist mill. 28 units; suites, $80-90. Shower baths; some kitchenettes; no air conditioning, TV, phones. Beach, hunting, swimming, hiking; guide service available. Fishing trips arranged. Gasoline and diesel. RV park, $15 per space. Restaurant; 6 am-9 pm; cocktails, bar. **(See ad page 249.)**

RANCHO SERENO BED AND BREAKFAST   ◆ Bed & Breakfast
1¼ miles south of the military camp at Km 196, then 1½ miles west of Hwy 1 on dirt road.
Phone (909) 982-7087.
US reservations agent: 1442 Hildita Ct, Upland, CA 91786.

All year [BP]   1P $45-50   2P $50

XP $10. 10-day cancellation notice. Ranch house on tree-shaded grounds. Electricity 9 am to 1 pm and 5 to 9 pm. 3 units. Shower baths; no air conditioning, phones. Kitchen and recreation room with cable TV. No smoking in guest rooms. Full breakfast served 8-10 am. Fishing trips arranged. Pets. ⊘

Santa Rosalía

Lodging

HOTEL EL MORRO   Motel
On Hwy 1, 1 mile south of Santa Rosalía ferry terminal. Mail: Apdo Postal 76, Santa Rosalía, BCS, Mexico.
Phone 01152 (115) 2-0414.

All year   1P $25   2P $30

XP $5; children ages 5 and under free. 10-day cancellation notice. 30 units; suite available. Spanish-style hotel overlooking Gulf of California. Some rooms with patios overlooking gulf. Shower baths, 2-bed rooms, some private patios. Pool. No pets. Dining room; Tue-Fri and Sun 7:30 am-10 pm, Sat and Mon noon-10 pm; cocktails, bar.

Tijuana

Lodging

GRAND HOTEL TIJUANA   ◆◆◆ Hotel
Al Bl Agua Caliente No 4500, ¼ mile east of Av Rodríguez adjacent to Tijuana Country Club. Mail: Box BC, Chula Vista, CA 92012 USA.
Phone 01152 (668) 1-7000, (800) 472-6385.

All year   1P $60-72   2P $69-79

XP $10. 3-day reservation cancellation notice. 23 stories. 422 units; suites. Cable TV, movies, radios. Heated pool, whirlpool, tennis. No pets. 2 restaurants, coffee shop; 24 hrs; cocktails; bar. AE, CB, DI, MC, VI. ⊘

HACIENDA DEL MAR HOTEL　　　　　　　　　Motor Inn
At Playas de Tijuana, 5 miles west of the border crossing. Mail: Box 120578, Chula Vista, CA 91912 USA.
Phone 01152 (663) 0-8603, (800) 425-2684.

All Year　　　　　　1P $34　　　　　2P $34

Quiet location near Oasis (Ernosto Contreas) Hospital and "Bull-Ring-By-The-Sea." 59 units. Cable TV, movies; some shower baths. Heated pool, guest laundry, meeting room. No pets. Restaurant; 7 am-11 pm. Cocktails, bar. AE, MC, VI.

HOLIDAY INN EXPRESS-TIJUANA AGUA CALIENTE　　◆◆◆ Motel
2 miles southeast of the border at Paseo de los Héroes #18818 via Rapida Ponient. Mail: Box 432808, San Diego, CA 92143 USA.
Phone 01152 (663) 4-6901; FAX 4-6912.
Reservations: (800) 465-4329.

All year　　　　　　1P $50　　　　　2P $50

XP $14. 3 stories. 140 units; suites with refrigerator, microwave & coffee maker, $87-100. Pool, hot spring whirlpool, sauna, exercise room. No pets. Coffee shop; 7 am-11 pm. AE, MC, VI.

HOLIDAY INN—PUEBLO AMIGO　　　　　　　◆◆◆ Hotel
At Via Oriente 9211 off Paseo de Tijuana. Mail: Via Oriente 9211, Zona Río, Tijuana, BC Mexico.
Phone 01152 (68) 3-5030, (800) 998-9668.

All Year　　　　　　1P $90-110　　　2P $90-110

XP $20. New 6-story hotel. 108 units. Cable TV, movies. Pool, gift shop, exercise room. Valet parking only. No pets. Meeting rooms. Restaurant; 7 am-11 pm; cocktails. AE, MC, VI. ⊘

HOWARD JOHNSON CONQUISTADOR HOTEL　　◆ Motor Inn
Just east of Av Rodríguez at Bl Agua Caliente 10750. Mail: Box 5355, Chula Vista, CA 91912 USA.
Phone 01152 (668) 1-7955; FAX 6-1340.
US reservations: (800) 446-4656.

All Year　　　　　　1P $50　　　　　2P $50

XP $5. 3-day reservation cancellation notice. Near Tijuana Country Club. 2 stories. 110 units. TV, movies, refrigerators, shower baths. Pool, whirlpool, sauna. No pets. Meeting room, data ports. Restaurant; 7 am-11 pm; cocktails; bar. MC, VI.

HOTEL LUCERNA　　　　　　　　　　　　　◆◆ Hotel
At Paseo de los Héroes and Av Rodríguez in the Río Tijuana development. Mail: Box 437910, San Ysidro, CA 92143 USA.
Phone 01152 (66) 34-2000, (800) 582-3762; FAX 01152 (66) 4-2400.

All year　　　　　　1P $58　　　　　2P $63

XP $12. Modern 6-story hotel. 167 units; suites $82-161. Cable TV, radios. Pool, tennis. No pets. Restaurant (see listing) and coffee shop; 7 am-midnight; cocktails, entertainment. AE, DI, MC, VI.

PLAZA LAS GLORIAS   ◆◆ Hotel
At Tijuana Country Club, Bl Agua Caliente No 11553. Mail: Box 43-1588, San Ysidro,
CA 92173 USA.
Phone 01152 (668) 1-7200; FAX 6-3639.
US reservations: (800) 446-4656.

All year   1P $54- 59   2P $54- 59

XP $9. 3-day reservation cancellation notice. 10 stories. 200 units. Color TV, movies. Pool, sun deck, whirlpool. No pets. Restaurant; 7 am-midnight; cocktails; bar. AE, MC, VI.

HOTEL REAL DEL RIO   ◆◆ Hotel
In Río Tijuana District, 2 blocks west of Av Rodríguez on Calle Velasco. Mail: Calle
Velasco 1409, Tijuana, BC 22320, Mexico.
Phone 01152 (66) 34-3100.

All year   1P $43   2P $44

XP $5. 5-story hotel. 105 units. Cable TV. Restaurant; 7 am-midnight; cocktails; bar.

RESIDENCE INN BY MARRIOTT/REAL DEL MAR   Suite Hotel
Off Hwy 1-D (toll road), 12 miles south by Real del Mar Golf Club at Km 19.5. Mail:
4492 Camino de la Plaza, #1246, San Ysidro, CA 92173 USA.
Phone 01152 (661) 3-3680, (800) 801-6038.

Fri-Sat [CP]   1P $99-119   2P $99-119
Sun-Thu [CP]   1P $79- 99   2P $79- 99

XP $10. All-suite hotel overlooking the ocean. 62 units. Cable TV, VCPs. Pool, whirlpool, exercise room. Dining room; 7 am-10 pm; cocktails. AE, MC, VI.

Restaurants

BOCCACCIO'S   ◆◆ Italian
Near the Tijuana Country Club at Bl Agua Caliente 11250.
Phone 01152 (66) 86-2266.

$10-28. Open noon-midnight. Closed major holidays. Seafood, steaks and pasta. Cocktails. MC, VI.

RESTAURANTE LA COSTA   ◆◆ Seafood
In the downtown area just west of Av Revolución at Calle 7A 150.
Phone 01152 (688) 5-8494.

$7-22. Open 10 am-midnight. Large selection including lobster, shrimp, oysters, whole and fileted fish. Cocktails. MC, VI.

TOUR DE FRANCE   ◆◆◆ French
On Calle Gobernador Ibarra and Hwy 1, across from Hotel Palacio Azteca.
Phone 01152 (66) 81-7542.

$9-18. Open Mon-Sat 8 am-10:30 pm, Fri-Sat to 11:30 pm. Closed Sun & last week of Dec. Charming setting with several small dining rooms and patio. Cocktails.

Todos Santos

Restaurant

CAFE SANTA FE   ◆◆ Italian
In the center of town at Calle Centenario No. 4.
Phone 01152 (112) 5-0340.

$9-12. Open noon-9 pm. Closed Tue and 8/1-11/9. Refined Italian dishes served in an attractively decorated dining room and lush tropical patio. Cocktails.

Campgrounds & Trailer Parks

For many visitors to Baja California, camping is an enjoyable and economical way to travel. In response to the need for information on campgrounds and trailer parks along the peninsula, and because it is generally inadvisable to camp in nondesignated sites along major highways, the Auto Club has prepared these listings as a convenience to travelers.

Camping Facilities

Camping facilities in Baja California range from primitive sites with no amenities to fully developed recreational vehicle parks. Since the completion of the Transpeninsular Highway, many fully equipped private campgrounds and RV parks have been built for vacationers in popular resort areas. Their facilities generally approximate those of their U.S. counterparts; rates are somewhat lower. In addition, the Mexican government has built several trailer parks along Highway 1 as a convenience to travelers. Trailer parks and campgrounds are authorized to lease rental space for long-term parking so that repeat visitors are able to leave their trailers and motor homes in Mexico between visits.

Despite the easy accessibility brought about by the Transpeninsular Highway, camping in Baja California requires careful preparation. Supplies are readily available only in the northern and southern areas of the peninsula; they are difficult to obtain in the sparsely populated midsection of Baja California. Campers should therefore plan to be as self-sufficient as possible. Potable drinking water is scarce and should be carried, along with plenty of radiator water. Campers will also find it convenient to carry their own disposable trash bags. Travelers with recreational vehicles should bring extra fan belts, hoses and other parts, as well as tools. Tires, including spares, should be in good condition and regularly checked for air pressure. Since Highway 1 is generally narrow and without turnouts or solid shoulders, it is a good idea to carry flares in case of breakdown. For a complete list of what to take, see the Suggested Supply Lists in the *Appendix*.

Trash and waste from recreational vehicle holding tanks should be disposed of only at designated locations. This makes collection easier and protects the scenic environment. Trash and litter of all kinds constitute an increasing problem in Baja California, particularly along the roads and on the beaches.

For more adventuresome (and self-sufficient) campers, the Mexican government has designated many spots along Baja California's scenic shoreline as *playas públicas* (public beaches). These primitive camping areas supposedly charge a small fee, usually $2 to $4 per night, but the fee is not always collected. Many have no facilities, but some have *palapas* (umbrella-shaped shelters built with dried palm fronds), trash cans and pit toilets. A few are operated by concessionaires; these generally have more facilities and charge a slightly higher fee. The most popular and accessible of the *playas públicas* are listed in this publication.

About the Listings

Each of the campgrounds and trailer parks listed in this section has been inspected by a representative of the Automobile Club of Southern California. Those which meet AAA standards are listed with the symbol ✓ before the name. All listings are as complete as possible, based on information available at our publication deadline. Considering Baja California's rapid rate of growth, however, travelers should keep in mind that changes may have occurred, particularly regarding rates and facilities.

Even at well-equipped trailer parks, facilities, maintenance and services may not be up to U.S. standards. Hookups occasionally aren't usable because of generator breakdowns; when this happens, the price is sometimes lowered. Many trailer parks lack telephones. Tap water is not suitable for drinking. Bathroom facilities are sometimes rustic and crowded. In addition, some of Baja California's campgrounds and trailer parks do not have English-speaking employees. Travelers should make use of a basic Spanish phrase book; some useful phrases and words are found in the Speaking Spanish section of the *Appendix*.

The Automobile Club of Southern California cannot guarantee the rates, services, maintenance or facilities of any campground or trailer park described in this publication.

Sites are listed alphabetically by city. The following abbreviations are used to denote hookups: **E**=electricity; **W**=water; **S**=sewer. All campgrounds and trailer parks are open all year unless otherwise noted.

In the mailing addresses of the following campgrounds, BC is the abbreviation for the state of Baja California and BCS stands for the state of Baja California Sur.

Bahía Concepción

BAHIA EL COYOTE (*playa pública*)
17½ miles south of Mulegé off Hwy 1; just after "Rcho El Coyote," turn at sign with beach symbol and go south ½ mile.
No phone.
$3-4 per vehicle. On shore of the bay. Pit toilets, cabañas.

EL REQUESÓN (*playa pública*)
27 miles south via Hwy 1 and unpaved road.
No phone.
$3 per vehicle. Attractive location on sandspit that links beach with offshore island. Pit toilets, cabañas, palapas.

PLAYA SANTISPAC (*playa pública*)
13½ miles south of Mulegé via Hwy 1 and unpaved road.
No phone.

$4 per vehicle. On Santispac Cove, part of Bahía Concepción. Flush toilets, showers, palapas, two cafes.

POSADA CONCEPCIÓN
15 miles south on Hwy 1. Mail: Apdo Postal 14, Mulegé, BCS, Mexico.
No phone.

$10 for 2 persons, $2 per each additional person. Overlooks the bay. 10 RV sites; area for tents. Hookups: EWS-10; electricity 10 am-10 pm. Flush toilets, showers, tennis, beach, skin diving, fishing.

RESORT SAN BUENAVENTURA
25 miles south of Mulegé via Hwy 1 at Km 94.5, on Bahía Concepción. Mail: Apdo Postal 56, Mulegé, BCS, Mexico.
Phone 01152 (115) 3-0408.

$8 per vehicle. RV/tent sites. Flush toilet, shower, beach, fishing, charter service, paved boat ramp, 15 palapas on beach. 3 bungalows with two cots, $20.

Bahía de los Angeles

GUILLERMO'S TRAILER PARK
On the shore of the bay. Mail: Montes de Oca No. 190, Fraccionamiento Buenaventura, Ensenada, BC, Mexico.
No phone.

$6 for 2 persons, $1 per each additional person. 40 RV sites. Hookups: EWS-15; electricity 7-11 am and 5-9:30 pm. Flush toilets, showers, beach, fishing trips arranged, boat ramp and boat rental, restaurant, bar, gift shop.

LA PLAYA RV PARK
On the shore of the bay. Mail: 509 Ross Dr, Escondido, CA 92029 USA.
Phone (619) 741-9583 (area code changes to 760 effective March 22, 1997).

$10 for 2 persons, $3 per each additional person. 30 RV sites; extensive area for tents. Hookups: E-30; electricity 7 am-9:30 pm. Disposal station, flush toilets, showers, fishing with guide, boat launch, ice, restaurant, bar.

Cabo San Lucas

CLUB CABO
3 miles east of town center; turn south off Hwy 1 on road to Club Cascadas. Mail: Apdo Postal 463, Cabo San Lucas, BCS, Mexico.
Phone 01152 (114) 3-3348.

$6 per person. RV park and motel rooms in open area. 15 RV/tent sites. Hookups: EWS-10, EW-5. Flush toilets, showers, pool, whirlpool. Palapa with TV, barbecue, ping pong. Fishing trips arranged. Shuttle to town.

EL ARCO TRAILER PARK
2 miles east of town on Hwy 1. Mail: Km. 5.5, Cabo San Lucas, BCS, Mexico.
Phone 01152 (114) 3-1686.

$10 per site. Open area with view of Cabo San Lucas Bay. 85 RV/tent sites. EWS-65. Flush toilets, showers, laundry, pool, restaurant, bar.

EL FARO VIEJO TRAILER PARK
¾ mile northwest of town center near Hwy 19, at Matamoros and Mijares. Mail: Apdo Postal 64, Cabo San Lucas, BCS 23410, Mexico.
Phone 01152 (114) 3-4211.

$12 for 2 persons, $3 per each additional person. Partly shaded area surrounded by wall. 19 RV/tent sites. Hookups: EWS-19. Flush toilets, showers, restaurant, bar.

✓ VAGABUNDOS DEL MAR RV PARK
1½ miles northeast of town center on Hwy 1. Mail: Apdo Postal 197, Cabo San Lucas, BCS, Mexico.
Phone 01152 (114) 3-0290.
US reservations: (707) 374-5511.

$16 for 2 persons, $3 per each additional person. 10-day cancellation notice. 65 RV sites. Hookups: EWS-65. Flush toilets, showers, laundry, pool.

Cataviña

CATAVIÑA RV PARK
On Hwy 1, ¼ mile north of Hotel La Pinta.
No phone.

$5 per vehicle. Open area with limited facilities. 66 RV/tent sites. Hookups: WS-66. Flush toilets.

Ciudad Constitución

CAMPESTRE LA PILA
1½ miles south of town center via Hwy 1 and ½ mile west on unpaved road. Mail: Apdo Postal 261, Ciudad Constitución, BCS 23600, Mexico.
Phone 01152 (113) 2-0562.

$8 for 2 persons, $2 per each additional person. Open area bordered by irrigated farmland. 70 RV/tent sites. Hookups: E-32, disposal station. Flush toilets, showers, pool, picnic area, snack bar.

✓ MANFRED'S RV PARK
½ mile north of city center on Hwy 1. Mail: Apdo Postal 120, Ciudad Constitución, BCS 23600, Mexico.
Phone 01152 (113) 2-1103.

RVs $11-13 for 2 persons; tents $9; $1.50 per each additional person. Nicely landscaped with flowering plants and trees. 32 RV sites. Hookups: EW-19; EWS-13. Flush toilets, showers, pool. Restaurant, motel rooms.

Colonia Guerrero

MESÓN DE DON PEPE
1 mile south via Hwy 1. Mail: Apdo Postal 7, Colonia Guerrero, BC 22920, Mexico.
Phone 01152 (616) 6-2216.

RVs $6-8 for 2 persons, $2 per each additional person; tents $4. Partly shaded area adjacent to highway. 35 RV sites, 20 tent sites. Hookups: EWS-35. Flush toilets, showers, fishing, restaurant, bar, tourist information.

POSADA DON DIEGO
1 mile south via Hwy 1 and unpaved road, past first RV park. Mail: Apdo Postal 126, Colonia Guerrero, BC 22920, Mexico.
Phone 01152 (616) 6-2181.

$9 for 2 persons, $1.50 each additional person. Pleasant area in rural setting. 80 RV/tent sites. Hookups: EW-80, S-60. Disposal station, flush toilets, showers, sports playfields, laundry, ice, restaurant, bar.

El Cardonal

EL CARDONAL RESORT
On the beach. Mail: El Cardonal, BCS, Mexico.
FAX 01152 (114) 1-0040.
Canadian reservations office: (514) 467-4700; FAX (514) 467-4668.

RVs with full hookups $25; campsite with hookup $8; campsite without hookup $6. 4 RV sites, 22 campsites. Hookups: 4-EWS, 5-EW. Flush toilets, showers. Fishing and local trips arranged. Restaurant. Motel rooms with cooking facilities $49.

El Pescadero

LOS CERRITOS RV PARK
1½ miles south on Hwy 19, then 1½ miles southwest via a dirt road.
No phone.

$4 per vehicle. Wide beach on shore of the Pacific Ocean. 50 RV/tent sites. Flush toilets.

Ensenada

CAMPO PLAYA RV PARK
1 mile southeast of downtown Ensenada, near intersection of Bl Lázaro Cárdenas and Calle Agustín Sanginés (Delante). Mail: Apdo Postal 21, Ensenada, BC, Mexico.
Phone 01152 (617) 6-2918.

$10 for 2 persons, $2 per each additional person. Fenced area near bay. 85 RV/tent sites. Hookups: E-60, WS-85. Flush toilets, showers, recreation room.

✓ **ESTERO BEACH TRAILER PARK**
8 miles south via Hwy 1 and paved side road (signs posted at turnoff). Mail: Apdo Postal 86, Ensenada, BC, Mexico.
Phone 01152 (617) 6-6225.

$12-16 for 2 persons, $3 each additional person. 3-day cancellation notice. Large seaside resort adjacent to Estero Beach Hotel. 70 RV sites, 50 tent sites. Hookups: EWS-58. Disposal station, flush toilets, showers, beach, boat launch, canoeing, horseback riding, fishing, tennis, playground, clubhouse, restaurant, bar. MC, VI.

PLAYA SALDAMANDO
On beach 10½ miles north via Hwy 1 and steep, winding dirt road. Mail: 3965 College Av, San Diego, CA 92115 USA.
Phone (619) 286-4289.

$6 for 4 persons, $1 per each additional person. 30 RV/tent sites. No hookups. Disposal station. Flush toilets, showers. No motorcycles.

SAN MIGUEL VILLAGE (VILLA DE SAN MIGUEL)
In El Sauzal, 8 miles north via Hwy 1-D. On Bahía de Todos Santos, just south of toll gate. Mail: Apdo Postal 55, El Sauzal, BC 22760, Mexico.
Phone 01152 (617) 4-6225.

$8-10 per vehicle. 30 RV sites, 100 tent sites. Hookups: EWS-30. Flush toilets, showers, beach, restaurant, bar, gift shop.

Guerrero Negro

MALARRIMO TRAILER PARK
1 mile west of Hwy 1 on east edge of town, next to Malarrimo Restaurant.
Phone 01152 (115) 7-0250.

RVs $10-12 for 2 persons, $3 per each additional person; tents $4 per person. Open area. 22 RV sites. Hookups: EW-22. Flush toilets, showers, restaurant, bar. Whale-watching trips arranged, $35 per person.

La Paz

✓ **AQUAMARINA RV PARK**
1½ miles southwest of city center, ½ mile off Hwy 1 on Calle Nayarit. Mail: Apdo Postal 133, La Paz, BCS, Mexico.
Phone 01152 (112) 2-3761.

$15 for 2 persons, $2.20 per each additional person. On the bay. 19 RV sites. EWS-19. Flush toilets, showers, laundry, pool, fishing trips, marina, boat ramp and storage, fishing trips, boat trips and scuba diving arranged.

✓ **CASA BLANCA RV PARK**
3 miles southwest of town center on Hwy 1, corner of Av Delfines. Mail: Apdo Postal 681, La Paz, BCS, Mexico 23000.
Phone 01152 (112) 4-0009.

RVs $13 for 2 persons, $2 per each additional person; tents $10. Partly shaded area surrounded by wall. 46 RV sites. Hookups: EWS-46. Fee for air conditioning & heater. Flush toilets, showers, laundry, store, pool, tennis, recreation room.

CITY VIEW RV PARK
On La Paz Bay, 10 miles before central La Paz when approaching from the north, at the town of El Centario, on Hwy 1. Mail: Apdo Postal 680, La Paz, BCS 23094, Mexico. Phone 01152 (112) 4-6088.

RVs $10 for 4 persons; tents $6. 80 RV/tent sites. Hookups: 40-EWS. Flush toilets, showers.

EL CARDON TRAILER PARK
2½ miles southwest of city center on Hwy 1. Mail: Apdo Postal 104, La Paz, BCS 23000, Mexico. Phone 01152 (112) 2-0078; FAX 2-1261.

$8-10 for 2 persons, $2 per each additional person. 3-day cancellation notice. Shaded area surrounded by wall. 80 RV sites, 10 tent sites. Hookups: EWS-80. Flush toilets, showers, laundry, ice, pool, recreation room, fishing trips.

✓ LA PAZ TRAILER PARK
2 miles southwest of city center off Hwy 1, on Brecha California, in residential area. Mail: Apdo Postal 482, La Paz, BCS, Mexico. Phone 01152 (112) 2-8787.

RVs $15 for 2 persons, $2 per each additional person; tents $10 for 2 persons. 3-day cancellation notice. 48 RV sites, 5 tent sites. Hookups: EWS-48. Flush toilets, showers, pool, fishing trips arranged, boat ramp nearby, laundry. AE, MC, VI.

OASIS LOS ARÍPEZ TRAILER PARK
On La Paz bay, 9½ miles before central La Paz when approaching from the north, in the town of El Centenario, on Hwy 1. Mail: Km. 15 Transpeninsular Norte, La Paz, BCS, Mexico. No phone.

$10 for 2 persons; $2 per each additional person. 7-day cancellation notice. 22 RV/tent sites. Hookups: EWS-29. Flush toilets, showers, laundry, beach, fishing, restaurant, bar.

La Salina

✓ BAJA SEASONS RV BEACH RESORT
On beach facing Pacific Ocean, 14 miles north of Ensenada off Hwy 1-D. Mail: Apdo Postal 1492, La Salina, BC, Mexico. Phone 01152 (662) 0-6070; FAX 0-6111. US Reservations: (800) 754-4190.

6/15-9/15 $30-35, 9/16-6/14 $25-30 for 4 persons, $3-5 per each additional person. 15-day cancellation notice. 134 RV sites. Hookups: EWS-134. Cable TV, flush toilets, showers, pool, whirlpool, sauna, steam room, tennis, laundry, groceries, restaurant, bar. MC, VI.

Loreto

✓ LORETO SHORES VILLAS & RV PARK
½ mile south of town plaza on beach. Mail: Box 219, Loreto, BCS 23880, Mexico.
Phone 01152 (113) 5-0629.

RVs with hookups $10 for 2 persons, $1 per each additional person; sites without hookups $8; villas $50-100. 42 RV sites. Hookups: EWS-42. Flush toilets, showers, beach, fishing.

PLAYA JUNCALITO (*playa pública*)
13 miles south of Loreto via Hwy 1 and unpaved road.
No phone.

$2 per vehicle. Attractive beach and view of mountains. No facilities.

VILLAS DE LORETO
½ mile south of town plaza on the beach. Mail: Apdo Postal 132, Loreto, BCS 23880, Mexico.
Phone 01152 (113) 5-0586.

$13.50 for two persons, $5 per each additional person. 13 RV sites. Hookups: EWS-13. Flush toilets, hot showers, fishing, windsurfing, horseback riding arrangements, laundry. 6 motel units, $50-60 for 2 persons; $14 for each additional person. MC, VI.

Los Barriles

✓ MARTIN VERDUGO'S TRAILER PARK
On beach of Bahía de Palmas, ½ mile east of Hwy 1. Mail: Apdo Postal 17, Los Barriles, BCS 23501, Mexico.
Phone 01152 (114) 1-0054.

$9-11 for 2 persons, $1 per each additional person. Partially shaded area. 69 RV sites, 25 tent sites. Hookups: EWS-69. Flush toilets, showers, pool, fishing trips arranged, boat launch, laundry, bar. Motel rooms $42.50-50. Restaurant adjacent.

✓ JUANITO'S GARDEN RV PARK
½ mile east of Hwy 1, one block from the bay. Mail: Apdo Postal 50, Buena Vista, BCS 23580, Mexico.
Phone 01152 (114) 1-0024; FAX 1-0024.

$10 for 2 persons, $4 per each additional person. 20 RV sites. Hookups: EWS-20. Flush toilets, hot showers, laundry, RV storage.

Mulegé

HOTEL SERENIDAD TRAILER PARK
Near mouth of river, 2 miles southeast of town off Hwy 1.
Phone 01152 (115) 3-0530.

$10 for 2 persons, $2 per each additional person. Partly shaded area next to the hotel. 15 RV/tent sites. Hookups: EWS-15. Disposal station, flush toilets, showers, pool, tennis, recreation room, boat ramp, fishing trips arranged, restaurant, bar.

✓ **THE ORCHARD RV PARK/HUERTA SAUCEDO**
½ mile south via Hwy 1. Mail: Apdo Postal 24, Mulegé, BCS, Mexico.
Phone 01152 (115) 3-0300.

RVs $13-16 for 2 persons, $2 per each additional person; tent site $5-6. Partly shaded area near river. 46 RV sites, 30 tent sites. Hookups: EWS-46. Disposal station. Flush toilets, showers, tennis, boat ramp, fishing, local tour arrangements.

✓ **VILLA MARIA RECREATIONAL PARK**
1¼ miles south via Hwy 1. Mail: Apdo Postal 5, Mulegé, BCS, Mexico.
Phone 01152 (115) 3-0246.

$12 for 2 persons, $2 per each additional person; tent site with palapa, $4.50 per person. Partly shaded area on river. 25 RV sites, 10 tent sites. Hookups: EWS-25. Disposal station, flush toilets, showers, pool, recreation area, fishing, boat launch, laundry, bakery.

Puerto Escondido

✓ **TRIPUI RESORT RV PARK**
15 miles south via Hwy 1 and paved side road, near Puerto Escondido. Mail: Apdo Postal 100, Loreto, BCS 23880, Mexico.
Phone 01152 (113) 3-0818; FAX 3-0828.

RVs with hookups $14 for 2 persons, $5 per each additional person; no hookups $5 per person. 3-day cancellation notice. 32 RV sites, 10 tent sites. Hookups: EWS-32. Flush toilets, showers, pool, groceries, gift shop, playground, restaurant, bar.

Punta Banda

LA JOLLA BEACH CAMP
8 miles west of Maneadero on BCN 23, on shore of Bahía de Todos Santos. Mailing address: Apdo Postal 102, Punta Banda, BC 22791, Mexico.
No phone.

$6 for 2 persons, $2 per each additional person. 120 RV sites, 80 tent sites. Hookups: E-20. Extension cords available. Disposal station, flush toilets, showers, beach, boat launch, tennis, recreation room, groceries, propane.

VILLARINO CAMP
8 miles west of Maneadero on BCN 23, on shore of Bahía de Todos Santos. Mail: Apdo Postal 842, Ensenada, BC 22800, Mexico.
Phone 01152 (667) 6-4246.

$10 for 2 persons, $4 per each additional person. 100 RV/tent sites. Hookups: E-50, W-100, S-50. Flush toilets, showers, beach, boat ramp, groceries, cafe.

Punta Chivato

PUNTA CHIVATO CAMPGROUND
On Punta Chivato, 13 miles north of Mulegé via Hwy 1, then 13½ miles east on graded dirt road.
Phone 01152 (115) 3-0188.

$5 per vehicle. On the beach, open sites. 40 RV/tent sites. No hookups. Disposal station, pit toilets, cold showers, fishing trips arranged in pangas, groceries, gasoline. Office nearby at Hotel Punta Chivato.

Rosarito

KOA ROSARITO
7 miles north via Hwy 1-D (San Antonio exit, east side of highway). Mail: Box 430513, San Ysidro, CA 92143 USA.
Phone 01152 (611) 3-3305.

$17 for 2 persons, $1 each additional person. 3-day cancellation notice. Grassy, partly shaded sites on bluff overlooking ocean. 65 RV/tent sites. Hookups: EWS-65. Disposal station, flush toilets, showers, playground, recreation room, laundry, curio shop, groceries, restaurant and bar nearby.

✓ OASIS RESORT
On ocean beach 3 miles north off Hwy 1-D, toll road (northbound, San Antonio exit; southbound, Oasis exit). Mail: Box 158, Imperial Beach, CA 91933 USA.
Phone 01152 (661) 3-3255, (800) 462-7472.

Fri and Sat 4/1-10/31 $43, 11/1-3/31 & Sun through Thu 4/1-10/31 $38, $6 per each additional person. 3-day cancellation notice. Beachfront park with both concrete and grass sites, built-in barbecue. 55 RV sites. Hookups; EWS-55. Flush toilets, showers, pool, sauna, whirlpool, beach, tennis, putting green, playground, gym, laundry, groceries, restaurant, bar.

San Felipe

CAMPO SAN FELIPE TRAILER PARK
In town on the bay shore. Mail: 301 Av Mar de Cortez, San Felipe, BC 21850, Mexico.
Phone 01152 (657) 7-1012.

$12-17 for 2 persons, $2 per each additional person; tents $10. 34 RV/tent sites; 10 additional tent sites. Hookups: EWS-34. Flush toilets, showers, beach, billiard room, ice.

CLUB DE PESCA TRAILER PARK
1 mile south of town center at end of Av Mar de Cortez. Mail: Apdo Postal 90, San Felipe, BC, Mexico.
Phone 01152 (657) 7-1180.

$12-15 for 2 persons, $2 per each additional person. Large landscaped park on gulf shore. 30 RV/tent sites; additional area on beach for large number of tents. Hookups: EW-30. Disposal station, flush toilets, showers, boat launch and storage, groceries.

FARO BEACH TRAILER PARK
On Punta Estrella, 10 miles southeast of town via paved road. Mail: Apdo Postal 107, San Felipe, BC 21850, Mexico.
No phone.

$25 per vehicle. Large, attractively landscaped park on terraced slope overlooking Gulf of California. 135 RV/tent sites. Hookups: EWS-135. Flush toilets, showers, pool, tennis, recreation room, ice, bar.

LA JOLLA TRAILER PARK
½ mile west of town center at Manzanillo and Mar Bermejo in residential area. Mail: Box 978, El Centro CA 92244 USA.
Phone 01152 (657) 7-1222.

$15 for 2 persons, $2.50 per each additional person. Sites with canopies. 55 RV/tent sites. Hookups: EWS-55. Flush toilets, showers, pool, spa, laundry, ice.

✓ MAR DEL SOL RV PARK
1½ miles south of town center on Misión de Loreto, adjacent to Hotel Las Misiones.
Phone 01152 (657) 7-1008, (619) 422-6900, in California (800) 336-5454.
US Reservations: 4126 Bonita Rd, Bonita, CA 91902.

$11-18 for 2 persons, $5 per each additional person. 3-day cancellation notice. Unshaded sites on attractive beach. 84 RV sites, 30 tent sites. Hookups: EWS-84. Flush toilets, showers, pool, boat launch, laundry. All hotel facilities open to campers. MC, VI.

PLAYA BONITA TRAILER PARK
1 mile north of town center via Av Mar de Cortez.
Phone 01152 (657) 7-1215, (909) 595-4250.
US Reservations: 475 E Badillo St, Covina, CA 91723.

3/1-10/31 $15-20 and 11/1-2/28 $10-15 for 5 persons, $2-5 for each additional person. Picturesque area on beach with rocky hills behind. 29 RV/tent sites. Hookups: EWS-29. Flush toilets, showers, fishing trips arranged. Condo suites available.

PLAYA DE LAURA RV PARK
In town at Av Mar de Cortez 333, San Felipe, BC, Mexico.
Phone 01152 (657) 7-1128.

$13-18 for 2 persons, $2 per each additional person. 45 RV sites, 10 tent sites. Hookups: EW-45, S-25.

RUBEN'S TRAILER PARK
1 mile north of town center via Av Mar de Cortez. Mail: Golfo de California 703, San Felipe, BC 21850, Mexico.
Phone 01152 (657) 7-1091.

$12-15 for 2 persons, $2 per each additional person. Picturesque area on gulf shore with rocky hills behind. 58 RV/tent sites. Hookups: EWS-58. Flush toilets, showers, beach, boat launch, fishing, laundry, restaurant, bar.

SAN FELIPE MARINA RESORT RV PARK
3 miles south of town on road to airport. Mail: 233 Paulin Av, Box 5574, Calexico, CA 92231 USA.
Phone 01152 (657) 7-1435.
US Reservations (619) 558-0295.

10/15-4/30 $22-24 and 5/1-10/14 $18 for four persons, $4 per each additional person. 3-day cancellation notice. Unshaded sites overlooking the marina. 143 RV sites (motor homes and trailers only). Hookups: EWS-143. Flush toilets, showers, TV hookups, pool, beach, laundry, groceries. MC, VI. **(See ad below.)**

VISTA DEL MAR RV PARK
¾ mile north of town center on Av Mar de Cortez overlooking the bay. Mail: 233 Paulin Av, Box 5366, Calexico, CA 92231 USA.
Phone 01152 (657) 7-1252.

$12 for 2 persons, $3 per each additional person. 21 RV/tent sites with shaded tables. Hookups: EWS-20. Flush toilets, showers.

San Ignacio

LA CANDELARIA TRAILER PARK
1 mile south of Hwy 1 off entrance road to San Ignacio. Turn right just beyond Hotel La Pinta, then go ½ mile southwest over rough dirt road.
No phone.

$3 per vehicle. Scenic area in a large grove of date palms. 30 RV/tent sites. Several palapas; no other facilities.

TRAILER PARK EL PADRINO
1 mile south of Hwy 1 on entrance road to San Ignacio, just beyond Hotel La Pinta. Mail: Ctra Transpeninsular Km 0.5, San Ignacio, BCS 23930, Mexico.
Phone 01152 (115) 4-0089.

$7-9 per space. 30 RV sites. Hookups: E-9, WS-20. Flush toilets, showers, restaurant, bar, tourist information.

San José del Cabo

BRISA DEL MAR RV RESORT
2 miles southwest of town center on Hwy 1. Mail: Apdo Postal 45, San José del Cabo, BCS, Mexico.
No phone.

$9-15 for 2 persons; $2 per each additional person. Fenced area on beautiful beach facing Gulf of California. 112 RV/tent sites. Hookups: EW-40, S-80. Flush toilets, showers, pool, laundry, restaurant, bar.

San Quintín

ENRIQUE'S/EL PABELLON RV PARK
9 miles south of Lázaro Cárdenas and 1 mile west of Hwy 1 via dirt road.
No phone.

$5 per vehicle. Open area with access to beach. 15 RV/tent sites; additional tent sites on beach. Hookups: W-27. Flush toilets, showers, fishing trips arranged.

Santa Rosalía

✓ LAS PALMAS RV PARK
2 miles south on Hwy 1. Mail: Apdo Postal 123, Santa Rosalía, BCS, Mexico.
Phone 01152 (115) 2-2270.

$10 RV and $6 tent for two persons, $2 each additional person. Grass sites. 30 RV/tent spaces. Hookups: E-5, W-30, S-21. Flush toilets, showers, laundry, restaurant, bar.

SAN LUCAS COVE RV PARK
9 miles south via Hwy 1 and unpaved road. Mail: Apdo Postal 50, Santa Rosalía, BCS, Mexico.
No phone.

$6 per vehicle. Open area adjacent to beach. 75 RV/tent sites. No hookups. Disposal station, limited shower and toilet facilities, beach, fishing, boat ramp, restaurant.

Santo Tomás

EL PALOMAR TRAILER PARK
North edge of the village on Hwy 1 in olive tree-shaded area. Mail: Apdo Postal 595, Ensenada, BC, Mexico.
Phone 01152 (617) 7-0650.

$10 for 2 persons, $2 per each additional person. 50 RV sites and large area for tents. Hookups: EWS-25. Flush toilets, showers, pool, hunting, tennis, groceries, restaurant, bar, curio shop, gas station.

Tecate

✓ RANCHO OJAI RV PARK & CAMPGROUND
13 miles east of town on Hwy 2. Mail: Box 280, Tecate, CA 91980 USA.
Phone 01152 (665) 4-4772.

$10-14 for 2 persons, $1 per each additional person. 41 RV sites. Hookups: EWS-41. Flush toilets, hot showers, hiking trails, clubhouse.

Todos Santos

EL MOLINO TRAILER PARK
At southern end of town near Hwy 19, behind Pemex station. Mail: Rangel y Villarino y Verduzco, Todos Santos, BCS 23300, Mexico.
Phone 01152 (112) 5-0140.

$10 for 4 persons. 21 RV sites. Hookups: EWS-21. Flush toilets, showers, laundry.

SAN PEDRITO RV PARK
5 miles south on Hwy 19 and 2 miles southwest via dirt road. Mail: Apdo Postal 15, Todos Santos, BCS, Mexico.
Phone 01152 (112) 2-4520.

Rate for 2 persons: RV $13, tent $3; $3 per each additional person. Open area on the shore of the Pacific. 71 RV and 25 tent sites. Hookups: EWS-71. Flush toilets, showers, pool, recreation area, laundry, restaurant, bar. 8 cabañas.

Index

The following is a complete listing of the attractions and place names that occur within this publication. **Places with names printed in boldface type offer lodging or camping facilities; detailed listings for some of these names appear in the** Lodging & Restaurants **and** Campgrounds & Trailer Parks **chapters.** A boldface page number denotes the primary reference of a particular place.

Index to Advertisers

Acknowledgements

Writer	George Yago III
Cartographer	Edward F. Davis
Graphic Artist	Barbara Stanfield
Cover Designer	Michael C. Lee
Editor	Kristine Miller
Photographer	Todd Masinter, except as noted:
page 216	Bill Cory
pages 24, 49, 50	Automobile Club of Southern California Archives